Succeeding as an
International Student
in the United States
and Canada

D1125168

Succeeding *as an* International Student *in the* United States *and* Canada

Charles Lipson

FOREWORD BY

Allan E. Goodman

The University of Chicago Press

CHICAGO AND LONDON

Charles Lipson is professor and director of undergraduate studies in political science at the University of Chicago.

The University of Chicago Press, Chicago 60637
The University of Chicago Press, Ltd., London
© 2008 by Charles Lipson
Foreword © 2008 by the University of Chicago
All rights reserved. Published 2008
Printed in the United States of America
17 16 15 14 13 12 11 10 09 08   1 2 3 4 5

ISBN-13: 978 0 226 48478 5 (cloth)
ISBN-13: 978 0 226 48479 2 (paper)
ISBN-10: 0 226 48478 5 (cloth)
ISBN-10: 0 226 48479 3 (paper)

Library of Congress Cataloging-in-Publication Data

Lipson, Charles.
    Succeeding as an international student in the United States
and Canada / Charles Lipson ; foreword by Allan E. Goodman.
        p. cm. — (Chicago guides to academic life)
    Includes index.
    ISBN-13: 978-0-226-48478-5 (cloth : alk. paper)
    ISBN-10: 0-226-48478-5 (cloth : alk. paper)
    ISBN-13: 978-0-226-48479-2 (pbk. : alk. paper)
    ISBN-10: 0-226-48479-3 (pbk. : alk. paper)
    1. Students, Foreign—United States. 2. Students, Foreign—
Canada. 3. College student orientation—United States. 4. College
student orientation—Canada. I. Title.
    LB2376.4.L57 2008
    378.1′982691—dc22
                                                        2007043033

♾ The paper used in this publication meets the minimum
requirements of the American National Standard for Information
Sciences—Permanence of Paper for Printed Library Materials,
ANSI Z39.48-1992.

To my dear friends, Lu Yichang

and her late husband, Professor Tang Tsou,

who began their life together during

World War II, when they were international

students in Chicago

CONTENTS

FOREWORD

Early in my tenure as a dean and graduate program director, an international student on a prestigious fellowship came to me with a series of problems. He was not sure what his professors were expecting: "Everybody assigns so much to read and then doesn't devote any time to discussing it." The student was also having difficulty writing: "I was taught to build to my conclusions, while my professors here seem only interested in them and not how I got to them." And the student, unable to find a comfortable living situation, was dismayed that the fellowship program offered little assistance and assumed greater reliance on the host campus. There were some interpersonal problems for which help was readily available. "I came here to study—not to be counseled—and think it best not to have the same institution do both."

None of these issues surprised me. Foreign students usually encounter some or all of them. What did surprise me was that the student was from England. It taught me that there are adjustment problems and systemic differences in educational systems and outlook even for those international students who may be completely fluent in the English language.

So for all my years in teaching, I wished I had Professor Lipson's book. And now that I am at the Institute of International Education, and see the issues that Professor Lipson discusses materialize for many students and on many campuses, I wish I had written his book. It is a very good one.

In 1959, the institute published a book called *Meet the U.S.A.* by the eminent American historian Henry Steele Commager. It was a brilliant treatise on the history, the people, and the geographic and political influences that shaped the American character. And it remains a valuable historic resource to help us understand what made the nation what it is today.

The book, updated for several decades but now sadly out of print, included a thirty-page "Practical Guide for Academic Visitors to the United States" as an appendix. Although much has changed in America and in the world in the last half century, I like to think that the institute's book is the spiritual predecessor to Professor Lipson's, and that Professor Lipson's book is the one we would have written if we had endeavored to publish our own guide for students in the twenty-first century.

Today, nearly 600,000 international students are in U.S. colleges and universities. Some 100,000 come to study in Canada each year. They come from over two hundred countries or places of origin, and work in every field from agriculture to zoology. Roughly half study at the graduate level, and all bring intellectual, economic, and cultural benefits to our campuses and communities. These students widen the perspectives of their North American classmates, contribute to vital research activities, and build lasting ties between their home countries and the United States or Canada after they return.

No other country attracts as many students or has the capacity to do so as the United States. The United States hosts over 200,000 more international students than the next leading host country, the United Kingdom, and more than double the number in Germany, France, or Australia, the next leading hosts. With roughly four thousand accredited colleges and universities and an international student population that makes up less than 5 percent of total enrollments, U.S. institutions also have a large untapped capacity to welcome more international students. Students can choose from among a much larger and more diverse group of higher education institutions than in the other leading destination countries to find a campus that meets their academic, financial, and personal needs.

America's highly decentralized higher education system and admissions procedures can be confusing to navigate, especially from afar. Students can and should visit EducationUSA advising offices (www.educationusa .state.gov) in their home countries to get to know more about the U.S. system of higher education and learn about specific colleges and universities. They can visit higher education fairs to meet representatives of the institutions and talk to alumni in their home countries to help identify the type of institution and the location that best meets their needs. And an extensive network of highly trained international education professionals and student advisers are in place at U.S. colleges and universities to provide ongoing support to students from other countries. All of these are invaluable sources of assistance to international students who come here to study.

But the information that Professor Lipson provides goes beyond even what these important resources offer. He provides a true insider's perspective on American higher education with a view from the classroom to help students find their way around and get the most out of their academic pursuits. This book is uniquely useful in providing detailed practical advice to help students truly immerse themselves in their campuses and communities. Professor Lipson guides them through the day-to-day details of student life in North America, and, more significantly, he explains with tremendous insight the nuances of the academic environments in which they will be working.

Writing to the students who come to North America about ways to increase their chances of academic success is important, but it is usually not done by those who play a major role in the academy. What makes this book even more compelling is that a person of considerable academic stature and with a large agenda of discipline-based research underway has taken the time to codify his experiences over the years as an adviser and program director to distill his best advice on topics of critical importance. We are all in his debt.

Dr. Allan E. Goodman
President & CEO, Institute of International Education

INTRODUCTION

Universities in the United States and Canada are vibrant, exciting places to study, and they attract outstanding students from around the world. This book is designed to help those students—to help *you*. It explains the biggest issues you will face as you attend class, write papers, work in labs, and meet professors. It also answers questions you might have about living in North America, from getting health insurance to renting an apartment or buying a car. It's a practical guide to studying and living in your new location.

You have some other excellent sources of advice, too. Your university's international student adviser works closely with students every day and knows all about your campus and city. At the adviser's office, you'll find experienced professionals who can answer most of your questions about living and studying in North America. For questions about classes, labs, research projects, and programs of study, you'll want to speak with your professors and fellow students. If you are an undergraduate, you'll also want to speak with your school's academic advisers, either in your department or in the dean of students' office. (At different universities, they are housed in different locations.) For questions about dormitories or off-campus apartments, you'll want to speak with your university's housing office. My goal is to complement them, to add to their useful advice. I hope my discussion will encourage you to talk with these deans, advisers, students, and professors, and that it will make your conversations more productive.

I have talked with many international students and listened carefully as they discussed the obstacles and opportunities they found. Over the years, I have worked with hundreds of students from Africa, Asia, Europe, Latin

America, and the Middle East. Besides teaching them and advising their research, I have met with them as director of both graduate and undergraduate studies in my department. I have served as faculty adviser to several student organizations and chaired a graduate program in international relations. So I have had plenty of opportunities to speak with international students and to answer the questions that really matter to them.

After these students have lived here for a few months and adjusted to their new environment, they are well equipped to answer one particularly important question: "What do you know *now* that you wish you had known when you arrived?" International students have great answers to that, as you might expect. I want to pass along their answers, plus some valuable guidance from deans of students and international student advisers. They have a wealth of experience. They've seen countless student issues, dealt with a few problems that crop up repeatedly, and thought carefully about how to resolve them. You can profit from their hard-won knowledge.

How the Book Is Organized

This book is designed to be accessible and easy to use. Most chapters are short and are focused on one or two issues. Within each chapter, the sections are clearly labeled. In addition to the table of contents (at the front of the book), there is an extensive index (at the end). Using these guideposts, you can go directly to any topic you want and skip over the ones that don't concern you right now. Feel free to do that. This book is meant to be a useful guide, not a novel to be read from cover to cover.

Part 1: Moving Here (Chapters 1–3)

The first three chapters—all of them very brief—explain how to move to the United States or Canada. They say what you should bring and what you should leave behind. They discuss visas and offer a quick list of things to do shortly after arriving, such as getting a local cell phone and meeting with the international student adviser. If you have already settled in comfortably, you can skim these chapters or skip them entirely.

Part 2: Succeeding at Your University (Chapters 4–9)

The next six chapters, "Succeeding at Your University," deal with academic issues. The first gives an overview of the most important issues. After that, each chapter focuses on one or two specific issues, such as the importance of creativity in U.S. and Canadian education (chapter 6).

Chapter 7 discusses the responsibilities of graduate students who teach course sections or assist faculty with research. (This book is intended for both undergraduates and graduate students but, naturally, some chapters are directed more to one group than the other.)

The next chapter explains plagiarism, cheating, and proper work in study groups. Academic honesty is a major issue for everyone at the university and occasionally a source of misunderstanding. It can be especially confusing for international students who may have been trained as undergraduates to repeat what their professors and other authorities wrote or said, without much concern for quotation or citation. The standards here are far different, and it is essential to know that from the start. Chapter 8 explains these standards and offers detailed examples to help you do honest work, as it is understood in North American universities.

Chapter 9 explains how U.S. and Canadian universities are organized and what values they seek to promote. It will help you adjust to a new academic environment and recognize many of the unspoken assumptions.

Together, these chapters map the terrain of North American universities so you can navigate it better. They are filled with specific suggestions to help you do your best academic work.

Part 3: Living in the United States and Canada (Chapters 10–25)

The chapters on living in North America are a guide to handling everyday tasks, such as getting identification cards, setting up bank accounts, finding a doctor, using public transportation, learning to drive, and so on. Each chapter deals with a specific issue, so you can turn to the ones you need and skip the rest.

Appendixes: Glossary and Abbreviations

Finally, I have included a detailed glossary of terms and a list of abbreviations used in universities. What does it mean to say someone is ABD, for example? (That's an informal term for those who have completed "all but dissertation.") There is also a table of U.S. and Canadian holidays, with brief explanations of how and when they are observed. The terms and abbreviations may be different from the ones in your home country, and the holidays certainly are. The clothing sizes are different, too, and I have included a table converting the ones you know to the ones used in North

America. You can turn to these chapters when you need a quick reference or definition.

The Goal of This Book

Although these chapters cover a wide range of topics, they share one overriding goal: to make it easier for you to live and study here. I want this to be a friendly, informative guide, one that helps you succeed in your classes, labs, and everyday activities.

Good luck!

Part 1

Moving Here

Chapter 1

What to Bring with You

If you are still planning your trip, here are some suggestions about what to take and what to leave at home. If you have already arrived, you can skip this chapter.

Pack light. That's always good advice when you travel, and it certainly applies when you travel abroad to study. Bring only the things you really need—items that are hard to replace, relatively small or light, or expensive to purchase here. Concentrate on the essentials, such as your passport, visa, and letter of university admission.

Here's a basic list, beginning with carry-on items. These are items you need as soon as you land or that cannot be replaced easily. Ask yourself this question: "If the airline loses my bags, what do I absolutely need to have?" Your answer tells you what to pack in your carry-on bag.

Start with some clothes suited to your new climate, medical records for your new doctor, and prescription medicines for the first couple of months (since you cannot refill them until you see a local doctor). Take enough cash and traveler's checks, if available, to cover the first few weeks. It may take that long until your new bank account is working and you have acquired local credit cards. Be sure to carry the letter admitting you to the university, as well as any scholarship offer and housing information. You will also want to carry your laptop computer, mainly because it could be stolen from your luggage, plus backup copies of all essential data. For the same reason, you should carry your digital camera, iPod, and PDA (such as a Blackberry) on board with you, if you have room. If not, pack them in your regular luggage.

Here's a full list, organized into things you should carry on board, things you should pack, and things you should leave behind.

Items to Pack in Your Carry-on Bags

- Immigration materials
  - ✔ Passports and visas for everyone traveling, plus any other documents required by immigration authorities
  - ✔ Birth certificates or certified copies (very useful, though not required)
  - ✔ Documents showing financial support while you are a student

- Money
  - ✔ Cash: at least $200 (Canadian or U.S. dollars, depending on your destination).
  - ✔ Traveler's Checks: at least $2000; more if possible. (You can use them as cash for purchases or deposit them in your new bank account here, where they are treated like a cash deposit.) If you carry nondollar currencies, you'll need to exchange them. That's easily done in large cities like Toronto or Los Angeles, where major banks have foreign exchange departments. It's much harder in small towns, where banks do not typically exchange currency. You can avoid that problem by exchanging funds at the international airport terminal after you have cleared customs.[1]
  - ✔ Cash card (for use in automatic teller machines): Major credit cards, debit cards, and bank cash cards can be used around the world to get local currency from automatic teller machines (called ATMs in the U.S., ABMs in Canada). Visa, MasterCard, Maestro, and American Express Cards work with nearly all machines in North America. So do cash cards from your home bank, *if* it is part of a global network of teller machines such as Cirrus or Plus. If you have such a credit card or bank card, you will have ready access to cash and can carry fewer travelers' checks, or perhaps none at all.
  - ✔ List of your credit card numbers and other vital financial information (Do *not* pack this list in any checked baggage, since it could be copied or stolen.)

- Health records and medicine
  - ✔ Record of required immunizations for yourself, your spouse, and children
  - ✔ Prescription drugs for two months
  - ✔ Medical records to give your new physician (translated into English, if possible)
  - ✔ List of allergies

---

1. Exchange rate calculators are now available free online. At Yahoo! Finance, for instance, you can not only look up exchange rates, you can easily convert specific amounts of any currency into another, including U.S. or Canadian dollars. The URL is http://finance.yahoo.com/currency.

- Important correspondence from your new university
  - ✔ Letter of admission
  - ✔ Scholarships or fellowships awarded to you
  - ✔ Housing assignment, if any

- Children's treasured items such as blankets and stuffed animals
- Children's school records, in English, if possible; otherwise, you may need to translate them yourself for school officials
- Laptop computer, unless you plan to buy one here
- Backup copy of all computer data and programs
- Small electronic gear, such as a digital camera, calculator, iPod, and PDA (if you have room in your carry-on bag; if not, hide them in your regular luggage)
- Clothing and toiletries: enough for a few days, in case they lose your luggage
- List of emergency phone numbers, addresses, and contacts in your home country and at your new university

Items to Pack in Your Regular Luggage

- Clothing
  - ✔ Clothes for school, suited to the climate where you will be living (unless you plan to buy them here)[2]
  - ✔ Two pairs of good walking shoes

- A backup copy of crucial computer data (unless packed in your carry-on bag)
- A few important books, particularly those that are hard to find in the United States or Canada
- Your children's favorite books and small toys
- Your favorite CDs and computer games
- Pictures of home and friends, plus other small mementos
- List of emergency phone numbers, addresses, and contacts at home and at your new university
- A large card with your new address in the United States or Canada inside *each* piece of luggage, as well as on the tag, in case the airline loses it. (If you do not have an apartment address yet, list the international students office at your university and its phone number.)

2. To know what kind of clothes you need, you need to know about seasonal weather patterns in your new location. For cities across the United States and Canada, you can find normal monthly temperatures, rain, and snowfall at www.weatherbase.com.

Items to Ship by Surface Mail

Surface mail is much less expensive than air mail, but it is also much slower. Use it for bulky items that do not fit in your luggage and are not needed immediately. Mail them several weeks before you travel, if possible.

- A few books that are
  - ✔ important to your studies, or
  - ✔ printed in languages that are hard to find in U.S. or Canadian bookstores

- Clothing you will not need immediately, such as winter jackets

Items to Leave at Home

Don't bother bringing things that are large, inexpensive, or delicate. It will be cheaper and more convenient to buy them in North America. So do *not* bring

- home appliances, such as toasters, irons, coffee makers, and so on,
- printers and scanners,
- glassware and anything else that is easily broken,
- spices (since they are now available online and often at local stores), and
- most books.

Chapter 2

Passports and Visas:
A Quick Overview

Each year, more than half a million international students come to the United States. Well over 100,000 come to Canada. The quality of university education in North America is as fine as any in the world, and it attracts wonderful students. They, in turn, enrich the education of their classmates and often contribute to new knowledge.

International students, like all visitors, must comply with U.S. and Canadian immigration laws. Those laws were tightened significantly after the terrorist attacks of September 11, 2001, when it was discovered that border security was dangerously lax and that some terrorists had entered North America legally, a few with student visas.

Since then, political authorities have tried to balance two goals: securing their national borders against genuine threats while still allowing legitimate students to come and go freely. Balancing these goals is a difficult task, one that has stimulated serious debate, some changes in law, and considerable inconvenience to international students.

Immigration policy continues to change. Today's laws could be transformed tomorrow by new legislation, court rulings, or administrative procedures. Heightened security threats or, worse yet, terrorist attacks, could lead to large-scale alterations. Since these laws and procedures are a moving target, I will not offer detailed advice. Instead, I will explain where you can get up-to-the-minute rules and regulations. Then, I will offer a few comments on the more enduring features of immigration law.

Visa Web Sites

Fortunately, both U.S. and Canadian immigration authorities maintain comprehensive Web sites and update them continually. It is wise to read this information carefully several months before you travel, if possible.

- United States: http://www.unitedstatesvisas.gov/index.html
- Canada: http://www.cic.gc.ca/english/study/study.asp

On these sites, you can find current rules and regulations, plus many of the visa forms you need to complete.

If you are coming to the United States, it's also a good idea to check for travel information at the Department of Homeland Security (http://www.dhs.gov/us-visit).

Naturally, you need a valid passport and appropriate student visas. Make sure your passport does not expire in the near future, since that can prevent you from getting a visa. Even better, have a passport that does not expire for several years and has an up-to-date photo. It's also important to check the medical requirements for visas. Inoculation against major diseases is a common requirement.

You will need to determine which visa is required for your studies and what restrictions are attached to it. A common restriction is that you cannot take paid jobs off campus while you are in North America on a student visa. That restriction may also extend to family members who come with you. Other common restrictions require you to be a full-time student and to perform well academically. In the United States, you must stay at the same university or inform immigration authorities if you wish to change. Sometimes, the requirements are even more specific, such as remaining in the same degree program listed on your visa application.

These are precisely the kinds of rules that vary between the United States and Canada and that can change whenever legislatures reconsider the issues or bureaucrats implement the policies. In any case, you must learn the current rules and regulations that apply to you. The place to begin is at the official immigration Web sites.

The earlier you review these online sites, the earlier you will find out what information you need to collect for your student visa. You may need to state (or even prove) where you have lived, what degrees you hold, where you have traveled, or what jobs you have held. The United States and Canada require different information, and, as I noted, their requirements can change. You need to stay abreast of the most recent official information.

If you plan to come with family members, find out what visas they require and what restrictions are placed on them. One, as I mentioned, is that your spouse might not be allowed to work off campus. There are some exceptions, though, so you'll want to check the current regulations.

On the positive side, your children are eligible for free schooling, the same as local kids. In North America, public schooling begins at about age five. For younger children, preschooling and day care are available, but you will have to pay for them. Some universities have subsidized arrangements.

The school year usually begins between mid-August and early September and ends in May. Schedules vary because they are set by the local school districts. If you have school-age children, you should check these schedules long before you travel, because they could affect your plans.

Visa rules can also affect your travel. A typical rule is that you can arrive up to one month before classes begin. Coming early gives you extra time to settle into your new surroundings and explore your new city. That's a wonderful opportunity, if you have time. By now, you know my advice: check the official U.S. and Canadian sites for current rules about early arrival.

Visa Information at the International Student Adviser's office

Besides these government Web sites, where else can you find answers about visas, children's schooling, and adapting to a new country? The international student adviser's office at your new university. Every university has one, and it's usually the first place to turn for nonacademic advice. (If you need *academic* advice, such as which courses to take, you should talk with professors and other advisers in your department.)

The international student adviser's office undoubtedly has a Web page for students, answering questions that are frequently asked, including those about visas. The site will also include contact information for university staff members who specialize in visas and immigration. You should let them know when you are arriving and get in touch with them immediately if there are any delays or other visa problems.

The staff at the international student adviser's office deals with issues like this every day, so they know the process well. They understand many other issues that affect international students, too. If they don't deal with a particular issue themselves—housing or medical care, for instance—they can certainly direct you to experts who do.

One thing international student advisers do *not* do is provide legal advice. If you need a lawyer to deal with immigration or visa problems, you'll need to hire one yourself. It is important to hire a specialist, someone who handles these issues every day and has earned a good reputation. According to an adviser who knows student travel and visa issues well, "the immigrant attorney bar is notoriously variable in its quality. Get a reference from your school or from the ABA [American Bar Association]. Check their credentials carefully." That's good advice.

Visa Interviews

Before you receive a student visa, you will probably be asked to meet with U.S. consular officials in your home country. Canadian officials have similar policies. What should you expect at this personal interview?

First, it will be brief—a few minutes at most.

Second, it is intended for you alone, not for your entire family. You are expected to answer the questions yourself. The interview will probably be conducted in English.

Third, you will be asked a series of questions designed to find out whether you are a legitimate student who does not pose a security risk and who plans to return home after your studies are complete.

To determine that, you may be asked

- why you plan to attend school in the United States,
- which universities you applied to and whether you were accepted,
- why you chose to study at the specific university you will attend,
- how you plan to pay for your education (loans? scholarships? gifts from your parents? funds from your home government?),
- where you will live in the United States,
- whether you plan to travel back and forth to your home country or elsewhere during your studies,
- whether your wife, husband, or children will travel with you or remain at home,
- how your family will support themselves, and
- what you plan to do with your degree.

Each interview is different, and these questions are only a general guide.

The best evidence that you are a legitimate student is that you have a coherent program of study that fits into your career plans. The best evidence that you are traveling to the United States to study, not to immigrate there permanently, is that you have deep, ongoing ties to your home country.

To make your case, give answers that are brief, candid, and to the point. You can supplement them with a few documents that show you are a legitimate student with a strong commitment to return home.

Expect the scrutiny to be more intense if you plan to specialize in a sensitive scientific field, if your country presents security risks, or if citizens from your country have earned a reputation for violating visa laws.

You must answer all questions fully and truthfully, of course, and provide whatever information and documents the immigration officials request.

If your visa is denied, you can reapply. You will need to check the rules for how soon you can do that.

Although Canadian immigration procedures are different, their basic goals in assessing applications for study permits are the same as those in the United States. They want to make sure you are a genuine student who poses no security risks and intends to return home after completing studies. Canada's visa office will review your written application and then decide whether to conduct a personal interview.

Chapter 3

The First Ten Things You
Should Do Here

Because there are so many things to do when you arrive, you will need to set some priorities. Here are my recommendations for what to do first.

1. Arrange for housing.
2. Meet with the international student adviser.
3. Get your university ID and e-mail account.
4. Set up a local cell-phone account.
5. Get a Canadian Social Insurance Number (SIN) or its U.S. equivalent, a Social Security Number (SSN) or Individual Taxpayer Identification Number (ITIN).
6. Set up a local bank account.
7. Establish utility accounts (electricity, heating, etc.) for your new apartment.
8. Make a list of emergency telephone numbers.
9. Apply for a credit card.
10. Be a tourist before classes start.

In part 3, you can find more detailed information about each of these tasks. What I want to do right now is focus on what you need to accomplish immediately.

Arrange for Housing

Before you arrive, make arrangements to (a) move directly into your apartment or dormitory room, or (b) live somewhere temporarily as you search for permanent housing. Most universities can provide temporary housing, but you should make arrangements before you come. The international

> ***Tip:*** To prove you are actually living at your new apartment or dorm room, mail yourself a letter at that address. Once the letter has been delivered, you can show it to banks, utilities, and others to prove you are a local resident when you set up accounts with them.

student adviser's office can help, if you e-mail them in advance. If you plan to rent off campus, explore the neighborhood *before* you rent. Is it safe? Is it close enough to your classes and labs? Is it close to public transportation? Is it served by the university's own bus system?

As soon as you find housing, even temporary housing, *mail yourself a couple of letters at your new address.* I know it sounds odd, but there's a good reason. To set up a bank account or get a driver's license, you need to show proof of your new address in the United States or Canada. A delivered letter is proof.

Meet with the International Student Adviser

Schedule an appointment soon after you arrive. Come prepared. Bring a list of questions and ask for whatever information you need. Ask when the next student orientation sessions will be held. There probably will be three different sessions worth attending:

- one for all new students,
- one especially for international students, and
- one to show all new students how to use the library.

For graduate students, there will be mandatory academic orientation for your department, division, or school. Some orientation sessions are optional, but you should attend all you can. They are valuable and will save you time and effort later.

Get Your University ID and E-mail Account

Be sure to check your university e-mail account regularly. It is how faculty, staff, and advisers will contact you for all university matters. If you maintain other e-mail accounts, such as those with Gmail or Hotmail, then you may wish to forward their mail to your university account or your university mail to them. Whatever you choose, you should have a regular, easy way to check your official university account.

Set Up a Local Cell-Phone Account

It is extremely valuable to have a phone while you search for an apartment and establish accounts at the university, bank, and credit card company. It also helps to give out your new number to friends, professors, administrators, and business people. You don't want to tell them, "I will let you know when I finally get a phone number."

Before you get a phone, compare companies and calling plans, including both local calls and overseas calls. The costs vary widely. (Later, if you decide to switch from one phone company to another, you can ask to keep the same phone number.)

Why not simply use your cell phone from back home? For two reasons. First, the technical standards for cell phones in North America are different from those in many other countries. Second, it is probably cheaper to set up a new account for use here, with options for calling internationally.

Get a SIN, SSN, or ITIN

If you are not eligible for a U.S. Social Security Number—most international students are not—see if you are eligible for an Individual Taxpayer Identification Number (ITIN). It works like a Social Security Number for identification but cannot be used for employment. There is no need for an ITIN in Canada, because they issue special SINs that cannot be used for employment. These numbers are helpful in setting up financial accounts. They can help in renting apartments, too.

Set Up a Local Bank Account

Deposit cash or travelers' checks so you have funds available immediately in your account. Your bank should treat a deposit of travelers' checks the same as a deposit of cash. That's why you should bring $2,000 or more in such checks, unless you can use a credit card or bank card from home to withdraw that amount from a local teller machine (ATM or ABM). After you have an account, you can

- order personalized checks from your bank;
- request an ATM card so you can withdraw cash and make deposits at banking machines;

- learn the bank's routing number, which is listed on their checks (you need that plus your account number to receive international wire transfers); and
- request a bank debit card, if you want one. I discuss those below and in chapter 15.

Establish Utility Accounts for Your New Apartment

As soon as you sign the agreement to rent an apartment, call the electric, gas, phone, water, and cable television/computer companies (known here as "utilities") and set up your new accounts. Tell them what day you want to begin actual service. If you delay setting up the accounts, you may be without these vital services for several days. Skip this if utilities are included in your lease, but only if *all* utilities are included. The lease may include some utilities, such as water, and not others, such as electricity.

You must set up new accounts for all utilities that are not included in the lease. To establish them, you may have to deposit several hundred dollars with each company. "Security deposits" like this are often required of customers who do not have a good local credit history. (The deposit should be returned to you when you leave the apartment if you paid your bills.)

Set up your utility accounts immediately after signing the lease, before you actually move in, and arrange to have services begin on the day you move in.

Make a List of Emergency Telephone Numbers

Store emergency numbers in your cell phone, PDA, and computer so you can find them quickly if you need to. Store one vital number under the name "ICE" (all capital letters). ICE stands for "in case of emergency." It is the number that doctors, ambulance drivers, or police should call in an emergency, such as finding you unconscious. It might be the phone number for your husband or wife, your parents, or a close friend.

Include the number for your country's embassy or local consulate, the international student adviser, the university police, your department, your health plan or physician, your utility companies (electric and heating, in particular), and any other numbers you might need in an emergency. (Remember that the general telephone number for all emergencies in the United States and Canada is 911.)

Print out a copy of your emergency numbers and keep it near your phone or in another prominent place. Update the list periodically.

Apply for a Credit Card

If you already have a credit card, be sure your billing address is up-to-date. To avoid temptation to overspend, limit yourself to one major credit card (MasterCard, Visa, or American Express). Get an alternative credit card if Visa, MasterCard, or American Express will not issue a card to you. It is sometimes difficult for international students to get a major credit card because they do not have a credit history in the United States or Canada. In that case, you should apply for

- a credit card from Wal-Mart, Target, or Sears, and from your local gasoline station, such as Shell or Exxon-Mobil. These retailers issue cards more readily than Visa or MasterCard. The cards are useful for shopping at those companies, but they cannot be used elsewhere. By paying these bills promptly, you can build a good credit history. Once you establish a good credit history in North America, you can get a Visa or MasterCard and cancel your others. *Or*
- a debit card from your bank. It deducts payments immediately from your account and does not require credit. Most banks issue them routinely to customers. Some people actually prefer debit cards, because they discourage spending and do not produce debt burdens. Debit cards do have one limitation, though: they do not help you build a local credit history, because you are not borrowing money.

When you do get a credit card, be careful not to overspend. Unless you are disciplined, you can dig yourself a deep financial hole.

Be a Tourist before Classes Start

Explore the campus, neighborhood, and city during good weather, before classes begin. Sign up for local tours offered by the international student adviser's office or the orientation office. Most universities offer them. Ask if they know about any self-guided tours, where you walk or drive a route that has already been mapped out for you.

If you have the time and money, consider a professionally organized city tour. In New York, for instance, there are personally guided bus tours in many languages. In San Francisco, Gray Lines offers dozens of tours, including ones with taped narration in German, Italian, French, Spanish, Japanese, Korean and Mandarin.

• • • •

Most of these recommendations are straightforward, but it helps to have a list. In the next few chapters, I will explain all of them in more detail and discuss many more. After you have reviewed my suggestions, you can set your own priorities. You'll have a better sense of what you want to do, how to do it, and what your alternatives are.

The following six chapters (chapters 4–9) provide information and advice specifically geared to academic life in North America. They should help you make a smooth transition from your educational system at home to your new one in the United States or Canada.

Of course, you are not only moving to a new educational system, you are moving to a new country, with its own rules for renting apartments, getting driver's licenses, buying health insurance, and more. Part 3 (chapters 10–25) offers detailed help on these practical aspects of day-to-day life. The appendixes include a glossary and a list of abbreviations to decode the terms commonly used (but rarely explained) in North American universities, as well as essential terms used in health care, banking, and shopping.

All these chapters share a common goal: to serve as a friendly, informed guide to student life on campus and off campus, across the United States and Canada.

Part 2

*Succeeding at
Your University*

Chapter 4

The Biggest Academic Challenges for International Students

When students study abroad, they move into a new academic and social environment. That means they have to deal with challenges they did not face at home, and a few challenges that do not face local students here. International students must adjust to a new country, far away from family, friends, and familiar places. They must read, write, and negotiate everyday life in a foreign language. And they must cope with a new and unfamiliar educational system, one that sometimes emphasizes different values from those they know at home, whether that home is in Spain, India, Brazil, China, or South Korea.

What's so different about North American universities? What do international students need to know to perform their best, to achieve the educational goals they set for themselves? What do they need to know to settle comfortably into their new surroundings, to find convenient places to live, shop, and worship?

To find out, I spoke with experienced international students and with the faculty, deans, and advisers who work closely with them. They understand university education here and have useful advice to share with undergraduates and graduate students coming to Canada and the United States. According to them, international students face three big issues in their academic work:

- mastering English,
- expressing their own viewpoints in papers, class discussions, and research, and
- learning the rules of academic honesty, as they are understood in the United States and Canada.

Handling these issues well will take you a long way toward academic success here.

In this chapter I will offer a brief sketch of these challenges. In the chapters that follow, I will fill in the details. Chapter 6 stresses originality in U.S. and Canadian classwork; chapter 8 explains our rules of academic honesty; chapter 9 explores the culture of North American higher education. In other chapters, I discuss everything from speaking up in seminars to serving as a teaching assistant. Later, in chapters 10–25, I discuss the personal side of moving to North America. In each chapter, I offer practical ideas to make your life easier and your academic work more rewarding.

What's New and Challenging?

When faculty and advisers are asked what academic issues are most pressing for international students, they often begin by saying how important it is to master English. You need to know it well to understand the assigned readings and join in class discussions. You need to know it well to understand what your professors and classmates say.[1] You need to use it when you teach course sections or supervise student lab work. To do your best work, you need to read, write, and speak English well. It's just as important for your life off campus, as well.

If you are here with a husband or wife, your spouse will also benefit from learning English. The social benefits are enormous. You can develop a much wider circle of friends, and your language will improve as you socialize. If you cannot speak English, your friendships will be limited to those who speak your native language.

While it is great to have friends from your home country, it is even better to have friends from there *plus* friends from around the world. Whether your new friends' languages are Arabic, Spanish, Hindi, or Mandarin, their common language here is English. The better you know it yourself, the easier it will be to engage them socially and intellectually.

Besides mastering English, faculty and advisers stress two other issues:

- the high value placed on original work, and
- the importance of acknowledging others' work whenever you use it.

---

1. The only exceptions are francophone universities in Québec.

U.S. and Canadian universities prize originality and creativity, not conformity and rote repetition. They encourage students to think for themselves, to develop their own informed viewpoints. The sooner you recognize this emphasis, the better your academic experience will be.

Of course, the quest for originality does not mean ignoring what the experts say. You should read assigned texts and articles carefully. Necessary as that is, it is not sufficient, especially in advanced classes. You also need to formulate your own perspectives, your own ideas about the materials. At the most advanced graduate levels, you need to push forward with your own distinctive research.

For some international students (and for some local students as well), this approach to learning feels unfamiliar or even disrespectful to the professor. That is *not* how it is seen, however, at the university level in the United States and Canada. It is considered desirable, not impertinent, for students to formulate their own ideas and pursue their own research. When others discuss their ideas, you are welcome to offer constructive suggestions and relevant comments. Nor is it disrespectful to differ with faculty or classmates, as long as you are thoughtful and courteous. The university is a place to explore new ideas and debate old ones. Students are encouraged to join that debate, to add their ideas to the mix.

The main point is that class discussions, papers, labs, and exams try to foster *both* expertise and originality. In chapter 6 ("Thinking Creatively"), I say more about how you can contribute your own ideas to class discussions and lab work.

All serious research builds on existing work and seeks to go beyond it. In doing so, it combines your work with the work of others. That brings us to the third major issue stressed by faculty and international student advisers. Everybody at the university—students and faculty alike—must clearly differentiate his or her own work from that of others.

Whenever you rely on others' work, you must acknowledge it openly. Whenever you use their ideas, research, or data, you must cite them. Whenever you use their words, you must quote them *and* cite them. Proper quotation and citation really matter here. Leaving them out, even if it is unintentional, is considered plagiarism and is a serious violation of our academic rules. Fortunately, it is easy to avoid these problems. I show you how in chapter 8 ("Avoiding Plagiarism").

Chapter 9 discusses broader issues about values, expectations, and behavior on campuses across the United States and Canada. Understanding them will help you navigate this new environment.

What Is Distinctive about U.S. and Canadian Universities?

The goal of all these chapters is to smooth your transition from studying in your home country to studying in North America. To help you make that transition, I ask two fundamental questions, "What's so different about university life here? How does it compare to university life in other countries?"

Let me offer a short list of my own answers here. In the chapters to come, I will fill out the details.

- Your participation in class is welcomed and is often required in seminars and discussion groups. You should not just sit quietly and take notes. Even large lecture courses have weekly discussion sections where you are encouraged to share your ideas.
- Critical discussion is welcomed. Class participation is not just a matter of repeating what your professor said or what the assigned readings covered. Of course you need to know those things, but you should do more than nod and agree. You should also feel free to question the experts. That includes questioning your professor's views, as long as you do it respectfully.
- Your own individual viewpoint is encouraged in class discussions, papers, and exams. That's especially true in more advanced classes, where your ideas should build on the foundations acquired earlier.
- Reading assignments at university level are extensive, much more than many international students are used to doing each week. In many classes, the assignments are too long to read everything closely. Instead, you have to read selectively, emphasizing some works more than others. You might analyze some works very carefully and skim others. Ah, but which ones are most important? That's a crucial question, and it's one you need to answer for yourself in many classes. In fact, learning which readings are vital and which ones are merely supplementary is an important part of your education.
- Class syllabi in U.S. and Canadian universities are more than a list of required readings. They set out the teacher's expectations for the course in some detail. They say when exams will be held, when papers are due, and, in many cases, what is expected on each assignment. "A syllabus here is like a contract between the teacher and student," one professor told me. "It spells out what is expected in the course."

- University students are continually evaluated on their performance, not just once at the end of the course. Most classes have several tests or assigned papers as the term progresses. Weekly problem sets are common in the sciences. In undergraduate classes, it is common for professors to give brief tests (quizzes) on the most recent work. These assignments spread out the workload and take some pressure off the final exam, since it is not the only grade for the course. But there's another benefit that is even more important. Because students are typically evaluated several times during the course, they get feedback while they can still use it. They find out what they are doing well and what they need to work on. That means tests, papers, and lab reports are not just measures of performance; they are valuable diagnostic tools for the student and professor.

- Academic performance is stressed. In some countries, admission to elite universities is sufficient to prove a student's abilities. Here, admission is only the beginning. There is a strong emphasis on performance *within* the program, even within the best programs. Performance may be measured by the faculty's evaluation of your papers, exams, and labs, or by your grade point average. Whatever way it's measured, the quality of your work has a major impact on the next stage of your career or education here.

- Pluralism is a fact of life in North American universities and a fundamental value shared by students, faculty, and the wider society. Tolerance for others is expected. Teachers and students here come in all shapes and sizes. They are citizens of all nations, members of all races and religions, men and women, gay and straight, old and young.[2] You do not have to embrace their ideas, values, or lifestyles, but you do have to treat everyone with respect and tolerance. They should treat you exactly the same way. That is a core expectation of living in a free, liberal society.

A Word of Reassurance

All this takes some getting used to. It may be confusing at first, especially if you were raised and educated with very different values. That's certainly what most international students say. But they usually move along the learning curve very quickly. What initially seems strange soon becomes familiar.

2. Gay = homosexual. Straight = heterosexual. Both "gay" and "straight" are widely used. Neither term is derogatory.

A few months later, you may hit a rocky patch. The newness will have worn off, class assignments will be bearing down, and the weather is beginning to turn cold and dreary. You may experience a sense of fatigue and homesickness. When you reach this low point, life here may seem more depressing than exciting. International students call it the "three month blues," since that's when it often strikes. As one student told me, "That's when it really hits you that you are a long way from your home, family, and friends."[3]

Remember, it's a bump in the road, not a permanent roadblock. With the help of supportive friends and advisers, with some intellectual challenges in class and some interesting activities around town, you can get back on track. I'll offer some practical suggestions.

Now, let's explore some of these issues in more detail.

---

3. To make matters worse, the holidays are beginning and local students are going home to their families. In late November, Americans celebrate Thanksgiving by gathering around family tables for traditional meals. (Canadians celebrate their Thanksgiving in early October.)

One experienced observer told me that it's a good time for international students to "take a trip, sometimes organized by the university or a [campus] club. Go home to roommates' family— see the real America around the [Thanksgiving table]. . . . Just sitting around the dorm when no one is there can be . . . a prescription for homesickness."

Chapter 5

Succeeding Academically

To succeed in American and Canadian universities, international students need to understand their new academic environment and adjust to its demands. You cannot meet these demands unless you know what they are.

This chapter will explain some of the challenges of being a student here, and some of the opportunities. It will focus on what's different about North American classrooms, how to cope effectively with this new environment, and, most of all, how to achieve real academic success here.

Improving Your English

The most obvious demand is to work comfortably in English. All your lectures, all your class discussions, all your papers, and nearly all your readings will be in English. It is essential, then, that you learn the language well and feel comfortable taking notes, writing papers, and explaining your ideas in English.

Some international students are already fluent. They come from countries where English is spoken, either as a first or second language, or they attended schools where instruction was in English. Indeed, you may have the advantage of being able to read research materials in several languages, while your classmates here are struggling. For others, though, learning the language is still a challenge. It is a challenge worth meeting head-on and mastering. The better your English, the better you will perform in classes, papers, and exams.

Universities here clearly understand the importance of knowing English. That's why they require international students to perform well on

> **Tip:** Working successfully in English requires more than reading well. You must be skilled at four distinct tasks:
>
> - listening
> - speaking
> - reading
> - writing
>
> Mastering all four takes practice. It helps to get skilled instruction, too, from courses in English as a second language (ESL). Chapter 12, "Learning the Language," suggests several ways to improve your English.

TOEFL, Test of English as a Foreign Language, or an alternative test, IELTS, the International English Language Testing System. In fact, they typically require students to do well on all parts of the exam, which are graded separately, as well as on the overall test.

A high score on TOEFL or IELTS is a good start, but it is only a start. Success at your new university requires more. You must be able to read rapidly and hone in on the key aspects of your reading. You must be able to understand speakers who, at times, talk too rapidly and use colloquial expressions. And you must be able to communicate your own ideas clearly and fluently, both orally and in writing. Each poses its own challenge.

Coping with Long Reading Lists

Whatever the subject, doing good work demands good reading skills—in English. Fortunately, nearly all international students have these skills. Still, the students I spoke with reported two major challenges coping with their reading assignments. First, they said, the load is formidable. Graduate students, in particular, say they were never assigned so many pages at home, where most were undergraduates. In Europe, Africa, Asia, South America, and the Middle East, the assigned readings are much briefer and more focused.

That leads to a second challenge: determining which readings deserve the most attention. In many courses, there is simply too much reading to devote close attention to everything. You need to concentrate on some readings and spend less time on others. That is especially true for graduate courses, where reading lists are long.

The teachers I spoke with added a third challenge. In upper-level

> ***Tip:*** Not all readings are equally important. Discriminate. Spend most of your time on the most important books and articles. Not sure which ones those are? Talk with your professors.

courses, they said, students need to take the initiative and choose their own supplementary readings. Doing these extra readings is particularly important if you are conducting research and writing papers. Faculty will offer suggestions if you ask, but you have to ask. The choice of what to read is ultimately up to you.

Of course, local students must complete the same heavy assignments. But they start with several advantages. First, they are working in their native language. Second, if they are graduate students, they already learned to cope with long reading lists when they were undergraduates. Third, as undergraduates, they also learned to take the initiative and choose additional readings in areas of interest.

While completing their BAs, they learned to pick and choose among assigned readings, skimming the less important ones so they could concentrate on the more significant books and articles. They also learned to focus on the main ideas, not the peripheral details. They learned to build their own reading lists for research papers, often finding ideas by looking closely at citations and bibliographies in the works they read.

These skills are crucial for graduate work in the social sciences and humanities, where students typically take three or four classes and must read one or two hundred pages per week for each. That intense pace continues throughout graduate school. Actually, it begins in upper-level undergraduate courses, which require substantial reading and research.

To keep up, international students not only need strong language skills, they need to discriminate intelligently among reading assignments. Not everything on every syllabus is equally important. Not everything needs

> ***Tip:*** International students face several challenges in their course readings.
>
> - They have never faced such long lists before.
> - There are too many readings to give equal care to them all.
> - The readings are in English, a foreign language for most international students.
> - It is often necessary to construct a supplementary, personalized reading list, especially in advanced courses.

to be read at the same pace or annotated with the same care. Focus on the most important items, take good notes on them, and make sure you understand the main points. That's the heart of the reading assignment. Then, if you are doing independent research, move on to the additional readings you have chosen.

Taking Good Notes

Effective notes are, by definition, *selective* notes. They capture crucial ideas and data, rather than scooping up everything the author writes or the professor says. Less important materials deserve less attention. You should be able to read them much faster (sometimes skimming them) and take fewer notes. One of your jobs as a student is to choose which materials are truly important so you can concentrate on them. Making these choices is a vital part of your education.

What about copying sentences and paragraphs directly from readings? That's fine, as long as you are careful. You need to watch out for three problems. First, if you copy too much, you will simply end up replicating the whole article. Remember, good notes must be selective. So copy only the most important materials. That's especially important to remember for online materials, which are so easy to drag and drop into your notes. Second, if you rely too heavily on copying, your notes will only repeat the author's ideas. Good notes should be more than that. They should summarize the key elements of the reading and include your own assessment. You should grapple with the materials, and your notes should reflect that mental work. Finally, when you copy text from online sources, you can easily lose track of the original source. A month or two later, when you look back at your notes, you may not remember which words belong to you and which belong to the published author. That's a serious problem when you use the notes to write papers. You could easily, if inadvertently, plagiarize. That is, you could claim you wrote something when, in fact, someone else did.

Good notes should make absolutely clear whether you are quoting someone else's words, paraphrasing them in your own language, or writing down your own original ideas. Fortunately, it is not hard to make these

> *Tip:* Taking good notes means taking selective notes, focusing on what's really important.

> ***Tip:*** Your notes should show clearly whether an item is a direct quotation, a paraphrase, or your own idea.

distinctions in your notes. I will show you how in chapter 8, "Avoiding Plagiarism."

Participating in Class

Joining in academic discussions is another vital part of your education. That discussion might happen in the classroom, but it also might happen at the lab bench or informally over coffee. Wherever discussions take place, they add immeasurably to your education and professional training.

Jumping into these conversations is a challenge for some international students. They might be uncomfortable speaking English. Or they might be new to the give-and-take of seminars, where professors toss out provocative questions and expect a variety of answers. In either case, international students need to adapt to this new environment, inside and outside the classroom. The sooner you do it, the better.

One of your highest priorities should be to understand this new academic environment. Figure out what is really important here and what is different from your prior schooling. Then strive to excel, just as you did at home.

One of the biggest differences, according to most international students, is that your own ideas really matter in classes here. When professors lead seminars, they expect students to formulate their own ideas and support them in discussion. Classmates sometimes disagree with each other or with the assigned readings. They might disagree with the professor. That's fine. In fact, it's encouraged.

For students educated abroad, this new classroom environment can be a shock. In some countries, students have been taught to defer to their professor's views and repeat them accurately. Doing that well has been a central goal of their education.

Although the same is sometimes true for North American high school

> ***Tip:*** Your own thoughts and observations are important to class discussions. In seminars and discussion sections, you are expected to join in the exchange of ideas.

> **Tip:** You are not expected simply to repeat the professor's views. Your own ideas are important, too. It's fine to disagree with your professor as long as you are respectful, do your homework, and keep an open mind.

students, that's not the goal of higher education here. *The goal is to develop your own, well-informed views, whether they match the professor's or not.* You are not here simply to learn the "right answers" or the "right methods." You are here to learn how to think analytically, to determine what is interesting and important, and, ultimately, to investigate these issues yourself.

Yes, it's important to understand what your professor thinks and what the assigned authors say. The better you do that, the better student you will be. But that is only halfway to your real destination: developing your own informed analysis.

To develop it, you need to complete your assignments, listen carefully to your professor and your classmates, and then raise your own questions and voice your own ideas. You are welcome to explore new ideas, including tentative ones you aren't sure whether you believe. Debate, discuss, explore, probe. That is *not* rude or disrespectful. It's expected, even if your views differ from the professor's or from other classmates'.

Of course, you should expect some debate in return. Your classmates or your professor might disagree with *you*. That's fine, too. It can lead to fruitful discussions and real learning. You might change your views as you confront counterarguments. Or you might hold your views with even deeper conviction as you explain their rationale and present your evidence.

Speak Up, Even If You Speak with an Accent

What if you have an accent? What if you haven't mastered all the details of English? My advice: Keep working to improve, but don't stop participating. Try to join the give-and-take of class discussions, even though you are still polishing your verbal skills.

"Don't be afraid to make mistakes when you speak," one professor told me. "That's a good way to learn. If you are afraid to make mistakes, you will just stay silent and won't improve." He spoke from personal experience. Raised in China, he arrived here as a graduate student in the social sciences. His competence in English grew alongside his academic studies, and he is now a leading scholar at a major American university.

> ***Tip:*** Don't let your accent stop you from participating in class. Contribute to the discussion—and keep working to improve your spoken English.

Many international students offered similar advice: don't be afraid to speak up, even though you are bound to make mistakes. "And don't be afraid to ask questions," one international student told me. "If you don't understand the professor's explanation or another student's comments, say so. Other students are probably confused, too."

Many students told me the same thing. Raise questions if you don't understand something. Contribute your own views to the classroom discussion and challenge those you disagree with. Be polite, be respectful, be constructive if you can, but be an independent thinker.

To participate in this way requires real effort, and a little bravery. You need to overcome your fear of questioning the professor. You need to overcome your fear of making mistakes. You need to overcome your fear of speaking in public or contradicting others' views. All these anxieties are understandable, but you need to overcome them for the sake of your own education.

As you do all this, you will find most local students are welcoming. They will support you as you settle into university life here. They want you to do well. That's what most international students tell me.

American and Canadian students appreciate how difficult it is to live in another country and navigate in another language and culture. In fact, many of them know these difficulties firsthand, since they have traveled to other countries themselves for a semester or a year. That's a popular option for undergraduates. Now, as more advanced undergraduates or graduate students, they are eager to study with classmates from Japan, Israel, or South Africa, for example, and eager to meet them socially outside class. They want to know about your background and compare it with their own. They want to know about your family's customs. They want to hear your views and understand your perspective.

In return, you should reach out to them in classes, labs, and social settings.

Keep Working on Your Language Skills

Besides practicing your English in class and in social settings, you can improve it by taking language courses or lessons. Instruction in "English as a second language" (ESL) can help with reading, writing, listening, and speaking.[1] There are also courses for students who already know the language well but want to reduce their accents. Most schools offer this kind of instruction (either free or at low cost), as do private companies and individual tutors (at somewhat higher cost).

If you can afford it, consider arriving a few weeks before classes begin so you can devote full time to studying English and exploring your new surroundings. (Student visas generally permit this). If you can, take a "total immersion" course, where you speak only English. Your language skills will improve rapidly.

Whatever route you take to improving your spoken English, it's important to keep practicing. Doing so will encourage you to participate in class and to make friends off campus. Later, if you want to teach or work here, your chances of being hired will be much better if you speak well.

Even if you return home, your English skills will prove valuable. After all, English is now the global language of education, business, science, medicine, and diplomacy. You have a golden opportunity to become truly fluent, but only if you really work at it.

Socializing in English

Besides taking classes, the best way to improve your English is to spend time speaking it with friends outside class. If all your friends speak Chinese, if all your lab partners speak Chinese, if all your family speaks Chinese, then your only chance to speak English will come in class. That's not enough. You simply cannot master a new language with such sporadic practice. At most, your English will improve very slowly.

The lesson here is simple: work on your English in special classes and social settings. Please don't wait silently in class, hoping to become a "perfect speaker" before you participate. Don't wait silently at your friends' apartments or at parties, either. Whatever level you've reached, start participating now.

---

1. ESL is the term used in the United States, Canada, and Australia. ESOL ("English for speakers of other languages") means the same thing and is used in the UK, Ireland, and New Zealand. EFL ("English as a Foreign Language") is slightly different, since it refers to teaching English in regions where it is not spoken. Students of the language are known as English language learners (ELL).

> ***Tip:*** Your English will stagnate if you use it only in class. It will improve much faster if you use it all day long—with friends, family, classmates, and room-mates.

Improving Your Written English

Writing skills are equally important. Universities know how valuable these skills are and have established "writing centers" to help all their students, graduate and undergraduate, local and international. Take advantage of the courses they offer and the writing tutors who offer individual advice.

To get that help, you need to meet with tutors at your university's writing center or study skills center. Give them a call or send an e-mail to set up an appointment. They can show you how to take better notes, keep up with your readings, and write more effective papers.

These centers do *not* offer instruction in your subject, whether that subject is economics, chemistry, or classics. That's up to your professors. Writing centers offer classes and individual instruction to help you write better papers and exams, whatever your subject. They can teach you how to organize papers more effectively, write clearer sentences and sharper paragraphs. They can show you how to edit your text. Their services are usually free, or very inexpensive, and they are available to all students. But, like all other services in the university, you have to ask for them. It's well worth the effort to seek them out.

> ***Tip:*** Every university has special centers to teach writing and study skills. They can be very helpful and typically work with students individually, at no charge. To get this tutorial help, e-mail them and set up an appointment.

Getting Help with Written English

While you are still improving your English skills, is it okay to receive assistance in writing your papers from someone who knows English well? That depends on how much assistance you receive, what kind, and whether you disclose that assistance. It's usually fine to discuss your work, at least at a general level, and it can be very helpful. But there are two exceptions. First, you can *never* discuss work during exams. Second, unless it is a group assignment, you cannot receive direct help without asking the professor and acknowledging the help, unless it is very minor.

If a friend reads your work and suggests a few small changes, that's seldom a problem unless your professor forbids it. But what counts as "small"? That depends on your professor and the standards in your field.

A computer scientist gave me an example recently. I asked her about assignments to write a computer program, assignments intended for each student individually. What assistance could a student legitimately receive from classmates? "They might double-check the program's syntax," she said, "but any help with the program's logic would cross the line." That's reasonable, but it wasn't clear to me before she said it.

Just to be on the safe side, ask your professor in advance, when the assignment is handed out. Let your professor know if you do receive assistance (or, better yet, ask before you do) and make sure it is only minor. If a friend corrects your grammar or word usage, watch carefully so that next time you can do it yourself. Remember, the main point of assistance is *not* to produce one better paper; it is to learn how to produce lots of better papers on your own.

You should not receive more substantial assistance on papers or other assignments *unless* you ask your teacher's permission and explain what kind of help you are receiving. Why? Because your teacher wants to know that the work she grades is actually yours. Receiving substantial assistance without faculty permission could lead to misunderstandings and perhaps to the serious charge that you received impermissible help. It could be considered cheating.

Of course, on exams, you cannot receive any help at all. None. That's true whether it's an in-class or take-home exam, whether it's "open-book" or closed.

Seminars Are Discussions, Not Lectures

Participation is essential in seminars. In fact, student engagement is what makes seminars work. Courses that depend on free and open discussion wither and die when students sit quietly in the back of the room, session after session, never contributing. Don't do it. Passivity harms your education, and it weakens the whole class.

As a teacher, I have found that students who speak up in the first few sessions will continue to participate throughout the course. If they remain

> *Tip:* In seminars and discussion sections, sit at the table. Be sure to speak at least once in the first two seminar sessions. After that, it will be much easier to participate regularly.

silent during the first few sessions, they seldom participate later. They lock themselves into a passive role, at least in that course.

You can easily avoid that, and you should. First, sit at the seminar table, not in the back of the room. Sitting at the table encourages you to participate mentally even when you are not speaking, and it prompts you to speak up when you have ideas. Second, in one of the early sessions, jump into the discussion at least once. Force yourself. Once you break the ice, you'll find it much easier to continue participating throughout the semester.

Getting Advice from Faculty

Everybody needs help occasionally. Perhaps you didn't understand part of the lecture. Perhaps you were confused about a particular reading. Perhaps you are trying to choose a paper topic or a course for next semester. All these are excellent opportunities to meet with faculty, pose questions, and chat informally. Take advantage of them. Try to overcome your understandable reluctance to meet individually with professors. Their assistance is an integral part of education here at all levels.

Once again, you'll need to be proactive. Professors and advisers seldom approach you and request a meeting, even if they see you are having difficulties. Perhaps they should, but they don't. So you need to seek them out whenever you have questions or need advice.

When should you meet with professors? The best time is during their weekly "office hours." All professors have them. They set up regular times to meet with students individually, such as Thursday afternoons or Tuesdays from ten until noon. Some use a sign-up sheet for appointments; others simply ask students to drop by. But don't expect the professor to mail you an engraved invitation. If you want to come, it's entirely up to you.

My advice: Find out when your professors hold office hours and sign up occasionally. Use these office hours to get to know the faculty, to raise questions about their courses, to get feedback on your work, or to seek advice.

A brief, businesslike visit—perhaps ten or fifteen minutes—can be very helpful. That's exactly what faculty office hours are designed for. If you can't come during regular office hours, perhaps because you have a conflicting class, you can usually arrange an alternate time. Be sure to come with a specific topic to discuss or question to ask. Meetings with faculty are friendly, but they are not social visits.

International students are often reluctant to meet with professors. "In their home countries, young people simply don't meet with prominent people unless they already know them," one South American educator told me. She's familiar with the problem because she runs a foundation that sends students to the United States for graduate work. "Our students don't meet with faculty very often. They won't do it unless they already know the professor well or have some kind of introduction. Many of them think that asking for help is a sign of weakness."

The perspective here in North America is different. It's not necessarily better; it's just different. Here, you don't need to know the teacher before you meet, and you certainly don't need an introduction. Nor is it a sign of weakness to ask for help or clarification.

Faculty members expect students to come to their offices and ask questions about academic work. It's part of their teaching, and it happens all the time. Faculty are accustomed to meeting with students they don't know well, and they are comfortable giving advice about courses, papers, and career objectives. All they ask is that you come during office hours if possible and come with an agenda or some questions you have considered before the meeting. A little preparation will make the meeting more efficient and productive.

One of your most important goals, as a newly arrived student, should be to meet faculty in your area of interest. To encourage that, let me urge

Tip: Set the goal of getting to know one faculty member each semester.

you to pursue one concrete goal. Get to know one new faculty member each semester for the first two years. That's not an unrealistic or impractical goal. You can easily achieve it *if you try.* It's well worth the effort and will give you good contacts with four faculty members at the end of two years. You'll learn from your discussions; you'll be well positioned to get advice for research papers or lab work; and, later on, you can get recommendations that will aid you on the job market.

I will continue this discussion of student-faculty relations in chapter 9, "The Culture of Universities in the United States and Canada."

Getting Help from Deans and Other Professionals

Faculty are not the only sources for information and assistance. University deans and advisers are also comfortable talking with students and dispensing advice, mainly about issues beyond the classroom, from scholarship aid to visa problems. As professionals, they know this terrain and respect each student's right to privacy and confidentiality. That's especially important in dealing with sensitive personal issues, such as medical problems, financial needs, or family emergencies.

Take medical help, for example. All schools provide medical care, not only for physical ills but also for psychological difficulties. These services are confidential and are usually covered by your student health insurance.

Some international students have told me how difficult it is for them to discuss emotional problems or seek help for them. Many come from countries where these problems are simply not discussed and where seeking psychological help is considered shameful or a sign of personal weakness. The attitudes on North American campuses are far different. Emotional difficulties are considered problems that should be treated by trained professionals, just as physical illnesses are.

If you aren't sure what health services are available or whether you qualify, just ask an adviser in the dean of students' office or an administrator in your department. If they don't know the answer, they can direct you to someone who does. Don't hesitate to ask for guidance so you can find the medical services you need.

> *Tip:* If you have medical problems or personal (psychological) issues, see your university's health service. They have specialists on staff, and all treatment is confidential. Even the fact that you sought treatment is a confidential matter, by law, whether you are treated or not.

Recognizing Cultural Differences

One theme of this chapter is that North American universities share some basic ideas about education, ideas that may differ from those of schools in other countries. The quicker international students recognize these differences and adapt to them, the more successful they will be.

One obvious difference, which we have not yet discussed, is the role of women. North American colleges and universities now enroll roughly equal numbers of men and women. There has been a steady rise in the number of women graduate students and a somewhat slower rise in women faculty. Although the percentages of women differ across fields, there is a broadly shared commitment—throughout the university and through most of the wider society—to ensure that women receive equal opportunity and equal treatment.

This commitment to gender equality has important implications for international students, especially those from societies where women are denied professional opportunities. Here, female students are supposed to have the same opportunities as males. That, at least, is our widely shared aspiration. Increasingly, it is the reality. There is no tolerance in the classroom or the academy for discrimination against women or, for that matter, against different races, religions, ethnic groups, or sexual orientations. That requires some adjustment for students who come from countries where women (or various ethnic groups or religions) are treated differently. Your classmates and teachers will be men and women of all colors and creeds. They rightly expect equal treatment.

Another important difference, according to some international students, is that American graduate schools are competitive. In some countries, admission to a top program marks the end of competition. Simply

> *Tip:* Equal treatment, regardless of gender, race, religion, sexual orientation, or country of origin, is a strong norm here. It is protected by law, as well as by the university's own rules.

Tip: Universities are both supportive and competitive intellectual environments. Your performance is important for the next step in your career, whether that is a job or further education.

listing the school's name on your résumé proves you are qualified. Here, admission to a good school is only the beginning. The next step is performing well. Your grade point average (GPA) matters.[2] So do your teachers' assessments of your work.

There are plenty of practical incentives for doing well at university. The best jobs in business and public service go to students who achieve strong academic records. The best jobs in teaching and research go to students who write innovative, important theses. So performance matters, whether you are an undergraduate or graduate student. It demonstrates your intellect, your mastery of the material, your willingness to work hard, your ability to work well in groups, and your skill at managing independent projects.

The point of this competition is not to defeat your fellow students but to do your own best work. That means there are crucial limits to competition. First, it should be fair. No cheating on tests; no faking lab results; no plagiarizing papers. Under no circumstances should you impede others' work. Second, striving for excellence should not degenerate into direct, one-on-one competition with other students. Your goal should be to encourage others as you learn yourself. There may be some intellectual competition, but there can be a lot of fruitful cooperation as well. As you move forward professionally, your old classmates will often be your strongest supporters.

If you work hard and study intelligently, your own performance will be just fine. In any case, it will be your personal best. If, on the other hand, you treat classmates mainly as competitors, you will lose the opportunity to learn from them and miss the chance to make lifelong friends and colleagues. In the process, you will shortchange your education.

2. Most schools calculate grade point averages on a four-point scale, where A = 4.0, A– = 3.7, and so on. That means a 3.5 average is a mix of A's and B's. Students, faculty, and administrators use GPAs as a quick way to calculate student performance.

Chapter 6

Thinking Creatively:
Going Beyond What the
Professor Said

Some years ago, my cousin Kathy traveled to Paris for her "junior year abroad." Along with her passport, she carried a typical American attitude toward higher education. She certainly knew it was important to listen to her professors and do the assigned readings. But, like most students here, she considered it even more important to analyze the materials herself and develop her own viewpoint. That's exactly what she had done as an undergraduate in Virginia, where she received high marks. Wouldn't this critical approach to learning work just as well in France?

No, it wouldn't. When her Parisian professor returned her first paper, he sternly announced, "Mademoiselle Liggett, l'originalité n'existe pas." (Miss Liggett, originality does not exist.)

His meaning was clear: do not strive for creativity in this class. "You are a newcomer," he was saying, "and I have studied these subjects for years. Nobody is interested in your half-baked ideas. Listen carefully to *my* ideas and *my* analysis. Take extensive notes when I lecture. Read the experts I assign to you. Then try to repeat my ideas and whatever facts I mention as accurately as you can."

Repeating the professor's viewpoint is a lesson already drilled into students in France—and in India, China, Mexico, and a hundred other countries. These students soon learn that, to succeed in class, they must replicate their professors' perspective, data, and methods in detail. "L'originalité n'existe pas."

This kind of repetition is not the route to success in North American universities, and the difference has real consequences for students who come here. They must reverse the path taken by my cousin Kathy. While

Tip: U.S. and Canadian universities emphasize creativity, in students as well as faculty. International students need to recognize these values and accommodate their work to them.

they are expected to understand their professor's views and the assigned readings, they are also expected to develop their own perspectives on the material they are studying.

Of course, it is still important to follow the lectures and the readings and to take careful notes. In fact, international students have a major advantage in performing these essential tasks because their education has always stressed them. U.S. and Canadian students, by contrast, are not always well prepared with these skills, and are more likely to skim the readings or skip the lectures—a very bad idea.

Reading and repetition are not enough. The goal is to develop your own understanding, your own synthesis of ideas, your own critique of readings and lectures. As you move into more advanced courses, you should develop your own sense of what are the most interesting problems and what are the best methods for analyzing them. In lab sciences, you should develop your own sense of how to perform experiments and how to generate your own data to test hypotheses.

No professor in Berkeley, Toronto, or Boston would ever announce, "Originality does not exist in my classroom." *The goal of a university education here is not only to master the assigned readings and to understand your professor's analysis; it is also to develop your own, well-informed perspectives.* You can pursue that goal whether you are writing a research paper, answering an essay exam, or conducting a lab experiment. In each case, you need to add your creative spark to your knowledge of the field. With time and sustained effort, you can develop true mastery of your subject: knowing the data and the analytic methods, knowing what others think, evaluating their views with care and rigor, and then developing your own distinctive analysis.

This view of education can come as a jolt to international students. But

Tip: Emphasizing creativity does not mean skimping on the readings or lectures. It means learning the assigned materials and then going further, developing your own informed perspective.

that's how higher education works here. Creativity and hard work are the keys to academic success in the United States and Canada, no matter what the subject.

Critiquing the Readings, Questioning the Professor

This emphasis on creativity has a profound impact on the way classes are taught. As international students soon realize, there are fundamental differences between classrooms in North America and those in, say, Germany, Pakistan, or Mexico.[1] To generalize broadly, classrooms in Africa, Latin America, the Muslim Middle East, and in some countries in continental Europe are more formal and hierarchical. In East Asia, the formality and deference to faculty is even stronger. To succeed in classrooms like these, it is crucial to know exactly what the experts say, beginning with your professor. Exams and papers require it. Teachers reward it.

The nickname for this style of education is "mug and jug." The professor is like a large jug, filled to the brim with knowledge. He pours it into the small mugs, his students.

This is not an attractive metaphor for higher education. It diminishes knowledge to the status of privileged information, passed from master to novice. Faculty in the United States and Canada overwhelmingly reject this mug-and-jug model in favor of a different one—one that encourages students to think originally and ultimately to develop their own insights and analysis.

One expert familiar with international students recommends an "analytical and questioning approach to knowledge rather than the received or rote learning style. Some students from some cultures will bring an uncritical reverence for the written word or the views of the teacher which might impede intellectual progress."[2] Following that theme, your goal should be to combine a thorough knowledge of the assigned materials (the best part of your prior education) with your own critical insights (the best part of your new education).

This more active style of learning takes some getting used to. But, as you'll soon discover, debate is a regular feature of higher education in

---

1. Classrooms in the UK, Ireland, Australia, New Zealand, and Israel are similar to those in U.S. and Canada. They emphasize student creativity and originality. They deemphasize rote learning and repetition of the professor's views.

2. Christine Humfrey, *Managing International Students: Recruitment to Graduation* (Buckingham, UK: Open University Press, 1999), 97.

North America, and professors' own views are part of it. Questions, skepticism, and even disagreements are actually encouraged. This brisk discussion fosters critical thinking and is not disrespectful to your professor or your classmates, *if* you treat everyone courteously and *if* you do the necessary homework (so your opinions are well grounded).

The real difficulty, then, is to balance two conflicting ideas about the professor's role as your teacher. On the one hand, she is the acknowledged expert. That's why she is the teacher and you are the student. On the other hand, she wants to teach you by fostering thoughtful discussion and independent ideas, not by creating little clones. Her own views are part of the discussion, not high above it. They are not beyond criticism and should not be accepted solely because of her authority. Her views, like everyone else's, must be supported and justified. Good teachers are prepared to engage in this kind of discussion and debate, rather than merely proclaiming the superiority of their views and indoctrinating their students. This tension between the professor's two roles, one as an acknowledged authority, the other as a participant in the discussion, is inherent in liberal education.

What Is Creative Work?

What does it mean to be a creative student—someone who does interesting and original work? The answer depends partly on your level of expertise and partly on your field of study.

In lower-level courses, such as first-year calculus or introductory microeconomics, you are expected to learn well-defined materials. No one expects you to do strikingly original work in these courses, much less contribute to new knowledge. First, you must learn how to differentiate an equation or find the market-clearing price. In courses like these, you need to learn the fundamental concepts, the basic theories, and the problems they address.

Yet even in these courses, students are expected to do more than absorb material and repeat it passively. You should understand what the main concepts are, why they are important, and how they are best applied. You should be able to explain these concepts clearly and manipulate them to cover new data. You should be willing to engage the course materials actively, challenge weak theories, and synthesize ideas from different parts of the course. In short, you should aim to be a curious and inquiring student, as well as a hardworking one.

The same rules apply to introductory lab sciences. Of course, you should be able to repeat well-defined lab procedures. But following an assignment is only a stepping-stone. The goal is to understand the logic of the experiments and their relationship to broader scientific theories. In basic courses, you should learn how particular experiments are normally conducted so you can perform them yourself. Later, you should be able to devise your own experiments and work out the sequence of tasks needed to perform them. At the most advanced levels, your goal should be to generate ideas, turn them into testable hypotheses, and then test them with appropriate techniques. The best students seek out interesting problems, develop hypotheses to illuminate them, and then generate original data to test their hypotheses.

> *Tip:* Creativity is just as important in lab sciences as in other courses. Doing creative work in the lab means identifying important problems, developing hypotheses, devising appropriate tests, and generating your own data.

As courses become more advanced and sophisticated, the demand for creativity rises. That's as true for comparative literature as it is for chemistry. Success in every field requires critical thinking, the ability to synthesize existing literature, and a capacity to develop your own questions and your own informed perspective.

> *Tip:* As you reach more advanced levels and do more sustained research, the demand for creative, original work also rises.

Intellectual Initiative

Learning that emphasizes rote memory and repetition discourages students from taking intellectual initiative. Learning that emphasizes creativity and originality, by contrast, stimulates intellectual engagement. This kind of engagement is the goal of university education. Students are strongly encouraged to pursue topics that interest them, conduct their own research, and choose their own readings to supplement class assignments. The more advanced the course, the more important your initiative and creativity.

Some international students have a difficult time making this intellectual transition, according to both professors and students themselves. "I

> *Tip:* Students here are expected to take initiative, especially in upper-level research courses. You are expected to choose interesting issues, compile your own set of background readings, and select an appropriate method to investigate them. Your professor will offer guidance and feedback.

have a hard time getting [a particular foreign graduate student who works with me] to build his own reading list for research," one professor told me. "He wants me to select every reading and he doesn't want to go beyond them. I keep telling him to look at footnotes and bibliographies in the articles he reads and pursue the works that look interesting and relevant."

She is making an important point. Creativity means more than just having a new idea. It means choosing an exciting topic, studying what others have already said about it, and selecting a fruitful approach to investigate it yourself. If creativity didn't matter, then professors could simply give you a topic, tell you what to read, and tell you how to research it. In many educational systems, that's exactly what teachers do. They do it here, too, in some introductory courses. But in upper-level courses, professors expect you to choose your own topics, readings, and research methods— all with their guidance. In short, you are expected to take the initiative in shaping your work. This combination of initiative and hard work is integral to creative learning.

Faculty Comments on Top International Students

To see what American and Canadian universities value, I reviewed hundreds of recommendations for top international students applying to graduate school here. These are the best undergraduates in Africa, Asia, Europe, the Middle East, and Latin America, and their professors want to see them admitted to the best graduate programs. To do that, their recommendations need to say not only that these are superb students, but that they also excel in ways that universities here really care about. That's what these recommendations do. As a result, these strong, successful recommendations tell you not only about the individual students. They tell you about values and abilities prized by North American universities. Here are some selected comments:

> She takes direction well, but has her own ideas. She is not a "what do I do next?" type of student.

[He] possesses one of the most essential qualities for becoming a first-rate researcher—originality.

Her capacity to absorb new material and identify important issues or problems is extraordinary. Her analytic skills are of the highest order. She writes with great intellectual maturity for someone at this stage of a research career. . . . She sets herself extremely high standards of personal integrity.

[This student] is not satisfied to simply regurgitate what she reads in the literature. Rather, she brings a keen analytical eye to every bit of her work.

[She has a] keen analytical and inquiring mind and excellent research skills . . . and was open to criticism and guidance.

He was consistently prepared and thoughtful in his approach to material. He has a fine critical facility, but also curiosity and imagination. He could be counted upon to take discussion beyond the immediate text, to consider implications and broader connections.

His in-class participation and exams demonstrated strong oral and writing skills, and a particularly acute critical distance and perspective toward the readings assigned for each session.

In class, he tended to offer the more perceptive comments, and they revealed a commendably deep engagement with the relevant literature.

Clearly, these are wonderful students, and the recommendations say that. In the process, they also underscore exactly what American and Canadian universities most value in their students.

Chapter 7

Working as a Teaching Assistant, Lab Assistant, or Research Assistant

Nearly all graduate students help teach undergraduate courses, supervise student labs, and assist faculty with their research. This chapter explains what these jobs are and what is expected when you perform them.

Assisting faculty in courses and labs can lead to a larger role: doing joint work and perhaps even publishing together. Working with leading scholars can be rewarding, but it occasionally leads to problems about who gets credit for joint work. I discuss these issues at the end of the chapter.

Serving as a Teaching Assistant or Lab Assistant

Most graduate students serve as teaching assistants (TAs), conducting weekly discussion sections and grading papers in large courses. Graduate students in the sciences play similar teaching roles in undergraduate lab courses.[1]

To succeed as teaching assistants, international students need to remember what helps them succeed as students in North America. First, it is crucial to communicate clearly—in English. Students find it hard enough to master calculus or organic chemistry under the best circumstances. It's much harder if they cannot understand what their teacher is saying. You can help them by speaking slowly and clearly and occasionally checking to make sure everybody understands what you are saying.

Second, encourage class discussion, questions, and even disagreements,

---

1. Different universities use different terms for teaching assistants. In the University of California system, for example, they are called graduate student instructors (GSIs).

> **Tip:** As a teaching assistant, it is vital that you speak clearly to the class. Prepare for each class session and encourage student participation, not repetition. Insist on academic honesty and explain your rules to everyone, in advance. If you have any problems or questions, take them to the head TA or the professor running the course.

not rote repetition. To facilitate this kind of class participation, you'll need to prepare for each session. Preparation doesn't take long, but you do need to think about what you want to cover and how you want to approach the material.

Third, insist on academic honesty. Your students should do their own work and follow the rules of citation, just as you do.

Fourth, remember that you are working under the direction of the class professor. Know how he wants papers and exams graded. If you have any questions about how to grade a paper or whether a student is cheating, talk it over with the professor. (In very large courses, there is often a head teaching assistant, with whom you might raise these issues first.) Remember, if you are not sure what to do, ask the professor.

There's one rule you won't have to ask about. All professors want you to grade students impartially, without preferential treatment for anyone. What counts is the quality of their work, not whether you like (or dislike) them. Whether you are grading participation in class or marking papers, try to give each student fair, evenhanded treatment. To do that, some professors and TAs actually hide the student's name from themselves when they grade essays or exams. They want to grade the paper, not the person.

Fifth, whatever rules you have for the class, explain them to the whole class before any problems arise. Make sure everybody understands the ground rules, and then apply them equally to all students. The same holds true for lab sections.

Maintaining Professional Relationships with Students

As a TA, you are a teacher. That's true even though you are still a student yourself. Being a teacher carries responsibilities, especially in dealing with students. Good teachers try to maintain cordial, professional relationships with all their students and avoid intimate friendships with any of them. As a teaching assistant, you should do the same thing.

As a teacher, you should

- act professionally;
- treat all students fairly and equally;
- avoid socializing privately with students enrolled in your class;
- attend every class session, unless you are sick or must deal with an emergency;
- show up for class on time;
- prepare your lessons in advance;
- give students useful comments on their work;
- turn in your grades promptly.

Graduate students are often surprised by the requirements of being a teaching assistant. They know they are supposed to teach a section and grade papers, but they don't think about any other obligations. In fact, these obligations are an essential part of teaching.

It can be difficult to be *both* a teacher *and* a student. You might find yourself teaching an undergraduate section in the morning and attending another course in the afternoon as a student. These dual roles can be confusing, since teachers and students have very different responsibilities. As a student, you are free to socialize with whomever you choose. As a TA, however, you should not socialize privately with students in classes you teach. It could lead some students to think you are playing favorites. In this case, your responsibilities as a teacher override your freedom as a student.

You can invite the *entire* class to join you for coffee or a pizza after class, but you cannot invite a few selected students. If you want to drink a cappuccino with a couple of students in your section, then you should make a similar opportunity available to their fellow students. Those who are not included in a social event will fear that you favor other students. Appearances matter. Your students should know that you treat them fairly and equally.

That's why, if you spend extra time helping one student with a paper or lab project, you should make sure everyone else is eligible for the same treatment—and make sure that they know it. Because you are responsible for grading your students, it is vital to avoid any conflict of interest, or even the appearance of conflict.

You certainly cannot date your students—for several reasons. It violates the basic principle that you should treat all students fairly and professionally, without favoritism. Is your date getting special treatment in

Tip: As a TA, you should treat all students equally. Avoid private socializing or any special treatment for students currently in your section or lab. It's vital that your students know you are fair.

class or labs? Other students would have every reason to wonder. Second, dating your students poses a conflict of interest. Your professional interest in teaching and grading fairly could easily conflict with your personal interest in developing a social relationship, perhaps an intimate one. The conflict of interest can be even worse if a relationship breaks up. Students who end personal relationships with faculty (or who refuse to begin them) might fear retribution in their grades or working relationship. Third, because teachers have power in the classroom and lab, students might not feel free to reject a teacher who requests a date. Given the inequality between teachers and their students, we cannot tell if a student's consent to a social relationship is really voluntary. For all these reasons, then, you should avoid dating or other private social activities with students in your classes or labs.

What if, by chance, you already know a student who is assigned to your section or lab? You *must* tell the professor who leads the course. Do it right away. She can decide whether to reassign the student, do the grading herself, or make some other arrangement. That's her choice to make. Once you tell her, you have discharged your responsibility.

Tip: TAs operate under the supervision of the course professor. If you encounter any problems in your section, bring them to the professor and ask for advice.

One final point, though it should be obvious: never use your authority as a teacher to coerce students or achieve personal ends. Be professional and scrupulously fair. Remember, as a teacher, it's important both to *be fair* and to *appear fair* to all your students.

Serving as a Research Assistant (RA)

Working as a professor's research assistant (RA) is one of the most common jobs on campus. It's also one of the best ways to forge a relationship with faculty and learn the nuts and bolts of research.

RAs work between five and fifteen hours each week and handle a wide

> **Tip:** As an RA, it's important to know what type of work the faculty member expects, how many hours you should work each week, and what kind of work product you should turn in. Discuss these when you begin the job. You should also make sure the professor knows your academic background and skills so he can take full advantage of them.

range of tasks, depending on the professor's research needs and the student's abilities. A student fluent in Arabic or Portuguese might translate materials for a professor who doesn't know those languages. A student who knows Stata or SPSS might be asked to run certain statistical tests. It all depends on your skills and the professor's needs.

Some RA work is routine and boring. We call it "grunt work." "Could you find this book in the library and photocopy pages 10–35?" "Could you encode this data for me?" Some assignments are a bit more challenging: "Could you find the best two or three articles on this topic I'm interested in?" Some is like writing a class paper: "Could you write a brief summary of this book and maybe find a good published review of it?" Or "Could you assemble a short reading list on this topic for me?"

Before you sign on as an RA, it's important to sit down with the professor and discuss exactly what the job entails. Is it mostly grunt work, for example, or is it mostly writing reports? Are you expected to take a lot of initiative or will you receive detailed instructions and close supervision?

Be sure to tell the professor about your skills and training. He can't take advantage of them if you haven't told him. Start by giving him a brief résumé, listing your educational background and pertinent skills. The résumé should launch a useful discussion during the job interview, one that may continue after you begin work.

In your initial discussions, you should find out what kind of working schedule the professor expects. Can you keep your own hours, or do you need to be in the office at certain times? He has undoubtedly had RAs before, and he will know what he wants.

He'll also have a good idea what kind of work product he expects. One professor might want brief reports submitted via e-mail. Another might prefer longer reports delivered in hard copy, with an e-mail backup. He'll know how quickly he wants various tasks completed. It helps to discuss all this as you begin the job. If you have any questions when you receive a new assignment, be sure to ask. That's the best way to avoid misunderstandings.

> **Tip:** If you are taking notes on books and articles for a faculty member, be sure that direct quotations are clearly indicated. Ask the professor how he wants you to handle this.

Finally, if you are taking notes on books or articles, ask the professor how you should handle direct quotes, as opposed to your own summaries. Mishandling direct quotations can lead to disaster. If your notes don't clearly distinguish direct quotations from paraphrases, then the professor's article (relying on your work) might fail to put quotation marks around another author's words. That omission can lead to charges that the professor plagiarized. My own advice is to put the letter Q at the beginning and end of each quotation. It's better than a small quotation mark, because it stands out. You are not likely to overlook it, and neither is the professor. (The following chapter, "Avoiding Plagiarism and Doing Honest Work," discusses this important issue in greater detail.)

Doing Joint Work with Faculty

Graduate students sometimes do research that leads to coauthored publications with their professors. It can be extremely rewarding—a chance for close collaboration and publications that advance your career. That's the good news.

The bad news is that not all joint work ends so happily. A few professors use their students' work without giving them full credit, or, worse yet, without giving them credit at all. That's abuse of authority. There are also more complicated cases, where it's unclear how to apportion credit and where the participants disagree about it. These problems sometimes arise in the sciences, where multiple authorship is common and where lab partners discuss their work freely. At what point does a comment or suggestion from the head of the lab (or perhaps from a fellow student) deserve authorial credit? Where should each participant's name appear in a coauthored paper?

These are difficult questions, and different specialties have their own norms (sometimes contested ones). The difficulties are compounded because lab members have different positions and different authority. Some, like the head of the lab, might hold the keys to your professional future.

I will not try to unravel these complexities here. Instead, I will offer one

> **Tip:** Before doing joint work with a professor, it's wise to discuss how credit is normally apportioned for such work. If you're unsure if his approach is fair and reasonable, check with friends in other labs and perhaps other faculty. Administrators who deal with academic integrity issues can also help answer these questions.

piece of straightforward advice. *If you are doing research in a laboratory or working collaboratively with a professor, it is best to discuss these publication issues in advance.* Do it early, before you have completed any research or produced publishable papers (or patentable inventions). Better yet, do it before you start the research. The faculty member will have some clear guidelines about how to handle credit for joint work. Discuss them openly. Be sure that you understand them and that you agree to these rules before you spend months or years on collaborative research.

If you are uncertain whether the professor's guidelines are fair and reasonable, ask faculty or friends in other labs. Again, it's best to do this at the outset, before you immerse yourself in the collaborative work.

Later, if problems or questions arise, you can take them to administrators who deal regularly with academic integrity issues. But it's far better to avoid these problems in the first place. The best way to do that is to discuss the issues openly and candidly at the outset of any research.

Chapter 8

Avoiding Plagiarism and Doing Honest Work

"International students can face an enormous cultural gap between what is expected here and what was expected in their home institutions," one experienced professor told me. "That is especially true of plagiarism. International students don't always understand that our rules are different [from those they may have had at home]. Some of them don't realize just how important plagiarism is here."

That's the nub of the matter. U.S. and Canadian universities flatly prohibit plagiarism and consider any violation a serious offense. Punishment can range from failing an assignment to expulsion from the university. Fortunately, there is a very simple solution: learn the rules of academic honesty here and follow them carefully. In this chapter, I'll explain the rules and offer plenty of practical suggestions to help you do honest work and avoid problems.

Cheating and Fraud

There's not much confusion about cheating. To take one obvious example, you cannot download material from the Web and pass it off as your own work. It's not, and you cannot pretend it is.

You cannot copy answers from other students, either for tests or problem sets. You cannot ask a friend for some help and then turn in the answer she wrote, pretending it's your own. That's fraudulent. Except for very minor help (such as making sure your punctuation is correct), you cannot receive any direct assistance for an individual assignment unless the professor permits it.

What kind of assistance is it proper to give or receive? Most faculty

> **Tip:** You cannot copy work from any person or source (such as a book, article, or Web site) unless your assignment permits it. If your assignment does permit it, then you must acknowledge others' work fully and openly. Otherwise, it's cheating or plagiarism.

would say you are welcome to talk with other students about any topic, including readings, issues, and questions. Teachers encourage such discussions as fruitful ways for students to teach each other. But you cannot copy any part of your work from someone else, unless you are doing a joint project and say so explicitly when you turn it in. Nor can you move from discussing issues, readings, and methods to getting—or giving—more concrete help with an answer, paper, or other assignment. General discussions are fine; specific help with an assignment is not.

Two Types of Group Work

Group work is commonplace in all the sciences and in some professional schools, such as business and public policy. Academic honesty in group work consists of the usual rules, plus one more: it is essential for you to understand whether the professor wants your group to produce a *joint product,* such as a coauthored report, or an *individual product,* such as a single-authored lab report, after some group discussions or joint work on the lab bench.

If you are supposed to produce a joint product, then your responsibility is to join in the planning and discussion and then contribute your fair share to the joint effort. You might write several pages of the group paper, for instance, or collect the relevant data for the group project. You might edit another member's work; you might pitch in with others to write the introduction and conclusion, and so on. At every stage, you can talk with other members of the group and collaborate on any details you wish.

The rules are completely different, though, if the assignment ultimately calls for individual papers, lab reports, or problem sets, after some group study. In this case, the group's goal is to teach each other and to think together about the main ideas. In a lab, you might be asked to do the experiments together but then collect the data individually and write up your own separate reports. You cannot receive detailed help on any part of the assignment that is supposed to be done individually. For assignments like this, it is vital to know exactly what the professor wants your group to

> *Tip:* Before you begin a group assignment, be sure you understand what the group is supposed to do together and what you are supposed to do on your own. If you are not sure, simply ask your professor.

do together and what she wants you to do by yourself. If you are not sure, just ask.

In fact, that's the most important advice I can give on all group assignments. Make sure you know what you are permitted to do together and what you are required to do individually. If you are not sure, ask your professor.

Plagiarism

Plagiarism is using materials—*any materials*—without proper attribution. That means presenting someone else's words, ideas, equations, research, or other work as your own. It really doesn't matter what type of work it is. It might be sentences or paragraphs someone else wrote. It might be architectural drawings or a musical composition. It might be lab data or computer code. If somebody else did it, you must say so openly. Give them credit. Otherwise, it looks like you are taking credit for work you did not do.

Believe it or not, you can even plagiarize yourself, although it is usually termed cheating instead of plagiarizing. Whatever the terminology, you cannot use your own previous work, written for another class, unless you explain it to your new teacher and ask permission.[1]

Plagiarism is a serious offense. When it's caught—and it often is—it leads to severe consequences, anything from failing a paper to failing a course. In extreme cases, it leads to suspension or expulsion. It's not a parking ticket. It's a highway crash. If it looks deliberate, it's a highway crash without seat belts.

Plagiarism is rare, but it does happen occasionally. A few students cheat deliberately.[2] Others make innocent mistakes. Students rushing to finish a paper may forget to include the necessary citations. Some students are confused about the rules. They may not understand that all quotations

---

1. This chapter is a good illustration. It incorporates ideas, materials, and text from my book, *Doing Honest Work in College,* 2nd ed. (Chicago, IL: University of Chicago Press, 2008). This citation is an example of full disclosure whenever an author draws on or directly incorporates his own prior work.

2. It is always wrong to use others' work without proper attribution. The most troubling cases involve intentional use of another author's work without full attribution. That is the classic definition of plagiarism. Some use a wider definition, which includes *unintentional* copying and

> ***Tip:*** You are expected to know the rules of academic honesty, as they are understood in the United States and Canada. Ignorance of the rules, or sloppy work habits, are not an excuse.

> ***Tip:*** It's important to get the "right answers," but it is equally important to say where you discovered them. Cite and quote your sources.

need to be identified with *both* quotation marks and citations or that original papers cannot be a patchwork of downloaded materials, pasted together. Some students are just sloppy. Perhaps their notes on a book or article are garbled or confused. Later, when they use these notes to write a paper, they could inadvertently treat the other author's words as their own. Even if it's an accident, it's no fun trying to prove that to a skeptical professor or dean.

Fortunately, this last problem is easily prevented. A little later in this chapter, I will show you a few simple techniques, beginning with Q-quotes, to keep your notes straight.

Another cause of plagiarism is that students don't understand the citation rules, or they come from academic systems with different standards, as many international students do. Perhaps they think (wrongly) that it is more important to get "the right answer" than to acknowledge the source. Actually, it is important to do both. The right answers certainly matter. But, at universities across the United States and Canada, it matters just as much to cite and quote the sources where you found those answers.

Whatever the cause, plagiarism is a serious violation of academic rules—for local students and international students, for undergraduates or graduate students, for faculty and postdocs. Misrepresenting someone else's words, ideas, or data as your own constitutes fraud.

The Three Principles of Academic Honesty

To avoid these problems, it helps to understand three basic principles of academic integrity. They are straightforward and easy to remember. First, when you say you did the work yourself, you actually did it. Second, when

---

borrowing. I call that "accidental plagiarism." Even if it's accidental borrowing—the spoiled fruits of sloppy notes rather than deliberate theft—it is still a serious problem. Whether or not you call it plagiarism, it's a major breach of academic rules.

> **Tip:** Academic honesty boils down to three fundamental principles:
>
> - When you say you did the work yourself, you actually did it.
> - When you rely on someone else's work, you cite it. When you use their words, you quote them openly and accurately, and you cite them, too.
> - When you present research materials, you present them fairly and truthfully. That's true whether the research involves data, documents, or the writings of other scholars.

you rely on someone else's work, you cite it. When you use someone else's words, you quote them openly and accurately. Third, when you present research materials, you present them fairly and truthfully. Quotations, data, lab experiments, and the ideas of others should never be falsified or distorted. They should never be fabricated.

Cite Others' Work to Avoid Plagiarism

Citation rules follow from these three basic principles of openness and honesty. If the words are someone else's, they must be clearly marked as quotations, either by quotation marks or block indentations, followed by a citation. (I'll explain block quotations in a minute.) It's not enough merely to mention an author's name. If it's a direct quote, use quotation marks and a full citation. If it's a paraphrase of someone else's words, use your own language, not a close imitation of the work being cited, and include a proper reference.

The same rules apply to visual images, architectural drawings, databases, graphs, statistical tables, algorithms, computer code, spoken words, and information taken from the Internet. If you use someone else's work, cite it. Cite it even if you think the work is wrong and you intend to criticize it. Cite it even if the work is freely available in the public domain. Cite it even if the author gave you permission to use the work. Cite it even if it is your professor's own work—and she obviously knows it's hers. All these rules follow from the same idea: acknowledge what you take from others.

The only exception, the only time you don't need to cite, is when you rely on commonly known information. When you discuss gravity, you don't need to footnote Isaac Newton.

What constitutes "commonly known information"? That depends on your field, your level of specialization, and your intended audience. A PhD dissertation on the Second World War can assume its audience is more so-

Tips on avoiding plagiarism: When in doubt, give credit by citing the original source.

- If you use an author's exact words, enclose them in quotation marks and include a citation.
- If you paraphrase another author, use your own language. Don't imitate the original. Be sure to include a citation.
- If you rely on or report someone else's ideas, credit that source, whether you agree with them or not.

phisticated than a sophomore paper on the same subject. The dissertation does not need to remind its audience that General Douglas MacArthur led U.S. ground forces in the Pacific. They already know that, and there's no need to reference a source for that common knowledge. The sophomore paper, on the other hand, is written for a more general (less specialized) audience, so it needs to provide more basic background information and needs to cite its sources for that information.

Quotation Marks and Block Quotes

When you quote an author, you not only need to cite the work, you need to cite it *and* include quotation marks.

As an example, let's take a sentence or two from a paragraph you just read. Let's say you want to use that in a paper you are writing. What's the right way, and what's the wrong way?

Example 1 (*correct* short quote): "A PhD dissertation on the Second World War can assume its audience is more sophisticated than a sophomore paper on the same subject."[Citation] Because the exact words are being quoted, they should be enclosed in quotation marks. A citation is needed to show where the quote originated.

Example 2 (*incorrect* short quote): A PhD dissertation on the Second World War can assume its audience is more sophisticated than a sophomore paper on the same subject.[Citation] Omitting the quotation marks here is a mistake. Because the exact words are being quoted, it is not enough merely to include a citation. You *must* include the quotation marks, as well as the citation.

Example 3 (*correct* paraphrase): Whether you are writing about World War II or nuclear fusion, you can assume the readers of a doctoral thesis are much more knowledgeable than a general audience.[Citation] This sentence

> *Tip:* The indentation for a block quote is the equivalent of quotation marks. It still needs proper citation. Block quotes are normally at least ten lines long.

does not need quotation marks (indeed, it cannot include them) because it is not quoting an author's exact words. Still, it needs a citation to show the source for this observation. In a table below, I'll explain paraphrasing in more detail.

Example 4 (*correct* block quote, showing a bit of regular text, followed by a long quotation):

Many students ask if they really need to cite everything. According to one expert, the answer

> depends on your field, your level of specialization, and your intended audience. A PhD dissertation on the Second World War can assume its audience is more sophisticated than a sophomore paper on the same subject. The dissertation does not need to remind its audience that General Douglas MacArthur led U.S. ground forces in the Pacific. They already know that, and there's no need to reference a source for that common knowledge. The sophomore paper, on the other hand, is written for a more general (less specialized) audience, so it needs to provide more basic background information and needs to cite its sources for that information.[Citation]

Longer quotes like this—several sentences or more—are set off from the regular text by an indentation. The indentation itself effectively serves as a quotation mark. You don't need to put quotation marks around the indented paragraph, and, in fact, you should not do so. However, you do need to include a proper citation, just as you would for a brief quotation.

Cite Others' Work to Avoid Plagiarism

There are serious penalties for violating these rules for proper quotation and citation. For faculty members, a violation can mean demotion or even loss of tenure. For students, it can mean failed courses and even expulsion. For international students, it can mean the loss of a student visa, which depends on being a full-time student in good academic standing. The penalties are harsh because academic honesty is so central to teaching, learning, and research. Across the university, we depend on the integrity of each others' work.

Being caught plagiarizing or cheating can affect students' subsequent careers, too. Employers are reluctant to hire someone with a record of ethical violations, and government licensing boards (such as those for lawyers, accountants, or architects) are reluctant to certify them to practice.

Taking Notes with Q-Quotes

Some honest writers find themselves in hot water, accused of plagiarism, because their notes are so bad they cannot tell what they copied and what they wrote themselves. You can avoid that by clearly distinguishing your words from those of others.

All you need is a simple way to identify quotes and keep them separate from your own words and ideas.

The common solution—using ordinary quotation marks in your notes—doesn't actually work so well in practice. For one thing, quotation marks are small, so it's easy to overlook them later when you return to your notes to write a paper. Second, they don't tell you which page the quote comes from, something you need to know for proper citations. Third, if there's a quote within a quote, it's hard to keep your markings straight.

There's a better way. To avoid all this confusion, simply use the letter Q and the page number to begin all quotations in your notes. To end the quote, write Q again. It's painless, and it's easy to spot the Qs when you read your notes and write your papers.

Begin your notes for each new item by writing down the author, title, and other essential data. You'll need this information for each book, article, and Web site you use. With this publication data plus Q-quotes, you'll be able to cite effectively from your own notes, without having to return to the original publication.

This system is simple, clear, and effective. It works equally well for typed and handwritten notes. It easily handles quotes within quotes. Looking at your notes, you'll know exactly which words are the author's, and which page they are on. You'll know if he is quoting anyone else. And you'll know that anything *outside* the Q-quotes is your own paraphrase.

Tip on using Q-quotes to identify exact words: Q157 Churchill's eloquence rallied the nation during the worst days of the war. Q

Tip on paraphrasing: Make sure your paraphrase does not closely resemble the author's words. When in doubt, double-check your wording against the original.

Because quotes can be complicated, let's see how these Q-quotes work in more detail. First, some quotes begin on one page and end on another. To show where the page break falls, insert a double slash (//) inside the quote. (A double slash stands out, just as Q does.) That way, if you use only part of the quote, you can cite the correct page without having to chase down the original again. To illustrate:

> Q324–25 Mark Twain's most important works deal with his boyhood on the river. He remembered // that distant time with great affection. He returned to it again and again for inspiration. Q

The first sentence is on page 324; the next one is on both pages; the third is only on page 325. Using Q-quotes with a double slash gives you all this information quickly and easily.

Quotes can be complicated in other ways, too. I explain how to handle them and take effective notes in my book, *Doing Honest Work in College.*[3]

Using the Internet without Plagiarizing

You need to be especially alert to these citation issues when you use the Web. Internet research is very efficient, especially when you don't need to read long stretches of text. You can do extensive targeted searches, quickly check out multiple sources, access sophisticated databases, click on article summaries or key sentences, and then drag-and-drop material into your notes. That's all perfectly fine. In fact, it's often the best way to conduct research. But it's also crucial to be a good bookkeeper. You need to use a simple, consistent method to keep straight what each author said and what you paraphrased.

The easiest way is to stick with the method you use for printed books and articles: *put Q-quotes around everything you drag-and-drop from electronic sources.* You can supplement that, if you wish, by coloring the author's text red or blue, or by using a different font. Just be consistent. That way you won't be confused in three or four weeks, when you are reviewing your notes and writing your paper.

One more thing: be sure to write down the Web site's address so you can cite it or return to it for more research. Just copy the URL into your notes. It's probably a good idea to include the date you accessed it, too.

---

3. *Doing Honest Work in College,* 2nd ed. (Chicago, IL: University of Chicago Press, 2008).

Some citation styles ask for it. If the item appears in a database and has a document identification number, copy that, too.

Quoting and Paraphrasing without Plagiarizing: A Table of Examples

A simple example can illustrate how to quote and paraphrase properly, and how to avoid some common mistakes. The following table shows the main rules for citation and academic honesty, using a sentence written by "Jay Scrivener" about Joe Blow. I'll use footnote 99 to show when that sentence is cited.

QUOTING WITHOUT PLAGIARIZING	
Joe Blow was a happy man, who often walked down the road whistling and singing.	Sentence in the book *Joe Blow: His Life and Times*, by Jay Scrivener
What's Right	
"Joe Blow was a happy man, who often walked down the road whistling and singing."[99]	**Correct:** Full quote is inside quotation marks, followed by citation to *Joe Blow: His Life and Times*.
According to Scrivener, Blow "often walked down the road whistling and singing."[99] "Joe Blow was a happy man," writes Scrivener.[99]	**Correct:** Each partial quote is inside quote marks, followed by a citation. The partial quotes are not misleading.
According to Scrivener, Blow was "a happy man," who often showed it by singing tunes to himself.[99]	**Correct:** Partial quote is inside quotation marks; nonquoted materials are outside. The paraphrase (about singing tunes to himself) accurately conveys the original author's meaning without mimicking his actual words. Citation properly follows the sentence.
Joe Blow seemed like "a happy man," the kind who enjoyed "whistling and singing."[99]	**Correct:** Two partial quotes are each inside quotation marks; nonquoted materials are outside. Citation properly follows sentence.
Joe appeared happy and enjoyed whistling and singing to himself.[99]	**Correct:** This paraphrase is fine. It's not too close to Scrivener's original wording. The citation acknowledges the source.
What's Wrong	
Joe Blow was a happy man, who often walked down the road whistling and singing. (no citation)	**Wrong:** It is plagiarism to quote an author's exact words or to paraphrase them closely without *both* quotation marks and proper citation. Acknowledge your sources!

QUOTING WITHOUT PLAGIARIZING

What's Wrong (continued)

Joe Blow was a happy man, who often walked down the road whistling and singing.[99]	**Wrong:** These are actually Scrivener's exact words. It is plagiarism to use them without indicating explicitly that it is a quote. It is essential to use quotation marks (or block indentation for longer quotes), *even if* you give accurate citation to the author. So this example is wrong because it doesn't use quotation marks, even though it cites the source.
Joe Blow was a happy man and often walked down the road singing and whistling. (no citation)	**Wrong:** Although the words are not exactly the author's, they are *very similar.* (The words "singing" and "whistling" are simply reversed.) Either use an exact quote or paraphrase in ways that are clearly different from the author's wording.
Joe Blow was a happy man. (no citation)	**Wrong:** There are two problems here. First, it's an exact quote so it should be quoted *and* cited. Second, even if the quote were modified slightly, Scrivener should still be cited because it is *his personal judgment* (and not a simple fact) that Joe Blow is happy.
Joe Blow often walked down the road whistling and singing. (no citation)	**Wrong:** Same two problems as the previous example: (1) exact words should be both quoted and cited; and (2) Scrivener's personal judgment needs to be credited to him.
Joe Blow appeared to be "a happy man" and often walked down the road whistling and singing.[99]	**Wrong:** Despite the citation, some of Scrivener's exact words are outside the quotation marks. That creates the misleading impression that the words are the writer's, rather than Scrivener's. This is a small violation, like going a few miles over the speed limit. But if such miscitations occur often or include significant portions of text, then they can become serious cases of plagiarism.
"Joe Blow was an anxious man, who often ran down the road."[99]	**Wrong:** The quote is not accurate. According to Scrivener, Joe Blow was not anxious; he was "happy." And he didn't run, he "walked." Although this misquotation is not plagiarism, it is an error. You should quote properly, and your work should be reliable. If such mistakes are repeated, if they are seriously misleading, or, worst of all, if they appear to be intentional, they may be considered academic fraud. (Plagiarism is fraud, too, but a different kind.)

QUOTING WITHOUT PLAGIARIZING	
What's Wrong (continued)	
Joe Blow "walked down the road" quietly.[99]	**Wrong:** The words inside the partial quotation are accurate, but the word following it distorts Scrivener's plain meaning. Again, this is not plagiarism, but it does violate the basic principle of presenting materials fairly and accurately. If such mistakes are repeated or if they show consistent bias (for example, to prove that Joe Blow is a quiet person or hates music), they may be considered a type of academic fraud. At the very least, they are misleading.

The table refers to single sentences, but some citation issues involve paragraphs or whole sections of your paper. Let's say you are writing about urban poverty and that William Julius Wilson's analysis of the subject is central to one section. Whether or not you quote Wilson directly, you should include several citations of his work in that section, reflecting its importance for your paper. You could accomplish the same thing by including an explanatory citation early in the section. The footnote might say, "My analysis in this section draws heavily on William Julius Wilson's work, particularly *The Truly Disadvantaged: The Inner City, the Underclass, and Public Policy* (Chicago: University of Chicago Press, 1987), 87–122." Or you could include a similar comment in the text itself. Of course, you still need to include citations for any direct quotes.

Paraphrasing

When you paraphrase an author's sentence, don't veer too close to her words. That's plagiarism, *even if it's unintentional and even if you cite the author.*

So, what's the best technique for rephrasing a quote? Set aside the other author's text and think about the point *you* want to get across. Write it down in your own words (with a citation) and then compare your sentence to the author's original. If they contain several identical words or merely substitute a couple of synonyms, rewrite yours. Try to put aside the other author's distinctive language and rhythm as you write. That's sometimes hard, because the original sticks in your mind or seems just right. Still, you have to try. Your sentences and paragraphs should look and sound different from anyone you cite.

If you have trouble rephrasing an idea in your own words, jot down a brief note to yourself stating the point you want to make. Then back away, wait a little while, and try again. When you begin rewriting, look at your brief note but *don't look at the author's original sentence.* Once you have finished, check your new sentence against the author's original. You may have to try several times to get it right. Don't keep using the same words again and again. Approach the sentence from a fresh angle. If you still can't solve the problem, give up and use a direct quote (perhaps a whole sentence, perhaps only a few key words). It should either be a direct quote or your distinctive rephrasing. It cannot be lip-synching.

Why not use direct quotes in the first place? Sometimes that's the best solution—when the author's language is compelling, or when it says something important about the writer. When Franklin Roosevelt spoke about the attack on Pearl Harbor, he told America, "Yesterday, December 7, 1941—a date which will live in infamy—the United States was suddenly and deliberately attacked. . . ."[4] No one would want to paraphrase that. It's perfect as it is, and it's historically significant. When you analyze novels and poems, you'll want to quote extensively to reveal the author's creative expression. Other phrases speak volumes about the people who utter them. That's why you might quote Lenin saying that "promises are like pie crusts, made to be broken." (For him, they were.) Or Samuel Johnson saying that "a decent provision for the poor is the true test of civilization." These are incisive and memorable lines, and they reveal something important about the speakers themselves.

Because there are so many times when direct quotations are essential, you should avoid them where they're not. Overuse cheapens their value. Don't trot them out to express ordinary thoughts in ordinary words. Paraphrase. Just remember the basic rules: cite the source and don't mimic the original language.

These rules apply to the whole academic community, from freshmen to faculty. A senior professor at the U.S. Naval Academy was recently stripped of tenure for violating them. Although Brian VanDeMark had written several well-regarded books, his *Pandora's Keepers: Nine Men and the Atomic Bomb* (2003) contains numerous passages that closely resemble other books.[5] Most were footnoted, but, as you now know, that doesn't eliminate the problem.[6]

4. President Franklin D. Roosevelt, Joint Address to Congress Leading to a Declaration of War against Japan, December 8, 1941, http://www.fdrlibrary.marist.edu/oddec7.html (accessed June 1, 2004).

5. Brian VanDeMark, *Pandora's Keepers: Nine Men and the Atomic Bomb* (Boston: Little, Brown, 2003).

6. Jacques Steinberg, "U.S. Naval Academy Demotes Professor over Copied Work," *New York Times* (national edition), October 29, 2003, A23.

Here are a few of the questionable passages, compiled by Robert Norris. (Norris compiled an even longer list of similarities between VanDeMark's work and his own 2002 book, *Racing for the Bomb.*)[7]

Brian VanDeMark, *Pandora's Keepers* (2003)	Richard Rhodes, *The Making of the Atomic Bomb* (1986) and *Dark Sun* (1995)
". . . Vannevar Bush. A fit man of fifty-two who looked uncannily like a beardless Uncle Sam, Bush was a shrewd Yankee . . ." (60)	"Vannevar Bush made a similar choice that spring. The sharp-eyed Yankee engineer, who looked like a beardless Uncle Sam, had left his MIT vice presidency . . ." (*Making of the Atomic Bomb,* 336)
"Oppenheimer wondered aloud if the dead at Hiroshima and Nagasaki were not luckier than the survivors, whose exposure to radiation would have painful and lasting effects." (194–95)	"Lawrence found Oppenheimer weary, guilty and depressed, wondering if the dead at Hiroshima and Nagasaki were not luckier than the survivors, whose exposure to the bombs would have lifetime effects." (*Dark Sun,* 203)
"To toughen him up and round him out, Oppenheimer's parents had one of his teachers, Herbert Smith, take him out West during the summer before he entered Harvard College." (82)	"To round off Robert's convalescence and toughen him up, his father arranged for a favorite English teacher at Ethical Culture, a warm, supportive Harvard graduate named Herbert Smith, to take him out West for the summer." (*Making of the Atomic Bomb,* 120–21)
"For the next three months, both sides marshaled their forces. At Strauss's request, the FBI tapping of Oppenheimer's home and office phones continued. The FBI also followed the physicist whenever he left Princeton." (259)	"For the next three months, both sides marshaled their forces. The FBI tapped Oppenheimer's home and office phones at Strauss's specific request and followed the physicist whenever he left Princeton." (*Dark Sun,* 539)

Source: Robert Norris, "Parallels with Richard Rhodes's Books [referring to Brian VanDeMark's *Pandora's Keepers*], History News Network Web site, http://hnn.us/articles/1485.html (accessed June 22, 2004). For convenience, I have rearranged the last two rows in the table, without changing the words.

Unfortunately, VanDeMark does not cite Rhodes or quote him directly in any of these passages. Some, like the last one, are virtual quotations and

7. Robert Norris, *Racing for the Bomb: General Leslie R. Groves, the Manhattan Project's Indispensable Man* (South Royalton, VT: Steerforth Press, 2002).

would raise red flags even if they occurred only once. A few others are a little too close for comfort, but raise problems mostly because there are so many of them in VanDeMark's book.[8] This is only one of several tables covering VanDeMark's poor paraphrasing or unquoted sources. Each was prepared by a different author who felt violated. According to the Naval Academy's academic dean, "The whole approach to documenting the sources of the book was flawed."[9] The dean and VanDeMark himself attributed the problem to sloppiness rather than purposeful theft (which is why VanDeMark was demoted rather than fired outright). Still, the punishment was severe and shows how seriously plagiarism is taken at every level of the university.

Plagiarizing Ideas

Plagiarizing doesn't only mean borrowing someone else's words. It also means borrowing someone else's ideas. Let's say you are impressed by an article comparing *Catcher in the Rye* and *Hamlet*.[10] The article concludes that these works are variations on a single theme: a young man's profound anguish and mental instability, as shown through his troubled internal monologues. If your paper incorporates this striking idea, credit the author who proposed it, *even if every word you say about it is your own.* Otherwise, your paper will wrongly imply that you came up with the idea yourself. Holden Caulfield would call you a phony. The moral of the tale: It's perfectly fine to draw on others' ideas, as long as you give them credit. The only exception is when the ideas are commonplace.

8. Besides copying words and phrases from Richard Rhodes and Robert Norris, VanDeMark took passages from Greg Herken, William Lanouette, and Mary Palevsky without proper quotations or full attribution. Some passages are *not* obvious cases of plagiarism—deliberate or accidental—but some are nearly identical to other works and still others are too close for comfort. The overall pattern is troubling.

These parallels between VanDeMark's work and other books are documented online with similar tables. See History News Network, "Brian VanDeMark: Accused of Plagiarism," May 31, 2003, http://hnn.us/articles/1477.html (accessed February 26, 2004). That page links to several tables comparing VanDeMark's wording to that of various other authors.

9. Nelson Hernández, "Scholar's Tenure Pulled for Plagiarism: Acts Not Deliberate, Naval Academy Says," *Washington Post,* October 29, 2003, B06, http://www.washingtonpost.com/wp-dyn/articles/A32551-2003Oct28.html (accessed March 5, 2004).

10. Although I thought of this comparison between Hamlet and Holden Caulfield myself, I suspected others had, too. Just to be on the safe side, I decided to do a Google search. The top item offered to sell me a term paper on the subject! After this depressing discovery, I decided to search for "Catcher in the Rye + phony." I was deluged with offers. What a delicious irony: to buy a term paper on Holden Caulfield's hatred of all things phony.

Distorting Ideas

A recurrent theme of this chapter is that you should acknowledge others' words and ideas and represent them faithfully, without distortion. When you paraphrase them, you should keep the author's meaning, even if you disagree with it. When you shorten a quote, you should indicate that you've shortened it and keep the essential idea.[11]

There are really two goals here. The first is to maintain honesty in your own work. The second is to engage others' ideas fully, on a level playing field. That's the best way to confront diverse ideas, whether you agree with them or not. That's fair play, of course, but it's more than that. It's how you make your own work better. You are proving the mettle of your approach by passing a tough, fair test—one that compares your ideas to others without stacking the deck in your favor.

The danger to avoid is setting up flimsy straw men so you can knock them down without much effort. That's not only dishonest; it's intellectually lazy. Believe me, your own position will be much stronger and more effective if you confront the best opposing arguments, presented fairly, and show why yours is better.

Conclusion: The Right Way to Paraphrase and Cite

The rules for paraphrasing and citation are based on a few core ideas:

- You are responsible for your written work, including the ideas, facts, and interpretations you include.
- Unless you say otherwise, every word you write is assumed to be your own.

---

11. To indicate that a quote has been shortened, insert an ellipsis (three dots) where the deletion occurs. Let's say a complete quote reads, "Emily eventually returned home, but only after she had walked down the block and spoken to a friend. I saw her as she finally entered the house." A shortened version might read "Emily eventually returned home, but only after she had . . . spoken to a friend." The ellipsis marks the deletion.

If the deletion chops off the end of a sentence, then you need to add an ellipsis and the missing period. So, a shortened version might read "Emily eventually returned home, but only after she had walked down the block. . . . I saw her as she finally entered the house." Notice the four dots: an ellipsis and a period.

Sometimes, you need to insert a word into a quotation to make it comprehensible or grammatically correct. Place any words you add in square brackets to show you have added them. For example: "I saw [Emily] as she finally entered the house." The word "Emily" was not in that sentence originally, so it is placed in brackets.

- When you rely on others' work or ideas, acknowledge it openly.

  - ✔ When you use their ideas or data, give them credit.
  - ✔ When you use their exact words, use quotation marks plus a citation.
  - ✔ When you paraphrase, use your own distinctive voice and cite the original source. Make sure your language doesn't mimic the original. If it still does after rewriting, then use direct quotes.

- When you draw on others' work, present it fairly. No distortions. No straw men.
- When you present empirical material, show where you acquired it so others can check the data for themselves. (The exception is commonly known material, which does not need to be cited.)

These principles of fairness and disclosure are more than simple rules for citation. They are more than just "good housekeeping" in your paper. They are fundamental rules for academic integrity. They promote real learning. They apply to teachers and students alike and encourage free, fair, and open discussion of ideas—the heart and soul of a university.

Chapter 9

The Culture of Universities in the United States and Canada

To do their best work, international students need to understand the beliefs, values, and behaviors that permeate North American universities. In this chapter, I want to highlight some of these widely shared cultural values.

This is not an abstract survey. It provides practical guidance and answers questions that international students often ask, such as "When should I meet with a professor?"

Like any brief overview, it paints with a broad brush. There are significant differences, after all, between the United States and Canada, as well as regional differences within each country. It's a long flight from New York to Arizona, or from Montreal to Winnipeg, and it's a long way culturally, too. But the similarities also run very deep, and it's those I want to concentrate on.

In highlighting some important aspects of culture, I do not mean to imply that they are somehow fixed and immutable. They are not. This is a dynamic environment—socially, economically, and politically—with changing values, jobs, and roles. Over the past two or three decades, for instance, discrimination against racial minorities has steadily declined, gay relationships have gained acceptance by the heterosexual community, and many more women have risen to prominent executive and professional positions.

Changes like these are surely important, and one could list many more, but they unfold over decades, not months. Since international students stay here for only short periods, they rarely see dramatic alterations. They may see changes in the making—this is not a rigid society—but they should consider the attitudes, beliefs, and behavior they find when they arrive as stable and slowly evolving.

My goal here is to clarify some key features of university life and show how they relate to larger social attitudes. I want to explore how Americans and Canadians understand their world, especially the world of higher education, how they behave, and how they expect others to behave. Most of all, I want to show how these attitudes and expectations matter to you as an international student. The goal, as I said, is to be helpful.

Informality

There is no "Herr Dr. Professor" here. Yes, professors are called "Professor" or "Doctor" and, yes, they are experts in their fields. But these titles do not emphasize hierarchy or erect barriers to informal, easy interactions between students and faculty.

Quite the contrary. Students are expected to speak with their professors after class, e-mail them occasional questions, and drop by during office hours to discuss academic topics. It's a great way to get feedback on your work, learn about exciting ideas in your field, and explore new avenues for research.

These informal connections with faculty can make invaluable contributions to your education. But they won't happen by accident. You need to take the initiative and seek out the faculty. They are *not* going to seek you out.

Faculty Office Hours

The best way to start forming relationships with faculty is to sign up for their office hours. Professors hold "open office hours" each week to meet any students who wish to come. All you need to do is sign up on the scheduling sheet, which is usually posted on the office door. Then come at the appointed time. You don't need to know the professor in advance, or even be enrolled in the professor's classes. If you cannot come to office hours because you have a conflicting class or job, ask if you can arrange an alternate time, but do that only if you need to.

A little planning will make these meetings much more productive. Come with your own questions and a clear agenda, and bring along some paper (or a laptop) to take notes. The subject matter is up to you.

> *Tip:* The best time to meet faculty is during their weekly office hours. Come with your own questions and agenda, and come to the point quickly.

Tip: When you meet with professors to discuss your writing, bring two copies—one for them and one for you. Be sure to include your name and e-mail address on the paper, and number the pages. If it's a longer paper, give it to them in advance.

Brief, Business-Like Meetings

Although meetings with faculty are informal, they are usually brief and business-like. That is, they have a specific purpose, such as discussing a paper or seeking a job recommendation. After a friendly greeting, they get to the point quickly. Some meetings are quite brief. They might take only a few minutes. That's all you need to get approval for a paper topic or ask what you should read for your research. Most meetings last a little longer, usually ten or twenty minutes, depending on the topic. If you need to schedule a longer meeting—say, thirty minutes to discuss a possible thesis topic—ask in advance.

International students often remark how different these expectations are from those in their home countries. Take these comments from a Spanish student who entered a doctoral program here after doing graduate work in his native country. "In Barcelona," he said, "you worked mainly with one professor. If you wished to see another faculty member and didn't already know him well, your professor would make a call and introduce you." Here, he said, you can see any professor during office hours. No introductions are needed. "But you are expected to talk about academic subjects," he added. "In Europe, where you work very closely with a single professor, you are expected to come to his office occasionally and just visit, sometimes for hours. That's not the case here. Here, you are expected to come to professors with a specific subject to talk about." He captured the differences perfectly.

Cordial and Professional Faculty-Student Relationships

Although faculty are not usually snobby or aloof, they are *not* normally part of a student's social relationships. They may join a group of students for coffee or lunch after class, but they are reluctant to go much beyond that. The reason is simple and practical: close friendships with individual students could lead to charges of unprofessional behavior or favoritism.

Even if those charges are wrong, the perception counts, so faculty wisely steer clear of private social relationships with their students. After all, students have a right to be judged equally, based on their work in class, not their friendships after class.

This equal treatment should include all grading and evaluation. The goal in North American universities is to grade students solely on their work, not on their personalities or their friendships with faculty. Knowing that helps answer a question some students ask. "Why did I receive poor grades when the professor seemed to like me?" The reason is that faculty here try to grade without favoring students they like or penalizing those they don't. Impartiality is the gold standard.

Show Up on Time

Informality does *not* imply loose scheduling of appointments. The expectation here is that you will show up on time, or very close to it. If you ask to meet a professor at 2 p.m., you should be there at 2:00, not at 2:15. If you schedule lunch with a classmate at noon, you should be there at noon. (By the way, we start the working day early, usually by nine, and eat early. Lunches typically start between noon and one, dinners between six and seven.) Daytime social and business meetings begin on time, or nearly so. If you are running late, it's polite to call, explain, and coordinate.

Classes start on time, too. If a professor is running behind, the class might start a few minutes late, but seldom much later. In any case, students expect their classes to start on time and arrive accordingly.

Exams *always* start promptly at the scheduled hour. Likewise, assigned papers are due by the deadline or before. If the paper deadline is 4 p.m., that's when you must turn it in. A few professors are more relaxed about deadlines, but most are not. Some are *very* precise. When they say a problem set or a lab report is due at 4 p.m. Thursday, they don't mean 4:15, and they certainly don't mean Friday. Turning it in late, even a few minutes late, can mean a lower grade unless you receive permission in advance.

If you are sick or face special difficulties meeting a deadline, such as several papers due the same day, you can seek an extension. Most professors are sympathetic and understanding, but that doesn't mean they will always grant an extension. It depends on the circumstances. You should

Tip: Show up on time to classes and meetings. Turn assignments in on time, too.

> **Tip:** Extensions for papers and other assignments may be granted for special circumstances. You need to explain those circumstances clearly to the professor. Unless it's an emergency, do that in advance.

explain your reasons clearly, and ask well before the deadline unless it's an emergency.

The only engagements where it's fine to be five or ten minutes late is for evening events *at another person's home.* If I'm having a weekend dinner party at my house and tell you it will begin at 8 p.m., it's perfectly acceptable to arrive at 8:10, but not much later. If the same party were held at a restaurant, the guests would actually arrive on time or, at most, a few minutes late. (The restaurant also expects you to arrive on time when they schedule reservations.)

Low Barriers to New Relationships

You will find it is easy to meet faculty and fellow students here. Your classmates hope to make new friends and want to meet students from around the world. When they go out to movies or a party, they're usually happy to include one or two new people in the group. If you take some initiative and ask to join, you can easily expand your circle of friends.

Another way to enrich your social life is to volunteer for various campus activities, such as tutoring neighborhood children or playing in the university orchestra. These extracurricular activities are rewarding in themselves, and you will probably make friends in the process. Volunteer organizations are commonplace on campus and a great way to meet students who share your interests.

Making these connections is easy—deceptively easy. A friendly smile and warm greeting are great, but they do not imply a more profound friendship, or even a continuing relationship. As one African immigrant put it, "Americans, they open their arms to welcome you, but they don't close."[1]

Forging friendships of real depth is never that easy. Wherever you live, it requires time, effort, and empathy. That's just as true in North America as it is elsewhere, despite the friendly greetings and willingness to befriend newcomers.

---

1. Amadou Tandina of Burkina Faso, in Jeff Libman, *An Immigrant Class: Oral Histories from Chicago's Newest Immigrants* (Chicago: Flying Kite, 2004), 9.

Social Hierarchies

The United States and Canada embrace the idea of democratic equality. But the issue is complicated because we also value individual initiative, personal choice, and economic competition. We are generally willing to tolerate inequalities that flow from fair competition. To put that another way, Americans and Canadians believe in equality of *opportunity*, not equality of *results*.

Both countries have established social "safety nets" for the poor, sick, disabled, young, and elderly (with Canada offering more generous benefits). These are, at best, limited protection against personal disasters. Their goal is to protect the unfortunate from falling too far, not to prevent the ambitious from rising too high. There is broad agreement that those who work hard and play by the rules should reap the rewards, including economic success.

The results are predictable. These are social systems with pronounced pyramids of wealth, power, and position, but also with many citizens who are deeply troubled by the disparities. One telling indication of this ambivalence is how nearly all Americans and Canadians describe themselves as "middle class." They rarely use terms like "lower class," "working class," or "upper class" to describe themselves or anyone else. They are reluctant to say—or even think—that they stand higher or lower than anyone else in social rank.

These attitudes have deep historical roots. Neither country emerged from a feudal past, and neither was governed by a hereditary, landed aristocracy.[2] Neither developed class-based electoral parties or the language of class struggle (or its mirror image, the language of class deference).[3] Rather, both countries stress equal opportunity, promotions based on merit, and the problematic role of high status, especially inherited status.

Hierarchies still exist, of course, but they are downplayed in public and may be "hidden in plain sight." It is this hidden dimension that sometimes fools international students. You might hear two people greet each other as "Hello, Joan" and "Hello, Barbara" as they leave the elevator, but Joan might be the bank's president while Barbara types her correspondence.

---

2. The exceptions are the patroons of the Hudson River Valley and the plantation squires of the Southern lowlands.

3. This is a central theme of Louis Hartz's influential book, *The Liberal Tradition in America: An Interpretation of American Political Thought since the Revolution* (New York: Harcourt, Brace, 1955).

That surface equality conceals real differences. At the university, the same casual greeting—"Hello, Joan"—could refer to a Nobel Prize winner, a new graduate student, or a janitor.

A European who lives in America told me that "at least in Germany it's very clear who's at the top and who's at the bottom. The hierarchy is very clear, visible, and well defined. Here, the differences are just as real, but they are hidden and difficult for newcomers to figure out."

This North American distrust of hierarchy and rank can also be seen in personal relations. Snobbery, conceit, and arrogance of position are considered mortal sins. We generally meet each other as equals.[4] That may be an inheritance from Protestant dissenters, who stressed individual faith without the intercession of a church hierarchy. They remembered the biblical text, even if they strayed from it: "Pride goeth before destruction, and an haughty spirit before a fall."[5]

Respect for Personal Achievement

Personal achievement and hard work are highly prized. To have risen from humble beginnings is considered *more* praiseworthy, not less, than to have inherited wealth or position. We call it "pulling yourself up by your own bootstraps," and we shower it with praise.

That's true in universities, too. There is more praise, not less, for a major scholar who came from, say, a small village in India and rose to the top because of his brilliance and hard work.

Merit and achievement count far more than ancestry. Candidates for political office emphasize their poverty-stricken youth, hoping that some of Lincoln's majesty will rub off on them. They compete to prove that they rose from even more humble beginnings than their opponents. In England, by contrast, Margaret Thatcher's rivals were slinging mud when

---

4. This is one area where regional differences matter. In the Old South and at prestigious universities on the East Coast, rank and status matter more than they do elsewhere in the United States.

5. Proverbs 16:18. In the Puritan-Calvinist tradition, this leveling sentiment is offset by a belief that God has chosen an elect for eternal reward. The sociologist E. Digby Baltzell argues that this elitist concept has a continuing influence in Boston, where it has fostered generations of leaders with a strong sense of their civic rights and responsibilities.

Deference in the South is quite different, in my opinion. It is based on a much stronger sense that society should be ordered and hierarchical. That was especially strong in Southern plantation life and can be traced, I think, to ideas about the gentry's proper role in early modern England.

For Baltzell's views, see *Puritan Boston and Quaker Philadelphia: Two Protestant Ethics and the Spirit of Class Authority and Leadership* (New York: Free Press, 1979).

they called her "a greengrocer's daughter." In North America, that would be a badge of honor.

Academic Ranks and Hierarchy in the University

These social values resonate within the university. There is virtually no concern with faculty members' social rank. There are no "Lords" or "vons" here. Nobody, beyond a few undergraduates, cares whether you are from a "First Family of Virginia." For faculty and graduate students, in particular, the only hierarchy that matters is one based on academic achievement.

It's no surprise, then, that academic titles matter far less here than they do in Europe. There are, however, two distinctions that do matter on the academic appointment ladder. One is whether a teacher is a member of the regular university faculty or not. Scholars with titles like "visiting professor" are not full members of the faculty. Similarly, lecturers, adjunct professors, and instructors are appointed for limited periods and are not considered full members of the faculty. They are considered faculty for some purposes, such as teaching, grading, and writing recommendations, but not for others, such as hiring new faculty or setting rules to govern the department or university.

A second important distinction is whether a faculty member is tenured or not. Tenured faculty hold permanent appointments and can be dismissed only for unusual reasons (such as serious misconduct, or when a whole department is eliminated). Also known as "senior faculty," these tenured professors help shape the university's curriculum, its rules and procedures, its hiring and promotion.

Junior faculty, who usually hold the title of assistant professors, are appointed for up to six years. Some are then evaluated for tenure, first by their departments and then by the university. Appointments eligible for such evaluation and promotion are called "tenure track." Other appointments are made only for specified terms (ranging from one semester to several years) and are not eligible for promotion and tenure. They are called "non-tenure track."

All tenured and tenure-track professors are considered full members of the faculty. But short-term appointments usually are not. These non-

Tip: Social rank counts for very little within the university. What counts is brains, hard work, and performance.

> ***Tip:*** While academic titles are less important here than in Europe, two categories do matter: Is a professor tenured or not? Is a professor a member of the regular faculty? Some appointments, such as instructors and visiting professors, do not hold faculty rank.

tenure-track faculty can be distinguished teachers and scholars, and they bear all the usual responsibilities for their courses and labs. But they do not typically participate in decisions about admissions, curriculum, or faculty hiring.

Most universities do not stress these differences among faculty, and they don't matter for most students' day-to-day work. They do matter, though, if students want to conduct extended research with a particular professor. A junior professor might be denied tenure and leave the university. An adjunct professor might leave after her contract expires.

Some departments permit visiting faculty to supervise theses; others don't. Some allow junior faculty to chair doctoral committees; others don't. Since the rules vary, it's wise to ask your department's administrator about them. You may also wish to speak privately—and candidly—with any faculty you hope to work with on long-term projects. Your future could be intertwined with theirs. Better to ask now than to be surprised later.

This discussion underscores two points. One is that professors come with different kinds of appointments. The other is that, even though some appointments rank higher than others, the faculty hierarchy here is far less pronounced than in Europe, Asia, or Latin America. In North American universities, status differences are based more on expert knowledge and recent achievements than on position or title.

Take junior faculty. In the great German universities, each field is traditionally led by one senior faculty member, who controls teaching and research in that specialty. He (and it is usually a man) appoints junior faculty who are, in effect, his assistants. Even today, this strong hierarchy persists in German universities.

Not here. Full professors, associate professors, and assistant professors are all expected to pursue independent research. They are hired as creative, original scholars with their own research agendas. The youngest may be called "assistant professors," but they are nobody's assistants.

There is an unavoidable difference between junior and senior faculty, even in North America, since senior faculty must ultimately decide who receives tenure and who does not. They decide the fate of junior faculty.

But universities try not to exaggerate this structural difference or project it onto their research and instruction. In particular, junior faculty are expected to play major roles (not minor, supporting ones) in research, publishing, teaching, and graduate training. Students are expected to take courses with both junior and senior faculty, without emphasizing rank or title. What really matters is how good your teachers are and how compelling their research is.

Performance, not Personal Background

This emphasis on achievement, not on social rank or family lineage, is strong and widespread in the university and in the wider society.[6] Most people and most businesses here care about your performance, especially your recent performance, not your personal background. They want to judge you on criteria that are relevant to the task at hand, not on extraneous factors such as race, religion, ethnicity, or country of origin.

> *Tip:* The emphasis on merit, not background, means you will be judged mainly on your performance, effort, and dedication, not on extraneous factors.

Prejudice does exist, of course, and you may occasionally confront it. Fortunately, it has little social support in the United States or Canada and even less within the university.

This emphasis on achievement, not ancestry, encourages hard work in several ways. First, it promotes the social value of work, which is rewarded (in every sense) if it is done well. Second, it undercuts the aristocratic value of conspicuous leisure. Indeed, in most cultures, aristocrats are defined precisely because they do not need to work, thanks to their wealth and social position. Their languid attitude inevitably spills over into elite education, especially when hereditary elites carry high status into the university.

North American universities are characterized by bourgeois and pro-

---

6. There are some exceptions. Family background counts for more among Southern elites and in small rural communities, where people have known each other's families for generations. Educational background—the "right schools"—counts for more in elite East Coast universities than in the Midwest, Rocky Mountains, or West Coast.

In general, wealth and family background matter much more for undergraduates than for graduate students. Professional schools fall somewhere in the middle, since family position may offer privileged entry into the job market.

fessional values, not aristocratic ones. That is particularly true of graduate and professional schools, where hard work and proficiency are highly valued. It is impossible to gain admission to *any* decent graduate school based on who your family is. Admission is based on undergraduate grades, writing samples, scores on standardized tests, and teacher recommendations. Professional schools also consider your job performance and career trajectory. What matters is not your family's achievements but your own.

That is less true at the undergraduate level, where social activities are more important and where students' background and family position carry more weight.

Recent Performance Counts Most

As important as your prior achievements are, you cannot rest on your laurels here. Graduate school admissions are a good example. It certainly helps to have attended a fine undergraduate school, one that admits only superb applicants. But that's not enough. To be admitted to a top graduate program here, you must excel as an undergraduate. Law schools, business schools, and doctoral programs all look carefully at undergraduate performance, not just at the university you attended.

Employers do the same thing. Nearly all of them would prefer a hardworking, successful student who received "A's" from Big State University to one who received "B's" from Prestigious Ivy University. The school's pedigree matters, but it is not a high priority. Employers and admissions officers care far more about your skills and ability. In evaluating them, they focus on what you accomplished in the last few years, not what you did five or six years ago to gain a spot at the university.

These values are nicely captured in a comment from the founder of Wikipedia, the online encyclopedia. "To me the key thing is getting it right," Jimmy Wales told an interviewer. "And if a person's really smart and they're doing fantastic work I don't care if they're a high school kid or a Harvard professor, it's the work that matters. And you can't coast on your credentials on Wikipedia . . . You have to enter the marketplace of ideas and engage with people."[7] His values are widely shared here.

---

7. Jimmy Wales, founder of Wikipedia, interviewed on the C-Span program "Q&A," September 25, 2005, transcript at http://www.q-and-a.org/Transcript/?ProgramID=1042 (accessed March 18, 2006).

"Fast Tracks" and Recruitment to Universities and Jobs

This emphasis on performance, especially recent performance, shows up in university admissions and professional recruitment. Universities here do not shunt students permanently onto "fast tracks" or "slow tracks," as they do in some countries. In France, for example, the fastest track leads up to the Grandes Écoles and then into senior levels of politics, bureaucracy, and business. The Grandes Écoles themselves recruit heavily from a few top baccalauréat programs. Likewise, in England, the most selective colleges at Oxford and Cambridge recruit heavily from a few leading public schools (what we call "private schools"). Although these systems are competitive and merit-based, they rely on a few high-quality "feeder schools," which send their smartest, best-prepared children to a few top high schools, which, in turn, send their best teenagers to the best universities. It's a rigid sequence. You must enter these fast tracks early, often before age ten. If you are not selected then, it's very hard to jump on later. Ask any third-grader in Japan.

In the United States and Canada, the tracking system is much looser and more flexible. It's certainly competitive, but recruitment is more broadly based and open to "late bloomers." It's possible to move into the most selective schools by excelling in high school or as an undergraduate, even if you did not attend the top schools or do so well before that.

It's true that an outstanding student at Phillips Academy Andover (a top private school) or New Trier High School (a top public school) still has the best opportunity to go to Yale or Stanford. But Yale, Stanford, and their peers recruit from thousands of schools across the country, indeed, around the world. The same is true at the graduate level. Students at the University of Toronto Law School or Harvard's Kennedy School of Government come from everywhere—educationally, socially, and geographically. The only common denominator is that they excelled at the previous stage.

Mobility between Different Types of Universities

Because the tracking system here is less rigid, it is possible to move from a two-year community college to an outstanding four-year university. In fact, California and many other states require their public universities to accept community college graduates. Likewise, highly selective graduate and professional schools regularly admit top undergraduates from

> ***Tip:*** Universities here recruit top students, regardless of where they were educated. There is not a rigid tracking system. Qualified students can always take the next step upward, even if they did not go to the "right" school.

universities that are less well known and less highly regarded. What matters is that these students show real promise. They have strong grades, outstanding recommendations, and top test scores.

This mobility is especially important for international students. I know many who began their education here at less competitive schools, such as a local branch of a large state university. They might not have gotten into the best schools at first. Or they might not have been able to pay for them. Or they might not have even heard about them. No matter. You can always transfer to a more competitive, intellectually challenging school in a year or two if your work here is first-rate. I know many students who have done just that. I know others who stayed at their initial schools, graduated with high marks, and then enrolled in leading graduate or professional schools. You are not shunted onto a permanent "fast" or "slow" track. You can always move up.

How can tell which universities are better? That's a hotly contested matter, as you might expect, but there are a number of rating services that try to measure the quality of education, social life, research, and other key dimensions of each university. The most prominent is the *U. S. News and World Report* rankings, published annually by that magazine. Basically, they classify all U.S. universities into categories, such as "major research universities" or "small liberal arts colleges," and then rank them by a formula that summarizes all their statistics. These numerical rankings are grouped into "tiers," and a university may be pleased to announce its move from the third tier to the second. *U.S. News* also organizes its ranking by regions, and ranks universities within a specific region like the Southeast United States.[8] Canadian universities are ranked by *Maclean's* magazine.

Emphasis on Continuing Improvement and Lifelong Education

Your education need not stop with a graduate or professional degree. The United States and Canada both encourage lifelong education. Some fields,

---

8. *U.S. News & World Report* not only ranks undergraduate institutions, it has publications ranking graduate schools and professional schools.

> **Tip:** Lifelong education is increasingly important in the United States and Canada. Many professions now require practitioners to take courses each year to maintain their licenses.

like law, medicine, and nursing, actually require practitioners to take short courses each year to maintain their licenses.

Continuing-education courses are part of a broader emphasis on life-long learning, especially for professionals. Universities have embraced this emphasis. Nearly all offer courses at night and on weekends for older students. Some of these students want to resume full-time schooling; others are looking for intellectual stimulation; still others want professional credentials or perhaps a change of careers. You might be one of them.

As a "continuing ed" student, the courses you take might lead to a recognized degree or certificate, or they might simply be interesting subjects you want to learn more about. Of course, you can list these courses on your résumé, which might help you land a job or gain admission to a degree program.

Businesses support this ongoing education for their employees and sometimes even pay for it. Many grant automatic pay increases to employees who earn additional degrees.

The larger point is that career advancement has many paths here. It continues over a lifetime and does not depend on undergraduate education at a few elite schools. What you did at age eighteen has a lot less impact on your success at age forty than it does in Europe or Asia. Old school ties are surely important, but they matter less than your recent performance, steady effort, and continued training.

The Individual, Not the Group; Individuality, Not Conformity

The performance that counts here is *individual*. Once again, the university's values mirror those of the wider society. The stress is on individuals, not groups. It is on individuality and creativity, not repetition or conformity.

This emphasis on individuality, creativity, and originality rises as students move upward, from high school to college, from college to graduate school. At lower levels, it's important to master basic techniques, such as grammar, computation, and lab procedures. At higher levels, professors expect more. They expect technical competence, to be sure, but they also expect students to develop their own well-informed perspectives on the material, to engage it actively, and sometimes to differ (politely but firmly) with the professor himself. This search for individual understanding and creative insight is especially important in doctoral programs, since PhD students aim to create new knowledge. The goal of doctoral programs, as one of my colleagues says, "is for students to move from being consumers of knowledge to being producers."

Study Groups and Individual Creativity

This stress on creativity and originality, on personal independence and individuality, does raise one problem. The world of business and policy-making is increasingly organized into small, fluid working groups. Take an advertising campaign, for example. No single person, no matter how talented, can create a major advertising campaign. Only a team can do it, drawing on different kinds of expertise. Some members might talk with consumers; others write advertising copy; still others produce commercials for TV, radio, and the Web. It takes a village, or at least a smooth-running team. The same could be said for developing major policy proposals. It's a group process.

For groups that produce a joint product, the trick is to couple effective collaboration with individual creativity. The investment bank of Goldman, Sachs is renowned for doing just that. Their goal shines through in their statement of business principles. "We stress teamwork in everything we do," according to one statement on the firm's Web site. "While individual creativity is always encouraged, we have found that team effort often produces the best results. We have no room for those who put their personal interests ahead of the interests of the firm and its clients."[9] Their work environment, they say, "is collaborative. We actively solicit ideas from one another, act on consensus wherever possible, and ensure that all team members get the credit for a job well done. True, our professionals are competitive, but they compete with the external marketplace—not with one another."[10] That statement perfectly captures the goals of joint working groups.

Business schools and public policy programs have adapted to this new

---

9. Goldman Sachs, "Business Principles," http://www.gs.com/our_firm/the_culture/business _principles.html (accessed March 18, 2006).

10. Goldman Sachs, "Desired Skillset [for New Employees]" http://www.gs.com/careers/ learning_center/articles/learning_center_963400.html (accessed March 18, 2006).

Tip: When you work with a study group, it is vital that you know what the professor expects from the group. Is it expected to produce a joint product, with each member contributing? Or is it a self-teaching group, with each member expected to turn in his own work, without direct help from others?

work environment by assigning some classwork to small groups. To do it well, students must figure out how to work together effectively. Complex lab work is conducted the same way.

Actually, there are two kinds of group work, and it's crucial to distinguish between them. In one, members study together but turn in their own individual work. Each person's work is graded separately. That means each student must do his own problem sets and other written work. Members can teach each other, discuss class materials, and explain how to solve problems—that's the whole point—but they cannot actually write the answers or solve the problems for another member of the group.

In the other kind of group, members actually produce a joint product and are given a single grade for it. They are expected to work together, divide some tasks, and edit each other's work. What counts as good collaborative effort in this case would actually be cheating for the other kind of group.

Little Deference to Age

Gray hair is not especially honored here. Experience and judgment are valued, of course, but there is little deference to older people as such. That's visible at the top of major corporations, where executives must retire by their mid-sixties so younger executives can move up.

It's visible on campus, too. Older professors need not retire—many remain active as scholars and teachers—but they are valued mainly for their ongoing achievements. Perhaps the most visible representation of these attitudes is that leading scholars here are often young. If their work is outstanding, they can rise quickly. Important publications can lead to rapid promotions and wide acclaim, regardless of age. Youth is no barrier to achievement, recognition, or position.

That's one reason why bright young researchers from around the world come to North America. They can pursue their own research, rather than follow that of a senior professor, and can move up as fast as their abilities and publications allow.

Mobility Is Commonplace and Upward Mobility Is Idealized

Moving up is a positive social value, and moving up quickly is even better.

Actually, several forms of mobility are encouraged, or, at least, considered enduring features of modern life. One is geographical mobility. Adult children do not necessarily live close to their parents. That's particularly true among professionals, who might grow up in Dallas, go to college in New Haven, take their first jobs in Chicago, and move to Los Angeles with their first promotions. Even if they remain in the same cities as their parents, they typically move to better neighborhoods or fancier suburbs as soon as they can afford it.

There is also considerable mobility between jobs. Children are not expected to follow their parents' careers, and they usually don't. Nor are they expected to stay with a single company, as they did in the 1950s. They are not even expected to remain in one type of job, thanks to rapid technological change and international competition. Movement between careers is not exactly welcomed, but it is not seriously resisted either. Instead, public policies attempt to cushion the shocks, train people for new opportunities, and encourage them to move wherever the new jobs are.

Universities and Job Mobility

This kind of mobility has several effects on universities. One is that universities recruit widely, from across North America and around the world. Most students still attend public universities in their home states or provinces, but it's commonplace to see the best students apply to elite universities, wherever they are. If you want to become an engineer, you probably hope to attend a top school like MIT or Cal Tech,[11] no matter where you live. If you want to become a journalist, you'll probably apply to Northwestern's Medill School or the University of Missouri. Students flood into these programs from all points on the compass.

While some hope to return home after graduation, many do not. They will look for the most rewarding jobs in the most interesting places. Faculty do the same thing. They seek out the best schools in their specialties and come from all over to work there. Recruiting for these jobs is not a

---

11. "Cal Tech" is the nickname for the California Institute of Technology, just as "Georgia Tech" is the nickname for the Georgia Institute of Technology.

> **Tip:** Job mobility and the demand for mid-career training has prompted universities to create new programs aimed at older students.

local affair, either. Academic job markets in the United States and Canada are national in scope and, in most fields, global.

Second, because so many people change jobs in their thirties or forties, universities have begun to tailor educational programs for them. Some of these older students are training for new careers. Others simply want a higher degree, perhaps an MA in teaching, business, nursing, or criminal justice, so they can move up the career ladder.

Third, it is widely assumed that individuals aspire to move up in their jobs, from a bank teller to manager, from manager to company vice president. University training and advanced degrees can contribute to this upward mobility. Large companies embrace this training and often pay their employees to pursue graduate degrees while they work. Every big city has dozens of programs targeted at such students, including many that allow students to keep their jobs and attend school on nights or weekends.

Competition Is Pervasive

Because universities recruit students and faculty from across the country and around the world, they often find themselves competing for the best ones. International students already know one side of this competition, that of student admissions. What is unusual here is the omnipresence of competition. Universities are rivals, in friendly but intense ways, not only for the best students but also for the best faculty and the money to recruit them.

How Universities Compete

How do universities compete for outstanding students and faculty? With salaries, scholarships, lab space, colleagues, and amenities. Top faculty are offered higher salaries, better research facilities, fewer classes, and a chance to work with other leaders in their fields. Top students are offered larger fellowships and a chance to work with leading teachers and researchers. If Stanford offers doctoral students free tuition plus a yearly stipend of $20,000, Yale cannot compete by offering only $13,000. That might work if Yale had a much finer program. But if both universities have excellent programs, then Yale has to match its competitors' offers to recruit the best students.

The same is true for recruiting and retaining top faculty. They want to work in the best-equipped labs, with the best colleagues and the best students.

How do Stanford, Yale, and Michigan get the resources they need for labs, faculty salaries, and student scholarships? By competing for government research grants, seeking donations from alumni and philanthropic foundations, and investing their donations wisely.

This kind of competition among universities is standard in the United States. It is a bit less common in Canada, which has far fewer universities and none of the rich private ones that characterize U.S. higher education. Still, Canadian universities must compete with each other and with U.S. schools for students, faculty, and resources.

There are two major points here. One is that competition is pervasive. All leading universities in North America open their doors each morning knowing that they must compete with dozens of other fine universities of their size and rank. Second, this competition is not just to recruit the best faculty. It's also to recruit great students, construct great facilities, and build great endowments to pay for it all. They compete on all fronts to do it. University presidents might speak in eloquent, muted tones, but they compete as intensely as executives at Nokia, Samsung, and Motorola.

More Competition Means More Choice

Competition implies real choice for students, faculty, and donors. Many countries have only one or two leading universities. Not here. Students and faculty can choose among several leading schools and sometimes more, no matter what their fields. To make that choice, they look closely at the scholarship funds they will receive, the teachers and researchers they will work with, the facilities they will use, and the quality of life they will enjoy outside the university.

Students and faculty also recognize that different universities are at the top of different fields. Although there is a general hierarchy among research universities, with schools like Harvard, Berkeley, and Toronto near the pinnacle, this ranking doesn't apply to all specialties. A university could have a great department in economics and a poor one in physics, or vice versa. They would undoubtedly love to improve their weaker fields, but they can do so only by recruiting stronger faculty and students. That

> **Tip:** Universities must compete for the best students and faculty. That means raising money to pay for them. Top students, including international students, reap the rewards. Not only can they choose which program to attend, they get better financing and work with better faculty in better facilities.

inevitably means raising the funds to pay for them and convincing top professors and students to join their programs.

In a way, then, the competition that is ubiquitous in the North American economy also characterizes university life. That does not imply hostility among competitors, any more than it does in the marketplace. Rather, it implies a dynamic environment, one that keeps students and faculty hard at work and offers them real options about where to live, study, and teach.

High-Quality Private Institutions, including Universities

Any roll call of top universities in the United States would include private universities like Columbia and MIT, alongside public universities like Michigan and UCLA. The presence of these private institutions is another characteristic of American society as a whole, which has a large, energetic nonprofit sector, funded by private donations.

Some parts of this private sector—but only some—are religious. In Chicago, for example, Catholics have built and financed a network of parochial schools, hospitals, social service agencies, and universities like DePaul and Loyola. Other faiths have parallel institutions.[12]

What is so striking about American charities and nonprofits, though, is how many are secular. That's certainly true of universities, but it's also true of food pantries, environmental groups, children's activities, hospitals, and cultural institutions.

These private institutions—secular and religious—are proof of a dynamic civil society, where people voluntarily organize to build, fund, and maintain a wide range of institutions. The institutions themselves are not controlled by the state or a dominant religion.[13]

12. Canada also has an important network of religious charities, especially in Catholic institutions in Québec, but it has fewer secular, private institutions than the United States.

13. Although most Americans and Canadians are Christians, they belong to many denominations. Most share a culture of tolerance for other faiths and, indeed, for agnosticism and atheism. There is certainly no state religion.

In its early years, Canada did have official churches in three eastern provinces (Nova Scotia, New Brunswick, and Prince Edward Island). The rest of Canada rejected the idea, and there are no official churches in Canada today.

> ***Tip:*** Higher education in the United States includes a mixture of public and private universities. Neither is intrinsically better; there are superb programs in both.

Overlapping Systems of Private and Public Education

The point is *not* that private institutions are better. Sometimes they are, sometimes they aren't. The point is that education, health care, and social services are all delivered by both public and private agencies, and frequently by private agencies that receive public funds or by public agencies that receive private grants. Some students at the University of Pennsylvania (a private university) receive federal support to study science or foreign languages. Some at Pennsylvania State University (a public university) receive scholarships from private foundations. Actually, most of Penn State's budget comes from a private source, tuition paid by student families, rather than from public tax dollars.[14]

These examples are not rare or unusual. In American higher education, the public and private sectors overlap, compete, and complement each other.

Education through high school is still overwhelmingly a public service in both the United States and Canada. Although some parents choose to pay for private schools, most children are educated at free public schools, beginning at age five or six and ending with high school graduation, around age eighteen.

After that, the educational system looks entirely different. Students must pay tuition bills—often high ones—in both Canada and the United States. The government still plays a major role, lending money to students and subsidizing public universities. (The Canadian system is almost entirely public. The U.S. has a mix of public and private schools.)[15] But, inevitably, the financial burden falls mainly on students and their families.

---

14. The U.S. university system is unique in imposing such high costs on students. Most other advanced countries pay nearly all those costs. The predictable result is that they must ration the scarce resource, since they cannot afford to pay for everyone who wants to attend university.

15. In recent years, a third option has begun to spread: for-profit universities. These generally focus on practical subjects, such as computer repair or fashion merchandising, striving to meet market demands. Many students want this kind of training, which traditional (nonprofit) schools don't provide. These for-profit schools typically hire teachers on a course-by-course basis and do nothing to promote faculty research. They are purely teaching institutions. Some offer instruction

Federalism and Education

There is no national university system in the United States or Canada. There are no national standards for admissions, tuition, or salary. Instead, each U.S. state and Canadian province runs its own system of higher education. They control it themselves and provide most of the funding.

Each state or province has its own flagship research university, such as the University of Virginia or University of British Columbia. In large states like Minnesota, Texas, Arizona, and Ohio, the biggest campuses have as many as 50,000 students in one location.

These flagship universities are only one element of the public system. There are also midsized state universities in virtually every city, and even more community colleges, with two-year degree programs. Each state decides for itself what kinds of universities it wants and how many dollars to pour into them.

The Wide Range of Public Universities

This decentralized system of higher education includes a wide variety of schools, designed to meet a wide variety of student needs. The best known are major research universities, which offer a full array of graduate and professional programs, along with undergraduate degrees.

Besides these prestigious schools, each state and province has teaching-oriented universities in all its major cities. Some are branches of the main state university; others are freestanding. There's a branch of the University of Wisconsin in Milwaukee, for instance, and a branch of the University of Colorado in Colorado Springs. They offer BA and BS degrees to undergraduates and some MA programs in areas of high demand, such as computer science, occupational therapy, and elementary education. Although many faculty are active researchers, the institutions rarely offer PhD's. (Doctoral programs are usually restricted to the flagship campus, such as the University of Wisconsin–Madison or the University of Colorado

---

in standard classrooms, some in work settings, such as auto repair facilities, and still others via computer (distance learning).

Not all these schools are fully accredited, but the better ones are. Accreditation carries two major benefits. First, it assures students and their employers that the education meets reasonable standards. Second, it opens the door for students to get subsidized educational loans, underwritten by the national government.

at Boulder.) Branch campuses focus on undergraduate education, with a strong practical flavor.

Unlike flagship research universities, where students live on campus or close by, these branch campus are often "commuter schools." Many students live at home and work full time or part time. To fit their busy schedules, courses are often given at night, on weekends, and online.

Not surprisingly, the students at these branch campuses differ from their peers at research universities. They are somewhat older and more concerned with career advancement. Many are studying part time to accommodate their work and family obligations. A good example of this type of campus is Ryerson University in Toronto, which calls itself "Canada's leader for career-focused university education." It has over 20,000 undergraduate students but only 700 graduate students. Even more striking, it has over 60,000 enrolled in continuing education courses.[16] The courses they take can lead to undergraduate degrees or certificates in specialized fields such as children's literature.

Finally, there are inexpensive local schools, known as community colleges, which offer two years of university education, culminating in an "associate's degree." Some students finish their education at that point; others transfer to four-year campuses to complete a bachelor's degree. Their community college courses transfer with them and count toward the higher degree.

The High Cost of Undergraduate Education

Higher education in the United States and Canada is expensive. It is costly to provide university education, and students themselves pay much of the costs. Tuition at public universities is $10,000 a year or more—often much more—and would be even higher without tax subsidies and private donations.[17] Important as these subsidies are, many families still cannot afford higher education for their children. Others must save for years to reach the goal. Fortunately, there are numerous programs to help defray the costs, including scholarship aid, subsidized loans, and on-campus jobs.

16. Ryerson University Web site, Quick Facts; http://www.ryerson.ca/news/quickfacts.html (accessed March 13, 2007).

17. Since each state pays for its own universities, it charges its own citizens (and taxpayers) lower tuition. Out-of-state students pay more, often much more. A student from Iowa, for example, will pay much less if she attends the University of Iowa than if she attends the University of Nebraska.

These programs are also available at two-year community colleges, where tuition is much lower to begin with.

If public universities are expensive, private ones are even more costly, upwards of $30,000 a year. They, too, have extensive scholarship and loan programs and use their endowments to provide support to needy students. Their aim is to create a diverse student body and recruit the best students, even those who cannot afford to pay.

The Cost of Graduate School: Differences between PhD and Professional Programs

Similar financial calculations apply to graduate programs. Tuition is lower at public universities, and there are grants and loans to cover costs at both public and private schools. It is important to draw a distinction between two types of graduate programs:

- doctoral programs, which train research scholars, and
- master's programs, which train professionals and executives.

Students in doctoral programs are heavily subsidized as part of the university's overall research effort. Their career choice may not be lucrative, but at least they get a free ride in graduate school. They receive scholarship grants to cover tuition, plus modest stipends to cover living costs. They can earn some additional income as teaching assistants or lab assistants, or by helping faculty with their research.

There is no free ride in professional schools and MA programs, such as law, business, and public policy. They charge tuitions similar to undergraduate programs and provide similar kinds of financial aid. Most students finance their MAs by taking out extensive loans, in addition to any undergraduate loans.

Although the loans are subsidized by U.S. and Canadian taxpayers, many students complete their MA degrees groaning under heavy debt burdens, which may take years to repay. These debts can be understood as investments in future earning power.

The High (Economic) Value of Education

Despite their high costs, North American universities are thriving, with long lines of students applying for admission. Top schools—graduate and undergraduate—have ten or more students vying for each place. Why? One obvious reason is that they provide an excellent education. If they

> ***Tip:*** Higher education is expensive, but it's worth it, in strictly financial terms. Lifetime earnings for BA and MA recipients are markedly higher than for high school graduates, even after deducting the costs of the degree.

didn't, they simply could not compete in the marketplace. They could not charge high prices and still fill their classes with outstanding students. After all, these students have plenty of alternatives.

One proof of universities' market value, beyond their piles of applications, is that their degrees markedly increase students' lifetime incomes, even after deducting tuition costs. The costs are high, but it still makes financial sense to pay them.[18] That's not true for all degrees—nobody gets a bachelor's in fine arts or a master's in social work for the high income—but it is true of most BA and MA programs.

The Diversity of U.S. Higher Education

There is no single type of university in the United States.[19] Rather, there are many types: public and private; nonprofit and for-profit; liberal arts and practical training; large and small; research and teaching; on campus and online; and much more. It is a remarkably diverse system, with schools of all shapes, sizes, and purposes.

One of the most striking (indeed, unique) features of the U.S. system is the prevalence of small private universities, with 1,500 to 2,500 students.[20] Called "colleges," they emphasize liberal arts teaching and are exclusively for undergraduates. Where larger schools use lectures and teaching assistants, these smaller universities use seminars and tutorials, taught by experienced faculty. Recent national surveys rank over two hundred of these small, four-year colleges, and some surveys rank still more.[21]

Virtually all these schools are private, supported by tuition dollars and

18. Gary S. Becker and Kevin M. Murphy have shown recently that much of the widening gap in incomes reflects the rising payoff for a college education and other skills. Becker and Murphy, "The Upside of Income Inequality," *American* (May/June 2007) http://www.american.com/archive/2007/may-june-magazine-contents/the-upside-of-income-inequality (accessed June 13, 2007).

19. I am focusing here on the United States because its higher-education system is much larger and more diverse than Canada's.

20. Even the term "college" is unusual. In the United States, but not in Canada, the term refers to schools devoted to undergraduate teaching. They may be stand-alone institutions, such as Amherst or Reed, or parts of larger universities, such as Yale College within Yale University.

21. U.S. News & World Report, *America's Best Colleges, 2006 edition;* Robert Franek, et al., *The Princeton Review's Best 361 Colleges, 2007* (New York: Princeton Review, 2006).

> **Tip:** There is no single model for university education in the United States. There are literally thousands of colleges and universities, aimed at different kinds of students and different needs, from liberal arts to practical training.

donations from alumni and private foundations. Schools like these simply don't exist in other countries. (There are a few in eastern Canada, mostly with religious affiliations.) Yet the United States has hundreds of them, educating students at high levels with lots of individual attention.

The result is a university system unlike any other in the world. Small liberal arts colleges exist alongside huge public universities; teaching institutions exist alongside research centers. Some emphasize the liberal arts, others the professions, and still others practical job training. Some do all three.

It would be an exaggeration to describe this network of U.S. higher education as a well-organized system. It is a vast, sprawling, decentralized collection of over 3,500 colleges and universities.[22] Yet this network produces real competition on many levels, offers real choices for students, faculty, and donors, and offers some of the world's finest higher education.

Emphasis on Civil Society and Volunteerism

The variety of universities illustrates another important feature of North American life: the vigor of civil society. It was not state planners or civil servants who founded these private universities. It was business and religious leaders, philanthropists and educators. The same civic groups pushed for law schools, business schools, and local branches of state universities to serve their communities. They value education in its own right and as an engine of economic growth.

This kind of voluntary organization, which Tocqueville considered so characteristic of American society, is ubiquitous on university campuses. You will find student organizations of every description, for virtually every kind of recreation, charity, and religion.

Volunteerism is a major feature of undergraduate life, in both the United States and Canada. Students join the symphony orchestra, the

---

22. Dan Lundquist, "A Parent's Guide to College Search: Why It Ought to Be an Enjoyable Year," in Robert Franek et al., *The Princeton Review's Best 357 Colleges, 2005 Edition* (New York: Princeton Review, 2004), 3. U.S. News & World Report, *America's Best Colleges, 2006 edition,* reviews over 1,400 schools.

> *Tip:* Volunteer student activities are a major part of student life at all universities. It's a great way to meet people, do things you enjoy, and contribute to the wider community.

chess club, the Model United Nations, the radio station, and the student newspaper. They play sports in intramural leagues. They tutor poor children, volunteer at soup kitchens, and read for the blind. Fraternities and sororities don't just hold parties. They also organize blood drives, charity raffles, winter clothing drives, and more. Participating in these volunteer activities is a regular part of student life.

That is less true for graduate students. Doctoral and medical students, in particular, are preoccupied with their studies. But students in law, business, public policy, education, and social work often participate in volunteer activities related to their professional training. They get a chance to socialize with fellow students as they contribute to the community.

Clubs for students from your home country or region bring together students from across the campus, from freshmen to advanced graduate students. Similar groups exist for every religion. They not only arrange worship, they join together for charity work and recreation.

Participating in these clubs and activities often carries weight on the job market.[23] When students apply for jobs, their résumés tell employers that they contributed to their universities and the wider community. These activities offer a rounded picture of students and may show their leadership abilities. In this case, what's good for the community is also good for you personally.

Leaders from Many Schools and Backgrounds

In some countries, leaders come from the same schools, the same faith, the same social background. Until the twentieth century, for example, England's leaders were drawn almost entirely from a narrow stratum of the landed classes. They began school together at Eton or Harrow, honed their debating skills at the Oxford Political Union, and worshiped from the Book of Common Prayer. Even now, England's leaders are drawn from a few "Oxbridge" colleges, France's from a few prestigious Grandes Écoles.

---

23. The one exception is for PhD's applying for academic jobs. For them, extracurricular activities count for very little. Of course, the activities may still be rewarding in themselves.

Not so in the United States and Canada. Political and business elites here are chosen from a wider, deeper pool. While some are educated at Harvard or Yale, many more are not. Some get their education entirely in their home states; others combine one degree from a state university with another from an elite national school.

This diversity in education contributes to diversity in national leadership. Whether it's business, politics, law, or medicine, the top people in the United States and Canada no longer come from a few top schools. Nor do they come from one class or one location. They come from all regions, multiple universities, and a variety of social backgrounds.

Women Expected to Play Leadership Roles

More and more of these leaders are women. Indeed, that is one of the most important social developments in North America over the past thirty years.

Universities have contributed to these changes and, in turn, been affected by them. As late as the 1970s, the overwhelming majority of students in professional schools were men. Today, about half are women. The same is true for PhD programs. Women are also moving steadily up the job ladder after graduation. Although women are still underrepresented in senior positions, their numbers are growing.

Discrimination and Harassment Are Unacceptable

This social transformation has wide support in the United States and Canada, and the support is virtually unanimous on university campuses. There are strong laws to prevent discrimination because of gender, or because of race, religion, sexual orientation, or national origin. It is flatly illegal to refuse to hire people because they are female—or because they are male, gay, black, Latino, Hindu, Muslim, Pakistani, German, and so on.

What counts are job qualifications. That's not just the law. That's what people really believe. According to polls, Americans and Canadians overwhelmingly agree that women should have an equal opportunity to suc-

> *Tip:* Women now occupy leading positions in universities, politics, business, and the professions. Discrimination against them *because they are women* is illegal and against the rules of every university.

> **Tip:** Sexual harassment is illegal and against university rules.

ceed in all fields, from law school to law partnerships, from business school to the executive suite, from graduate school to full professorships. They also acknowledge that some women may wish to work part time or stay home to raise children.

What does this mean for you, as an international student? If you are female, it means you should find role models to emulate and an open path to your career goals.

It also means that, if you do face discrimination or harassment, you will find well-established procedures at the university to help you personally and to combat the problem more broadly. You can discuss any complaints or raise any questions confidentially with a responsible university official. Every university has an office to deal specifically with these issues.

The same rules apply to discrimination based on race, religion, national origin, and sexual orientation (that is, whether a person is gay, lesbian, or transgendered). National laws and university regulations require equal treatment and prohibit harassment. That includes protection against a hostile work environment.

It means your professor could be a woman. So could your teaching assistant or lab supervisor. That's a new experience for some men, who come from countries where women rarely hold positions of authority. Most international students adjust easily, and, indeed, support the idea that men and women should be treated equally at work. But even if you have a different opinion, you are still expected to behave professionally and courteously toward women in the academic workplace.

Treat women students, faculty, and researchers the same way you treat men. Use the same professional standards for students and faculty of all races, religions, and backgrounds. Nobody can tell you what to think, but universities can, should, and do tell you how to behave in the classroom and workplace. On that point, they are sending a clear message: "Everyone is entitled to equal treatment."

> **Tip:** Laws and university rules prohibit discrimination based on race, religion, ethnicity, country of origin, or sexual orientation. You are expected to behave courteously and professionally toward teachers and students from all backgrounds.

Male-Female Friendships

Men and women are not only mixed together in the classroom, they often socialize as colleagues, professional associates, or friends. An invitation to lunch with a lab partner is commonplace. It is not a date, or at least it doesn't have to be. The assumption here is that men and women can meet for casual conversation and professional discussion outside the office.

It's also fine to form deeper relationships, whether they are close friendships or romantic partnerships. What is *not* permitted is to date anyone you teach or supervise. If you have any responsibility for a person's grades, academic evaluation, or financial awards, it is extremely unwise—and probably against your university's rules—to have an intimate relationship with him or her. At some universities, the rules go further, saying that faculty cannot date *any* student, even if that student is an adult from a different department.

Although the rules vary from university to university, they all have the same rationale. First, personal relationships between professors and students, or between supervisors and employees, open the door to favoritism. Even if the relationship is completely voluntary, it may be unfair to third parties (or may seem unfair to them) if they don't receive equal treatment. Second, any intimate relationship between a boss and employee (or between a teacher and student) raises the possibility of abuse of authority. The lower-ranking person may be coerced, or feel that way. Third, there could well be trouble if the relationship ends. When partners break up, they often feel upset, hurt, and angry. If the former partners work together, these emotions can easily seep into the workplace. That's uncomfortable for everybody and troublesome if one has authority over the other.

> *Tip:* Casual friendships between men and women are commonplace in North American universities. What is not permitted is a relationship between a teacher and his (or her) student.

Same-Sex Relationships

The rules and guidelines that apply to male-female relationships apply equally to same-sex relationships. Most (but not all) universities offer tangible support for same-sex couples and extend them the same benefits they offer married couples. If spouses are entitled to health benefits, for instance, then so are gay partners.

> ***Tip:*** In most universities, same-sex couples receive the same benefits as married couples. They are also subject to many of the same rules, such as the prohibition against teaching or supervising your partner.

They are also entitled to the same protections against sexual harassment and coercion. Just as the rules prohibit a man from harassing a woman (or vice versa), they prohibit a man from harassing a man, a woman from harassing a woman. Whether it is gay or straight, sexual harassment is sexual harassment.

The rules that prohibit you from dating your students apply to same-sex relationships, as well. So do the rules about not teaching or supervising your partner. You should not have control over the grades, pay, fellowship awards, or performance ratings of your partner. It is fundamentally unfair, and it can easily lead to abuse. That's why universities prohibit it.

Coercion and Threats Are Forbidden

Coercion, threats, and sexual harassment are strictly forbidden. University rules prohibit them, and so do public laws. That applies to everyone at the university and to all relationships, from freshman to faculty, from staff members to senior administrators. If you confront any threats or abuse, report it to the university, which has confidential procedures to handle the problem.

> ***Tip:*** Coercion and sexual harassment are forbidden, both by university rules and by law. All universities have confidential procedures for reporting any problems.

Accepting Personal Differences: Race, Religion, Sexual Orientation, Country of Origin

The same basic principles—tolerance and, indeed, active acceptance— apply to relationships with faculty and fellow students of different races, religions, sexual orientations, and countries of origin.

These are more than rules and regulations. They are widely shared values in North America and their acceptance is virtually universal on university campuses. There is general agreement that it should not matter if you are Christian, Muslim, or nonreligious; if you are physically handicapped;

if you are black, white, Hispanic, or Asian; if you are gay or straight. In your classes, labs, and housing, these factors are simply irrelevant. It's your work that counts.

You are welcome to hold your own views about any of these issues. You may think it is profoundly wrong, for example, for someone to be an atheist. So be it. Those are your views. But you must respect the rights of others in classroom, the dormitory, and workplace, whether they are an atheist, Hindu, Jew, Buddhist . . . whatever.

In turn, others should show you the same toleration and respect. If they don't and you cannot resolve the problem yourself, speak privately with officials at the university, who can help resolve any complaints or misunderstandings.

Openness to Foreigners, Ignorance about Their Countries

Universities here are welcoming to international students, and so is the wider society. Unfortunately, that doesn't mean we actually know anything about your country. We don't. Well, occasionally we know a little, but more often we are clueless. We do speak your language, *if* it is English. Or maybe Spanish or French. Otherwise, we don't.

Don't mistake this ignorance for intolerance. Americans and Canadians are actually very accepting of foreigners. We want to know more about you and your country. It's just that we don't know very much right now. "If you are from Africa," one adviser told me, "expect to be asked about lions and tigers."

Yet both countries have accepted wave after wave of immigrants and, indeed, think of themselves as built upon successful immigration. Neither has a narrow definition of a "true American" or "true Canadian." If you arrived in San Francisco from China and just took your oath of citizenship, you are just as American as your neighbor, whose family arrived from Ireland in 1849. That's not just an aspiration. It is a bedrock value.

Most of the time, teachers and fellow students are eager to learn about your background and ready to accommodate your needs. A typical example is a religious holiday. If you need to take a day off to observe Yom Kippur (the Jewish Day of Atonement), for example, your request will certainly be approved. No one expects you to be in class or at the lab bench that day. If you need to take an exam, it will be rescheduled. Just let others know well in advance so they can make arrangements. That's essential. It's up to you, not them, to initiate these arrangements.

If you want to discuss your customs and your faith, you will find many teachers, fellow students, and coworkers are interested in learning about them. If you want to celebrate your country's national day or another local holiday, you'll find many friends here who would love to attend. Along the same lines, they would enjoy showing you how we celebrate our holidays, such as Thanksgiving.

You will also discover that Americans (in particular) are patriotic. They wave the flag on the Fourth of July. That doesn't mean they blindly accept their country's policies or agree with the president or congress. But they do love their country, its values, and its democratic processes. They expect immigrants and long-term residents to learn the language and to recognize and accept its core national values, such as religious tolerance.[24]

Do Not Proselytize in the Classroom, Lab, or Workplace

As you discuss these customs, ideas, and attitudes, you should observe one important limitation. Do not use the classroom or lab to proselytize. If you hope to convert others to your faith or your politics, do it outside the workplace. And be sensitive to others' feelings.

The same limitations apply to them. Fellow students and staff members should respect your feelings and avoid proselytizing you in the workplace. On the other hand, it's perfectly fine for them to approach you in social settings and ask if you'd like to join them for religious services or a church-related social event, such as a dinner or talk. Invitations like these surprise some international students, especially those from countries where one religion dominates. But they are not unusual here. You are welcome to accept and explore the opportunity, or simply say "no, thanks."

Tip: The university is very accepting of diversity. You will find that other students are interested in learning about your background, experiences, faith, and customs. But you should *not* proselytize in the workplace, classroom, or lab.

Some Differences between Universities in Canada and the United States

In many ways, Canadian universities resemble their American counterparts. Their academic standards and scholarly values are identical. So are

24. There is also a rising concern about illegal immigration, which has reached unprecedented levels in the United States

their multiple missions, which range from teaching and basic research to professional and job training. In both countries, the national government subsidizes student loans and restricts them to its citizens. Both educational systems are decentralized, with public universities aligned to their federal political structures.

Strong as these similarities are, there are also a few significant differences between the two systems. The first is that America has many more private universities, not just in total numbers but in proportion to its population. The Canadian system is almost entirely public. Second, the United States has countless small undergraduate schools, strongly committed to liberal arts education. Almost all of them are private rather than state-sponsored. Canada has no equivalent. Third, although both systems have a federal structure, Ottawa plays a larger role in university education than does Washington. There is no U.S. version of "Canada Research Chairs," for example. Nor does Washington provide ongoing support for university operating budgets, as Ottawa now does.[25] Finally, as the Canadian educational system grew, it swallowed a number of private universities. McGill is the most prominent example. In the United States, by contrast, only a few private universities have become public. Most others have kept their status as private schools.

Close Ties between Universities and Industry

U.S. and Canadian universities, like their counterparts everywhere, are deeply involved in national life. That begins, naturally, with training future leaders. But it doesn't end there. Increasingly, universities are engaged in all aspects of the economy, since growth depends on high technology, continuous innovation, and high levels of human capital.

North American universities have long played major economic roles, from student internships and job recruitment to faculty consulting and sponsored research. Most undergraduates expect to take summer jobs for income and experience. That's even more common for graduate students in the professions, such as business, law, engineering, nursing, or public policy.

Faculty in business, law, and engineering often consult with corpora-

25. U.S. government agencies, such as the National Science Foundation, do provide what is called "indirect cost recovery" related to specific research grants. That is, if the NSF awards a professor $500,000 to study the impact of tornados, some of those funds will be used to pay the university's costs for providing office space, equipment, and staff support for the research.

> **Tip:** Universities are closely tied to the United States and Canadian econo-
> mies at every level. Their graduates become leaders, entrepreneurs, manag-
> ers, and researchers. University-based research contributes to public policy
> and private firms.

tions, nonprofits, and government agencies, and then bring their practical
experience back into the classroom. At a broader level, universities are
sensitive to growing areas of the economy, such as software development,
health-care management, and e-business, and often develop programs to
train students in these areas of high demand.

Universities' Central Role in High-Technology Economies

The relationship between universities, business, and government is growing deeper because of basic changes in the economy. One way to see these
changes is to look at how inventions are made. In the early nineteenth
century, they came mostly from inspired tinkering by lone individuals.
The cotton gin, mechanized textile production, and improvements in the
steam engine were all products of self-educated mechanics. By the late
nineteenth century, systematic research began to complement haphaz-
ard experiments. Sometimes, as in Thomas Edison's workshop, it was
self-taught inventors who conducted these systematic investigations. But,
increasingly, it was inventors steeped in the natural sciences. The clearest
examples are the German chemical and pharmaceutical industries, which
emerged from Germany's new research universities.

By the early twentieth century, General Electric and other large corporations began to establish their own research laboratories, focusing (naturally) on product development. Their scientists became a bridge between
basic scientific work, conducted mainly in universities, and applied work,
conducted mainly in corporate labs.

The pace of this work has quickened since World War II. Innovation
after innovation has emerged from engineering and the physical sciences
and, more recently, from computer science, materials technology, and
molecular biology. In all these areas, university research is essential.

Corporations draw heavily on this research—in two ways. The most
important is by hiring university-trained scientists. All major companies
now have their own research facilities, which recruit PhD's and collaborate
with universities and university hospitals. Second, when university scien-

tists make breakthroughs, they license them to firms that can bring the ideas to market. While universities have a comparative advantage in basic research, business firms have a comparative advantage in applied research, product development, and marketing. So it makes sense for universities to transfer ideas and the legal rights to develop them to companies that can profitably exploit them.

From Research to Economic Development

This collaboration between university and commercial research is growing ever closer as technological change accelerates and the economy moves away from basic manufacturing. Firms in the United States and Canada now depend on the flow of new products and processes. They need highly educated managers to run their operations and handle their finances. They need highly skilled researchers to assess the market. They need imaginative scientists to create the next generation of products. Since universities are devoted to this kind of sophisticated research and training, they are situated at the very heart of these economic changes. They are uniquely positioned to transfer knowledge and provide skilled employees to private firms and public agencies.

Whole industries, such as financial services and futures markets, are founded on university research, led by the economics departments and business schools at the University of Chicago, Harvard, Stanford, and MIT. University science and technology programs help drive regional economic development. The most obvious examples are Silicon Valley, which grew out of Stanford's science and engineering programs, and Boston's Route 128, which grew out of similar programs at MIT.

Advanced medical centers, like those in Houston, Seattle, and San Diego, depend on the same kind of links to the biological sciences. These hospital complexes have become focal points for biomedical research, patient care, and employment.

Their payrolls are now major sources of urban income. Chicago is a good example. For decades, the largest employer on the city's south side

> *Tip:* As technology grows ever more sophisticated and basic research ever more important, the links between universities and the economy are bound to grow stronger.

was the Union Stock Yards, which slaughtered cattle for the nation. Now it's gone. The biggest employer today is the University of Chicago Hospitals. The butchers have been replaced by surgeons.

Nor is Chicago unique. In dozens of cities, university medical centers are major sources of employment and technological development. They are busily engaged in developing new drugs and new treatments. Their largest source of funding is still the national government, but pharmaceutical companies are providing an increasing share of research support, as well as hiring top graduates.

Technology Transfer

Whatever the source of funding, medical researchers are eager to translate their findings into standard treatments, available to everyone. That's not just true for medicine; it's true for all university research. If scholarly work has practical applications, then it's likely to be commercialized quickly—for two reasons. First, universities, departments, and individual scholars are alert to the possibilities of profit and want to capture them. As I noted earlier, universities compete for funds and top researchers. It is not considered beneath the dignity of scholars here to seek profits from their work *as long as the work itself meets the highest academic standards and is directed toward scholarly ends.* That means professors, graduate students, and other academic researchers are expected to remain disinterested as they conduct experiments, evaluate data, and publish their work. If they fail to meet these standards—if they bias their findings for profit motives—they violate basic standards of academic integrity.[26]

---

26. These standards apply to university-based research. Faculty and advanced graduate students sometimes consult for companies, governments, and nonprofit agencies. Some become deeply involved, particularly when the organizations rely on the faculty member's inventions.

Universities have two principal interests in such cases. First, they want to make sure there is no conflict of interest between these outside activities and the professor's scholarly work and university commitments. To minimize these conflicts, universities have explicit rules about conflicts of interest and generally require faculty to disclose any activities that might conflict with their university responsibilities. Second, universities want to make sure that full-time faculty devote their time mainly to teaching and research, not consulting, running companies, or trying court cases. Most universities limit how much consulting or other outside work faculty members can do. One day per week is a common limit.

Each university sets its own rules, but they share some common features: full disclosure of possible conflicts of interest, explicit limits on time spent on outside activities, and integrity in all scholarly work.

> **Tip:** Universities are increasingly interested in commercializing their discoveries.

Second, U.S. law now encourages universities to commercialize any results from federal grants. The law, known as the Bayh-Dole Act, says, in effect, "The public paid for this research and should benefit from it." In practice, this means research must be published and any useful findings, products, and technologies must be made available to the public. The inventors can do that either by taking out patents or by putting the material in the (free) public domain.

New Laws to Encourage Technology Transfer

Until the Bayh-Dole Act, the U.S. government held all rights based on its sponsored research. Unfortunately, it was woefully ineffectual in passing on the results to industry and the public. The Bayh-Dole Act changed all that. It gave clear property rights to the grant recipients, such as university scientists. That allowed academics and universities to profit from their inventions.

To profit, however, they need to translate lab results into products that succeed in the marketplace. That almost always means finding a commercial partner. The public benefits by gaining access to these new products and by the products' broad stimulation of the high-technology economy. If universities or individual researchers choose not to pursue the commercial possibilities of their federal research, they must allow others to do so.[27]

The Bayh-Dole Act has been extraordinarily successful because it recognizes and reinforces the central facts of modern economic life.

- Advanced economies are built on innovation and research.
- It is vital to foster this research and its commercialization.

---

27. The Bayh-Dole Act is officially called the Patent and Trademark Law Amendments Act (December 12, 1980), P.L. 96–517. The Office of Management and Budget subsequently gave directions on its implementation (OMB Circular A–124, issued on February 10, 1982). The Reagan administration expanded the act through a Presidential Memorandum on "Government Patent Policy" (February 18, 1983). Finally, in 1984, Congress modified the act in a few ways, making the Commerce Department the chief agency for administering it (P.L. 98–620, November 8, 1984) These laws, memoranda, and regulations are consolidated in 37 CFR 401 and 35 USC §§ 200–212 ("Patent Rights in Inventions Made with Federal Assistance").

- One important way to do that is to promote the efficient transfer of ideas between universities and firms.[28]

Modern, wealthy, growing economies are built on high technology. High technology, in turn, is promoted by strong relationships among academic scientists, government agencies, and private firms. Since universities are central to innovation and training knowledge workers, they are positioned at the fulcrum of the modern economy.

28. Council on Governmental Relations, *The Bayh-Dole Act: A Guide to the Law and Implementing Regulations* (October 1999), http://www.cogr.edu/docs/Bayh_Dole.pdf (accessed September 18, 2005).

Part 3

Living in the United States and Canada

Chapter 10

Settling In

Moving to a new country, finding the right place to live, and settling in comfortably are exciting and challenging. I know. I spent time in several countries as an undergraduate and again as a faculty member. I know what it means to try, in a broken tongue, to order steak and actually be served pigs' feet. Really. Somewhere, there are still waiters wondering what I wanted to eat. (Short answer: *not* pigs' feet.) And yet, it was a great experience, except for the feet.

In this chapter, I'll help you get started here. I have already discussed what you should do immediately after arriving (see chapter 3, "The First Ten Things You Should Do Here"). Now, I'll turn to what you should do next.

In subsequent chapters, I'll offer detailed information about the most important aspects of student life in the United States and Canada, from transportation and personal finance to housing and health care, and much more. Each chapter addresses a specific aspect of living—and thriving—in North America, so you can easily find the information you need.

Dial 911 for Emergencies

For emergencies, there's a single phone number to dial anywhere in the United States or Canada: 911. Dial it to report a fire, reach the police, or summon an ambulance and emergency medical technician. The number costs nothing to use and works from both cell phones and landlines.

Dial 911 only for emergencies. If a problem can wait, such as a complaint about parking tickets, call the police department's regular phone

> *Tip:* Dial 911 for police, fire, ambulance, and other emergency needs. It works in both the United States and Canada.

number, not 911. If you don't know the regular number for the police, look it up in the phone book or online, or dial 411 for directory assistance.

Equally important, never call 911 as a prank or joke. It wastes precious resources, and it's a criminal offense.

Campus Police

Nearly all universities maintain their own police forces to protect students, faculty, and staff, as well as campus buildings. Because they regularly patrol the university, campus police officers may be able to reach you quickly in an emergency.

You should write down the phone number for the campus police and program it into your cell phone. You should also check around campus to see if there are "emergency call boxes," which are connected directly to the campus police office.

For more on campus police services, see chapter 25, "Dealing with Problems."

> *Tip:* Add the campus police number to your cell phone. As you walk around the campus and the neighborhood, check to see where emergency phone boxes are located.

Compile a List of Emergency Numbers

Besides 911 and the university police, there are several other phone numbers you might need in an emergency. You should compile a list, post it in your apartment, and store it in your cell phone, computer, and PDA.

Begin with "ICE," which stands for "in case of emergency."[1] That is the number you want police, fire, or emergency medical technicians to call if they find you unconscious and cannot ask you directly whom to call and

---

1. In another context, ICE has a very different meaning. It stands for "Immigration and Customs Enforcement," a branch of the U.S. Department of Homeland Security. Still, on your cell phone, emergency workers know what it means. It tells them exactly who to call if you cannot tell them yourself.

notify. It is probably the number for your husband or wife, your parents, or a close friend. Be sure it is labeled ICE.

Next, add the phone numbers for the electric company, the gas company (that is, natural gas, not petrol), your doctor, the emergency room at the local hospital, the university police, and your insurance agent. If you don't have all these names yet, you soon will, and you should add them to your emergency list as soon as you do.

You'll want to include people you might need to reach quickly: family members, close friends, next-door neighbors, the landlord, the international student adviser, and so on. For some you might want to include both cell phone and landline numbers. You might need these numbers in a hurry.

If you have children, your emergency list should include their doctor, the pediatric emergency room, and poison control (that is, the number to call if anyone swallows poison).

Be sure to include the number for your home country's embassy and for the local consulate, if there is one. If legal problems or immigration issues arise, you may want to contact them. You also have a right to call them if you are arrested.

In addition to phone numbers, your list should include numbers for your passport, your insurance policies, and your HMO card or health insurance. In an emergency, you won't want to search around for this critical information.

It helps to add a few explanatory comments next to some of these entries. That way, your list can be used by a baby-sitter or houseguest if there's trouble at your apartment. For example, my list says "Bob Lipson (Charles's brother in Seattle)." As it happens, I already know that Bob is my brother. But a housesitter wouldn't. At the top of the list, write your own address, phone number, and cell phone. That way, if a baby-sitter needs to call an ambulance, she can tell them where to send it. If she needs to reach you on your cell phone, she can.

To construct this list, you will need to look up a few numbers. Nobody

---

Tip: Compile a list of phone numbers you might need in an emergency, everything from the hospital emergency room to the gas and electric companies. Include the numbers for some vital documents, such as your passport and health insurance card. Then enter the list in your cell phone and post a copy in your apartment.

remembers the phone number for the gas company or the hospital emergency room. Few people remember their passport numbers, either. Go ahead and compile that list now. Why wait? Print out several copies and update it when numbers change.

Items to Carry with You

There are several items you should carry with you at all times. They prove you are here legally and, in case of an accident, that you are properly insured. *All* international students should carry

- a photocopy of your passport (while keeping the original in a safe place),
- your health insurance card or HMO card, and
- any visa papers required by immigration (see their Web sites for details).

If you drive, you should carry three more items:

- your driver's license,
- the registration for your car, showing you paid for the license plate, and
- your automobile insurance card (insurance is required for drivers)

If the police pull you over, the first thing they say is, "Please show me your license, registration, and insurance." You don't want to mumble, "Officer, I really have them, but I left them at my apartment."

Items to Keep Safe

Some items, like your passport, are too valuable to carry around all the time. You should keep a photocopy with you and put the number on your emergency list. As for the passport itself, put it in a secure place, either in your apartment or in a "safe-deposit box" at your bank.

You can rent a small box at a local bank for $50–100 a year, and you don't need to be a bank customer to do it. This safe-deposit box is completely private and will protect your vital documents, jewelry, and other valuables from fire, theft, or flood. The box is protected against fire, theft, and flood and can be opened only by using two keys simultaneously, one from the bank and one from the customer. Even though the bank must assist in opening the box, they don't look inside. The contents are private. The bank provides small, private rooms where customers can add and remove items from their boxes. The only drawback, aside from the cost, is that access to the box is limited to regular banking hours. If you are traveling to Rio or Seoul on Sunday evening, you must remember to retrieve your passport the day before, when the bank is open.

An alternative is to put your passport and other small valuables in a safe place at home. To guard against fire, you can buy a small fireproof box at a locksmith, hardware store, or discount store. The boxes come with a lock, but a thief could simply steal the box and open it later. Still, they're a useful safeguard against fire.

Preventing Identity Theft

Some numbers are so valuable that you shouldn't carry them at all. You should simply memorize them and keep the numbers in a safe place. The most important is your Social Security Number, or, in Canada, your Social Insurance Number. That, and the numbers from your bank account and credit cards, are the main targets of identity theft. The same is true for an Individual Taxpayer Identification Number. An ITIN is similar to a Social Security Number, though it cannot be used for employment. It is used by visitors to the United States who don't qualify to work (so they cannot get a Social Security card) but who need a similar number for tax documents, credit card applications, and the like.

Write down the following numbers and store them in a safe place:

- Social Security Number or Individual Taxpayer Identification Number (in the United States),
- Social Insurance Number (in Canada),
- credit card numbers,
- bank account numbers, and
- the vehicle identification number for your car.

Remember, don't share these numbers casually, and don't carry them around with you. And don't be tricked into giving them out in response to fraudulent phone calls or e-mails, a vile practice known as "phishing." Believe me, no matter how authentic or legitimate these pleas may sound, nobody in Nigeria really wants to give you $5 million.

Thieves also phish by pretending to be your bank or credit card company. Their goal: to steal your identity and use it to withdraw money from your account or make false charges on your credit card. To do that, they pretend to be a legitimate business and invent a story that requires you to send them personal information ("we lost your data" or "you need to send us updated information"). Then, they conveniently provide you a Web link

> **Tip:** Protect your Social Security or Social Insurance numbers, along with other sensitive numbers such as credit cards and bank accounts. Don't respond to e-mails asking for those numbers or other personal financial information.

where you can send that information. It's a scam and a crime. The "convenient Web link" actually belongs to them, not to your bank or credit card company. *Never* go to the Web sites provided in these e-mails. They just want to steal your identity and then your money.

Along the same lines, protect your credit card information. Don't include the card numbers in e-mails, for example, since they aren't secure. When you charge items online, use sites you know are legitimate and secure (encrypted). When you charge something at a store or restaurant, keep the receipt, which may contain your credit card number, or rip it up. Don't leave the receipt lying around.

Victims of Identify Theft

If you are ensnared by identity theft—if you discover any suspicious bank withdrawals or credit charges—notify the bank or credit card company immediately. Ask them for details about the transactions, dispute them if they are not yours (or if you are unsure), and ask the company which law enforcement officials you should notify.

Although it helps to take these precautions, you still might be a victim. If that happens, you need to act promptly.

- Close any accounts you think were tampered with or were opened fraudulently in your name.
- Report the identity theft to your local police. Be sure to get the number of the police report and obtain a copy of it, if possible. You will need them later when you deal with credit card companies, banks, and others.
- Contact the three credit rating agencies, Equifax, Experian, and Trans-Union, and explain the identity theft:
  - ✔ Equifax.com 1-800-525-6285
  - ✔ Experian.com 1-888-397-3742
  - ✔ Transunion.com 1-800-680-7289

In the United States, you should also contact the Federal Trade Commission (FTC), which maintains a Web site concerning identity theft: www .consumer.gov/idtheft/. You can also phone them at 877-438-4338. At their Web site, you can download an identity theft affidavit, which you fill out and return to the FTC. The FTC works with law enforcement agencies to track down the thieves.

The Canadian government maintains a Web site for replacing lost or stolen identification cards: http://canada.gc.ca/cdns/wallet/wallet_e.html. To notify them about misuse of your Social Insurance Number, you should contact

Social Insurance Registration
PO Box 7000
Bathurst, NB E2A 4T1
E-mail: sin-nas@hrdc-drhc.gc.ca

Personal Safety

Valuable as your financial information is, it pales beside your personal safety. The best way to protect yourself is to know your surroundings, take prudent precautions, and avoid undue risks.

It is possible, however, to be *too* cautious. Some students never venture far from campus because of unrealistic fears. They're safe, but at the cost of never knowing their neighborhood or city, never fully experiencing the country in which they are living.

That's a real problem for some international students. They come to America (and, to a lesser extent, to Canada) with genuine fears about their personal safety. That's understandable, since some of them come from countries where cities are very safe. Too often, though, their worries about crime here are exaggerated. Crime is certainly a threat, and you need to take precautions, but excessive fears can stifle visitors' curiosity, trap them at home, and limit their enjoyment of a new country.

How can you balance reasonable concerns about personal safety with a desire to explore your new surroundings? The best way is to know the *real* risks, not the hype, and take sensible steps to limit them.

How can you differentiate among neighborhoods in your new city, sorting out the desirable from the dangerous? The best approach is to ask people who know the city intimately, the people who live there, not other international students. If you are from Mumbai or Munich, you certainly know those cities better than any visiting student. Well, the same is true here.

> **Tip:** Personal safety depends on knowing your surroundings and avoiding undue risks. Take prudent precautions and explore your new community. Don't stay trapped at home because of unrealistic fears.

Let me give you a personal example from Chicago, but one that applies to all cities. There are many neighborhoods worth seeing around Chicago, but some are too risky after dark, at least for me. I'd be perfectly happy to go there at noon, but not at midnight. Some places I might be willing to go with a group of friends but not by myself. There are many other neighborhoods I don't know well enough and would need to ask someone before I went there. Finally, there are some areas I avoid entirely, no matter what time it is. I wouldn't go there with a police escort.

When you ask a local resident about your new city, she might reply, "It's fine to go up to 47th Street, and it's really interesting. But don't go to 37th Street." That's valuable advice, and it avoids two problems. Unless you asked, you might wander up to 37th Street and return without your wallet. The other, less obvious problem is that you might stay home, fearing (wrongly) that it is too dangerous to go to 47th Street. Both errors carry a real price tag. You can avoid them by asking people who know the territory.

Home Safety

Speaking of safety, you need to take some precautions around your apartment, too. The most important is to have working smoke detectors—not just smoke detectors but *working* smoke detectors. Your apartment, dorm, or house will almost certainly come with a few smoke detectors already in place. There should be one in the kitchen and one in or near every bedroom. If any are missing, buy and install them. They are inexpensive and can be found at any hardware store or drugstore.

They won't protect you, however, without fresh batteries. Buy some as soon as you move in. Detectors usually require 9 volt batteries, which should be changed twice a year. A good rule of thumb is to change them in the spring, when daylight savings time begins, and again in the autumn, when it ends. Start this cycle by installing fresh batteries in all smoke detectors as soon as you move in.

If you live in a large building, you should plan your escape in case of fire. It's a wise precaution. It takes only a few minutes to make a plan, and it could save your life. If you have older children, make sure they understand exactly what to do.

Tip: Make sure your apartment or dorm room has smoke detectors with fresh batteries. Replace the batteries twice a year.

> **Tip:** Ask fellow students if the university police respond quicker than the city police. Call the faster one first.

Earlier, I mentioned that you should call 911 if you smell a fire or need immediate police assistance. Now, let me add one more piece of local knowledge. If you live near campus, your first call might be to the university police, even before you call 911. At some universities (including mine), the campus police actually respond faster than the city.

When you call the university police, they not only respond themselves, they often relay your request to the city police so they can respond, too. Since different universities handle these calls differently, you need to know what your university does and how well they do it. Ask fellow students who have some experience or ask the international student adviser. Then figure out, in advance, whether your first call should be to 911 or the university police.

Keep Your Immigration Status Up-to-Date

Another necessity of international student life is keeping your immigration status up-to-date. I already discussed that in chapter 2, "Passports and Visas: A Quick Overview." But let me remind you of three things. One is that you *must* keep a valid passport. If yours is about to expire, renew it. Second, if you hold a student visa, you need to remain in school and continue to make satisfactory progress toward your degree.[2] If you change schools or academic programs, you might need to update that information with immigration authorities. Their Web site will explain the rules. Your international student adviser's office will also know them. Finally, if you leave the country and intend to return, be sure you have the proper visas. "Leaving the country" includes trips between the United States and Canada. You might be able to fly from Tampa to Toronto but not reenter the United States. Don't leave without securing the necessary visas.

If you have questions about these immigration and travel issues, check the appropriate government Web sites. And be sure to stay in close touch with your international student adviser about all immigration processes.

---

2. Most international students are enrolled full time. But regulations may permit you to study part time *if* you follow appropriate government procedures. For details, see the official immigration Web site and check with your international student adviser.

Chapter 11

Learning the Terrain

You may have come here to study, but you'll enjoy your stay a lot more if you get out and explore your neighborhood, your city, and points beyond.

If you have a little time before school starts, after you've rented an apartment and unpacked, you can do some things that will make your life here more rewarding. I'd put two items at the top of my "to do" list: traveling around your new hometown and perfecting your English. Perhaps you can do both simultaneously. Perhaps you need to give priority to one. Let me begin with being a tourist and then take up language training in chapter 12.

Tip: If you have time before school starts, you can spend it profitably by

- exploring your new hometown, beginning with your neighborhood, and
- working on your English.

Exploring Your Neighborhood

The best time to start exploring your campus, neighborhood, and city is soon after you arrive, before the chill of winter, before the crush of classes, papers, and labs. Since most universities begin in August or September, you'll come at a good time to walk around the neighborhood and drive around town. You'll be learning the terrain during warm weather. A few months later, when it's cold and rainy, you will already know the route to your favorite restaurant or coffee shop.

The place to start exploring is near your apartment or dorm. Where are

> **Tip:** Explore your campus, neighborhood, and city while the weather is good and before class assignments bear down on you.

the best places to shop for groceries, clothes, and office supplies? Where's the post office? Where are the best restaurants and movie theaters? You'll want to discover the convenience stores, twenty-four-hour stores, pharmacies, and larger food markets. You'll want to test a few local restaurants and perhaps a place to dry clean your clothes. For all these choices, it helps to ask your friends, advisers, and acquaintances in the neighborhood. The best options for you will depend on your tastes, income, location, and transportation.

In my neighborhood, for example, there are two small groceries within easy walking distance. They are more expensive than large groceries and carry fewer brands, but they are *so* convenient. They're great when we run out of milk or eggs, or when I hunger for some "health food," like ice cream or candy.

When I need to buy more groceries, I can drive a few blocks to a medium-sized supermarket (a large grocery) and a pharmacy. This pharmacy, like most large "drug stores" in North America, carries a wide variety of items—food, candy, cosmetics, school supplies, small appliances, and much more. It is open twenty-four hours a day and has a banking machine where I can get cash or make deposits.[1]

If I wish, I can drive another fifteen minutes to shop at a huge supermarket with a befuddling array of choices. This behemoth has its own discount card, which is free to customers who request it. It knocks a dollar or two off some items, but it's not a credit card. It's a discount card. Many chain stores have discount cards like this, but you need to ask for them.

Shopping

Although neighborhood stores are convenient, you'll probably need to travel a little farther to buy clothes, furniture, electronics, and other essential items. That means you need to drive or take public transportation (a bus or subway).

In most cities, it's a trip well worth making. You'll discover a wide vari-

---

1. In the United States, these machines are called ATMs, or automated teller machines. (The name refers to a bank teller, the person who handles your deposits and withdrawals.) In Canada, the same machines are called ABMs, automated banking machines.

ety of retail outlets, some locally owned, some branches of large national chains. Of course, you also can shop online for many of the same products. I'll discuss these options in chapter 16, "Spending Money: Shopping at Local Stores, Malls, and Online."

What matters now is that you begin exploring some of these alternatives before you are weighed down with classes, labs, and assignments. Since you need to buy food, furniture, office supplies, and books anyway, why not use the opportunity to look around at different stores?

Restaurants

It's also a good time to check out local restaurants, with either your family or fellow students.

Every university town has its motley collection of fast-food joints: McDonald's, KFC (chicken), Taco Bell (Mexican), Subway (sandwiches) and, in Canada, Tim Hortons, Mr. Sub, and others. Some, like Pizza Hut and Domino's Pizza, will deliver to your door.

If you want to step up a bit in décor and quality, you can eat at moderately priced chains like Applebee's, Bennigan's, Chili's (Mexican), or Olive Garden (Italian), which have full table service.

Most students find it fun to go beyond the chain restaurants and try some locally owned places, especially those that provide regional cuisine, such as Cajun cooking in New Orleans or seafood in Seattle, or dishes from around the world. Good ethnic restaurants abound, even in smaller cities. After all, Canada and the United States were built on immigration, and some of these new arrivals started restaurants with food from their home countries.

Sometimes, you'll find more than one or two good ethnic restaurants. You'll find a whole neighborhood full. There are "Chinatowns," for example, in dozens of cities across North America, from Boston and Toronto to Los Angeles and Vancouver. There's a "Little Italy" in Boston, New York, and San Francisco, and its equivalent (by other names) in several other cities. There are Latino districts in countless cities, with restaurants ranging from inexpensive to fine dining. Although metropolitan areas have more dining options (there are great Afghan and Ethiopian restaurants in

Tip: Go beyond chain restaurants. Look for good, locally owned restaurants, including those that feature ethnic cooking.

> **Tip:** It's a good idea to make reservations at popular dining spots. You are expected to show up on time. If you are running ten or fifteen minutes late, call the restaurant and explain.

Washington, DC, for instance), you can find good ethnic restaurants in most university towns. In some, you can even find ethnic grocery stores so you can cook for yourself and friends.

If you are not sure whether a restaurant is too expensive, too noisy, or too formal for your tastes (or your family's), just call and ask. You are welcome to ask about price, too: "What does a full meal, without wine, usually cost?" They'll be glad to tell you. They will also tell you if they are located near public transportation and whether they have a parking lot, street parking, or valet service (where an attendant parks your car for a few dollars).

At better restaurants and more popular locations, it's wise to make phone reservations well in advance. That's especially true if you are dining out on Friday or Saturday night. The restaurant may call you back later to confirm. They expect you to show up on time.

When you make dining plans, remember that North Americans dine earlier than Europeans and Latin Americans. The peak dinner hour in restaurants is 7:00 p.m., and many close their kitchens at 9:00 or 10:00 p.m.

Most restaurants now prohibit smoking. Virtually all are accessible to people in wheelchairs, which means they are also convenient for parents with strollers.

Tipping in Restaurants, Taxicabs, and Elsewhere

Restaurant bills in the United States and Canada seldom include the gratuity (also known here as a "tip"). When you dine out, you should add another 15–20 percent to the bill for the waiter, either in cash or on the credit card slip. A few restaurants add it themselves, mainly for large groups, but they are the exception. Review your bill to see if the tip is already included. If not, be sure to add it.

If a valet parks your car, it's customary to tip a dollar or two, in addition

> **Tip:** Tips for the restaurant staff are not normally included in the bill. A standard tip is 15–20 percent.

to the parking fee. Give a similar tip to a coatroom attendant who checks your coat, briefcase, or backpack.

Gratuities are normally offered for several other services. Taxi drivers are given an additional 10–15 percent of the fare, perhaps a little more if the driver helps with your luggage. Tips for barbers and hairdressers are in the same range. Porters who handle your luggage at a hotel or the airport are usually given one or two dollars per bag.

Public Transportation and Cars

Unless you order your pizza to be delivered and your books online, you'll need to ask friends where to shop and then drive there or take public transportation. If you don't have a car, you'll want to learn quickly about the bus and subway routes. Which streets do they serve? How good is the service? How safe? How late do they run? How much do they cost? Do you need to pay with exact change? Are there special discounts for students or monthly cards for frequent riders? There usually are.

Be sure to ask whether your university has its own transportation services, not only around campus but also around town. Some universities run regular shuttle buses to popular locations off campus. They may run extra shuttles to the airport at the end of the semester.

If you drive, and especially if you plan to drive to school regularly, you should learn about parking arrangements immediately. Most universities set aside parking for students, but they charge several hundred dollars for the privilege. Students need to buy an annual sticker showing that their cars are allowed to park on campus.

Not all parking stickers are alike. Some allow you to park only in certain areas, say in Lot C but not in Lots A or B. Ask about the arrangements on your campus and try to purchase a sticker that allows you to park near your classes or department. The sooner you ask, the better your chances of getting the parking spot you want.

I'll continue this discussion in chapter 18, "Getting Around: Cars."

Tip: Learn which public transit routes and university buses serve your needs.

Tip: Check on university parking arrangements, and try to buy a sticker for a parking lot near your department.

Exploring Your City and Region

Before school begins, consider traveling around the larger area where you live, just for fun. If there are parks or historical sites nearby, think about visiting them. If downtown is interesting, make a trip and stroll around—while the weather is good and before you are saddled with academic assignments. If your town has a company like Gray Lines, which offers guided tours, consider going on one. It takes only a few hours, and it offers lots of valuable information and historical background.

What you learn now about your new city will pay dividends throughout your stay. Some universities offer tours like this themselves, primarily for new students. If yours does, take advantage of it. Also, ask if your city offers self-guided walking tours. Many do, and they cost nothing. You simply pick up a pamphlet at a central location and follow the mapped route. Chicago, for example, has an architectural walking tour that features the city's historic skyscrapers. Boston has the Freedom Trail, which covers important sites from the Revolutionary War. In the summer, they even station guides along the route to explain the locations, give a little history, and answer questions. Montreal has an information center in the oldest part of the city, Vieux Montréal, and a wonderful historical museum in the area. Consider taking a tour like this before school starts, and ask some fellow students to join you. You'll learn about your new surroundings and strengthen your new friendships in the process.

> **Tip:** Be a tourist in your new surroundings. Check out the historic sites and popular attractions. Do it while the weather is good, before school assignments pile up.

Learning the Laws

As you learn about your neighborhood and your city, you should also learn about the laws. Those vary from city to city, state to state, province to province. Both the United States and Canada have strong traditions of federalism (decentralized government). What's legal in one jurisdiction may be illegal in the next. In most cities, for example, it's perfectly legal to talk on cell phones while driving. But in several cities, including Chicago, it's not. You must use a hands-free phone or risk getting a ticket. Every state has its own speed limits and its own minimum age for drivers. Some

> *Tip:* You are responsible for knowing the laws, even if you are new to the area.

cities permit smoking in restricted sections of bars and restaurants, while others ban all smoking indoors, except in private homes. These differences are the product of federal political structures that emphasize local control instead of uniform national laws.

What doesn't vary is your responsibility for knowing the laws, both local and national. Ignorance of the law does *not* constitute a defense. If you are driving eighty miles per hour and a policeman pulls you over, you are going to get a ticket. It won't help to explain that you didn't know the speed limit. I speak from experience.

It won't help to hand the officer $20 and ask him to forget about it. That may have worked when Al Capone was running amok, and it's still standard procedure in some countries, but it isn't here. In fact, offering a bribe can land you in jail. There are easier ways to learn the local customs.

Local Newspapers

One of the best ways to learn about your new hometown is to read a local newspaper. Today, most students read them online, and that's fine. For international students, though, I recommend subscribing to a newspaper, at least for the first few months. Thumbing through all the sections will give you a great sense of what's happening locally. What are the major controversies? What really matters to people around here?

There are some concrete benefits to subscribing, as well. The paper will quickly pay for itself because it includes discount coupons for shopping and countless advertisements for sales. Subscribing shouldn't be expensive, and there are usually discount rates for students. As you read the paper day by day, you'll begin to feel less like a visitor and more like a resident.

> *Tip:* Subscribe to a local newspaper. Even though you can read it online for free, there is a real benefit to reading the physical paper, especially in your first few months.

What Should You Wear?

You probably won't worry much about what to wear to class, parties, or other events, and you'd be right. Years ago, there were fairly strict codes: professors wore business attire (suits and ties for men, dresses for women). Students dressed fairly formally, too. Nicer restaurants refused to let men dine without a coat and tie.

Those days are long gone. Today, Americans and Canadians dress much more informally, though there are still some regional variations. (Eastern Canada and the U.S. East Coast and South are a bit more formal, in manners and dress, than the West Coast, Plains, and American Southwest.) Your best guide to appropriate dress is to observe what your classmates are wearing and follow along.

There are a couple of occasions when you should dress up a bit. The most important is for a job interview. If you are presenting a job talk at a university or interviewing at a corporation or law firm, you should wear subdued business attire (a dress or pant suit for women, a tie and dark suit or jacket for men). You should wear something similar if you are presenting a paper at a convention. If other conventiongoers are dressed more informally, you can always remove your coat and tie.

If you are going to a *very* fancy restaurant, you might ask in advance if there is a dress code. There probably isn't one, but it's worth checking.

One suggestion: if you are unsure what to wear to an event and don't know whom to ask, err on the side of being a bit "overdressed."

> ***Tip:*** Informal dress is usually fine for class and social occasions, but wear business attire for job interviews and convention presentations.

Religious Symbols and Apparel

One area of dress that concerns some international students is religious apparel, such as headcoverings. Let me offer some reassurance. Canada and the United States are socially and religiously diverse, and they value toleration. They not only accept different religions, they accept the garments and symbols that accompany them.

This tolerance is commonplace at universities. Many students and faculty are secular, but it's not unusual to see an observant Jewish man wearing a small headcovering (kippot) to class or an observant Muslim woman wearing a headscarf (hijab). It's even more common to see students wearing a small pin or necklace bearing a cross, proclaiming their Christian faith.

How do other students react? With overwhelming agreement that it's a personal matter. Beyond that, most students on most campuses are simply indifferent to your display of belief. Of course, a few will warmly welcome these symbols and a few others will look askance. Whatever their opinions, it's entirely up to you whether to wear a religious symbol or garment. It's a personal choice, not a highly contested political act, as it is in some countries.

How to Find a Place of Worship

Where can you find a church, mosque, synagogue, or other place to worship? Easy: just ask the international student adviser or the dean of students. Their offices will have a list of worship sites around the city and religious groups on campus, including their addresses and contact numbers. These lists are usually posted online as well.

At many universities, there is also an umbrella organization for all religious groups. At Yale, for example, the university chaplain's Web site gives information about more than a dozen religions on campus, as well as places of worship around the city. There may be a similar organization at your university.

Become an "Amateur Anthropologist"

In this chapter, I have offered some ideas about social life in North America and suggested a few ways to learn more. You'll learn a lot simply by talking with fellow students. You'll learn some more, I hope, by reading the chapters that follow. But perhaps the best way is learn is by being an active observer. To put that another way, I urge you to become an "amateur anthropologist." Even if you are training to become an astrophysicist, you can mimic the anthropologists and learn about local habits. It's fun. All you need to do is pay attention and reflect on what you see. For example:

- How do people meet and greet each other?
- How far apart do they stand when talking?
- Do they tend to be formal or informal, especially compared to your home country?

- What do they do for recreation?
- When they celebrate, do they invite friends to their homes?
- Do people arrive on time?
- Do they give each other elaborate gifts, small tokens of esteem, or nothing at all?
- How do men and women relate to each other in classes, the library, and the dining hall?
- How religious (or secular) are most students at your university? Is that different from the wider society?
- How tolerant are they of different cultures and religions?

The more you observe, the more you will learn. The more you learn, the more enjoyable and profitable your stay will be.

You can become a skilled observer, no matter what your age or interests. I learned this some years ago by watching my twin sons, Mike and Jon, who were three years old when we lived in London. I can still remember their fascination with automobile headlights, which were at eye-level for them. They quickly discovered that, in rainy England, many cars had wipers on their headlights. They knew that American cars did not. Oh, the joy of this discovery! They were fascinated by the difference between American and British headlights, and their discovery led to countless comparisons between London and Chicago, between Cambridge, Massachusetts, and Cambridge, England.

That's street-level anthropology, as practiced by three-year-olds. You can do it yourself as a twenty-three-year-old, with your own interests and sophistication. Use your time in a new country to observe, compare, learn, and enjoy.

> **Tip:** Become an "amateur anthropologist," closely observing your new surroundings.

"How Are You?"

Let me give you your first assignment as an amateur anthropologist. Find out what the natives mean by asking, "How are you?" It is the single most popular greeting, at least in the United States, and it comes with several local variations that mean essentially the same thing:

- "How are ya?"
- "How's it going?"
- "What's up?" or its slang version, "Wassup?"
- "What's happening?"
- "What's cookin'?"

Southerners often ask, "How are y'all doing?" Natives of New Orleans sometimes say, "Where y'at?" (as in, "Where are you at?").[2] These greetings, and the responses to them, are so familiar that Americans never stop to think how puzzling they are. International students do. And they are not sure how to solve the puzzle.

My Answer to "How Are You?"

Let me offer a native's view. Compare it with what you discover.

"How are you?" is a friendly greeting that can mean two things. Among true friends, it is an invitation to answer with your personal feelings, *but only if you wish*. That is, you can choose to answer the questions "Are you feeling well? Are you facing any serious problems? Are things going well for you at home and at work?" Among friends, you can answer those if you wish, but you don't have to. If you prefer, you can respond briefly and impersonally and then move on to discuss other things. Second, among acquaintances who are *not* close friends, "How are you" is simply a polite welcoming statement. It's not a question; it's just a way to say, "hello." It expresses an interest in the other person *without seeking any detailed personal information*. That's what business associates mean when they say "How are you?" That's what local students mean when they greet classmates.

When you hear the question, how should you respond? You already know how to respond to true friends. In fact, that's what's so puzzling about the question. It seems odd and intrusive to hear it from somebody who is more distant. What are they asking, and how should you respond?

If it's a casual acquaintance, you can always respond, "Hi, there. I'm doing just fine. Nice to see you. How are *you*?" Or you could answer with a little more personal information without going too far. Here are a few examples:

---

2. "Y'all" is a good Southern expression for "you all." It can be addressed to one person or several. That is, "How are y'all doing?" can be addressed to you alone or to you and a group of friends. In New Orleans, the local greeting of "Where y'at?" is so distinctive that natives are occasionally called "Yats."

- "Oh, I stayed up late writing a paper. What about you? How are you?"
- "I'm a little tired, but not too bad. I just moved to a new apartment. So, how are you doing?"
- "I've been reading all day and night for my economics exam. What's up with you?"
- "Great. I just got back from a trip home to visit my family. How are you?"

Normally, you would not share many details or indicate any serious problems unless you were talking to a friend. When others ask, they are not requesting intimate details. They are just greeting you.

The advantage of saying you are writing a paper, moving to a new apartment, working hard in a course, or just back from visiting your family is that it opens the door for the other person to begin a discussion. In the process, you learn more about each other and perhaps, after many such conversations, become real friends—the kind who sincerely want to know, "How are you?"

> **Tip:** When close friends ask "How are you?" they invite a personal response, but they don't require it. When acquaintances ask, they are merely expressing a polite interest in you. You should respond pleasantly, without offering too much personal information, and express the same interest in them.

Chapter 12

Learning the Language

Immersing yourself in a new country means immersing yourself in its language. Except for Québec, where French is dominant, that means learning to speak, read, and write English.[1] Learning the language is vital to your success—in the classroom and in your new community.

Since English is now the world's "second language" and the first language of science, business, and scholarship, your skill in using it will serve you well long after you complete your degree. A solid command of English will pay dividends throughout your professional life.

Even if you already read and write English well, it still pays to improve your speaking and reduce your accent. "The more skilled you are at speaking English," one international professor told me, "the more confident you will be in speaking up. You will participate more in class, and you will learn more." That's sound advice. The best way to follow it is to take language classes while you are here.

ESL Programs

Fortunately, there are excellent programs to help you learn English as a second language (ESL).[2] The best ones use experienced teachers and give you lots of practice and feedback. Almost all universities offer programs

1. French and English are *both* official languages throughout Canada, but French is used regularly only in the province of Québec. If you study in that province, you'll want to learn French (the local dialect is called *québecois*), even though English is widely spoken in Montreal. Although learning French is valuable in its own right, the language does not have the truly global uses of English, which yields advantages throughout your professional career, no matter where you live.

2. What the United States and Canada call ESL (English as a second language), some countries call ESOL (English for speakers of other languages). Both terms mean the same thing.

> *Tip:* Learning to communicate effectively in English is crucial to academic success here. ESL programs can help with reading, writing, and speaking. If you have a strong native accent, there are special programs to help you reduce it.

like this, either free or at low cost. They are not for academic credit. You can also take classes with tutors, at private firms, or at nonprofit social service agencies, especially those that work with new immigrants. Other options are to take online courses or buy inexpensive ESL computer programs or CDs, which you can use in your spare time. There are also free podcasts, available at the iTunes store, to help English language learners (ELLs).[3]

Some courses teach the basics, others are more advanced. Still others specialize in reducing your accent, making it easier for others to understand you. To find the best options for you, ask the international student adviser or your school's ESL staff. For a complete list of programs in the United States, see *Intensive English USA,* published in annual editions by the Institute of International Education (available at http://www.iiebooks.org/inad.html).

The Importance of Learning English for Spouses

Throughout this book, I have emphasized the importance of learning English for international students. It is equally important for student *spouses* to learn English, even if they aren't working or studying.

Why does it matter? Why shouldn't a husband or wife just speak Chinese or Korean or Arabic at home? Why should spouses take courses to improve their English? For three reasons. First, taking English allows them to escape the narrow social confines of their houses and their friends from back home. It widens their horizons. It's fine to socialize with friends from home, but it's also valuable to meet people from other countries and other backgrounds. Second, it will encourage their children to become bilingual, a wonderful asset for them now and later in life. Third, it will have a tremendous impact on the spouse who is in school. If a student speaks English only for an hour or two in class and then returns home each night

---

3. The Online Writing Lab (OWL) at Purdue University maintains an excellent list of online resources for ESL students. Their URL is http://owl.english.purdue.edu/handouts/esl/eslstudent.html.

Tip: Spouses as well as enrolled students should learn English while they are here.

to speak Hindi, Turkish, or Polish, that student's English will not improve very fast. The same is true for international students who select roommates from their home countries. They will inevitably speak to each other in their native language. Their English will suffer.

"Use It or Lose It": Your English Won't Improve Unless You Use It

When students communicate mainly in their native languages, their English remains awkward, broken, and heavily accented. As a result, they are reluctant to speak up in seminars or join friendly discussions after class. That, in turn, sharply limits their social and intellectual experiences. Because their friendships are limited, they don't get many chances to practice their English. It forms a vicious circle.

Working with international students, I've seen all these difficulties firsthand. If they don't speak English regularly *outside* the classroom, they won't improve their speaking and writing *inside* the classroom. Don't fall into that trap yourself, and don't let your spouse fall into it.

The Language of Lab Partners

The barriers to using English regularly are even higher in some sciences, where there are heavy concentrations of international students. With so many gifted international students, especially from Asia, it is possible to choose lab partners who communicate only in their native languages. The lure is certainly understandable. It's comfortable, and you can concentrate on science rather than on English.

But the short-term advantages are offset by significant long-term costs. Doing lab work in Chinese, Japanese, or Korean while studying in North America sharply limits your intellectual universe. It will remain a burden to interact with English-speaking students and faculty—the vast majority of fellow scientists. That burden won't grow any lighter over the years. After all, your English won't improve if you speak only Chinese in your lab. In a world where scientists communicate in English, poor language skills can be a major obstacle to publishing, presenting papers at conventions, and advancing in your chosen field.

> *Tip:* Speak English regularly in classes, labs, social settings, and, if at all possible, at home. If laboratory work is a major part of your studies, choose a lab where you and your partners communicate in English.

One effective solution is to pick lab partners from different countries. Again, your partners need not be native English speakers. What matters is that you communicate with each other in English. That's the best way to improve your language skills.

Believe me, I'm not saying this to discourage any international student. Quite the contrary. I'm saying it to help you avoid problems and achieve real success. If you foresee the difficulties, you can take specific steps to overcome them. The rewards are great.

Five Ways to Improve Your Language

How can you solve the language problem, then? First, take ESL courses. Choose courses that are aimed at your level and stick with them. They can be given at your university, a nonprofit organization, or a company that specializes in language instruction. You can take regular classes, individual tutorials, or online courses. You can even buy full ESL courses on CD or DVD. It's your choice. Do whatever suits your pocketbook, learning style, and schedule.

Second, if you are not married, try to live with roommates who will speak English. That could mean living with Americans, Canadians, Australians, or South Africans, but it doesn't have to. It could mean living at a dorm for international students, a regular dorm (where some students are native English speakers and others mostly use that language), or an off-campus apartment, *if* your roommates do not share a native tongue.[4] If you speak Dutch and your roommate speaks Spanish, you will inevitably speak English to each other. That's enough to do the trick. Although neither of you is a native English speaker, you will both steadily improve your language skills.

Third, whatever your living situation, try to develop friendships and engage in social activities where you speak English. Gathering for a daily cup of coffee and an occasional pizza with friends who speak English will work wonders.

---

4. For more on dorm living, see chapter 19, "University Housing and Meals."

Tip: Here are five ways to improve your English:

- Take ESL courses.
- Choose roommates who do not speak your native language.
- Engage in social activities where you speak English.
- Pick partners for your lab or study group who will communicate in English.
- Encourage your spouse to take ESL courses and socialize with some friends in English.

Fourth, if you have a choice among partners in labs or study groups, select ones who will speak English with you. Again, they don't have to be native English speakers.

Finally, if you are married to someone who speaks your native language, encourage your spouse to take ESL courses. Equally important, encourage your spouse to make friends outside the circle of parents and children from your native country. It's fine to have friends from Brazil or Thailand or wherever you are from. That's understandable, and it's perfectly fine. In fact, it's great to have friends and social support from back home. But it's not so great to limit yourself to those friends. You'll miss the opportunity to experience the true diversity of North American university life. Your language skills will suffer, too.

Creating a Virtuous Circle: Improving Your English by Using It

All five suggestions are based on the same principle: the more English you speak, the better you'll become. The better you become, the more you'll speak. It can become a virtuous circle.

As your language improves, you will find it easier to make friends here, speak up in class, and write papers in fluent English. That, in turn, will open up a new world of possibilities for you, personally and professionally.

Now that you know the importance of improving your English, let's turn to a few other tasks that you need to handle shortly after you arrive: getting ID cards, setting up a bank account, and applying for credit cards.

Chapter 13

Identification Cards

Whether you are opening a bank account, renting an apartment, boarding an airplane, or checking out a library book, you'll need some kind of identification card to prove that you really are who you say you are. What kinds of ID cards do you need? Which ones are most useful in your everyday life? How do you get an ID card when you've just arrived from Hong Kong, St. Petersburg, or São Paulo?

The most useful identification cards are:

- a photo ID from your university, and
- some kind of government-issued photo ID, such as a driver's license.

You'll need both. If you don't drive, you can get a similar ID for non-drivers from most states and provinces. You will need a couple of local IDs, since many places ask for two. They prefer at least one to be issued by the state, province, or country where you currently live. They want to see a card from the government of Alberta or Alabama, not from Albania.

University IDs

You can get your university ID quickly and easily. The usual procedure is to go to the registrar's office and bring a document proving your identity. Your passport is the best proof. The university registrar should already have a record of your admittance, but it's smart to bring along your letter of acceptance and your immigration documents, just in case they have trouble finding your files. The registrar at your university might have slightly different procedures—it's worth checking—but the ones I've listed are fairly common.

If you are not sure where to go for your university ID or what proof to carry, ask the international student adviser or dean of students.

Driver's Licenses and State IDs

School IDs are essential within the university, but they are not nearly as useful off campus. In the world beyond the university, the most useful identification card is a driver's license or its equivalent for nondrivers. The reasons are straightforward. Driver's licenses have a photo and are difficult to counterfeit, thanks to holograms, signatures, and, increasingly, biometric data. Businesses see these state IDs every day so they know them well and can detect fakes.

So, it's worth trudging down to the state department of motor vehicles, standing in a long line, and getting your license or an identity card for nondrivers. Do it before classes start, while you have time.

In chapter 18, I will discuss the driving tests you need to pass. For now, let me concentrate on the proof you need to obtain the card. The principle items you should bring are

- your passport,
- your immigration documents from the United States or Canada,
- a document showing your current local address, such as a lease agreement or utility bill,
- your Social Security (or Social Insurance) Number or its equivalent, such as an Individual Taxpayer Identification Number. Some states will issue a temporary license for visitors (such as international students) with a letter from Social Security stating that you are not eligible for a Social Security Number.

If you have other official documents, such as birth or marriage certificates from your home country (or certified copies of them), bring them along. You want to avoid the necessity of making a second trip just because some bureaucrat asked for another document.

There is a fee for the driver's license, so you'll need to bring some cash or a check since they may not take credit cards.

> **Tip:** Soon after you arrive, get a University ID and a driver's license, or its equivalent for nondrivers. When you apply for them, be sure to carry documents proving who you are and where you live locally.

> ***Tip:*** For identification, you need a local driver's license or its equivalent for nondrivers. It is the single best form of local ID.

The necessary documents vary by state or province (remember, these are federal systems), but they are fairly standard and easy to determine online. Just do a computer search for "driver's license" plus the name of your state or province. The agency that issues licenses will have its own Web site and will explain which documents you need.

A local license is valuable even if you can drive with an international license, as some students can. An international license might work on the highway, but it won't work for general purposes of identification. For that, you need good *local* identification, including some kind of government-issued photo ID. A driver's license is your best option.

Fake IDs

Never use false identification papers. If you are caught using them, you may be arrested. Still, some illegal immigrants use them to "prove" they are here legally. Some teenagers use them to "prove" they are old enough to enter a bar and buy liquor. Don't try it. It's a crime to use a false ID, and it can result in serious immigration and visa problems.

> ***Tip:*** Never use false identification papers. It's a crime that carries serious consequences for your immigration status and student visa.

Chapter 14

Earning Money

So far, we have talked mainly about spending. Now, let's talk about getting the money you need to pay the bills. The usual ways are jobs, scholarships, fellowships, and loans. Some fortunate students also receive funds from their home governments or gifts from their families.

Roadblocks to International Student Funding

In funding their education, international students face two major obstacles that local students do not. First, both the United States and Canadian governments provide a wide range of scholarships to their own citizens and permanent residents, but not to foreigners. For example, international students are not eligible for U.S. government programs that pay for campus work-study jobs or foreign language training. Nor are they eligible for government-subsidized student loans. Only citizens and permanent residents can apply for them. The politicians who passed the laws have said, in effect, "These programs are paid for by our nation's taxpayers and that's who should reap the rewards."

Second, visa regulations make it difficult—sometimes impossible—for international students to hold ordinary jobs off campus. Of course, different visa categories, such as those for student spouses, may have different restrictions. Still, the immigration laws are generally crafted so that international students are welcome to come *as students*, not as competitors for local jobs.

If this cloud has any silver lining, it's that your home country might have its own programs to support citizens studying abroad. You probably know about some of these opportunities already, but it's worth double checking. Ask the international student adviser's office and your embassy, as well as other students from your home country.

Local Jobs

Both the United States and Canada restrict the jobs international students and their family members can hold. Naturally, the details differ for each country, and they can change whenever policymakers revisit the issues. Since immigration and visas are hot political issues, the changes could come at any time.

To keep up with current rules and regulations, the best advice is to go to the immigration authorities' Web sites.

- United States: http://www.unitedstatesvisas.gov/index.html
- Canada: http://www.cic.gc.ca/english/study/study.asp

It's also an excellent idea to check with your university's international student adviser. Staff members in the adviser's office deal with these issues every day so they have plenty of useful information and advice. Be sure to check the adviser's Web site, too. It may already have answers to your questions.

> *Tip:* Immigration laws in the United States and Canada make it difficult for international students and their spouses to earn income off campus. But some kinds of work might be allowed if you apply.

Don't Work Illegally

Some students try to evade the rules and work illegally. That's a very bad idea. If you are caught, you are in deep trouble. It's not only a violation of immigration laws, it's a violation of tax laws unless you pay taxes on the illegal earnings. At the very least, you will lose your student visa and will be unable to continue your studies here.

Staying an Extra Year for Professional Training

On the positive side, international students are often allowed to stay for an extra year after graduation and work *if* their jobs contribute to their academic training. This kind of practical training is considered educational,

> *Tip:* You can apply to stay for an extra year and work after you complete your degree *if* you can show that the work is educational and is part of your professional training.

so it fits into the United States and Canadian student visa programs. Of course, you need to apply for this extension and explain how the employment adds to your education. Again, the international student adviser's office will know the details and can help.

Learning about Funding Opportunities at Your University

Because of visa restrictions, most international students cannot earn income off campus. Instead, they support themselves with scholarships, fellowships, research positions, campus jobs, and gifts from home.

Scholarships and fellowships are hard-won prizes, and they are major sources of student support. Once awarded, the funding normally remains stable from year to year, though dramatic changes in a student's performance could have some impact.

What does change, once you enroll in a university, is your *knowledge* of local funding sources. You will undoubtedly learn about more fellowships, research positions, and teaching assistantships at your university and, if you are a graduate student, in your specialty.

On-campus jobs as research assistants, lab assistants, and teaching assistants (TAs) are great ways for international students to earn money. These jobs are not restricted to local citizens. International students are eligible for them as an integral part of your education. You should ask faculty and students in your department about them. The more people you ask, the better your chances of finding additional support. Be sure to ask faculty if they need research assistants. Working as an RA is the best way to combine paid work with specialized research in your field.

As with all immigration issues, you need to check the specific rules that apply to your visa category. You can do that online or at the international

> *Tip:* Research assistantships (RAs) are good jobs because they combine learning and earning. Because they're on campus, international students are eligible for them. Be sure to ask professors you work with if they need an RA.

> **Tip:** The dean of students and international student adviser have specialized staff who know about student scholarships, loans, and campus jobs. It's vital to talk with them if you are seeking funds to pay for your education.

student adviser's office. Fortunately, the adviser's office handles these question every day, knows the details, and can give you a quick response.

The adviser's office and the dean of students' office are also good resources for learning about scholarships, fellowships, and other funding opportunities. International students, like all students at the university, need help sorting through the vast maze of potential funding sources. If your current funding is inadequate, be sure to talk with staff in both the adviser's and the dean's offices.

Besides talking with staff, you'll want to read about funding opportunities. The best place to start, if you are studying in the United States, is *Funding for United States Study: A Guide for International Students and Professionals.* Published annually by the Institute of International Education, it is detailed and comprehensive. You can find it and other IIE publications at http://www.iiebooks.org/index.html You may be able to find some of their publications at your university library or international student adviser's office.

Another very useful resource is EducationUSA, sponsored by the U.S. State Department. It runs a Web site with information to help international students finance their U.S. education. Go to http://www.petersons.com/educationusa/ and look at the section on financial aid and scholarships. It has separate resources for graduate students and undergraduates.

If you are studying in Canada, the best place to begin researching scholarships and fellowships is Education@Canada: International Gateway to Education in Canada, sponsored by the Council of Ministers of Education, Canada (CMEC). The relevant Web page is http://educationcanada .cmec.ca/EN/Study.php. Another valuable resource is DestinEducation, sponsored by the Canadian Bureau for International Education. Their Web page on scholarships for international students is www.destineducation.ca/resource/annex-g4_e.htm.

What Do Professors Know about Student Funding?

Do your professors know much about student funding sources? Yes and no. They do not know the full range of these funding sources. After all,

> **Tip:** Although professors and department administrators don't know the full range of student funding opportunities, they do know about specialized resources in their own fields.

they are experts in Shakespeare, organic chemistry, or computational biology, not in student finance. But their specialized knowledge gives them an edge in knowing about funding *in their own fields* and *in their own departments*.

This specialized knowledge is most applicable to graduate students and some advanced undergraduates. It's a very good idea, then, for graduate students to ask their professors and their department director of graduate studies about funding possibilities. These faculty members should know about scholarships, fellowships, postdocs, and other opportunities, as well as RA and TA positions. For the same reason, you should speak with the staff member in your department responsible for graduate student affairs.

Income Taxes

Some scholarships are taxable, and all wages are. It doesn't matter whether you are a citizen, permanent resident, landed immigrant, international student, temporary visitor, or visitor from another planet. What matters is where you earn your income, not your immigration status. That's true for both the United States and Canada. If you earned taxable income in either country, then you must file tax returns at all levels of government: federal, state or provincial, and city. (Most cities don't levy income taxes, but a few do. That means you need to check on the city where you earn your income.)

The tax laws are an impenetrable bog, and I, for one, threw up my hands in despair long ago. Unfortunately, existential despair is not considered a legitimate tax deduction. So I'm afraid most of us decide to buy tax preparation software, such as TurboTax or TaxCut, or use a tax prepara-

> **Tip:** Everyone who earns income, including international students, must pay taxes on it. Immigration status is irrelevant. What matters is where you earned the income, how much you earned, and how the tax authorities treat this type of income.

tion service, such as H&R Block or Jackson Hewitt. None of them is very expensive. If you have substantial income or complicated tax issues, it may be worth hiring a tax accountant.

Insurance

Just as students rarely think about paying taxes, they rarely think about buying insurance. That's understandable. You don't need most types of insurance, and one you do need—health insurance—is available from your university. I discuss health coverage in detail in chapter 22, "Health Care."

What other kinds of insurance do you need?

If you drive, you certainly need automobile insurance. The law requires all drivers to have some insurance, known as "minimum coverage," but you may wish to purchase more than the minimum. A good insurance policy can replace a wrecked car and pay for medical treatment after an accident. Your policy will also cover you when you rent a car on an out-of-town vacation. I discuss all that in chapter 18, "Getting Around: Cars."

Most students don't need life insurance, though you might want to buy it if you have children. It's far less expensive to buy "term life" than "whole life." Term life is pure insurance, without any savings or investment component, and it's the cheapest way to buy several hundred thousand dollars of coverage. That may seem like a lot, but it could be crucial to your family if you die. It will help pay for their living expenses and your children's education. If you don't have those obligations, then you don't need life insurance.

Students rarely need long-term disability insurance. Its purpose is to pay your wages if you are incapacitated. Since you don't have any wages to replace, you don't need it. Finally, there is long-term care insurance, which is normally purchased by older people, concerned about costs of nursing home care. You should know about these types of insurance, but you probably don't need any except auto, health, and, possibly, life.

You can buy all this coverage from private insurance agents or online, but, before you do, check with your university. Their human resources department or employee benefits office will know the issues. Better yet, the university has probably arranged group rates for many of these policies. Students, faculty, and staff can buy at preferred rates. (The exception is auto insurance, which you must purchase privately.) Ask for the university's booklets explaining the options, or access them online. After review-

> ***Tip:*** If you drive, you need auto insurance. If you have children, you may need life insurance. If you breathe, you need health insurance.
>
>   Universities don't provide auto insurance, but they provide almost everything else. Check with the benefits office before buying a policy. Universities often have the cheapest coverage, and, in any case, can advise you about the choices.

ing the options, you might wish to speak with a benefits counselor and get advice before making your choices.

Information Privacy?

When you apply for insurance, jobs, bank accounts, or credit cards, you will often find yourself answering personal questions—*very* personal questions. What happens to this information about your finances, health, and family? Does it stay private?

The answers are less than reassuring, especially to Europeans who have stricter laws and different traditions about information sharing. In the United States, and to a lesser extent in Canada, private firms collect and share massive amounts of personal data.

There are exceptions, naturally. Some firms promise to keep any personal data private, and they tell you so in advance. *Nearly all health service data must be kept private by law.* That even includes whether you have visited a doctor, psychologist, or other health professional.

But those are the exceptions, rather than the rule. Many firms routinely share personal data with each other, with credit agencies, with firms specializing in "data mining," and sometimes with the government.

You can prevent some of this sharing, but you must specifically "opt out" of it. You must fill out a company form, if you can find it, explaining that you do not want your information shared. As you can tell, that's not easy.

Unless you opt out, the default is that your data can be shared, although different states have their own restrictions. In general, though, personal data is less private in North America than it is in Europe.

Chapter 15

Managing Money: Bank Accounts, Debit Cards, and Credit Cards

Once you've obtained your identification cards, you're ready to set up a checking account and apply for credit cards.

Bank Accounts

You should set up a local checking account as soon as possible. U.S. and Canadian banks have similar arrangements, but Canadians use the British spelling: chequing account.[1] Most students need only a straightforward checking account, nothing fancy. You can use your account to deposit scholarship funds, receive wire transfers, make cash withdrawals, and pay bills, either electronically or by personal check.

To set up the account, you need at least two pieces of identification, preferably picture IDs, plus one item with your local street address (not a post office box number). A utility bill in your name or a letter mailed to you at that address will prove you live there. Canadian banks want to know your Social Insurance Number. U.S. banks want your Social Security Number or ITIN, but they understand that most international students are not eligible for them, and they will usually establish accounts without them. To prove that you are in the country legally, you should bring your passport and visa. With these documents, plus some cash to deposit, you are ready to establish a new bank account.

Every city has multiple banks competing for your business. Which one

1. Most banking terms are the same in the United States and Canada, but a few are different. In the United States, a single deposit made for a fixed period of time, such as one year, and returned with interest at the end of that period, is called a "certificate of deposit," or CD. In Canada, the same arrangement is called a "guaranteed interest contract," or GIC.

should you choose? To find out, you need to look at the services they provide, the charges they impose, and the convenience they offer, primarily
their branch locations and their network of automated teller machines,
or ATMs. (In Canada, the same machines are called ABMs, or automated
banking machines.)

All banks offer similar services as part of their basic checking account.
The only difference is how much it costs and how convenient it is. You
should be able to get the services you need at a low monthly cost or even
free, without any requirement that you keep a minimum account balance. Some bank accounts offer more services but require you to keep a
minimum balance, perhaps $100 or $200. If you fall below that amount,
even for a day, the bank charges you a monthly fee. To avoid needless
charges, you'll want to compare accounts, consider what services you
need, and determine whether you are likely to maintain the minimum
balance.

To find the right bank, you should see which ones have offices near
your apartment or university, and, equally important, which ones have
their own automated machines near you. Banks typically allow their customers to use their own ATMs without cost, but they charge customers
from other banks for the service. You'll face the same charge when you use
ATMs from other banks. In fact, when you use other banks' ATMs, you
often pay two fees: one from the ATM you're using and another from your
own bank. Ouch! Over the course of a year, these fees add up, so you'll
want to find a bank that has its own ATMs near where you live, study, and
shop.

You'll also want to choose the type of account that fits your needs. All
banks offer basic accounts that provide essential services all allow you to
maintain low balances. If you need more than that, you can opt for a premium account at the same bank. But you will need to maintain larger
bank balances and will be charged if you fall below them.

All banks have brochures explaining the options. You should review
them, then sit down with a customer service representative and discuss
your needs.

My advice is not to worry about the interest rates you receive on deposits unless you expect to maintain large balances. The difference of 1 or 2

Tip: Choose a bank that has locations and ATMs near you. Select a bank
account that fits your needs and won't pile up needless charges and fees.

percent in annual interest won't amount to very much each year. It's far more important to receive the services you need, avoid charges and fees, and bank at a convenient location.

Checklist of Bank Services and Costs

Here's a simple checklist for basic (or student) accounts. Use it to compare costs and services at local banks:

Minimum opening deposit	$0 for most basic accounts; none should be over $100
Minimum balance to avoid fees	$0 for most basic accounts; $100–$250 for accounts with more services
Monthly service fee	$0 at most banks; $3–$10 per month at some
Checking fees	Unlimited free checking transactions at many banks; at least 10 free transactions monthly at all banks, with small fees for each check after that
Printed checks with your name	Free for first order at some banks; charge for subsequent orders
ATM fees	Your own bank's ATMs: unlimited, free use is typical Other banks' ATMs: $1.50–$3 fee from the other bank; possibly an additional fee from your bank
Online banking and bill payment	Free at some banks, a monthly charge at others
Fees for bounced checks (checks returned because of insufficient funds)	Most banks charge fees if their customers write bad checks (which cannot be paid from their current funds) or if they deposit bad checks from others
Overdraft protection	Available at a few larger banks for a fee or as part of premium accounts; rarely included in basic accounts with low minimum balances

International Wire Transfers

All banks can handle wire transfers, but they don't all handle them equally well. Citicorp, Chase, and Bank of America process millions of these transactions each month. Your small corner bank does not. If you plan to wire funds often, or receive them, it may be worthwhile to have your account at a large international bank that can smoothly deliver the services you want.

> *Tip:* If you plan on sending or receiving international wire transfers fre-
> quently, set up your account at a larger bank that handles such transactions
> frequently.

Banking in a Foreign Language

Banking is one area where, if your English is still shaky, it is advisable to
speak your native language. You don't want to make financial mistakes
because you are still mastering English.

Fortunately, banks know this and have employees who speak different
languages. But not every branch bank has employees who speak every
language. You need to check. If you prefer to do your banking in Chinese,
Hebrew, or Portuguese, you should inquire *before* you select a bank. Ask
fellow students from your home country; they'll know.

If you want to do your banking in Spanish, you're in luck. Because
Spanish is so commonly spoken in the United States, almost every bank
office has representatives who can work with you. In Canada, the same is
true of French.

> *Tip:* If your English is less than fluent, it makes sense to bank in your native
> language. For some languages, you may need to look around the city, includ-
> ing its ethnic neighborhoods, to find a bank that can serve you.

Overdrafts

Most banking transactions are similar to those in your home country. But
there are two exceptions worth mentioning: overdraft protection and the
widespread use of paper checks.

Banks in many countries routinely protect their customers against over-
drafts. If your bank balance turns negative, they provide you with instant
credit to cover it. If a customer has $500 in her account, for example, and
writes her landlord a check for $800, the bank will draw on the customer's
credit line, pay the extra $300, and charge the customer interest for the
loan.

Not here. Most consumer accounts do not have attached credit lines
like this. It is certainly not standard. Your bank might honor the check, but

Tip: Banks in the United States and Canada do not routinely offer overdraft protection to customers. If you write a check that's larger than the funds available in your account, the bank will refuse to honor your check. You'll pay extra fees for bounced checks like this, and you'll get grumpy phone calls from the people who tried to cash them. If you need overdraft protection, ask your bank whether they offer the service when you set up your checking account.

they will not do it regularly, and they will charge you punitive fees. More likely, they will simply refuse to pay the $800. The check will be sent back to the landlord, marked "insufficient funds." Your bank will charge you a fee for the bounced check, and the landlord's bank will charge him a fee for submitting a check that could not be cashed. He will pass that fee on to you, probably in an irate call demanding the rent and the fee. You can avoid that by watching your bank balances carefully and making sure you have funds available to cover each payment you make.

If you really want overdraft protection, you can find it at a few larger banks—for a fee, usually a few dollars a month. It is not part of a basic student account, but it may be included in some fancier accounts, which provide more services but require higher minimum balances. You should ask about it when you set up your account.

When you do, be sure to ask about fees. Some banks charge an annual (or monthly) fee for their services; others charge an implicit fee by requiring higher balances. You should also ask whether they charge an additional fee when you actually use the overdraft feature. Of course, all banks charge interest for money you borrow, whether it is for an overdraft or anything else. Be sure you have a complete picture of all these costs before signing up for overdraft services.

Electronic Payments

There are several ways to make payments from your new bank account. The easiest ones are electronic. Actually, there are several ways to make electronic payments. You can send payments online, use debit cards, or pay regular bills like electricity by automatic monthly withdrawals. These electronic payments are secure, and they deduct the funds directly from your account. Or you can pay bills the old fashioned way, with paper checks.

Writing Checks

Many international students are so used to paying with electronic transfers that they don't know much about paper checks, which are still popular here. Let me go over the basics.

A physical check looks like this:

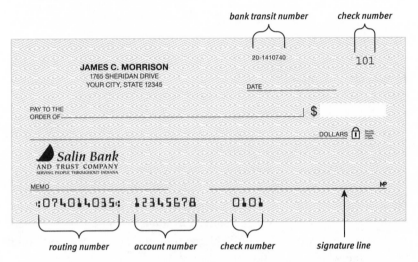

This is a (fictional) check that James C. Morrison ordered from the Salin Bank and Trust Company in Indiana. All personal checks look very similar. Mr. Morrison's name and address are printed at the top, on the left side. He might also have included his wife or partner's name if they shared the account, and he could have added his phone number. Across the bottom of the check are three numbers.

- Routing number (074014035). This number is unique to each bank, identifying it so other financial institutions can move funds to or from that bank. In other parts of the world, banks use a similar identifier, known as a SWIFT number.
- Account number (12345678). Mr. Morrison's account number ensures that funds are withdrawn from his specific account.
- Check number (101). The number for this particular check. Notice that this number appears again at the top of the check, in the right corner

These numbers are machine readable.

The routing and account numbers are essential if your family, friends, or business associates want to wire money to your account.

Now, let's fill out this blank check to pay for groceries at the "Local Food Mart."

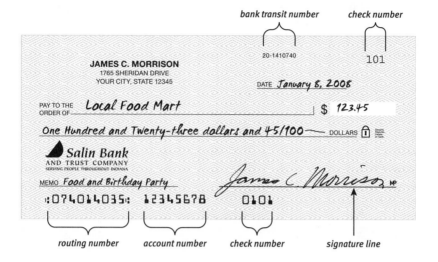

Checks like this are normally filled in by hand, in ink. The date of January 8, 2008, has been written in the upper right-hand corner. The name of the recipient, Local Food Mart, is written next to "Pay to the order of." (Sometimes, a recipient might ask that you make out the check to "cash." He will endorse it by signing his name on the back and depositing it to his account.) Mr. Morrison's signature is on the line in the lower right-hand corner. In the lower left corner, there's a spot labeled "memo," where you can write a note to yourself, such as "food for birthday party." That's purely optional.

This check is made out for $123.45. That amount must be written twice, once in digits and once in words, as protection against fraud or mistakes. Next to the dollar sign, the amount is written in numerals: $123.45. For safety's sake, you should write the first digit close to the dollar sign. That way, no one can fraudulently insert another digit, changing the amount to, say, "$5,123.45." That's too much food for a birthday party. On the next line, immediately below the recipient's name, you must write out the same amount in letters: "one hundred and twenty-three dollars and 45/100." Since spelling out this amount did not take up the whole line, Mr. Morrison wisely added some dashes at the end. That way, no one can insert anything else on the line.

That's how you fill out a paper check to pay someone.

Making Bank Deposits

Now, what if someone gives you a check like this and you want to deposit it in your bank account?

First, make sure the check has been properly filled out and signed. Without a signature, it's worthless. Then, on the back of the check, sign your own name. Immediately under that, write, "For deposit only," followed by your account number and the name of your bank. It is smart to write your name and account number again on the front of the check, at the very top. (That's just to be certain it gets deposited to your account.) Here's a sample, showing Mr. Morrison's signature on the back of a check for deposit in his account:

After that, you should fill out a deposit ticket from your bank. (Some banks call it a deposit slip. There's no difference.) When you buy checks from your bank, you will receive some personal deposit tickets, which include your account number. If you don't have them handy when you want to make a deposit, take blank slips *from your bank* and fill in your personal account number.

Here's the front and back sides of a sample deposit ticket:

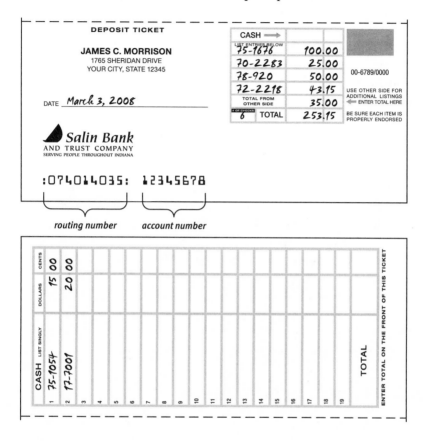

routing number   account number

Each ticket lists the checks and cash you are depositing in your account. In this example, Mr. Morrison is depositing six checks and no cash. He can list the checks in any order. The first one here is for $100.00. Notice that it has a hyphenated number beside it: 75-1676. That is called a "bank transit number," and it's very similar to a routing number that appears at the bottom of each check. If you look at the check Mr. Morrison wrote to the Food Mart, for example, you'll see it has a small number "20-1410740," near the top. That's the bank transit number for the Salin Bank, which Mr. Morrison uses. It can be listed as either 20/1410740 or 20-1410740. On the deposit slip, you should include bank transit numbers for every check you deposit. It identifies each one. If two or three checks come from the same bank, they will have the same transit numbers.

This deposit ticket has room for only four checks on the front. On the back, though, it has room for many more. So Morrison lists four checks on the front and two more on the back. He subtotals the checks listed on the back, which come to $35, and carries that over to the appropriate spot on the front. Then he adds up the four checks on the front, plus the subtotal from the back and the cash he wants to deposit, if any. Then, he writes out the total: $253.05.

Having filled out the deposit ticket, Mr. Morrison gives it to his bank, together with the checks, at either a branch office or an ATM. The bank will then credit the funds to his account. Notice that the deposit ticket, unlike a check, does not have to be signed.

When Mr. Morrison reviews his bank balance, he'll find this $253.15 added to his account. Unfortunately, he cannot withdraw this money immediately. In banking lingo, the $253.15 is not yet considered "available funds." That's because his bank must still present the checks to the banks on which they were written, collect the funds, and deposit them in Mr. Morrison's account—a process that can take several days. Until the funds have actually been collected, Mr. Morrison can't access them. He can withdraw only the funds that have already been collected in his account—the "available balance." If he deposited $500 last month and $253.15 today, he can withdraw only the $500 until the new deposit clears.

Debit Cards

When the funds finally are available, one way to withdraw them is with a debit card. Although the card looks like a credit card, it's different. A credit card provides short-term loans to the user; a debit card does not. Instead, it withdraws funds directly from the user's bank account. It is, in effect, an electronic check—one that is cashed immediately.

Let's say Mr. Morrison uses a debit card to pay for $75 worth of prescription drugs at his pharmacy. When the pharmacist swipes the debit card through the machine, it instantly withdraws $75 from Morrison's bank account and transfers it to the pharmacy. It's exactly like writing a check, except that it's electronic and instantaneous.

Since a debit card provides no credit, it builds no credit history. Like a paper check, it can be used only to withdraw "available funds" from a

> ***Tip:*** Debit cards are like electronic checks. They are a convenient way to pay for purchases, but they don't provide credit or build a credit history.

user's bank account. Because it's similar to a check, many banks provide debit cards to any customer who asks. International students can apply for them when they set up their checking accounts.

Credit Cards

Getting a credit card can be difficult for new international students because they don't have a local credit history. That means they cannot prove they actually pay their bills on time. Unfortunately, as far as banks, landlords, and credit card companies are concerned, "no local credit history" is the same as "bad credit history."

So how can a newly arrived international student acquire a credit card? There are three ways. The first is to ask the credit card companies that flock to your campus during orientation week. They know thousands of students will be arriving, eager to purchase everything from books to blankets, and they are just as eager to supply them with loans. (Whether it is wise for students to take these loans is another matter entirely. For many students, it's all too easy to borrow more than they can repay. The result is like a lobster trap. It's enticing for lobsters to crawl in, but it's impossible for them to crawl back out. You'll feel the same way if you charge too many lobster dinners on your credit card.)

When school is beginning, card companies set up application tables in prominent locations on campus and promote their cards. To apply for them, students fill out a page of personal information and financial data. The companies run the data through their own computers and those of credit rating companies. If the credit scores are high enough (that is, the local credit history is good), then applicants are accepted and receive their new cards in the mail.

If you don't qualify for a card that way, you can apply for a "secured" credit card. These cards come with low credit limits and require you to maintain an associated bank account. If you deposit, say, $600 in the bank account, they will issue you a credit card with a $600 limit. If you fail to pay your credit card bill, they simply withdraw the money from your bank account and pay it off. The bank account fully secures your credit.

Tip: Because international students have no credit history in the United States or Canada, they often find it difficult to get major credit cards such as MasterCard and Visa. There are three approaches to getting these cards.

- Apply for an ordinary credit card during your university's orientation week, when card issuers are soliciting new accounts on campus.
- Apply for a secured credit card, which requires an associated bank account.
- Apply for "store cards," issued by major chain stores and gas stations.

Store cards and secured credit cards are useful in their own right and can help you build a good credit history. Building that history, however, means not borrowing too much and paying your bills promptly each month.

You can use such a card the same way you use a regular credit card, and at the same places. It looks like a standard Visa or MasterCard, and, indeed, it is one. The only difference is that it has a bank balance standing behind it.

Why use a secured card? Why not simply deposit $600 in a regular bank account and use a debit card to access it? Because a debit card does not build credit history, and a secured card does. If you use the secured card wisely and pay off your charges each month, you can build a positive credit history in three to six months. With that history, you become eligible for an ordinary (unsecured) credit card with a higher credit limit.

If you don't have the funds to pledge for a secured card, there's one other alternative. You can apply for a "store card," issued by companies like Target, Wal-Mart, and Sears. All major petroleum companies issue cards, too, for use at their gas stations.

The good news is that a lot of companies issue such cards, and it's easier to qualify for them than for Visa, MasterCard, or American Express. The bad news is that each card can be used only for purchases at the company that issues them. You can't use a Target card to buy gas, and you can't use an ExxonMobil card to buy clothes—or to buy gas at Shell, for that matter. Still, these cards are useful in their own way, and, by paying your bills promptly each month, you can build a credit history.

Remember, to get these cards or to set up a bank account, you need to present good identification and proof of your local street address. So you need to acquire those documents first (see chapter 13, "Identification Cards").

Lost or Stolen Credit Cards

What happens if a card is lost or stolen? The answer is good news for consumers. U.S. and Canadian laws protect consumers against the misuse of their cards. As long as the consumer reports the problem promptly, he is not responsible for large purchases made illegally with his card. (He may be legally responsible for a small amount, but many credit card issuers protect consumers against even that liability.)

Most credit card companies offer their users other protections as well. If you order a pair of shoes online and they send you two left shoes, you should first try to resolve the problem with the seller. If that fails, you can call the credit card company, dispute the charge, and you probably won't have to pay it. The credit card company protects you against faulty merchandise and fraudulent transactions by sellers. Debit cards generally offer some protections, as well, but they are not always so extensive.

A Word of Caution about Credit Cards

Credit cards are a double-edged sword. They are an extremely convenient way to make purchases, but they are also an extremely easy way to borrow more than you can repay. Use them carefully, and don't let them seduce you into overspending.

Let me offer two pieces of advice:

- Get only one or two credit cards. You don't need more, and having too many may tempt you to spend too much.
- Pay off your entire balance each month, or as much of it as you can. By paying fully and promptly, you will avoid high interest charges and onerous late fees.

Keep a watchful eye on your expenses. If you notice that your credit card debts are slowly increasing, or if you cannot pay off the entire balance most months, then you are spending too much. It's time to rein in those expenditures.

> **Tip:** Don't carry more than one or two credit cards. Don't use them to overspend. Pay off your entire balance (or as much as possible) each month, and pay it promptly.

Chapter 16

Spending Money:
Shopping at Local Stores,
Malls, and Online

As you familiarize yourself with your neighborhood and city, you will undoubtedly want to learn more about local shopping. In this chapter, I'll discuss various types of shopping, from downtown stores to large malls to small "strip malls." I'll also discuss some well-known national stores, especially discount stores, with prices that suit student (and faculty!) budgets. And, of course, I'll discuss shopping online.

My goal is to explain the practical aspects of shopping in North America. Are local sales taxes included in the marked price, for instance? Which prices are negotiable and which ones are not? How often do stores hold special sales, when prices are reduced? Are some stores open late at night, after you finish studying? Can you get delivery of large items, like mattresses or refrigerators? Will the stores install complicated equipment, like a large-screen TVs? What kinds of warranties are available on electronics and appliances? Are there any reliable guides to product quality? How can you find out which brands and which models are the best values for your money? What about purchasing used items, which are often the cheapest way to furnish student apartments? Where can you find them?

That's a lot of territory, but I'll try to cover it briefly and efficiently so you can buy what you need without inadvertently buying yourself a headache or breaking your budget.

Shopping Malls, "Big Boxes," and Other Options

After you have visited the stores in your neighborhood and near campus, you'll want to check out downtown shopping (if you live in a large city) and local malls. Actually, there are two kinds of malls. One is a small, neighborhood "strip mall," with four or five stores in a row (that is, a strip) and off-street parking. The other is a large indoor shopping center—sometimes called a regional mall—anchored by several major department stores. When people say, "I'm going to the mall," they mean these indoor shopping centers. The smaller ones have only two anchor stores, with an aisle of specialty stores and kiosks between them. Bigger malls have four anchors or more, plus dozens of smaller stores. All of them have acres of free parking and many places to eat, usually a "food court" with fast-food places plus some chain restaurants with table dining, either in the mall itself or nearby.

Most large malls are aimed at the vast middle class, but a few feature high-end fashions and expensive jewelry. Some are like Honda Civics, others are like Mercedes. There's a quick way to tell: look at the department stores. Are they mostly medium-priced stores like Sears or Macy's, or expensive ones like Bloomingdale's and Neiman Marcus? Later in this chapter, I'll list the stores and give you a sense of their products and price ranges.

Near these malls, but separate from them, are other large "discount stores" or "big-box retailers." (They are called "big boxes" because the stores themselves resemble giant boxes.) They emphasize low prices, which fit student budgets nicely. Some, like Wal-Mart and Target, carry a wide range of merchandise, everything from clothes and small appliances to dishes and detergents. Their largest stores ("megastores") include full supermarkets, so you can shop for paprika and printer paper at the same time.

Most big-box chains specialize in one or two areas. Staples, for example, sells office equipment and supplies. Toys "R" Us sells clothes and toys for infants and older children. Best Buy and Circuit City feature TVs, computers, and music systems; Bed, Bath & Beyond sells towels, sheets, and household accessories; Barnes & Noble and Borders carry large inventories of books and music. All of them price aggressively and compete directly with online retailers like Amazon.com.

With so many chain stores in so many categories, the best way to show them to you is in a table. I have included major online sites, which are important for everybody, but especially for international students, who often want to buy products that are not available locally. Let me give you a couple of examples: exotic spices and men's clothing. Cooking dishes from your home country requires the right ingredients, including the right spices. In large cities, you can find them easily. But what if you live in Ames, Iowa (the University of Iowa) or College Station, Texas (Texas A&M)? You might need to buy your ingredients from an online store.

You could face the same problem finding good shirts and pants if you

are not as tall—or as wide—as most Canadians or Americans.[1] It's easy
to find these clothes online, where several stores specialize in fitting men
under 5'9" (175 cm). For women, there are similar sites with "petite sizes."
I have grouped stores like these in their own categories.

The table doesn't include every store, but it is extensive and does mention the most prominent ones. I have added the term "online" when the
retailer lacks a physical store. Remember, too, that every community has
good local stores.

Type of store	Some major brands	Explanation
Department stores, expensive, high-quality	Bloomingdale's Eddie Bauer (outdoor clothing) L.L.Bean (online) Neiman Marcus Nordstrom Saks Fifth Avenue	High-end clothing and house-wares. Some have discount divisions that sell overstocks, such as Nordstrom Rack, and Off 5th (Saks). Check your local Yellow Pages and see if any leading chains have outlet stores or clearance centers in your area.
Department stores, moderately priced	Dillard's (U.S. South) HBC: Hudson's Bay Company ("The Bay") (Canada) JCPenney Kohls Macy's Mervyns (U.S. Southwest) Sears	Full range of men's, women's, and children's clothing; housewares; furniture, rugs, and appliances in some stores
Clothing, moderately priced	Abercrombie & Fitch Anthropologie Banana Republic Gap H&M J.Crew JoS. A. Bank (suits and dress clothing) Lands' End (online) The Limited Men's Wearhouse (suits and dress clothing) Old Navy Urban Outfitters	Good quality clothing at moderate prices. Some stores are at the high end of the moderate price range; others are at the low end. Some retailers carry a wide range of clothing. Others specialize. Old Navy sells casual clothing for young adults while Men's Wearhouse sells business suits, dress shirts, and ties.

1. If you visit Web sites for Americans traveling in Asia, you'll see the other side of this "size"
question. Americans in Japan, Korea, China, and India often ask where they can find larger
clothes than those available in local stores.

Department stores, discount prices	Big Lots KMart Target Wal-Mart	Discount clothes, plus office supplies, housewares, packaged foods (especially snack food), and some hardware. Often the best place to buy everyday plates, pots and pans, soft drinks, and even clothing.
Outlet stores	Multiple stores at special outlet malls Online links to multiple outlet stores at http://www.outletsonline.com/shop.html	Malls with stores from different manufacturers, selling their own new products at significant discounts. The products are either current overstocks, last year's models or factory "seconds" with slight imperfections (marked as such).
Dollar stores	Dollar General Family Dollar	Discount stores that concentrate on consumables (like soft drinks and snack foods) and other low-priced items, including clothes. Called "dollar stores" because, in the 1950s and 1960s, all items cost $1 or less.
Warehouse stores (discount)	BJ's Wholesale Club Costco Sam's Club	Deep discounts on food, electronics, clothing, jewelry, and some furniture. Food is often sold in large packages, so you might have to buy a six-pack of soup instead of one can. The savings are significant. Requires an annual membership for a small fee, but you can browse the store first to see if you want to join.
Discount clothing stores	Burlington Coat Factory DSW (shoes) Fashion Bug Filene's Basement Foot Locker (shoes) Marshalls Payless Shoes Ross Dress for Less Stores T. J. Maxx	Mid-quality clothing at sharply reduced prices. Some items are overstock or last year's newest fashions purchased from high-end stores and marked down significantly.
Large-size clothes	Casual Male XL Lane Bryant (women's) Rochester Big & Tall Men's Clothing	Full line of designer clothing for taller or heavier adults. The term "XL" stands for "Extra Large."

Small-size (petite) women's clothes	Ann Taylor Loft Macy's Talbots and many others	Many stores and catalogs offer petite sizes for women, including Lands' End, JCPenney, Chadwick's, and others.
Small-size men's clothes (online)	For the Fit Napoleon's Tailor Short Sizes	Online stores that carry a full range of clothing for men under 5′8″ or 5′9″ (175 cm).
Discount housewares, sheets, towels	Bed Bath & Beyond Linens 'n Things	Good sources for sheets, towels, decorative accessories, and other small household items.
Mid-priced furniture and housewares	CB2 Crate and Barrel Ikea Pier 1 Imports Value City	Wide range of household items and furniture, many bearing the dire phrase "some assembly required."
Electronics, music, TVs, stereos	Amazon.com (online) Best Buy Buy.com (online) Circuit City hhgregg iTunes (online music, audio books) Overstock.com (online) RadioShack Sam Goody (music)	Before buying, get reviews of all the latest electronic products at cnet.com and other sites. Many bookstores and electronic stores also sell music.
Computer Retailers	CompUSA Dell.com Hp.com Micro Center Other electronic stores	They also sell many accessories, such as printers and scanners, and other products that use computer processors, such as digital cameras.
Office supplies	Office Depot OfficeMax Staples	All have both physical stores and online sites.
Discount hardware stores ("home improvement")	Home Depot Lowe's Menards	Big box stores with huge selections of low- to mid-priced items including tools, garden equipment, light bulbs, shelving, paint, electrical supplies, houseplants, etc. You'll need extra time to park, shop, and stand in line to pay. If you just need a hammer or window fan, you'll find it easier to pick one up at a neighborhood hardware store or a large drugstore like Walgreens.

Second-hand ("thrift") shops; Consignment shops	Goodwill Salvation Army Local consignment stores	Goodwill and Salvation Army sell clean used clothes and other inexpensive used items, with all their profits going to charity. Consignment shops are run by both charities and for-profit companies.
Online classified advertisements, for electronics, furniture, etc. (new and used)	Craigslist.org eBay Local newspapers, such as *Chicago Tribune* classified ads, print and online Classified ad sites within your university	eBay is the largest online auction site in the United States and Canada. It charges fees but offers some protection for buyers and sellers. Craigslist.org is a good way to search for products and services in your community. Many universities also maintain "marketplace" sites where students, faculty, and staff can buy and sell to each other.
Drugstores	CVS Longs Drugs Rite Aid Shoppers Drug Mart (Canada) SuperValu Walgreens	"Drugstores" offer much more than prescriptions and over-the-counter (nonprescription) medicines. Many are open 24 hours a day, 7 days a week, selling household supplies, small electronics, photo processing, and some packaged foods.
Books, new	Amazon.com Audible.com (audio books) Barnes & Noble Border's Chapters Indigo (Canada) iTunes (audio books) Local independent stores	Some booksellers, including Amazon, have divisions in other countries so you can easily order books published in Europe or Asia, as well as in the United States or Canada. Many bookstores sell music, too.
Books, used (including textbooks)	AbeBooks Alibris Amazon.com	AbeBooks is an excellent online site for used books. At Amazon, all book searches automatically include both new and used editions.
Textbooks (online)	CollegeBooksDirect.com eCampus.com Half.com Textbooks.com Other online bookstores	Textbooks are so expensive that students often search online for used books or discounted new ones. But shipping takes time, so order before the start of the semester. Be sure you buy the assigned edition, not an earlier, out-of-date version.

Movie rental	Blockbuster Hollywood Video Netflix (online only)	Blockbuster and Hollywood Video have thousands of neighborhood rental stores, plus online divisions. Netflix mails DVDs (with excellent service) and has a wide selection.
Children's stores, including toys (discount)	Toys "R" Us	Wal-Mart and Target also have extensive selections of children's clothing, toys, and video games.
Auto parts, tires, batteries	Advance Auto Parts AutoZone Canadian Tire Discount Tire Pep Boys Tire Rack	Several have very useful product reviews at their online sites.
Jewelry (mass market)	J. B. Robinson Sterling Jewelers Zale's	Retail outlets in most larger malls.
Eyeglasses, contact lenses	LensCrafters Pearle Vision	For eyeglasses and contact lenses, using your doctor's prescription. They have a wide selection of frames.
Shoes (online)	Zappos	Extensive selection of men's, women's, kids, athletic, and jogging shoes.
Sporting Goods	Dick's Sporting Goods Sports Authority	Products for all sports and outdoor activities, including athletic shoes.
Pet Supplies	PetSmart	Toys, treats, pet food, and other products for small animals, birds, and tropical fish.
Convenience stores	7-Eleven Circle K Cumberland Farms Sheetz Wawa Stores at larger gas stations	Quick in-and-out stores for milk, potato chips, or beer. Frequently located at gas stations. Often open very late or around the clock.
Global, ethnic foods and spices	Penzeys.com The Spice House (online)	Excellent sources for exotic spices, which are probably not considered exotic in your home country. Be sure to type the full title of "thespicehouse." Otherwise, you get a different site.

		In addition to these sites, many ethnic cookbooks list their own sources for ingredients. Look in the back of the cookbook.
Travel agencies (online)	Expedia Orbitz Priceline Southwest.com Travelocity	Expedia, Travelocity, Orbitz, and Priceline all offer airline tickets, rental cars, and hotel rooms for specified prices. Priceline has an additional service called "name your own price," where you can bid on air travel, hotel rooms, rental cars, and full vacation packages. Southwest Airlines offers inexpensive flights, but only if you book well in advance and use their Web site. They do not list flights on any other companies' sites.
Self-storage facilities	Door to Door Storage Extra Space Storage Public Storage U-Haul International U-Store-It Many other local facilities and national chains	These companies rent locked storage units on a monthly basis. Some units are the size of a small closet; others are much larger. You might rent one if you are going away for the summer and lack a safe, dry place to store your books, furniture, or even your car. All of them sell boxes and other packing materials.

Are Prices Negotiable?

In nearly all these stores, the prices are labeled and are not negotiable. This isn't eBay—well, except for eBay and its competitors. Everywhere else, you pay the marked price.

There are three important exceptions to this rule of a single, fixed price. One is that most stores have special sales, lasting a day or a week, when they mark down prices on selected items or everything in the store. The prices are still fixed, but they have been reduced. All clothing stores, furniture stores, and electronics stores have sales like these and advertise them heavily.

Unlike stores in many countries, which hold special sales only once or twice a year, retailers in the United States and Canada often have sales. The "post-holiday sales," you'll soon discover, begin almost as soon as the "pre-holiday sales" end. You'll see advertisements for sales named after every conceivable holiday: Memorial Day, Labor Day, Mother's Day, Father's Day, President's Day, and just about every other day except your birthday.

You can find these sales advertised in the weekend newspapers and at store sites online. If you are considering a large purchase—say a music system or a washing machine—ask the salesperson when their next sale is coming and whether it includes the items you want. Sometimes they know, sometimes they don't.

Second, many stores and consumer brands offer rebates or discount coupons, available in newspaper advertisements or online. Some, like Walgreens and Target, leave a stack of these ads near their store entrances. You can pick them up when you come to shop. Other rebates come in various shapes and sizes. The most convenient are instant, "in-store" rebates, which reduce the price you pay at the store's cash register. Others entail more effort. They require you to mail a coupon and sales receipt to the manufacturer, who will then mail you a rebate check.

The coupon or ad may offer a dollar off the price of a small item or perhaps $50 off a larger one. This amounts to a special sale on that item, sometimes for all customers, sometimes only for customers who bring in the coupon. Supermarkets and drug stores use coupons like this constantly—literally every week. Some also give customers a "special value card," which works like a permanent electronic coupon on that week's specials. They hope these "value cards" will encourage you to shop at their store regularly.

The third exception to fixed prices is for very expensive items, from high-end TVs to cars. Their prices *are* negotiable. Sometimes, the negotiations are direct and straightforward: "Because I like you," the salesman whispers, "I'm going to take $100 off the price." "Make that $150 off," you reply, "and it's a deal." Other times the negotiations are more subtle and indirect: "These suits have a fixed price, but if you buy one today, I'll toss in a tie." "Make that two ties and you've sold me a suit."

Tip: Except for the most expensive new items and all used goods, prices in the United States and Canada are seldom negotiable. But there are regular "sales," when prices are marked down, and there may be discount coupons for some items. For very expensive items, such as cars, the prices are almost always negotiable.

By the way, these negotiations are usually pretty quick and straight-forward. They certainly don't resemble the elaborate, ritualized offer-and-response of merchants in Middle Eastern bazaars.

Buying at Flea Markets, Second-Hand Stores, and Pawn Shops

The general rule about fixed prices does *not* apply to flea markets and second-hand stores, which sell used items.[2] Haggling for a better deal is exactly what they expect. You won't get the best price without doing it.

Most cities and many smaller communities have weekly flea markets. They are sometimes known as "swap meets" because they began as gatherings to trade and barter. Today, however, they are populated by dozens of small merchants, who sell everything from T-shirts to CDs. Most items are new. A typical merchant might buy twelve dozen white socks from a wholesaler and then sell them to customers in packs of three or six. Many flea markets are outdoor affairs, operated only in the summer. Some operate year-round and move into large warehouses during the winter.

Although flea markets do have some used items, you'll find many more at second-hand stores and online auction sites. In the United States and Canada, the most common second-hand stores are run by two charities, Salvation Army and Goodwill Industries. In some cities, various local charities operate second-hand stores to raise money. (When charities run second-hand stores, they are also called "thrift stores.") The clothes, desks, couches, lamps, dishes, and appliances they sell are used, but they are clean and in good condition.

Where do they get these items in the first place? From people who are cleaning out their houses, throwing out clothes that no longer fit, or packing up their apartments for a move. In fact, when it's time for you to move, you might want to donate some items yourself. You'll feel a lot better about it than simply throwing your old winter coats in the garbage.

Consignment shops and pawn shops also sell used clothes, furniture, electronic equipment, and more. Consignment shops are small, locally owned stores that accept items from their owners. The people who bring in items still own them, even after the shop displays them for sale. If they sell the items, they split the proceeds. If they can't sell the items, they return them to the owner.

2. Why is the term "flea markets" used for outdoor bazaars with dozens of small merchants? One story is that they got the name centuries ago because the used clothes they sold were infested with insects. Who knows? Fortunately, those days are long past.

Tip: Besides online auction sites, you can buy used goods at second-hand stores, consignment shops, pawn shops, and flea markets.

Consignment shops are more common in larger cities than in small towns. Although the goods are used, they are typically better quality, more expensive items than those in ordinary second-hand stores. A consignment shop might sell fur coats, wedding dresses, designer clothes, fine porcelain, and other items that are still in good condition and were costly when new. A number of antique stores also operate "on consignment."

Another source for used goods is pawn shops. They sell everything from guns and gold watches to guitars and stereos. Some even sell cars and motorcycles. People bring in items and either sell them to the pawn shop or borrow money based on their resale value. (That is, they use the items as collateral for loans.) If the borrowers repay the debt, they will get the pawned items back. If not, then the shop becomes the legal owner and can sell the items.[3] In all cities, you'll find a mix of locally owned shops and national chains like Cash America or Mister Money.

Pawn shops and consignment stores occasionally have fixed prices, but almost all of them are willing to bargain.

Factory Outlet Stores

There's one more inexpensive shopping option to consider: factory outlet stores. The stores themselves are owned by manufacturing companies, which sell new items at greatly reduced prices. Sometimes their products are this year's excess inventory; sometimes they are last year's models or colors; sometimes they have slight imperfections, known as "factory seconds."

Factory seconds are always marked as such. The defects do not affect the items' use and are often hard to notice. In fact, you'll find more blemishes on a perfect jacket after you've worn it a couple of times than on these "seconds."

Entire malls are devoted to outlet stores, usually in smaller communi-

---

3. The police, naturally, want to make sure that pawned items came from their rightful owners, not thieves. I hope you do, too. That's why it's important to shop at reputable stores.

ties or the far suburbs of large cities. They offer considerable savings. Some outlet stores are now online. You can find links to many at Outlets Online .com.

Buying Used Items Online

Today, most used items are bought and sold online. The biggest marketplace, by far, is eBay. Although the site began with individual sellers who were cleaning out their closets, it is increasingly filled with "power sellers," that is, businesses with "electronic storefronts" to sell new products.

EBay has strong incentives to make sure its sellers are reputable. They kick miscreants off the site and offer some limited protection to buyers. Still, it's important to check the seller's reputation before transferring any payment to them. You do that by looking at feedback reports on the seller, which are posted on eBay.

Among the other online auction sites, one of the most useful is Craigslist .org. What makes it so valuable is that you can find lots of local goods and services, such as rental apartments, baby-sitters, tickets to concerts, and more. To find them, go to Craigslist.org and click on your city or the type of service or product you are interested in. Unlike eBay, the listing is free and there are no sellers' fees. That's the good news. The bad news is that there is no buyer or seller protection. Scammers lie in wait, hoping to separate you from your money.

You can also find used items advertised in your local newspaper. These "classified ads" have appeared in local papers for years. Now, they have migrated to the papers' online sites.

Finally, your university may have its own online marketplace, limited to students, faculty, and staff. Sites like these can be especially useful for finding apartments near campus, furniture from students leaving town, or services such as baby-sitting or housecleaning. The University of Chicago

> *Tip:* Buying used items can save real money, but it does carry risks. The goods almost never come with guarantees. Also, some sellers at online auction sites may misrepresent their products or try other scams. Some buyers run scams, too. Be careful, investigate the other party to any transaction (look at their feedback), and, if possible, try to shop at sites that offer you some protection.

has a site, for instance, that proclaims it is "the premier online listing of goods for sale within the University of Chicago community." That's a bold claim, but it just might be right. It is, after all, the *only* online site listing goods for sale within the University of Chicago community.

Delivery? Setup? Installation?

Sharp competition means that retailers offer many optional services to their customers. One of the most important is home delivery for large items. If you buy a complicated product, like a home theater system, you might want professionals not only to deliver it, but to install it. Similarly, you might want furniture to be assembled or carpet to be professionally installed.

It's all available . . . for a price. The best time to ask about the price is *before* you complete the purchase. Why? Because, as I said earlier, more expensive items typically allow for some price negotiation. The store might not be willing to lower the price of the TV, but they might be willing to "throw in" some extras, like delivery or setup at a reduced cost. It doesn't cost you anything to ask! But you need to ask before agreeing to the purchase. Once you say "yes," the bargaining is done.

You also want to ask the store about delivery dates and times. Sometimes, they can hurry up a delivery, but that's unusual. Usually, it has to be scheduled several days in advance, and the sales staff may have very little to say about it. A different department or a subcontractor handles deliveries.

> **Tip:** Delivery, setup, and installation are almost always available for larger products or more complicated items. But these services cost extra and need to be scheduled several days in advance.

Warranties and Repair Services

Product warranties are an important aspect of many purchases, especially for expensive items. They not only protect you against unexpected repair costs, they give you some indication, when you make the initial purchase, whether the manufacturer is truly confident about the product's quality and durability. After all, the manufacturer is offering to pay for repairs—an expensive proposition if the product is poorly made.

You need to know several things about any warranty.

- What does it cover and what does it exclude? Does it cover the entire product or only some portions?
- If repairs are needed, does the warranty cover all parts and labor, or only parts? For the portion it does cover, does the warranty pay for all costs or do you pay a fraction?
- How long is the warranty period?
- Can you purchase an extended warranty for an additional fee? If the factory warranty is for thirty days, for instance, can you extend it for another year or longer. (Extended warranties are actually high-profit items for retail stores, so check the price carefully.)
- If a product needs repair, do you have to mail it or take it in for service? Or can you sit at home while the repair technician comes to you? That's an important question if the warranty is for a large-screen TV or other bulky product. Hauling them to a shop is no fun at all.
- Can the warranty be transferred to another owner if you sell the product? That's very important if you buy durable goods like a washer and dryer. You may want to sell them when you graduate and move, and you'll get a better price if you can assure the buyer that they are still under warranty.

Gray-Market Products

Some legitimate, new products, which are normally sold with manufacturers' warranties, are occasionally sold for lower prices without them. What's up? It's likely they are being sold on the "gray market." Unlike a "black market" product, it's *not* a fake, counterfeit, or stolen item. The product itself is fine. But it is being sold by a retailer or other distribution channel that is not authorized by the manufacturer. In such cases, the manufacturer may not be willing to honor the standard product warranty.

Gray markets arise in a couple of ways. One is that a store wants to sell a particular product line but, for some reason, cannot become an autho-

---

Tip: Gray-market dealers sell legitimate, new products, not fakes. But the dealers are not factory-authorized sellers and so may not be able to provide factory warranties. To compete with authorized dealers, they have to offer lower prices.

rized dealer. If it can acquire products through other channels, perhaps through another dealer, it becomes a gray-market dealer. Or perhaps the product costs much less overseas. By purchasing the product there and shipping it to the United States or Canada, the retailer might be able to undercut local prices. Indeed, he'd have to. Otherwise, consumers would buy from an authorized dealer where they would also receive a manufacturer's warranty.

Gray-market dealers do not announce their status. You have to observe it, perhaps by noticing that they do not display an "authorized dealer" sign. Or you can ask directly if they are authorized dealers. Even if they are not, you may still want to buy from them, but you would surely want a discount for doing so. You'll also find they might offer their *own* warranty for the product.

Sales Taxes

Unlike prices in Europe, which include VAT (the Value Added Tax), marked prices here do *not* include state or provincial sales taxes. If you see a sweater marked $100, for instance, you must add another $5–8 for those taxes and perhaps another dollar or two for city taxes. In Canada, you can add another 7 percent for the national sales tax, called the goods and services tax (GST). (The United States does not have a national sales tax.)

You pay these sales taxes on almost everything you buy in stores and restaurants, from books to computers to sandwiches. Remember, they are *not* included in the posted price.

There are a few exceptions to this rule: some items already include the tax or are not subject to sales taxes. The marked price of gasoline, cigarettes, and alcohol already includes heavy taxes. Other items, like groceries and prescription drugs, are exempt from sales taxes in some states but not in others. (Sales taxes are passed by each city, state, and province, so they vary.)

There are no state taxes on Internet purchases *if* you purchase from a vendor in a different state. So, if you are studying in California and order a laptop from Dell in Texas, you'll save $80 or $100 in sales taxes, which should more than cover the cost of shipping.

Tip: Sales taxes are not included in the marked prices for most items.

Returns

Nearly all retailers allow you to return products, not just defective ones but those you simply decide you don't want. Perhaps the clothes you ordered don't fit or the new lamp doesn't look good in your apartment. You can usually return them for a short period after purchase. The store will either offer you a replacement, return the purchase price, or offer you a "store credit" (that is, a voucher that can be used only for purchases within that store or store chain).

If the product malfunctions after several weeks, it will probably be considered an issue for the manufacturer, under the terms of the warranty. Still, it's a good idea to contact the retailer first. A few retailers don't allow returns at all. They post signs near their registers saying "all sales final."

But those stores are the exception. Most others have fairly generous return policies. Each store determines its own rules, but they all share two features. First, you must return the item promptly. For some stores, that might be three days; for others, it might be thirty. Second, you must return the item in essentially new condition. You can't return a dress after you've worn it to a party, or a novel after you've finished reading it. What you can do, without a problem, is try on the dress or examine the novel. You can take a new toaster out of its package and see how it looks. You should be able to return any of these items *if* they can still be sold as new.

Online retailers have the same policies. In fact, they are usually more accommodating, because they understand that you cannot try on a jacket or examine a vase until you receive it.

Beyond that, store policies differ. Some want returns to be made very quickly, in one or two days; others give you more time. Most pay for return postage; some don't. Some give you back your money (the purchase price plus sales taxes); others give you a "store credit." A few companies hit you with a "restocking fee," perhaps 10 percent of the purchase price.

Retailers who sell used books, second-hand clothes, and other used items are a major exception to these return policies. They almost never allow them. When you buy a used shirt or used china, you buy them "as

> *Tip:* Retailers generally allow customers to return products they don't want *if* they are returned promptly and in new condition. Each seller's exact policies are different, so you should ask in advance.

> ***Tip:*** Companies that sell used products seldom permit returns.

is." Once you pay, they belong to you and cannot be returned. There is usually a sign saying exactly that.

Whatever the policies, they are normally well established for each retailer. If there's a chance you might want to return the item, ask for details *before* you purchase.

Clothing Sizes

One of the most frustrating aspects of shopping in another country is finding the right size clothes. When you cross borders, you often need to convert your old, familiar sizes into a new metric. Actually, it's a bad pun to say "metric," since Americans notoriously refuse to use the metric system—for clothes or anything else. To take a typical example of the size conversions, a standard American men's shirt, size 15, would be marked 38 in Europe, Japan, and other countries. The reason: the neck opening measures 15 inches, or 38 centimeters.

In appendix 2, "Abbreviations, Acronyms, Nicknames, Holidays, Floor Numbering, and Clothing Sizes," I provide charts for men and women to convert international clothing sizes into their North American equivalents.

> ***Tip:*** When you find clothing that fits in North American stores, write down your "new" size. It won't solve all your problems, because clothing sizes vary so much, but it should help you when you shop the next time.

How to Research Product Quality

A final word before you start clicking on Web sites or trudging off to the mall: Do some product research before you buy. Know which brands are most reliable and which models offer the best value. Know which ones to avoid.

A good place begin is *Consumer Reports* magazine. Their motto is "Expert. Independent. Nonprofit." That's exactly right. They do serious testing, refuse to run any advertisements, and have earned a strong reputation for fair, unbiased evaluations. Each issue covers several types of consumer products and rates all the makes and models. Their annual *Buying Guide* summarizes the reports. It's worth subscribing or at least reading the magazine at the library. For a small additional fee, you can subscribe to their online service, ConsumerReports.org.

Besides *Consumer Reports,* there are fine guides, online and in print, for most products. CNET, for instance, provides excellent reviews of new electronic gear. Audiophile magazines do the same for new music systems, as do photography magazines for cameras. Whatever the product, you will probably find helpful reviews, as well as discussion threads in online forums.

As a student, you should be good at doing research like this. It's worth your while to do it in this case, especially if the product is costly. As one student reminded me, "It's not just about getting the best price. It's about knowing what you are buying."

Chapter 17

Getting Around: Buses, Bikes, and Taxis

Earlier, I urged you to explore your neighborhood and learn about public transportation and university bus routes. Let me underscore that advice and add some details. After that, I'll discuss taxis, shuttle buses, bikes, and other transport options before turning to automobiles in the next chapter.

Let's start by looking at one of the least expensive ways to get around: public transportation.

Public Transportation: City Buses, University Buses

Nearly all cities have regular bus service between the university and areas where students live and shop. Most have special, money-saving cards for anyone who uses public transportation frequently. Students may be eligible for even better cards at deeper discounts. These arrangements vary by city so you'll need to check the Web site for local public transit or ask your advisers at orientation.

Frequently, the university itself runs buses along popular routes. The buses are free, or very inexpensive, to students, who are usually asked to show their university ID when they enter the bus. You can find out the routes and schedules at orientation, or ask the international student adviser or dean of students. They may also have pamphlets or maps about city buses (and subways in large metropolitan areas).

> *Tip:* Transit systems sell discount cards to riders who use the bus or subway every day. Most offer additional discounts to students.

Be sure to find out when the last buses run. Students often study or play late, and you don't want to be caught watching the last bus disappear into the night.

Airport Shuttles

For most students, one regular destination is the airport. Taxicabs can take you there, of course, but there are usually much cheaper ways. Your university might run special buses there at busy times, like the beginning and end of each semester. Commercial operators run airport vans and shuttles throughout the year, usually at half the cost of taxis. Although the price is appealing, there are drawbacks to consider. Unlike taxis, the vans don't leave as soon as you climb onboard. They wait for more passengers or leave at a fixed time. (You can ask the driver how long the wait will be.) They don't drive straight to your destination, either. They drop off each passenger along the route. That can mean a long ride if you are the first to board and the last to exit. So, in choosing between taxis and shuttles, you'll be making a familiar trade-off: time versus money.

> *Tip:* The cheapest and easiest way to get to the airport is usually a special van or bus. See which ones operate from your campus, and see whether you need a reservation.

Other University Travel Options

Besides airport shuttles and university bus routes, most universities help their students find partners to share rides to nearby cities and more distant locations. These "share-a-ride" arrangements are particularly popular as vacations approach. At Ohio State, for example, there are literally thousands of students traveling to Cleveland, Cincinnati, Dayton, Pittsburgh, Indianapolis, and other cities. Some are already driving with friends, but others would be happy to include one or two fellow students, partly for company, partly to share the costs. They may offer round-trip rides (that is, to the destination and back) or one-way. Other students need rides and post ads on campus requesting them: "Need ride to New York. Prefer to leave December 6–8 and return January 3–4. Please call xxx or e-mail."

Before the Internet, these requests were written on small sheets and posted on bulletin boards at popular locations such as dining halls or stu-

> **Tip:** Share-a-ride advertisements offer an inexpensive way to ride to nearby cities. They are especially attractive when the supply and demand is high, at the beginning and end of semesters. Check the electronic bulletin board at your university.

dent activity centers. Some still are. But today, the most popular bulletin boards are online. Some are limited to people at the university. Others, like Craigslist, are open to the public.

What are the financial arrangements for these shared rides? Generally, the passengers offer to pay for gasoline. Arrangements differ, but the passengers either pay for all the gas or split it with the driver. Since fuel is only part of the cost of driving, it's certainly reasonable for passengers to fill the tank.

Some universities also help out with local transportation, especially for student activities. As I've already noted, many have their own bus routes, serving the campus and nearby neighborhoods. Some also have university cars or vans, which seat eight to ten people, for student organizations to use. You may wish to see if your university has such vehicles and who can use them. Do you need to be part of an official organization? What's the cost? When they are available?

Taxis

Taxicabs are available in all university communities. (They are called "taxis" in some cities, "cabs" in others.) The cost often surprises international students. It is not a happy surprise. The fares at home are typically much lower. One reason for the high costs here: most cities restrict the number of cab licenses and charge high fees to those who get them. In some cities, a cab license (or "medallion") sells for tens of thousands of dollars. You, the lucky rider, pay for that.

You can request cab service in several ways. The most common is to call the company. It is listed in the Yellow Pages and online. The dispatcher will ask for your address, your phone number, and where you are going, before telling you how long you should expect to wait for the cab. Obviously, the wait is much longer during peak times, morning and evening, or when the weather is bad (because more people request cabs then). If you are eating at a nice restaurant and need a ride home, you can ask the restaurant to request a cab for you. Or you can walk onto a busy street and hail one yourself. Simply raise your arm and signal to passing cabs. Finally,

> **Tip:** If you need a taxi very early in the morning or late at night, it's often hard to find one on the streets. Your best bet is to call the company and request a taxi.

you can usually find cabs lined up and ready for passengers outside busy hotels and major hospitals.

Cabs are always available at the airport. Some, like New York's LaGuardia, offer an option to customers. You can take a cab by yourself or save money by sharing one with other passengers going to the same area, such as Manhattan's Upper West Side. The airport cab dispatcher will explain the cost differences and assemble groups who want to share rides.

What Do Taxis Charge?

For some trips, such as a ride to the airport, there may be a fixed charge such as $35 or $40, plus tip. More often, cabs simply charge by the mile. In most cities, there is an initial charge (perhaps $2.50) when you enter the cab, a small charge for each additional passenger and each piece of luggage, and then a standard fee for each tenth of a mile driven. There is also a charge for time, so it costs more to travel ten miles at rush hour than at midnight. All these charges appear on the meter, which should be turned on when you enter the cab. If there are any tolls on your route, such as bridge or airport tolls, they will be added to your bill. These charges are standardized in each city, probably by local regulators rather than free-market competition.

Payment is normally in cash, although cabs take credit cards in a few cities. You should tip the driver about 15 percent of the bill (but not less than $1) when you pay. You can request a receipt, if you wish.

Occasionally, cab drivers try to cheat their passengers. It's rare, but it does happen. One way is for them to take a circuitous route to your destination. Sometimes, the driver is new to the area and simply doesn't know the route. More often, though, the long trip is deliberate fraud. Another trick is to drive without turning on the meter and then make up a fee when you arrive, "Oh, the regular charge is $75." The victims are mostly people from out of town, including international visitors.

How can you protect yourself? I have three suggestions. First, you should learn the approximate fare to your regular destinations. If you are a student at USC or UCLA, for instance, you should know the cab fare to LAX (Los Angeles International Airport). If you don't, just ask some friends or the dispatcher at the airport. Second, make sure the meter is turned on. If it is not, ask what the fixed charge will be *before* you travel more than a block or two. If you are unhappy with the proposed charge, ask to stop and get out. Third, appear knowledgeable. If you look like you've made this trip many times before, you'll be driven straight to your destination. If you look like this is your first trip outside Uzbekistan, you might take a very long and expensive cab ride.

Bicycles

Lots of students and plenty of professors ride bikes between home and class. It's a cheap and convenient way to commute. You can buy a new bike at a shop near campus or a used one from a fellow student. (Ads for used bikes are a regular feature of university bulletin boards.) There are racks all over campus so you can lock up your bike while you attend class or study at the library.

If you ride a bike, you need to watch out for two problems, aside from rain and snow. One is personal safety. The other is theft.

Bike safety begins with a good, strong helmet that fits you snugly. *Never* ride without one. It is required by law nearly everywhere, and it's a good idea in any case.

Be *very* careful riding on city streets. You cannot ride on sidewalks, since it is too dangerous for pedestrians. In some cities, you can use special bike paths that exclude cars. If your city has them, and the path is convenient, you'll find it's the safest way to ride, and often the prettiest.[1] Other cities maintain special traffic lanes for bikes. These lanes run outside the moving traffic, next to the parked cars. (That's where you should ride on city streets, whether or not the bicycle lanes are marked.) Cars are not supposed to drive in these marked lanes, but some do anyway, and all of them must cross the bike lanes when turning.

Even with special lanes, then, city streets can be dangerous for bicycle riders. When a bike tangles with a car, the car always wins. Sometimes, the driver causes the accident, sometimes the biker. I've seen countless bike riders sail through red lights and stop signs, assuming cars will see them and yield. It's a risky assumption. Drivers don't always see bicycles and, even if they do, they may be going too fast to stop quickly. Sometimes, the

---

1. If you do ride on special bike paths, watch out for the pedestrians who share the path. Bikes can reach high speeds on these paths, and collisions with pedestrians are very dangerous to both riders and walkers.

> *Tip:* Bikes are among the cheapest forms of basic transportation. You can find used ones locally on bulletin boards or Web sites like Craigslist.

> *Tip:* Always wear a bicycle helmet and remember to lock up your bike, even if you are just leaving it briefly.

fault lies with poorly maintained roads. Potholes, bumps, and bad pavement can trip even a good cyclist, so you need to be alert. Sometimes, the fault lies with car passengers, who open their doors without first checking to see if a cyclist is approaching. The message is simple: if you ride a bike, be watchful and cautious.

This warning applies equally to country roads, where cars are typically driving fast and there is seldom a special lane for bikes.

The dangers are real. In recent years, 700–800 U.S. bike riders died in crashes each year, and about 90 percent of the deaths were caused by collisions with cars. More than 45,000 bike riders suffer serious injuries annually, and ten times that number require visits to the emergency room.[2]

Jane Brody, a reporter for the *New York Times* and a bicyclist herself, offers several excellent ideas to lessen the dangers:

Signal all turns and stops and make full stops at stop signs.

Never ride on the sidewalk.

Ride in a straight path.

Try to make eye contact with drivers before you change lanes or turn left.

Don't weave in and out of parked cars.

Be visible. Wear brightly colored clothing in daylight; when riding in the dark, wear light-colored clothing and a reflector vest.

If you cycle at night, have a white headlight and red taillight (preferably a blinking one).

Do not cycle wearing headphones.[3]

And be sure you always ride in the same direction as traffic.

2. These statistics are compiled by the U.S. Department of Transportation and are reported by the Bicycle Helmet Safety Institute, http://www.helmets.org/stats.htm (accessed June 16, 2007).

3. These suggestions are quoted from Jane E. Brody, "Personal Health: Cars and Bikes Can Mix, When the Rules of the Road Are Clear," *New York Times*, June 5, 2007, http://select.nytimes .com/search/restricted/article?res=F20C15FA3A540C768CDDAF0894DF404482# (accessed June 16, 2007).

Equipment theft is another major issue. Every large city has its share of bicycle thieves, equipped with bolt cutters to slice through chains and flimsy locks. To thwart them, you *must* buy a strong lock. Use it every time you leave your bike, even if its "just for a minute."

Lock your bike on a rack, if possible, rather than a pole or other object. You'll find racks everywhere on campus, along busy shopping streets, and even at some malls. My advice is to lock your bike in a very visible location, where thieves cannot operate unseen.

Motorcycles

My advice for motorcyclists is similar. Always wear a helmet. Always lock your bike and do it in a visible location. Be very careful on city streets and highways, where road conditions and other motorists pose constant hazards.

One important difference between motorcycling and biking is that motorcyclists need a state license. An ordinary driver's license won't do. There's a separate test (written and on-road) for motorcycles, and you'll need to pass it to get your license. Before taking the test, you can get a "learner's permit," which allows you to practice driving under limited conditions. These licenses are issued by states and provinces, and each has its own rules, posted on its Web site. Search for the "Department of Motor Vehicles" or "Motorcycle Licenses" plus the name of your state or province.

Chapter 18

Getting Around: Cars

Modern cities and their suburbs are built around automobiles, for better or worse. That's especially true of the fast-growing cities in the American South and West.

Universities are integral parts of this larger society and they, too, depend on automobiles. Many students need cars to get from home to class or to buy groceries, books, and clothes. If that includes you, then you'll need a car, driver's license, and insurance.

I'll cover all these topics in this chapter. I'll explain how to get a driver's license, buy or rent a car, purchase insurance, and handle other aspects of car ownership. I'll also explain how to rent a truck or van so you can pack up and move to another apartment, across town or across the country.

Driver's Licenses

You probably came here with a driver's license from your home country. With that plus an easily obtained international license, you may be able to drive here. But I don't advise it. Even if it's legal—check your local laws to see if it is—most police don't know about it. So you'll need to carry a copy of your state's "rules of the road" booklet to show them, in case they pull you over. The booklet is available from your state department of motor vehicles (DMV). Explaining the law to a policeman is no fun, and it's not advisable. You, a newcomer, will be explaining the law to someone who has been enforcing it for years. You may be right, but why not avoid trouble if you can?

Frankly, it's smarter to get a local driver's license. Police know what it means, and, just as important, it's the best form of local identification. If

Tip: Even if you can drive with a license from your home country, it's wise to get a local driver's license. Police know what it means, and it's the best form of local identification. If you don't drive, you should get a personal identification card from the state department of motor vehicles.

Tip: To get a driver's license you must pass a written test to prove you know the laws, a vision test to prove you can see the highway, and a road test to prove you can drive safely. For the road test, you'll need to supply a car.

you don't drive, you should get a personal identification card from the state motor vehicle agency. Although it doesn't permit you to drive, it works fine as an official ID. (For more details, see chapter 13, "Identification Cards.")

To get a driver's license, you need to pass a series of tests. One covers state or provincial driving laws. You can get a copy of the relevant laws at the DMV or download it online. The department of motor vehicles will give you a straightforward multiple-choice test on these laws, followed by a basic vision test. If they find problems with your eyesight, the license might require you to wear glasses or contact lenses when you drive.

Finally, an officer from the department will accompany you on a road test. You need to supply a car for this test. The state or province does *not* provide a car, so you'll need to bring your own or borrow a friend's.

With the officer riding along and observing, you will drive around local streets and cope with real-life situations. Then, you will hear the dreaded words, "Could you please parallel park?" If you pass all these tests, you'll pay a fee, have your picture taken, and get your license then and there. It does not need to be renewed for several years and, even then, will not require another test.

Driving Safely in a New Country

The challenge is not so much passing the test; it's driving safely after you get the license. That's a challenge for everyone, but it's more difficult for international students for a couple of reasons. First, many have not driven extensively before. It takes practice to drive well. You wouldn't expect to play tennis well if you'd never picked up a racquet before and spent some time on the practice court. Well, the same is true for driving a car. You need to practice to drive well. Second, even experienced drivers from Indonesia or Italy must learn to deal with different conditions here, in Indiana or Idaho. International students are unfamiliar with the way people drive in the snows of Toronto, on the freeways of Los Angeles, or, heaven forbid, around and around the traffic circles of Washington. These are not hypothetical challenges. They are real, and they are dangerous.

Driving School: A *Very* Good Idea

There is a solution, and I urge all international students and spouses to take it. *Attend a local driving school* before you take the driver's test.

Every university town has driving schools. They provide a valuable service, not only in teaching you the traffic laws but in teaching you how to drive safely. They work with novices who have never driven before, and with experienced drivers who want to adjust to driving here.

Although driving schools charge for the service, it's worth the price. The instruction will make you a better driver, and a much safer one. It pays for itself quickly, too, since auto insurance companies give you a discount for completing the course.

One way driving school helps is by showing you what to expect from other drivers. To preserve life and limb, you need to understand how they actually behave. These informal rules of the road differ from city to city. Montreal is not Boston. Actually, nowhere is like Boston, where drivers seem to think basic rules of the road are merely suggestions.

One other point about driving schools. You might be able to find one where instructors speak your native language. I know I have consistently encouraged you to practice and improve your English whenever you can. That's still a good rule, but learning how to drive is an exception to it. If you feel insecure or uncomfortable using English, it's fine to receive driving instruction in your native language. The reason is the same one I gave for using a bank where they speak your language. A mistake at the bank or behind the wheel can be much more serious than one ordering dinner or asking directions. Fortunately, most cities and university towns have

Tip: It really helps to take driving lessons. Private schools offer them in every city. They'll go over the laws, prepare you for the test, and give you plenty of supervised practice on local streets. Most of all, they'll make you a better, safer driver.

Tip: There may be driving schools that teach in your native language. It's a useful option if you are not yet comfortable in English.

driving schools with instructors from various countries. To find the right one, ask someone from your university's human resources department or turn to the Yellow Pages (in the phone book or online). Look under "Driving Instruction," and start calling around.

Buying a Car

You may need to buy or lease a car for your everyday needs. A car is essential in suburbs, smaller towns, and most cities across the southern and western United States and the Canadian plains. These towns are built on the self-fulfilling assumption that everyone goes everywhere in a car. Nobody walks. Nobody uses public transportation. That's not true in most cities on the East Coast and Great Lakes and a few on the West Coast, notably Vancouver, Seattle, and San Francisco. These cities have good bus and subway systems. In most other places, though, you'll need a car.

Buying one is rarely a happy experience. The cars are expensive, the salesmen sleazy, and the prices negotiable. Very negotiable. All too often, the salesman offers you a "special" deal. "I'll tell what I'm going to do," he might say. "If you want to buy this little beauty today, then I can make you a great deal. I'm telling you, these cars are hot, and I can only promise it to you today." Yeah, sure.

Whether you buy a new Ford, Toyota, or Hyundai, you may have to engage in such negotiations, and—who knows?—you may get a good car at a good price. But before you negotiate, you should go online and get three kinds of information:

- product evaluations for the car you want, compared to others in its category,
- the car's wholesale price, equipped the way you want it, and
- incentives currently being offered, such as lower interest rates or "cash back" (that is, factory-authorized rebates).

Arrive at the dealer armed with this information.

For car ratings, the best places to go are three free sites, Edmunds.com, Vehix.com, and Yahoo! Autos, and one that requires a paid subscription, *Consumer Reports* (either the magazine or the online service). *Consumer*

Tip: Before you buy a car, do some research. Basically, you need to know two things. One is how good the car is, compared to others in its category. On average, what is its quality, reliability, comfort, gas mileage, and other performance characteristics. Second, you need to know not only the average retail price but what the dealer actually pays so you can negotiate a good bargain.

Reports is published by a nonprofit organization. It takes no advertising and is not trying to sell cars.

As for rebates and other incentives, the dealerships themselves display this information prominently on their Web sites and in their ads, especially the advertising sections in weekend newspapers. (Dealers advertise on Saturdays and Sundays because that's when most car buyers shop. If you can shop during the week, you'll find it much easier and less rushed.)

Dealers try to keep their wholesale prices secret, for obvious reasons. In fact, they blow smoke in your eyes. One way is by showing you their "dealer invoice," which is less than the "full sticker price" on the vehicle window. (Nobody pays full sticker price *unless* it is a very popular new model in short supply or is sold only at a one-price, no-bargaining dealership, like Saturn.) Since the invoice is lower than the sticker price and since it actually says "invoice," you might think it's the dealer's price. You'd be wrong. It's a bargaining gimmick. To get a more realistic sense of what the car you want really costs the dealer, go to Edmunds.com or ConsumerReports .com. Be sure you look for a model equipped the way you want it.

My advice: if you are purchasing a new car, first purchase the "New Car Price Report" from *Consumer Reports*. It is customized for the specific make and model car you are considering and gives several critical pieces of information:

- the true dealer invoice price for a vehicle,
- the dealer price for any optional equipment or packages,
- any hidden incentives given to dealers by the manufacturers, and
- specific guidance on what you should pay.

The report costs less than $20 and, quite literally, can save you thousands.[1]

Some Web sites compete with dealers by offering to sell you a car at a

---

1. *Consumer Reports* estimates the average consumer saves $1,900 by using the New Car Price Report. It can be ordered at 1-800-693-5524.

very competitive price. They actually deliver it to your door. Others provide your name to local dealers, who then send you bids by e-mail or phone. You can accept those bids, ask for better ones, or take them to a dealer and ask him to beat the best price.

If you hate negotiating, there is an alternative worth considering. You can buy from a dealer that sells for fixed prices. There is no haggling, no back-and-forth between you, the salesman, and the sales manager. This is *not* simply a dealer saying "I won't negotiate." It's a company policy at several brands and at the largest used car dealer, CarMax.

Used Cars

If you decide to buy a used car (what dealers euphemistically call "pre-owned"), be sure to check its background. There's a simple way to do that: type in the vehicle identification number (VIN) at Carfax.com.[2] A report from Carfax should document everything that has happened to that car, from maintenance to damage reports, from theft to normal upkeep. It does have one limitation, though. Carfax can only report what repair shops and insurance agencies have told it. It's always possible that some repairs were made but not reported, so it pays to check carefully before buying any used car. Carfax itself charges for its reports, but dealers often provide them free to customers. Ask before you buy.

> *Tip:* If you buy a used car, be sure to ask the seller for the complete vehicle history.

You'd be right to worry about a dealer who wouldn't provide a vehicle history report like this. Don't buy that car. In fact, don't buy any used car without carefully examining its documented history. You want to make sure the car has received regular service and has never been in a major accident.

If the used car is relatively expensive, consider taking it to your own mechanic for an inspection before you buy. You can hire auto mechanics to inspect your vehicle and report any problems to you. Some mechanics actually specialize in these inspections. If you can't do that before the purchase, you should do it immediately afterward.

2. The Vehicle Identification Number (VIN) is stamped on the car in several spots, including the engine bay, the dashboard, and the door on the driver's side. Ask the dealer to point out the number and be sure to write it down.

Why inspect a car *after* you've bought it? Because many dealers offer a seven-day, money-back guarantee. Even if they don't, many jurisdictions give you the legal right to return the vehicle and get your money back for the first few days after purchase. (These laws differ from state to state, so it's important to check before you buy.) If your mechanic says the car has serious, hidden problems you should return it.

Except for CarMax, which has a no-bargaining policy, all used car prices are subject to intense bargaining. As a buyer, you are at a disadvantage because the seller knows the vehicle much better than you do. Of course, you can see whether the car looks clean and has low mileage.[3] What you don't know, but the seller does, is what lies hidden below the surface. Was the oil was changed regularly? Did some accidents go unreported? Was the car driven mainly on highways or in harsh, stop-and-go traffic?

You'll never know as much as the seller, but you should at least try to minimize your disadvantage before making an offer. Besides checking the Carfax damage report, you should check the *Kelley Blue Book,* which reports standard prices for all years and models. In fact, it is so widely used that buyers and sellers simply refer to "blue book value." (It also shows price differences for cars in better or worse condition.) Along the same lines, you should access online auction sites. Ideally, you'd like to find prices for the same model, year, condition, and mileage as the car you are considering. Finally, it helps to know whether the seller has only recently begun advertising the car or has been trying to sell it for weeks. The longer a car languishes unsold, the more flexible the seller will be on price.

Warranties

Whenever you buy a used car, you need to know whether the vehicle is being sold with a warranty or "as is" (that is, with whatever defects the car already has, with no promises to repair them). Dealers might provide a warranty for one week or one month, and they usually can provide longer warranties for an additional fee. Private sellers might be able to transfer their existing warranty to you. These arrangements vary widely, and you definitely need to ask.

All new cars come with warranties, though the length and coverage varies. You can extend the coverage for more years or miles by purchasing an "extended warranty" from the dealer before taking delivery of the car.

---

3. Changing the miles on an odometer is a serious crime. It used to be a common, if unscrupulous practice. Now, it's rare, but not entirely unknown.

Whether it's a regular warranty or an extended one, whether it's for a new car or a used one, you need to know which repairs are covered and which ones are not. For the covered repairs, you need to know what fraction of the costs the warranty pays and what fraction you pay. You also need to know whether you can transfer the warranty to another owner when you sell the vehicle. That certainly adds to the vehicle's resale value.

Borrowing or Paying Cash for a Car

Whatever kind of car you buy, you should compare the costs of buying it for cash, buying it with loans (from the dealer or a bank), or leasing it for several years. You can't compare these alternatives in the abstract. You need to look at the costs for a specific car at a specific time. When you do, go beyond a simple comparison of monthly payments and look at the total costs for the car you want.

Beware of false comparisons. A car lease might come with low monthly payments but carry some hidden charges. The payments might cover only the first 10,000 miles per year. After that, you owe 20¢ a mile. That "little surprise" will greet you when you return the vehicle after the lease. The lease also assumes the car comes back with only normal wear. But who judges that? An unscrupulous dealer could exaggerate the necessary repairs and sock you with extra charges. That's why you should work with a reputable dealer and buy on terms that fit your needs.

> **Tip:** To buy a car, you need to price alternative vehicles and alternative ways of financing them. Come to the dealer knowing the car's wholesale price, which you can find on the Web.

Two Car Accessories Worth Considering

One way dealers make money is by adding "extras" to the car. These accessories come with high profit margins. You can skip most of them, such as underbody rust protection, but you might want to buy a few others, such as leather seats or a top-quality music system. That depends on your taste, your wallet, and your commuting time each day. If you have a longer commute, you'll want a nicer car.

You can order accessories directly from the dealer or from an "after market" supplier, who sells and installs sound systems, car alarms, and other parts. Once again, it pays to compare prices, quality, and service.

Tip: Car alarms are a valuable accessory in most locations. Satellite navigation is useful if you sometimes drive on unfamiliar routes.

Two accessories worth considering are satellite navigation and car alarms. Navigation systems are worth the price if you expect to take long trips or drive regularly in unfamiliar areas. If you mostly drive back and forth between school and your apartment, it's a waste of money. Car alarms, on the other hand, are a good idea in many areas. Most cars come with basic antitheft devices, such as electronic keys, but complete alarm systems offer more protection. They can be installed by the dealer or a company that specializes in car alarms.

Car Insurance

If you own a car, you *must* have insurance. In fact, you need it as soon as you drive off the dealer's lot.

Car insurance is designed to cover several kinds of risks. Your car might be stolen or damaged in an accident. You might damage someone else's car or property. Far worse, you could injure yourself or someone else. If these injuries are serious, the medical costs could be astronomical.

When you buy auto insurance, you buy coverage for each of these risks as part of an overall package. State laws require that you buy at least basic insurance, known as "minimal coverage." Beyond that, you can choose the level you need. If you need your car for daily commuting, for example, you should buy insurance that provides a rental car while yours is being repaired after an accident. If you have extensive assets, you should buy more liability coverage to protect yourself against lawsuits, especially large claims for personal injuries.

Naturally, it takes some time to decide how much insurance you need and to shop for the best price and service. You don't have time to do that while you're still at the car dealer. But you do need insurance, even for that first ride home. What's the solution?

Actually, there are two solutions. If you already own a car, your insurance probably covers the new vehicle for several days, while you shop for more insurance. To find out whether you have this coverage and how long

Tip: If you need a car for daily commuting, then buy car insurance that provides a rental car while yours is being repaired after an accident.

it lasts, ask your current insurance company before you go car shopping. If you don't already have car insurance, you have to take a second approach. Buy short-term insurance from the car dealer. It's called an "insurance rider" and lasts seven to ten days. (Dealers work with an insurance broker who provides the actual coverage.) They might charge $50 or so for the service, or they might throw it in "free" to clinch the deal for the car itself. With this short-term coverage in hand, you can drive off the dealer's lot and shop for a regular insurance policy.

Lowering the Cost of Car Insurance

If you are worried about the annual cost of car insurance, you can lower it in several ways. The most important is to comparison shop. You can purchase automobile insurance online or by phone from dozens of companies. Geico, Nationwide, and Progressive are among the best known, but there are many, many others.[4]

Low cost is obviously important, but so is good customer service. When you actually need their assistance—when you're sitting beside the road Saturday night after an accident—you want the company to be there for you. You don't want a recorded voice that says, "Your business is very important to us. Please stay on the line until Monday morning."

Wherever you buy insurance, you can lower the cost if you

- buy renter's insurance from the same company (see chapter 20);
- raise the amount of "the deductible";
- drive less than 10,000 miles per year;
- install a car alarm system; *or*
- take a driver's education course.

There are discounts for all of these, but to get them, you need to ask the agent. You can save money with a higher deductible because you pay more of the costs for any accident. If your deductible is $100, then you pay the first $100 of any damages. If your car needs $1,500 in repairs, the insurance company will pay you $1,400. If your deductible is $500, the insurance company will only pay you $1,000, but the policy costs much less. Finally, believe it or not, there also may be discounts for good grades in school. Why? Because insurance data show that good students also have good driving records.

---

4. You can find them at geico.com, nationwide.com, and progressive.com.

> ***Tip:*** To drive legally, you must purchase auto insurance. It covers auto thefts, injuries to you and others, damage to your car, and damage to others' cars and property. Every state mandates minimum coverage, but you may wish to purchase more. In choosing an insurance company, look at both costs and customer service, and tailor the policy to your needs.

Car Rentals

Until now, we have been talking about buying or leasing a car for long-term use. What if you only need a car for a few days? You can rent one.[5]

Cars are available for daily or weekly rental at every airport and many city locations. The big rental companies are familiar names around the world: Hertz, Avis, Budget, National, and many more. All of them carry a wide variety of cars, from subcompacts to giant SUVs. To find the best prices, go to their Web sites or those of major travel agencies, such as Travelocity, Expedia, Orbitz, or Priceline.

The rules for renting cars in the United States and Canada are similar to those elsewhere, but it's worth going over some of them. For students, the most important rule is that you must be twenty-five or older to rent. The car rental companies say that this restriction is based on accident records and the high costs of insuring younger drivers. Whatever the reasons, all major companies have the same age restriction. It's conceivable that some small, independent companies have different rules, but you'll have to look very hard to find them.

> ***Tip:*** You can rent a car only if you are twenty-five years old or older.

Let's assume that you are flying to Boston and want to rent a car at the airport. You've gone online, picked the type of car you want, found a good price, and reserved a vehicle for a specific period. So far, so good. Now, let me explain what you need to do when you arrive at Logan Airport in Boston.

First, you need to go to the rental company's local office. That's easy. At

---

5. For most purposes, renting means the same thing as leasing. For automobiles, however, the two terms are used differently. Car "rentals" are for days or weeks. Car "leases" are for many months (perhaps two or three years), and the price should be compared to that of an outright purchase.

Tip: The only people who can drive your rental car are those who sign the initial rental agreements, unless the company rules say otherwise. Some companies allow your spouse to drive without signing the agreement.

every airport, car rental agencies either have offices in the terminal or run shuttle buses from there to their offices nearby.

When you arrive at the office, you will fill out and sign an agreement with standard provisions to obey driving laws, pay all tickets, and return the car in the same condition you borrowed it. You will need to present a valid driver's license and may be asked for a second form of photo identification. The agreement specifies when and where you will return the vehicle, such as noon the following Saturday at the same location. You can always return it earlier. If you want to return the car at another location—perhaps you are driving one-way from Boston to Philadelphia—you can arrange it, but you'll need to do so in advance and may have to pay a surcharge, sometimes a high one.

The only people who can drive the rental car are those who sign the initial rental agreement *unless* the company permits it. Some automatically permit your spouse to drive without signing the contract. Others require a signature if your spouse wants to drive. All other potential drivers need to cosign the agreement and, like you, need to be twenty-five or older, licensed, and able to provide photo identification.

You should ask about mileage charges. Some agreements allow you to drive unlimited miles. Others allow you to drive 100 or 200 miles per day and then charge 20–30¢ per mile after that.

If you expect to drive to another state or province, or across the U.S.-Canadian border, be sure to ask the company in advance. Some rental agreements permit it. Others don't.

Although most provisions in the rental agreement are standard, you do need to make a couple of choices. You don't need to make them in advance. You can do it when you sign the agreement.

One is about paying for gas. All rental cars come with a full tank of gas. One option is to pay, in advance, for the whole tank. That's very costly if you don't expect to drive far. You might drive only ten miles, but pay $40 for the gas. On the other hand, if you expect to drive much farther and return with the tank nearly empty, you've gotten your money's worth. The alternative is to agree, in advance, that you will return the car with a full tank. That means you'll need to stop at a gas station just before you drop off the car. If you forget or don't have time, the rental company will fill the tank for you and charge you an outrageous price.

You also need to choose whether or not to buy insurance from the rental company. All drivers need insurance against certain risks. You, your passengers, or others could be hurt in an accident. Your car or someone else's could be damaged. Other property might be damaged. A thief could break into your car and steal your iPod or laptop.

Once again, the rental agreement offers you a basic choice. You can allow the rental company to insure you against some or all of these risks, for a daily fee. The fee is high, but the service is very convenient. The alternative is to "decline coverage." You should do this *only* if you already have adequate insurance on your own car and if it covers you for rentals. Most car insurance does, but you need to check with your insurance agent. A quick call should get the answer.

When you sign the rental agreement, you actually accept or decline four separate types of insurance coverage, for

- collision damage to your car ("collision damage waiver"),
- liability in case of lawsuits by other injured parties ("liability coverage"),
- loss or theft of any personal items ("personal effects"), and
- injuries that require medical treatment ("personal accident insurance").

To decline them, you will be asked to write your initials at several places on the rental agreement.

Once you have signed the agreement, you will pick up your car in the company lot. It's tempting to turn the key and drive off. Don't do it quite yet. There's one more thing to do. You should quickly walk around the car, inspecting it for damage. If you notice a dent on the trunk or a large scratch on the driver's door, make a note of it. You do that on a sheet provided by the rental company, showing the generic outline of a car. Using that drawing, mark an X on the door and trunk to identify the damage. As you drive off the company lot, you'll stop at the gate and show the guard your rental contract. (The guard is there to prevent theft and inspects all contracts.) Ask the guard to confirm your report of minor damage. The guard will then initial your drawing or the contract to confirm that the damage existed before you rented the car. Why is that important? Because

Tip: If you don't have your own car insurance, or if it doesn't cover rentals, you should purchase the daily insurance from the rental company.

> **Tip:** If you have any problems with your rental car or wish to keep it longer than your agreement states, call the company's toll-free number. It's listed on your rental contract.

otherwise, when you return the car, the rental company might think *you* caused the damage, and they would charge you accordingly.

After you drive off the lot, you may decide, unexpectedly, that you would like to keep the car for another day or two. That's usually possible, but you must call the rental company and ask. (The rental contract, which you should keep with you, provides their toll-free number.) Be sure to ask what the additional costs will be.

What if the car has a flat tire or mechanical break down? You are *not* responsible. Call the company, and they will send someone to fix the flat or repair other small problems. If the problems cannot be fixed immediately, the company will pick you up, provide another rental car, and tow away the troublemaker. The best rental companies have a reputation for handling such problems efficiently.

One final point about car rentals, but a very important one: drive responsibly, just as you would with your own car. Don't speed or drive recklessly. Don't drink or use drugs and drive. It's too dangerous, for you and everyone else. Safety counts, no matter whose car you are driving.

Renting a Truck, Van, and Trailer

If you are moving, either across town or across the country, you probably need to rent something larger than a car. To pack all your books, furniture, and household items, you might need a truck or van, or perhaps a trailer that can be hitched to your car.

Several major companies specialize in rentals like these. The biggest are U-Haul, Penske, and Ryder. Some car rental companies, such as Enterprise and Budget, also rent trucks, vans, and trailers.

The bad news is that these trucks and vans cost more than rental cars, per day and per mile. The good news is that you can rent them if you are eighteen years old or older.

The rental procedures are similar to those for cars (described above), though the companies are certainly not as finicky about dings and scratches. The equipment is covered with them.

To get started, go online or visit a dealer to determine what kind of

> **Tip:** If you are moving during a busy season, like the end of the school year, you need to reserve your moving truck and equipment well in advance.

vehicle or trailer you need and what the prices are. Then reserve those items for specific dates and locations. For example, you might want a fourteen-foot truck, on May 16–17, to move from Austin, Texas, to Houston. If you are moving during a busy time, such as the end of the school year, you should make your reservations early.

The company will quote you a price, which, in this case, includes renting the truck in one location and dropping it off in another. The price includes a specific number of miles, which should be more than enough to make the trip. If you drive farther, you will pay a fixed price for each additional mile. Likewise, if you need to keep the truck longer, you can call and arrange it.

Be sure to ask who is eligible to drive the truck and who is legally responsible for any damage. Your car insurance probably does *not* cover moving equipment like this, although it's always a good idea to check. If your regular car insurance does not cover you, then ask the rental company what kinds of coverage they offer.

Companies like U-Haul and Ryder do more than rent trucks and trailers. They provide a full range of moving supplies. They sell cardboard boxes, in case you can't find enough free ones at local stores. They sell bags of foam "peanuts" to protect your ceramics and glassware. They rent heavy blankets and pads to protect your furniture from scratches. They rent baggage carts and hand trucks so you can move heavy items like refrigerators. They rent hitches and trailers so you can tow your car or motorcycle.[6] They even rent storage facilities in case you need extra space.[7]

The trucks themselves range from small pickups and to twenty-six-foot vans, big enough to move a four-bedroom household and tow your own

---

6. If you plan to tow a vehicle or a trailer packed with household goods, be sure your car or truck has enough horsepower for the job. Towing a heavy load with an undersized four-cylinder engine will rapidly destroy the engine and transmission.

If you are unsure how much weight your vehicle can comfortably tow, ask an experienced car dealer or a rental company like U-Haul. Since U-Haul, Ryder, and other companies spend all day renting hitches and trailers and trucks to pull them, they should be able to help you figure out what weight you can pull.

7. A number of chains provide clean, dry self-storage facilities. They compete on price, service, and location. You can find them in every city and even in smaller communities.

car behind it. You can drive these vehicles with a regular license. That is, they are not large enough to require a commercial driver's license (CDL).

Believe me, none of these trucks is luxurious. But they do generally come with an automatic transmission, a radio, and air conditioning.

Traffic Tickets

Whether you are driving a rental truck or your own car, you already know: police are out there lurking, waiting to give you a ticket if you accelerate past the speed limit or park too near a fire hydrant.

The best advice is to obey the traffic laws and, if you get a ticket anyway, to pay it promptly. In large cities, you can pay online. In smaller cities, you have to mail them a check.

If you think the ticket was *their* mistake, not yours, you can contest it in traffic court. For smaller tickets, you can do that on your own. You don't need a lawyer to explain you were only traveling forty miles an hour, well under the speed limit. But for more serious charges, like drunk driving, you should hire an attorney to represent you. You'll want one who specializes in traffic tickets, auto accidents, drivers' licenses, and DUI ("driving under the influence" of alcohol).

Two Types of Traffic Tickets

There are two types of traffic tickets: "parking" and "moving." The cost of parking tickets varies widely, by city and by violation. In a small town, you might pay $5 for staying too long at a meter. In a big city, you'll pay five times that amount, and far more if your car is towed.

You must pay these tickets promptly or you will accumulate overdue fees and additional fines. If you pile up a few hundred dollars in unpaid fines, the police will tow away your car or lock its wheels so you can't drive. (They use a clamp known as the "Denver boot," after the city that invented it.) To drive your vehicle again, you must clear up all the unpaid tickets, plus pay some additional fines and late fees.

Moving Violations

Moving violations, such as running a red light, are much more serious than parking tickets. They are expensive because the violations are so dangerous. Not only will you pay high fines, you will lose your license if you accumulate several of them.

> **Tip:** Moving violations are more serious than parking tickets. For a parking ticket, you pay a fine. For moving violations, you not only pay a fine, you may face jail and the loss of your license.

Most states measure your driving record by giving you "points" for each moving violation. (You don't lose any points for parking tickets.) The more serious the violation, the more points are deducted. Accumulate too many points and your license will be suspended or revoked.

There is one way to erase some of these points. You can attend traffic school. The sessions last about five hours and are devoted to safe driving. Not all states offer them, but many do.

After most moving violations, you pay your ticket but you don't need to appear in court. For more serious violations, however, you must appear before a judge, who will hear the case and impose a fine. If you fail to appear, the judge will issue a warrant for your arrest. Finally, after some especially dangerous violations, such as reckless driving, the police will take you into custody immediately unless you can post bond. (The bond amount differs in each jurisdiction, but it usually ranges from $100 to $400 for small infractions, more for serious violations.) The bond is to make sure you appear in court. If you do appear, the bond is returned to you. If you fail to appear, the bond is forfeited and an arrest warrant is issued.

Since drivers may not carry enough money to post cash bonds, they sometimes carry "bail bond cards" provided by their insurance companies. Members of the American Automobile Association (AAA) and Canadian Automobile Association (CAA) have membership cards that can be used as bonds (though not all jurisdictions accept them).

These bonding requirements are just one indication that moving violations are treated seriously. They can lead to large fines, jail time, court hearings, and loss of driving privileges. These sanctions should be reason enough to obey the traffic laws. But they are not the most important one. The main reason to obey the traffic laws is to keep yourself, your loved ones, and everyone else on the highways safe.

> **Tip:** After some moving violations, such as racing on the highway, drivers may be taken to jail and released only after posting bond. After several moving violations, drivers' licenses will be suspended temporarily or revoked entirely.

Car Accidents

If you are in an accident, *call 911 immediately if there are any injuries.* If the accident is only minor and no one is injured, call the regular (nonemergency) police number.

When an officer arrives to investigate, it is your responsibility to obey instructions and provide any information requested. You may be asked to take a "Breathalyzer" test to determine if you are sober. You can refuse to take the test, but, if you do, the legal presumption is that you were drunk.

If you are in an accident, it's important to get some basic information at the scene. You should write down the name of the investigating officer and the number of the police report. You'll need those when you contact your insurance company.

It's a good idea to exchange information with the other driver: names, driver's license numbers, license plates, insurance companies, and insurance policy numbers. You should *not* discuss the amount of your insurance coverage or what type of coverage you have. Announcing that you have $1 million in personal injury coverage is a good way to get sued for $1 million. Try to be as calm and courteous as possible. Your insurance company certainly hopes you don't admit the accident was your fault. That apology could add to their financial liability—and yours.

If you think the other driver was at fault, take some pictures to show what happened. They will buttress your case later.

If your car is too damaged to drive away from the accident, then you need to be towed. The police may come with their own tow truck, or you may have to call one yourself.

It's a good idea to speak with your insurance company first. They need to know about the accident as soon as possible. They can also give you valuable information, like whether your policy covers towing and whether it provides a rental car while yours is being repaired. If your insurance policy includes towing, be sure to follow the insurance company's instructions. They will tell you how far the car can be towed, for example, and perhaps which tow truck operator to use.

Even if your insurance does not cover towing, it will be covered if you are a member of AAA or CAA. That benefit is one reason why drivers join.

Tip: If you are in an accident, call your car insurance company right away. They can often advise you on what to do immediately.

If you need towing or other minor assistance, such as fixing a flat tire, call their number and they will dispatch a truck.

Actually, your car may need to be towed twice. The first time is to get it off the road and into a safe location, such as a fenced-in lot. The second time, a few days later, you will have to move it to a good repair shop—ideally, one that specializes in models like yours. In the days after the accident, you'll have time to find a repair shop.

Fill 'er up: Buying Gasoline

Driving means visiting the gas station. Not so long ago, stations used to check your oil and tires, clean your windshield, and fill up your car. Those halcyon days are gone. Now, "full service" means little more than having a desultory clerk fill your tank while you pay an extra dime per gallon for the privilege.

Self-service means doing everything yourself. The rules are simple. You pay first. You can go inside the station and give the attendant $10 or $20 and say, "I'm at pump number 5." Or you can swipe your credit card or debit card at the pump itself. Then you fill the tank and try not to spill gas on your new shoes. If you are unsure what to do, just ask the customer at the next pump.

Some stations also offer car washes. Again, you can pay at the pump or inside the station. If you want to check your tire pressure (it's a good idea to do so periodically), then you're on your own. Most gas stations have a coin-operated machine where you can put air in the tires, but you'll need to buy a tire-pressure gauge from an auto-supply store.

You should change your oil regularly, at least every 3,000 miles. The cheapest way to do that is at places like Jiffy Lube or Oil Express. Every town has them. You can drive in without an appointment.

For more extensive checkups, say every 10,000 miles, you should return to your dealer. Make an appointment several days in advance. These appointments can take several hours, so bring something to read, perhaps one of Tolstoy's longer novels.

> **Tip:** Most drivers fill up their own cars at the gas station. You pay first, either at the pump (with a credit or debit card) or inside the station (with a card or cash). You should check your tire pressure occasionally and have your oil changed regularly.

You may also need to visit your dealer for tune-ups and pollution controls. Both Canada and the United States require cars, trucks, and SUVs to pass regular "vehicle emission tests." You will be sent notices every few years telling you to bring in your car for tests. If you don't pass, your car must be repaired and retested. That's where the dealer comes in.

Drive Sober, Drive Safe

One final but crucial point: always drive sober. Even a couple of drinks slows your reaction time and degrades your skill behind the wheel. More drinks or drugs only make the problems worse.

If you're going to a party and expect to drink, you should think about how you will get home. Take a bus or taxi. Or ask a friend to avoid alcohol and act as the "designated driver." Whatever the solution, don't get behind the wheel after you've had several drinks.

"Driving under the influence" is a serious crime precisely because it's so dangerous. If you are caught, the consequences are severe. You can lose your license and go to jail. Your insurance costs will skyrocket. And, of course, you are far more likely to be involved in a serious accident.

Tip: Don't drink and drive. Ever.

Chapter 19

University Housing
and Meals

There's a world of difference between living in a nice place in a safe neighborhood, close to campus, and living in a shabby apartment in a dangerous neighborhood, isolated from your friends.

Before choosing any living arrangements, you should review your budget and decide what you can afford. Consider the price range for student apartments and find out what your rent money buys in different neighborhoods. How nice are the units in various price ranges? What kinds of neighborhoods are they in? How convenient are they for your school work and social life?

Finding a Place to Live in Three Stages: Temporary Housing, Your First Year, and Longer Term

It's impossible to answer all these housing questions when you've just unpacked your bags, before you really know the city. How can you possibly compare neighborhoods and prices? That's why it's helpful to think about housing issues in three stages. The first is when you arrive in town. During the first few weeks, before classes begin, you'll need temporary housing as you search for a more permanent place and perhaps for roommates. The second stage is when you lease your first place and move in. Once you have lived there for a year or so, you'll have a much better sense of the entire area—your own neighborhood and others—and the options they afford. You'll know where your friends and classmates live, where the good restaurants and entertainment are, and how important it is for you to be near campus—or to get away from it each night. You'll know the transportation options for each area. That brings us to the third stage, when you

> **Tip:** There are three stages in finding a place to live:
>
> - temporary housing for the first week or two after you arrive,
> - a room or apartment for the first year, as you settle into your new surroundings, and
> - longer-term housing after you know the area well.

make longer-term housing decisions, based on your greater knowledge. You may decide to keep your apartment, move to another one nearby, or move to a different neighborhood entirely. You may decide to continue living with the same roommates or look for different ones. In any case, you'll have a much clearer sense of your alternatives.

By the time you reach this third stage, you'll have enough solid information to make good housing choices. So I'll concentrate here on the first two stages: temporary accommodations and your first apartment.

Temporary Accommodations

The key to finding temporary housing is to communicate with the international students office in advance. You should contact them long before you board the plane, and you should remain in contact. Tell them your tentative arrival date and, if you need temporary housing, ask for their advice.

Some students don't need short-term housing. They have friends at the university and will stay with them as they search for a place to live. Or they don't need it because they will live in a dormitory. They have already returned the necessary paperwork and been assigned a room.

If you plan to live in a dorm, you still need to know when your room becomes available. A few dorms stay open year round, but most close for the summer and reopen a week or two before classes begin. What if you plan to arrive a month early? Can you move into your dorm room, or will you need a temporary place to stay? You need to know. There are probably rooms on campus for students who need short-term housing before school. But don't assume that rooms are available. Ask before you travel.

Speak with the international students office several weeks before you arrive and ask specifically about temporary accommodations. They should be able to help you avoid the high costs of staying in a hotel as you look for an apartment or wait for your dorm to open. If you can't find temporary housing on campus, consider an inexpensive alternative like a youth hostel. Again, the international student adviser's office will know. Work with them.

> *Tip:* Before you arrive, you should maintain close contact with the international students office. If they know when you are coming, they can help arrange temporary housing, probably in a dorm.

The same advice applies to winter break. Many dorms close in December, after the end of the autumn semester. If you plan to arrive then, or you are already enrolled but plan to remain on campus, then it's vital to check with the international student adviser or the University Housing Office.

Dorms as First-Year Housing

What about housing for your first year here? For undergraduates, the best option is unquestionably a dorm room. Most residential universities (as opposed to commuter schools) require undergraduates to live on campus for the first year or two, although they make exceptions for those who are older or married.

Why does the university want new undergraduates to live on campus? For several reasons, aside from the rental income it generates. Living on campus helps students connect with their classmates and make new friends. It provides them with a full range of services, including food. It allows university staff to keep an eye on students as they adjust to university life. And it allows the staff to communicate easily and informally with those who need help.

Dorm advisers and resident assistants or resident aides (RAs) can watch out for students, because they live in the dorms themselves. That means RAs are nearby to listen to student problems, arrange some social activities, and offer practical advice—without being too intrusive.

RAs are on hand to talk informally with students and assist them with everyday problems, such as homesickness or unruly roommates. Since RAs live close to the students, they can spot problems early, such as a student who won't eat or won't leave her room. When they see problems like these, or when students ask them for help, they might offer some advice or direct them to professional resources on campus.

RAs are *not* trained psychological counselors, like those at the medical center or student mental health center. (I explain these medical services in chapter 22, "Health Care.") What RAs can do is listen to your concerns, offer informal advice, and steer you to the right resources on campus, perhaps the dean's office or health clinic.

RAs are closely connected to these resources because they are part of

Tip: For new undergraduates, dorms are the best idea and are required by many schools.

the university's larger arrangements for student housing, services, and activities. These arrangements vary from campus to campus, but most are supervised by a dean with overall responsibility for student life. The goal is to integrate dorm living with all the other services provided to students.

Graduate student dorms are another part of this system. They don't have resident assistants, because the students are older, more experienced, and more self-sufficient. Even so, many graduate students say that dorms provide valuable services and are a good choice for incoming students. That's particularly true for international students who are learning their way around a new country and adjusting to a new educational style.

The Advantages and Disadvantages of Dorm Living

Dorms have three advantages for international graduate students. The first is location. They are either on campus or very close, so you never have to worry about commuting or parking. You can concentrate on your studies and meeting fellow students. That brings us to the second advantage. University housing provides a ready-made social environment, a supportive place to make friends from the United States, Canada, and around the world. I know lots of international students who have lived in dorms, and all of them say how many good friends they made there. Finally, it's a simple, easy place to eat, sleep, study, and hang out. You don't have to hunt for an apartment in the first place, and you don't have to worry if the heat breaks down in mid-January. It's all taken care of.

The downside is that you don't have as much space or privacy as you do in an apartment. You might prefer to live in another neighborhood, away from campus. There might be cost differences, too. You'll want to consider these trade-offs when you choose whether to live on campus or off.

If you do want to live in a dorm, be sure to ask what options the university has. Can you choose among several dorms? What makes one different from another? Are some popular with international students? Do men and women live in the same dorm, perhaps on the same floor? Is there a convenient place to park?

At most universities, the dorms are coed. Not long ago, that was unheard of. Now it's commonplace. Men and women live on the same floor and

Tip: For new international graduate students, dorms have several advantages. The location is great. The services and upkeep are provided. And it's an easy place to meet other students and make friends. On the other side of the ledger, the rooms don't have as much space or privacy as some students want.

may even share the same bathroom. That can be disconcerting for some, especially for international students who grew up with greater separation between the sexes. For others, it's perfectly fine. In any case, you should know about arrangements like these when you consider dorm life. If you have any concerns, just ask what options are available. You may be able to find an all-male or all-female dorm if you prefer, but you'll need to ask.

You'll also want to ask about the cost and lease arrangements. What if you change your mind after a few months and want to live elsewhere? Can you do that? Or are you committed to a lease that lasts for the entire school year, as you would be in a regular apartment? You will undoubtedly have questions of your own, and it's worth asking them before you make a decision.

Campus Meal Plans

You should also ask about the meal plan. The first question is: are students who live in dorms required to buy some meals in the dining halls? These arrangements vary considerably from school to school. Some require students who live in dorms to buy as many as two meals a day; others have no requirements at all.

Most universities offer students a range of meal plans. One student may want to purchase only five meals a week. Another wants fourteen. An increasingly popular way to satisfy these varied preferences is by using "flex dollars." Students deposit cash with the registrar and, in return, receive flex dollars to buy meals or snacks whenever they want. The funds are accessed through the student's ID card, which works like a debit card on campus. In fact, it is sometimes called a "campus cash card."

The campus dining hall is undoubtedly the least expensive place to eat unless you have a kitchen and enough time to prepare meals yourself. There's a social side to eating in the dining halls, too. Because people sit at large tables, they're a good place to meet new people and get together with old friends.

Complaining about dining hall food is a favorite subject, but the complaints are a bit overcooked. Dorm food is hardly three-star cuisine, but it has steadily improved. There is now more variety, more ethnic foods, and more salads, fruits, and other healthy options. Options that were once rare, like vegetarian or vegan meals, are now commonplace. So are meals designed to meet religious needs, like kosher meals for observant Jews and halal meals for Muslims. Still, not every dining hall offers these options, so it's wise to ask.

Questions to Ask about Campus Meal Plans

Before signing up for a campus meal plan, you'll want to understand the costs and options. Here are some questions to ask.

- What are the minimum requirements? That is, do you have to eat at least five or ten meals on campus each week? Or do you have to buy a minimum number of flex dollars for meals?
- Beyond that, what options do you have? For example, does the university offer plans with five, ten, or fourteen meals per week? What options are available for breakfast? If you want a quick snack, can you get it as part of the plan?
- Can you eat at any dining hall or only one or two? Can you eat at one near your classes, lab, or dorm? In other words, how convenient will it be for you to eat on campus?
- If you have special dietary requirements, can you meet them in the dining halls? Some students want vegetarian or vegan meals, for instance, while others want kosher or halal. The offerings may be great, lousy, or nonexistent. If these options matter to you, then you need to ask about them.
- Is the food tasty? Is there much variety?
- What do the various plans cost?

> *Tip:* If you are thinking about living on campus, ask about the dining options and whether you are required to purchase a meal plan. If you are, see if the plan fits your needs.

Married Student Housing

Most universities have special housing options for married students. These are not dorms. They are regular apartments, owned by the university. They do have one thing in common with dorms, though. The residents are all connected with the university and have a variety of shared interests—education, travel, children, and more. The housing provides a welcoming community for newcomers and an easy way to meet other student families and form friendships in a new country. All in all, this may be the best choice for married international students in their first year and perhaps for their entire stay.

In fact, married student housing is so attractive that, on many campuses, it is oversubscribed. There are too few apartments for the families who want to live in them. If you are interested in this option, then it's important ask about it as soon as possible. If you like what you hear, put your family's name on the waiting list immediately.

> *Tip:* Many universities rent apartments to married students. The location is usually convenient, and the apartments offer a simple, easy way to meet other couples and families. Because there may be a waiting list for these apartments, you should find out about them as soon as possible and, if you are interested, immediately put your name on the waiting list.

Chapter 20

Apartment Rentals

Even if you don't live in a dorm or university apartment, your school can provide valuable help as you seek housing. Most universities have a housing office with two branches. One deals with dorms and university-owned properties, the other with privately owned apartments off campus. You should work closely with them as you search for a place to live.

The university housing office is a central location that collects information about the local housing market and helps students navigate it. From years of experience, they know which areas are safe and convenient. They know what renters can expect for their money in different neighborhoods and price ranges.

The housing office can help you compare the costs of living in a dorm and living in an apartment. They'll know which landlords are more reliable and which ones you should avoid. They'll know which brokers and agents to deal with. They collect ads for local units and can suggest which ones to look at first. They don't rent apartments themselves, other than the university's own housing, but they can guide you to places that do.

The housing office can help in another way. Most of them collect student requests to find roommates. (By the way, the advertisements for roommates and apartments use lots of abbreviations. I'll help you decode these ads in appendix 2, "Abbreviations, Acronyms, Nicknames, Holidays, Floor Numbering, and Clothing Sizes.")

With so much information and expertise on hand, the university housing office should be the first place you go if you want to rent a place off campus.

Let me pass along some basic advice to complement the suggestions from your university housing office.

> *Tip:* For new graduate students, the most important housing decision is whether to live in a dorm or an apartment off campus. It's important to understand the options and the costs before you choose. That information is available from your university's housing office.

The Value of a Good Location

The three most important things in real estate, according to an old joke, are location, location, and location. That's why many students live on campus, and it's a major consideration if you live elsewhere. Location means more than proximity to the university. It also means neighborhood safety, the availability of stores, groceries, and restaurants. If you have children, it means the quality of local schools and playgrounds.

Location also means access to transportation. Even if an apartment is far from school, it could still be convenient if parking is easy or local buses run directly to campus. I speak from hard-won experience. I once lived in a great place but had to walk several blocks to the subway and then transfer from one line to another. It took about forty-five minutes to get to school and another forty-five minutes to return. It was daily agony. You are welcome to learn from my mistake.

Looking at Apartments

When you look at apartments, be a little skeptical. Run the water in the shower. Is it strong and steady, or does it dribble out? Flush the toilet. Turn on the stove. Open the windows. Ask if the unit is already wired for broadband and cable TV. Listen to how noisy the unit is. Is there much soundproofing between the rooms and between apartments? Does street noise seep into the building, ready to interrupt your studies or your sleep?

If you are seriously considering a particular unit, ask others in the building what they like about it and what they don't like. Ask what they think about the landlord. It's especially important to inquire about things that are hard to discover for yourself, like whether the heating and air conditioning work well and whether repairs are made promptly. Ask residents about the neighborhood's safety and whether there have been crimes recently in the building or nearby. Police cars with lights flashing in front of the building are a bad sign.

Tip: Before you rent a unit, check on the details, from plumbing to parking. Check on noise and traffic at various times, not just when the rental agent shows you the apartment. If you are seriously considering a place, speak with others who live in the building. Ask what they like and don't like. Ask about things that are difficult to observe for yourself. And be sure to ask about the landlord.

If you have time, return after dark and see what the area is like. After all, you won't live there only in the daytime.

Leases: What You Need to Know about Renting an Apartment

The lease itself is a long and forbidding document. A nonlawyer (like me) can't fathom the technical language. That means I am *not* giving legal advice here. In fact, lawyers themselves find it hard to give general advice about renting because, as one told me, "Real estate laws are *extremely local.*" Another said, "I cannot emphasize enough how the specifics will vary from place to place." They vary from Maine to California, from city to city, and, of course, from Canada to the United States.

Still, if you are going to sign a lease, you need to know what your basic obligations are and what you'll receive in return. You should be able to figure that out, even though it's obscured by pages of legal boilerplate. What really matters are a dozen or so key elements, which should be comprehensible. You need to understand them before you sign on the dotted line.

Here are the most important clauses in any lease, beginning with the financial ones:

Clause in rental agreement	Questions and comments
Monthly rent	Straightforward
Day of the month when rent is due	Some dates may be more convenient for you than others. If you receive funds on the first day of each month, for example, you might prefer to pay the rent a couple of days later, after your check has been deposited and cleared. The landlord might be willing to change this date in the lease.
Number of grace days to make late payments; penalties when you pay later than that	If the rent is due on the first day of the month, you might not incur penalties if it is paid before, say, the third or the fifth. Different leases give different grace periods. Even so, you should pay on time. Do not pay late routinely.

Security deposit	Do you need to give the landlord a security deposit to cover any damage that might occur to the unit? If so, how much is the deposit and who holds it? In most areas, there is a standard amount, and you should know what it is. In some cities, it's a month's rent; in others, it's a half-month. Whatever the amount, your deposit should be returned promptly at the end of the lease *if* you leave the apartment in good condition.
Broker's fee	Do you owe anything to the broker or agent who listed the apartment and showed it to you? Or is that already included in the rent?
Payment for the last month of the lease	Do you need to pay the last month's rent (or a half month's rent) in advance, when you sign the lease? That payment comes in addition to the first month's rent. Legally, you cannot use the security deposit as the final month's rent, but it's not uncommon for renters to try.
Initial payment upon signing the lease	All rentals require the first month's rent in advance. If they also demand a security deposit and the last month's rent, you would owe *three* months' rent when you sign the lease. That's a large sum, but it's standard in some markets, such as Boston. You'll need to have the cash in your bank account.
Cosigner or guarantor	Do you need someone to sign in addition to you and your roommates to guarantee payment? Some rentals not only require a cosigner, they require someone who lives locally and has good credit. Remember, unless the lease says otherwise, everybody who signs is individually responsible for the entire rent.
Utilities	Does the rent already include gas, electricity, water, and perhaps cable TV? Which utilities are included, and which ones are not?
Length of agreement	Does the lease run for an entire year or only for nine months (the school year)? Sometimes, landlords offer a choice, but they charge more per month for six- or nine-month leases.
Early termination	Although a lease may run for a year, it might also contain a provision for early termination, either by the tenant or the landlord. Normally, these require thirty or sixty days' written notice. Some leases have this termination provision; others don't. Check to see what terms are in your lease.

Occupancy date	When can you move in?
Number of people permitted to live in the apartment	Can you have only one roommate? Or can you have three or four if you wish?
Sublet rights	If you wish to move out during the summer or leave before the end of the lease, can you sublet the unit to other tenants? Or are you stuck with the full payment yourself? If you sublet the unit, you still have important legal responsibilities. First, you may need the landlord's approval for the people to whom you sublet. Second, if they damage the apartment or fail to pay the rent, you are ultimately responsible. To protect yourself, you may want to ask for a security deposit from the people who are subletting.
Children	In most cases, rentals cannot prohibit children, but there are some exceptions. If this affects you, be sure to check.
Pets	Rentals *can* prohibit pets. Some leases do, others don't. If pets violate the lease, don't try to sneak Rover or Fluffy in. You could lose the apartment, along with your security deposit.
Furnishing	Does the apartment include any furniture or do you need to purchase everything yourself?
Refrigerator	A refrigerator is normally included in the apartment and is not considered furnishing. But you need to make sure, since it's an expensive item. Check the refrigerator's quality when you view the unit.

Signing a Lease

When you are ready to sign a lease, you should ask for a copy to examine *before you sign.* It helps to have a day or so to review the important clauses. You should clearly understand the items I've listed. They are the guts of the lease. If you need any help figuring them out, ask the university

> *Tip:* Don't sign a lease until you've reviewed it and understand the key elements, listed above. When you do sign, remember that your initial payment can be very large, as much as three months' rent. Be sure you have the funds available. Remember, too, that everyone who signs the lease can be held legally responsible for the entire rent.

> **Tip:** Any changes to the lease should be made in writing. All parties to the lease need to agree and initial each change.

housing office or the broker who showed you the unit. You shouldn't need a lawyer unless you are buying a place or the rental is very complicated or unusual.

Sometimes, you'll need to change the wording of a specific clause before you sign the lease. First, everybody needs to agree. Then you need to write the changes on the lease. It's not enough to agree over the phone, or even in person. All changes should be in writing, and each one should be initialed by all the parties, including the landlord.

Here's an example, showing the standard way to do that (using arbitrary initials for the renter and landlord). In this case, the standard lease begins on September 1, 2008. We have agreed that it should begin on September 15:

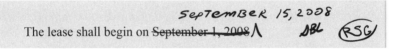

Some communities have passed laws governing landlord-tenant relations. It's worth checking to see if yours is one. The laws are normally attached to the lease itself and cover general items such as whether security deposits should receive interest payments.

When you're ready to sign the lease, you need to bring along immigration documents to show you are in the country legally. Some brokers might want to see these documents before they show you the apartment. Of course, you should also bring your checkbook. The first payment is due when you sign the lease.

Occasionally, renters lease their apartments without written agreements at all. That's called by various names, such as "month-to-month tenancy." The landlord and tenant agree on the price and the move-in date, but, beyond that, their relations are governed by local laws. For example, the law may permit either party to end the tenancy by giving thirty days' written notice.[1] If the landlord and tenant had a written lease, they could agree

---

1. Giving thirty days' written notice is not as straightforward as it sounds. To begin with, it doesn't really mean thirty days. It usually means I must give notice in the calendar month before the lease will end. If I want the last rental month to be October, then I must give notice during September.

on different terms, perhaps sixty days' notice or no right to cancel at all. Without a lease, though, they are bound by local laws on such matters.

Roommates

If you want roommates, or you need them to share the rent, check the notices around campus and post your own, online and on bulletin boards. Tell everyone you know and talk with the housing office, which may help you find potential roommates. Although the international students office is not the housing office, they may know other students who are looking for a place to live, and they might have a bulletin board for notices. The university housing office certainly will.

In choosing roommates, the crucial issues, aside from ability to pay, are reliability and compatibility. Can you count on your new roommates to do what they say they will? Can you rely on them to shoulder their fair share of the responsibilities, everything from cleaning the dishes to vacuuming the floor?

Spend as much time as you can with potential roommates before deciding whether to room together. People can be great friends but not great roommates, and vice versa. For most of us, it doesn't matter if a friend likes to play loud music at home and leaves the place a mess. It matters a lot in a roommate. Your friends might love to stay up late, partying, talking, and drinking every night. That could be exactly what you want in a roommate. Or it could be exactly what you want to avoid. It helps to discuss these issues plainly, in advance, before you choose someone to room with.

Your ability to communicate will also serve you well later, after you've moved in together. The willingness to talk about issues, to approach them in friendly rather than confrontational ways, and to seek resolutions, rather than brooding silently or complaining to others, is vital to living together comfortably as roommates.

Besides a willingness to talk about issues and reach compromises, the key to living with roommates is everyone's willingness to do their share, and do it without griping.

> *Tip:* Good roommates should be reliable and compatible. They don't necessarily have to be close friends. They do have to be willing to talk about problems and work toward joint solutions.

Setting Up Your Place

Once you have rented an apartment, you'll want to make it comfortable to live in. That means a trip to the furniture store for a bed, sofa, desk, and chair; the hardware store for paint and appliances; and perhaps the computer store for a new printer. You probably brought your laptop from home. If not, you'll want to shop for one online or see if the university has special deals. Other students will know the best places to buy sturdy, inexpensive furniture. Be sure to ask about delivery and set-up charges. One of the most ominous phrases in the English language is "Some assembly required."

As for appliances, don't bother lugging anything on the plane. Toasters, coffee pots, irons, and even microwaves are so cheap you should buy them here. The only expensive appliance is a vacuum cleaner, but you really do need one. Your place won't clean itself. You might as well buy it immediately, because that's when the dust starts to pile up.

None of these items will work unless you turn on the electricity. Seems obvious. Actually, it's not so obvious. Unless utilities are included in the rent, it's your responsibility to call and set up service for electricity, gas, water, phone, and cable TV.

Many renters forget that detail until they arrive in the apartment. That's when they discover they can't turn on the lights or cook on the stove. It may take several days to turn on the gas and electricity and a week or more to install cable or DSL. That's why you should speak with the utility companies as soon as you sign the lease. Let them know the date you will be moving in and arrange to have service begin at that time. They will work with you to set up your account. If you don't have a credit history, they might require a security deposit. That's standard.

> **Tip:** Contact the utility companies as soon as you sign the lease. Set up your account and arrange to have electricity, gas, water, phone, and cable service begin the day you move in.

Safety First

Another item deserves immediate attention: smoke detectors. Intuitively, it seems that a hot, smoky fire ought to wake you up. But it won't . . . until it's too late. That's why smoke detectors are essential. Install new batteries

> **Tip:** It's vital to have working smoke detectors. Make sure you have one either in your bedroom or nearby, and be sure to change the batteries twice a year.

in them when you move in and remember to change them each autumn and spring. If you don't already have a smoke detector in your bedroom or nearby in the hallway, buy one right away. They're cheap, and they're essential.

Give Your Neighbor a Key

We all get locked out of our houses sometimes. It's a good idea to swap keys with a friend or neighbor who you know and trust.

Renter's Insurance and Security Alarms

You might want to buy renter's insurance. It's inexpensive and protects you against losses from fire or theft. It also covers damage you might do to someone else's property. That's not very likely, but it could happen if, say, your bathtub overflowed and the water spilled into the apartment below. It also covers you if someone slips in your apartment and sues you for a broken leg. For about $12–$15 a month, you get $20,000–$30,000 in coverage for losses, and another $250,000 or more in liability coverage.

Make sure the insurance covers your laptop. You might need to list it separately on the policy. In fact, you might want to insure your computer even if you don't want to insure your whole apartment. Companies like Safeware.com sell coverage against theft, accidental damage, power surges, and more. For a new laptop, annual coverage costs about $70.

If you own expensive electronics, furnishings, or jewelry, you not only need insurance, you might want a security alarm. You may be able to set up a simple one yourself, but more elaborate systems need professional installation. In either case, you need to pay a company to monitor the system. If the alarm goes off because of an intruder, fire, or malfunction, the system will call the monitoring company automatically. They, in turn, will call you to see if everything's okay. If you say "no," or if they don't receive an answer, they will call the police. You have to pay each month for that monitoring service.

If you install a security alarm, make sure a trusted neighbor has the code and a key to your apartment. That's important because you might not

> ***Tip:*** Give a trusted neighbor a key to your apartment, in case there's an emergency or you are locked out. If you install a security alarm, be sure your neighbor has the code and a key to let the police in, if necessary.

be at home when the alarm goes off. A neighbor can shut off the alarm and let the police into the apartment, if necessary.

The Most Important Spot in Your Apartment (And No, It's Not Your Bed)

Since you've come here to study, the most important part of your apartment is the space where you do that. Try to find a quiet spot for your desk, computer and printer, and possibly a reading chair. Don't shortchange yourself here. If you intend to work at home, you need a good place to do it.

You should set up your workplace as soon as you move in—the desk, bookcase, and whatever else you need. If there are several electric outlets nearby, that's great. If not, buy a surge protector with an extension cord and multiple outlets. If you are using Wi-Fi, set that up right away. Be sure to install a security firewall, with password encryption. If you rely on hardwiring, be sure your desk is near the DSL or cable wall connections. If you plan to do a lot of reading at home, buy a good reading chair. It's a splurge, but it's worth it.

As long as you're setting up a study space at home, try to find a good one on campus, too. That will probably be in the library, in an area used by friends from your department. When you're ready to take a break, you'll find classmates nearby. But be wary—at school and at home—of study spaces that morph into social spaces. To do serious work, you need a quiet place to read, write, and reflect without interruptions and distractions.

> ***Tip:*** You *must* set up a study space in your apartment and find a quiet place on campus to study regularly. Do both by the end of your first week in school.

Chapter 21

Kids and Family

Housing choices are intimately linked to your family situation. If you are married, you can't live in ordinary dorms, though you may be able to move into university-owned apartments. Many universities offer these units to same-sex couples as well.

School Choices for Children

School and preschool are leading considerations for all families with children. Elementary school begins with first grade, around age six. It is free to everyone, including the children of international students and academic visitors. Citizenship or permanent residence is *not* required.

What is required, by law, is that you send your child to school. There are several options:

- public schools, paid for by taxpayers and available free to local residents;
- private schools, paid for by parents and private contributions;
- parochial or religious schools, paid for by parents and religious charities; and
- home schooling, paid for by parents, who teach their children at home.

In recent years, some parents have opted to educate their children at home, either because they are unhappy with school quality or because they want to give their children more religious and moral instruction. This home schooling is subject to local standards governing all education.

Younger children almost always go to neighborhood schools. Unfortunately, the quality of these schools varies dramatically, not only from city

Tip: The quality of local schools varies dramatically and often depends on where you live. If you have children, you should investigate the schools they would attend before choosing a place to live.

to city but also within them. There might be an excellent school on 57th Street and a terrible one on 67th Street.

The implication is clear: if you have children, you should look carefully at the quality of local schools and consider them when you choose a neighborhood.

How can you know which schools are good? As a rule of thumb, wealthier towns and neighborhoods have nicer schools. That's true because the kids come to school better prepared and because richer communities can devote more resources to education. Prosperous suburbs use local taxes to pay for first-rate schools. But there is considerable variation. It is important to talk with other parents, the international student adviser, and the staff at your university's housing office, which should know the terrain.

When you speak with them, ask about "magnet schools" and "charter schools." Both are public schools that recruit students from beyond their neighborhoods and are empowered to develop specialized curricula. They might emphasize math and science, for instance, or the arts.

Magnet schools usually restrict admission to top students, who must pass entrance exams or meet other stringent criteria. This makes them attractive to gifted, highly motivated children who thrive on challenging courses.

Charter schools are an effort to create more educational choice and greater competition within the public school system and to give educators more flexibility in hiring staff and developing curricula. Unlike elite magnet schools, charter schools do not require entrance tests. Instead, they have to compete with ordinary neighborhood schools, which are required to educate all children.

To determine which schools are best for your child and your family, you need to go well beyond these general descriptions. You need to find out much more about the schools in your neighborhood and city. That's why it is so important to talk with other parents and knowledgeable university staff. Since the best schools may not have many openings, it helps to begin these conversations as soon as possible.

Documents Needed to Enroll Your Child in School

To enroll your children in school, you need to show their birth date, their school records, and proof of immunization against major diseases. A passport or birth certificate will show their age. If they attended school in your home country, you should bring a copy of their school records. You may need to translate these records into English (or French in Québec) so local school officials can understand what preparation your children already have. Finally, check with the local school district to find out which immunizations they require. Standard ones include measles, mumps, rubella, tetanus, and diphtheria. Some schools now require polio vaccinations. International students may need to show that their children don't have tuberculosis. (These vaccinations and tests are discussed in chapter 22, "Health Care.") The common theme is that all these diseases are highly contagious. If one child is infected, all the others are at risk.

Preschool

Although standard schooling starts around age six, many communities offer free "preschool." The most common option is kindergarten for children who will start elementary school the following year. Some communities provide it free, as an adjunct to public schooling. Others do not. Nursery school, for younger children, is not part of the public schools and must be paid for by parents. It might be considered "educational daycare."

Not all nursery schools have the same daily schedule. Some hold one session in the morning and another in the afternoon. Others take children for the entire day. If you want your child to attend nursery school, you'll want to investigate these options.

> *Tip:* Regular schooling for children starts with first grade, around age six, and requires proof of age and immunization. Children do *not* have to be citizens to attend free public schools. Some school systems—but not all—provide free schooling for children in the year before first grade (kindergarten). Again, the children of international students are eligible.

Daycare

Daycare for infants and toddlers comes in many forms, all of it paid for by parents. Most communities have a variety of nursery schools and countless private baby-sitters. There has been increasing pressure on universities to provide their own childcare services, but it hasn't always yielded results. Faculty, staff, and students need childcare that is convenient, stimulating, and well supervised. The problem is cost, and, not surprisingly, universities are reluctant to provide large subsidies. As a result, many universities don't provide any childcare at all. For those that do, parents bear most of the costs.

Location, cost, hours of operation, and quality of care are all major considerations in choosing nursery schools and daycare. A convenient location depends on where you live and study. You might want to drive to a prospective daycare center to see just how easy (or difficult) it is to get there. Do it at times you actually expect to drop off and pick up your child.

You'll also want to compare the costs and quality of different daycare options. The best information undoubtedly comes from other parents. Ask the parents you meet—not just international students but all parents. Besides speaking with parents individually, speak with support groups for parents and student spouses. Most universities have them, and they are an excellent source of information. So are members of your local church, synagogue, or mosque. Finally, speak with the human resources office or benefits office at your university. They should know about daycare options at the university and in the community. (The international students office doesn't usually handle these issues, but they may have some information and know the names of other parents to contact.)

As you learn about good daycare centers, call them and arrange an interview. Ask about how many children are supervised by each staff member and what kinds of training and degrees staff members have. Ask about children's activities and whether they ever go to playgrounds, museums, and events away from the daycare center. Check on the different plans they offer, such as half-day and full-day care, discuss their cost, and ask when openings might be available. If possible, stay and observe the childcare they actually provide.

Tip: Before first grade, children may attend nursery school, then kindergarten. Nursery schools are private. Parents must select and pay for them themselves. Some kindergartens are part of free public schools; other are private. Most universities do not provide preschool care, but some do. Again, parents have to bear most of the cost.

> **Tip:** Other parents are the best source of information about daycare. They may also be willing to swap some baby-sitting chores with you.

Private baby-sitting is relatively expensive, and most student families cannot afford much of it. Some student spouses offer to baby-sit, usually because they are already watching a child of their own. Others swap services informally. "I'll take your daughter this afternoon if you can take mine tomorrow." With so many young parents around, there are plenty of opportunities to help each other.

Student Spouses: Coping with Loneliness and Social Isolation

One of the most vexing issues for international student families is the spouse's isolation and loneliness, far from friends and family. While the student is busy with classwork assignments, labs, and exams, what is the husband or wife to do?

In most cases, it is the husband who is in school, making connections with fellow students. Meanwhile, his wife stays at home, looking for friends and activities and often tending to a young child. It's a recipe for loneliness and unhappiness—for the spouse and for the whole family. There's an American T-shirt (and a country music song) that makes the point, "If mama ain't happy, ain't nobody happy." The grammar may be bad, but it's the thought that counts.

This is not just a problem for international students. Spouses of local students face the same isolation, especially if they are young parents. But they have some marked advantages. They know the language. They don't have to deal with visa restrictions on working. And, if they are from the area, they may already have family and friends to help them.

Given the difficulties, what solutions work best for spouses of international students? First, study English as a second language. Without some ability to negotiate your new world in English, you are trapped. You can associate only with people who speak your native language. It's great to have friends who speak Chinese, Hindi, or Arabic, but it's limiting to have *only* those friends. The ESL class itself is an opportunity to get out of the house, meet new people, and engage in a new and challenging activity. (For more, see chapter 12, "Learning the Language.")

Second, if you are eligible to work, look for a job that is stimulating and offers opportunities to make social connections. If your budget gives you some flexibility, you might be willing to make a little less money if the job itself is more interesting.

Third, reach out to other student spouses. When you do, follow the advice I gave earlier: don't limit yourself to families from your home country. You will find that many other student families have just moved here, too. They are looking to forge new friendships, just as you are. They want to meet you as much as you want to meet them.

Fourth, if you have children, try to arrange some time for yourself. That means getting regular childcare, perhaps at a nursery school or perhaps by swapping baby-sitting duties with other parents. A little time off is vital for your social life—and your mental health. When you do get a little time off, try to get out of the house and treat yourself to some activities you really enjoy. That might be a trip to the museum, a walk in the park, a visit to the library or the gym—whatever strikes your fancy and lifts your spirits.

Fifth, join some activities around the university and the community. They are rewarding in their own right and an excellent way to make new friends. There are lots of choices. The important thing is to embark on one or two of them. The sooner, the better. You might participate in volunteer groups, discussion groups, spouse support groups, and, if you are religious, any number of activities at your church, synagogue, or mosque. Actually, all religions have groups on campus, such as Hillel for Jewish students and Newman Centers for Catholics. They welcome student spouses and have a variety of social activities, study groups, and charity work. You can also join a regular congregation in the community, where you'll meet people of different ages, backgrounds, and occupations.

Joining groups and activities is the single best way to meet others in the community and form meaningful friendships. Doing so will make a world of difference in how much you enjoy your stay.

> **Tip:** Student spouses often feel isolated. That's especially true for wives who accompany their husbands to universities far from home. You can lessen that isolation by working on your English-language skills, reaching out to other spouses, and joining activities around the university.

Chapter 22

Health Care

Every country has its own distinctive arrangements for health care. All of them are complex systems, filled with bureaucracy and government regulation, designed to allocate scarce and expensive resources. But, beyond that, crucial elements differ.

Take the United States and Canadian systems. Both offer high-quality, high-technology, high-cost health care, but they pay for it very differently. In the United States, individuals pay for their own care, at least indirectly, through insurance or HMOs (health maintenance organizations). In Canada, the government pays for health insurance (which means individuals pay for it through taxes). The system doesn't use HMOs, which are central to U.S. medical care. Because Canada's coverage is so straightforward, their doctors have far less paperwork. Because it is a far less litigious society, their doctors don't practice medicine with lawyers looking over their shoulders.

These differences have some impact on international students. The biggest is that students in the United States may need to choose between an HMO and health insurance. In Canada, insurance is the only option. Other than that, international students find the two systems very similar. Even Canada's "single payer" health insurance has little effect, because it rarely includes international students. Provinces and territories have the option of covering international students, but they avoid it because of the cost.[1] International students in Canada, like those in the United States, must pay for their own health insurance. It's not cheap.

1. Citizenship and Immigration Canada, "Studying in Canada: A Guide for Foreign Students," section on health insurance, http://www.cic.gc.ca/english/resources/publications/study .asp (accessed June 22, 2007).

Leaving Home and Finding New Health Care

In discussing health coverage for international students, it helps to distinguish between short-term issues—the ones you face when you arrive—and longer-term issues.

The first stage is preparing yourself properly *before* you leave your health-care system at home. You need to collect your medical records, prescription medications, and proof of vaccination and bring them with you. These records will ease the transition to your health-care provider here.

The second stage is arranging your health care here. You need to sign up for an HMO or health insurance and then find the right doctor, pharmacy, and dentist. The two stages are closely linked, of course, but they are not identical.

When you first meet your doctor here, bring all your medical records. If you've been treated in Scotland for high blood pressure or Korea for high cholesterol, your new doctor needs to know. You'll want to explain these issues to the doctor yourself, but it is also important that you bring along the technical records, in English if possible. That means you need to ask your doctor at home for the records before you leave for North America. If your records are in Mandarin or Urdu, you may need to have them translated.

Medical records are important enough to take in your carry-on luggage, if there's room. If you are already here and don't have your records, ask your doctor at home to send you a copy.

You should also pack a couple of months' supply of prescription medications. It might take that long before you see a doctor here and have your prescription renewed or replaced. (Your prescriptions might be changed here for two reasons. First, your new doctor might think there are better treatments. Second, your old medications might not be approved for use in the United States or Canada.)

It's essential to tell your doctor about any medications you are taking (to avoid harmful interactions with other medications) and any allergies you have. Some, like a reaction to penicillin, can be deadly. It also helps if you inform your doctor about any food allergies.[2] If your English is still a little shaky, write down this information and give it to the doctor. Or ask

2. When you dine out, remember to tell the restaurant staff about any allergies. That means you need to know the English words for whatever affects you. At least your task is easier than a friend of mine who is allergic to bell peppers. She travels widely and can't possibly remember the right word in every language. So she carries a picture of bell peppers.

Tip: It is essential to communicate clearly with doctors, nurses, and other health-care professionals. Many medical centers have translators on staff or can arrange for them, if you give advance notice.

Tip: Before leaving home, you need to handle three medical tasks.

- Get a copy of your medical records, in English if possible.
- Bring several weeks' supply of your prescription medications.
- Get the immunizations required for your new school and bring the records with you.

if the medical facility has translators available. Some do, but it's best to ask in advance.

Finally, before you come to the United States or Canada, check on the immunizations you need. Different jurisdictions and universities have their own requirements. California, for instance, requires all university students to be immunized against mumps, measles, and rubella, and requires students under twenty-one to be immunized against hepatitis B. Washington, D.C., has a much longer list of requirements.

You Need Immunizations, But Which Ones?

The best way to find out which immunizations you need is to check with the international students office. They probably sent you a list in their information packet, but they can easily send you another copy. You might need immunizations for the following diseases.

- mumps
- measles (rubeola)
- rubella (German measles) (The MMR vaccine protects against all three: measles, mumps, and rubella.)
- hepatitis B (HBV; a three-dose sequence for immunization)
- meningococcal meningitis (Two vaccines are currently used against five different types of meningitis, but they do not give complete protection.)
- varicella (chicken pox) (You will need either immunization with two doses of Varivax or a blood test that shows you are immune because you already had the disease)
- polio

■ tetanus and diphtheria (You will need a record of immunization or a booster shot within the past ten years.)

You might also be required to show that you don't have active tuberculosis. That can be done with a tuberculosis skin test (PPD, by Mantoux).

In most places, students cannot register for classes until they have received all required vaccinations. Of course, you must be registered to stay in compliance with your visa.

Finding Health Care Here: The Basic Issues

Having arrived with your immunizations, prescription medications, and medical records, you now need to find good health care. In practice, that means purchasing health insurance or joining an HMO. In fact, all universities require their students to have medical coverage. They won't allow students to enroll without it.

If you come here with other family members, you should provide coverage for everyone. Yes, it's expensive, and yes, you may have to pay for most of it yourself, but there is no good alternative. You really need it for everyone in your family.

Universities generally offer students, faculty, and staff a choice of several health-care plans. The cost and coverage vary, but there are some common features. All the plans cover basic medical care, preventive care, diagnostic tests, and emergencies. Nearly all of them cover prescription medicines. None covers dentistry, ordinary eye care (such as glasses), hearing aids, or long-term care in nursing homes. Your health plan might have arranged discounts on some of these services, such as eyeglasses, but you still have to pay for them yourself. If you want full coverage for dentistry or long-term nursing, you may be able to buy separate insurance from your university.

For students coming to the United States, the first decision you need to make—and the most fundamental one—is whether to join an HMO or buy health insurance. That's easy if your university has a campus health center. Normally, you simply purchase the health insurance or HMO plan required for the health center. On larger campuses with major hospitals

Tip: Despite the costs, you should purchase medical coverage for yourself and everyone traveling with you.

nearby, you have more choices. To decide which one is best for you, you need to understand the main differences between HMOs and health insurance. What are the advantages and disadvantages of each?

First, I'll discuss campus health centers. Then I'll turn to HMOs and finally to health insurance. Remember, Canada does not use HMOs, so that section applies only to the United States.

Your Campus Health Center

At many universities, especially those without major research hospitals, students rely on a campus health center. It is set up to meet your needs, and you have full access to it when you purchase student health insurance. It should be your first stop for most illnesses and for advice about staying well. You can schedule an appointment or use the drop-in hours for an unexpected illness. If you have a medical problem at night, when the center is closed, you simply phone the center's doctor or nurse "on duty."

All campus health centers are staffed with a variety of medical professionals. Smaller centers typically have several nurses and nurse-practitioners, and perhaps a health educator, nutritionist, or fitness expert. Larger centers have all those plus doctors who specialize in internal medicine, gynecology, or family medicine. For mental health issues, they have psychologists, nurses, social workers, or doctors, either at the center or at a separate campus location. A few centers have dentists, and all of them can refer you to dentists in private practice. Some centers dispense medicines, but most work with pharmacies close to campus, as well as Internet pharmacies.

One of the center's most important jobs is to screen patients, to decide who should be treated at the center and who should be seen by outside specialists. If you need a specialist, your insurance should cover it. I'll discuss that later. Screening (or triage) is important because the center can handle most day-to-day health issues efficiently and at low cost. That keeps student health costs from rising even higher.

The campus health center performs basic medical tests, treats minor illnesses, and prescribes medicines and contraceptives. Most centers offer a variety of "wellness" classes to help you stop smoking, eat better, or get more exercise. They often organize student support groups, led by experienced professionals, to deal with alcoholism, drug use, eating disorders, or other problems.

Although it's easy, fast, and cheap to use the center for most of your medical needs, it is not set up to handle more complicated diagnoses, treatments, or hospital care. The center's screening will determine if you need those services. If you do, your doctor or nurse at the center will provide a referral and help you set up an appointment.

Your insurance covers the specialist treatment, but it may not cover *all* the costs. Since medical costs here can be jaw-dropping, you should read the section below on insurance and read your specific policy carefully. There is usually a pamphlet that explains the key elements.

Health Maintenance Organizations (HMOs)

Unless you are signed up with a campus health center, you need to decide what kind of health coverage to buy. In the United States, health maintenance organizations are a popular choice.

An HMO provides its members with a full range of medical care, from regular checkups and diagnostic tests to major operations. It has its own facilities, usually near campus, and its own physicians, nurses, and other health professionals on staff. As a member of the plan, you choose a primary care physician on their staff. Adults see an internist, general practitioner, or gynecologist. Children see a pediatrician or family doctor.

Whomever you choose as a primary care physician, you should see that doctor regularly for checkups and preventive care, not just for illnesses. If you are sick and can't wait for an appointment, you can always come to the HMO's walk-in clinic during day-time hours and see the physician on duty.

Whether you use an HMO or health insurance, you cannot use the hospital emergency room for ordinary medical care. It's not designed for that. It's for real emergencies, as the name implies. If you do need to go there, perhaps because you've been in an accident, the emergency-room staff will phone your HMO for approval before treating you. That's why you should always carry the HMO's 24-hour number, which is on your membership card. That's also why it should be programmed into your cell phone.

Most of your medical care will be handled at the HMO itself. Normally, you pay a small fee (perhaps $10–$20) each time you see a doctor or fill a prescription. If you want to use a brand-name drug rather than its generic equivalent, you will pay a little more. These copayments are your only costs besides your regular monthly fee.

What if you suffer from a more complicated illness, such as a kidney infection, irregular heartbeat, or eating disorder? Then you will need to see a specialist on the HMO staff. In that case, you will need a medical referral. HMOs are stingy about handing them out.

There's a straightforward reason: cost. Specialist care, emergency room

Tip: HMOs have the advantage of comprehensive coverage for a fixed amount, but you have to use their physicians and you may be denied the specialist care you seek.

visits, and hospital stays are all very expensive. If HMOs didn't control access to them, they would need to charge sky-high monthly fees or go broke. On the other hand, HMO patients sometimes feel they are being denied specialist care or hospital treatment for financial reasons, not medical ones. There are standard procedures to resolve such disputes, but they don't always leave patients smiling.

Your university may offer a choice among several HMOs. You might prefer a doctor at one of them or the location of another. The monthly fees and copayments might differ, too. The University of Chicago, for example, offers employees a choice of three HMOs. If a member needs hospitalization, two of the HMOs pay all the costs. The third requires a copayment of $100 per day for the first three days. You'll want to consider differences like these when you choose a plan.

The main advantage of HMOs is that they are a convenient, low-cost, single location for nearly all your medical needs. There's no annual deductible, and you never have to fill out complicated claim forms. Your costs are effectively fixed. Unlike an insurance plan, there is no preset limit to how much the HMO will spend on your lifetime medical care.

The disadvantages are equally straightforward: your principal physician must be someone on their staff, and you depend entirely on that physician and the HMO bureaucracy for your access to specialized care. If they deny you a referral to see a cardiologist, you can't see one. (Or, rather, they won't pay for it, which is effectively the same thing for everybody except Bill Gates.) If they do give you a referral, you'll see only the cardiologist they have on staff—good, bad, or indifferent—not a specialist you pick.

The alternative is to buy health-care insurance. Your university has already arranged for several insurance options, just as they arranged for several HMOs. Your task is to choose among them, based on your needs and their costs and services.

Health Insurance Plans

A typical health insurance plan, such as one offered by Blue Cross/Blue Shield, gives you tremendous flexibility in choosing doctors. That's the principal advantage of insurance compared to HMOs. You can choose any doctor or licensed medical provider you wish, both for primary care and specialist treatment. You don't need a referral to see a specialist. It's your choice. You don't need the insurer's permission for emergency room care or hospitalization. You're covered.

But that coverage and flexibility comes at a price, beyond the monthly premiums. First, while the insurer pays some costs for any care you receive, it pays far more if you use one of its "preferred providers." The insurance company has enrolled hundreds, perhaps thousands, of preferred medical providers in its network. They include hospitals and clinics, plus the full range of health-care professionals, from physicians and psychologists to physical therapists. But not every hospital and every doctor belongs to every network. The ones you want to use may not be part of your insurer's network. If they are not, you can still use them, but it will cost a lot more.

When the insurer signs up providers, it also negotiates rate schedules with them, usually at significant discounts from their full fees. Providers agree to charge these lower rates so they can gain access to the insurer's large pool of patients. In return, the insurer agrees to pay a high percentage of the agreed rates directly to the providers. A doctor who is outside the network can bill patients at higher rates (above the agreed rates) and will be reimbursed a smaller percentage by the health insurer. In either case, *the patient owes the doctor whatever is not paid by the insurance company.*

This means patients who use doctors outside the network are hit with much higher charges. A simple illustration shows the difference. Take two cardiologists who normally charge $1,000 for a heart exam and diagnostic tests. One is a member of your insurer's network, one isn't. How does that affect your out-of-pocket costs?

Let's say the insurance company has a scheduled rate of $600 for this particular heart procedure, and every cardiologist in the network has agreed to accept it. In return, the insurance company agrees to pay 80 percent of this scheduled rate. The insured patient pays the remainder. Because the insurance company pays the doctor directly, there's no need for patients to submit a claim form. So, if you see the cardiologist who is a preferred provider, you would pay 20 percent of $600, or $120.

Now, let's say you prefer a different cardiologist who is not part of the network. You are welcome to go there—you might receive superb treatment—but, as your insurance policy clearly states, it only pays 65 percent of the cost for providers outside the network. (This percentage varies in different plans, but it's usually between 60 and 70 percent.) Remember, though, your cardiologist will not be charging you the lower scheduled

> **Tip:** Health insurance plans give you much greater flexibility than HMOs in choosing doctors, including specialists, but you pay about 20 percent of the costs each time you see a doctor in their network and much more if you see someone outside the network.

rate of $600. She'll be charging her normal fee of $1,000. After you receive the exam and a bill from the doctor, you fill out a claim form and submit the paperwork to your insurance company. They will pay 65 percent of $600 (their scheduled rate, not the doctor's full rate), or $390. You are stuck with the remainder of the bill, $1000 − 390, or $610. As you can see, there is a heavy penalty for going outside the preferred provider network. In this case, it costs five times as much.

The direct costs of doctor visits and monthly fees are not the only charges you face. All health insurance plans have "deductibles." That might be, say, $200 for each hospital admission. In other words, you are expected to cover the first $200 of the hospital bill yourself. Deductibles like these vary among insurance plans. You also pay a small amount for each prescription medicine.

The only good news about deductibles is that each policy sets a maximum amount you have to pay out annually. Once you spend that amount, you don't have to pay any more deductibles.

Finally, all health insurers set a maximum on the total benefits they will pay out during any patient's lifetime, perhaps $2–3 million. As far as deductibles and maximum lifetime payouts are concerned, it doesn't matter whether the medical care is received inside or outside the insurer's network. HMOs don't have deductibles or lifetime maximums.

Choosing the Right Coverage

Your choice, then, is not just between health insurance and an HMO, it's between several insurance plans and several HMOs. Insurers differ in their deductibles, lifetime caps for coverage, and, of course, doctors and hospitals in their networks. HMOs differ in the doctors on staff, convenience of locations, waiting periods for appointments, and difficulty of getting referrals. You need to compare the full range of insurance plans and HMOs before selecting one.

It's not a simple task, as you can see. For new students, the choice is even more difficult because they lack good information about local alter-

> *Tip:* Your choice of medical care is not just between health insurance and an HMO. It's typically between several insurance plans and HMOs. Deciding among them is a complicated task. Beyond the generic differences between insurance and HMOs, you need to evaluate the advantages, disadvantages, and costs for each option your university offers.

natives. Since you haven't seen any local doctors or hospitals, how can you possibly decide which HMO or health insurance company is best for you? Naturally, you'll ask other students and perhaps advisers, but you really won't know what's best for you until you've actually used the services yourself, and perhaps not even then.

Fortunately, you are not locked in. You can change your medical coverage each year. There is an "open enrollment" period when you can select a new plan. So you aren't stuck for years with the choice you made your first week in school.

Dentists and Pharmacists

Besides finding health coverage and a personal physician, you need to find a local dentist and pharmacy. It's important for everyone to see a dentist twice a year for cleaning and checkups. A visit costs around $80–$120, more if they start drilling. It's tempting to postpone these appointments— visiting the dentist is rarely a cause for celebration—but you should go there anyway. It's much easier to prevent problems than to repair them, and it's much easier to repair them sooner than later.

You will probably have to pay for these visits yourself, but it may be worth buying dental insurance if you need extensive work. There might be one low-cost alternative. If your campus has a dental school, it might have a dental clinic that serves students and community residents, often at discounted rates.

Most health plans give you a wide choice of pharmacies. A local pharmacy might be near your apartment, or it might deliver to you for a small fee. You might appreciate the personal service you get. You might prefer a large chain because it's open around the clock and you can shop for groceries in the same store. Or you might prefer to order prescriptions from an online pharmacy. The costs are low and they deliver to your door. You can choose whichever pharmacy you like, as long as they have signed up with your provider.

> **Tip:** Besides choosing a health-care plan and a doctor, you need to select a dentist and a pharmacy. The standard recommendation is to see a dentist twice a year for checkups and cleaning. You'll have to pay for that yourself (about $80–$120) unless you purchase special dental insurance. Most plans give you a wide choice of pharmacies, so you can choose the one that is most convenient. If you *don't* have prescription coverage, then you will certainly want to shop for the lowest-cost pharmacy.

> **Tip:** Arrange automatic refills for any prescriptions you receive each month.

One suggestion: if you receive the same prescription each month, ask your pharmacy to set up an automatic refill. They will notify you every month when the pills are ready.

Mental Health Services

Leaving home and family for university studies is a major life transition. The transition is more formidable if the university is thousands of miles away, in a different country, in a different culture. It's not unusual for students facing this transition to report being upset, anxious, depressed, or unable to sleep. They may report binge drinking, binge-and-purge eating, or other behaviors that genuinely trouble them.

You may face problems like these yourself. Many students occasionally do. The problems may be temporary—short-lived responses to a difficult moment—and you may have good friends to discuss them with. On the other hand, you may find your problems linger and worsen. You may feel isolated on your new campus, without good friends to share your thoughts and feelings (or at least friends who can help you with these issues). You may find that your problems impair your ability to function well, academically or socially. They may be affecting your health.

Perhaps the problems are mainly about adjusting to a new environment. Perhaps they are related to a specific situation, such as coping with a difficult roommate, a broken relationship, or decisions about sex. Perhaps they are developmental issues, like living on your own or choosing a career, which arise for the first time in young adulthood. Perhaps you need a little help dealing with chronic problems, like diabetes, that you could manage well when you lived at home. Now that you are living in a dorm, with a new schedule and dining hall food, you have to figure out how to regulate your insulin all over again.

Whatever the problems are, if they are continuing, if you feel alone in dealing with them, or if they are harming your ability to function the way you normally do, you should consider seeing a professional. It is often helpful to share your concerns with an experienced psychiatrist, psychologist, or clinical social worker. They are not only available to talk with you, they can recommend useful coping strategies. They have lots of experience doing exactly that. They also may know if any medications can help. Physicians on staff can prescribe them.

Deans and advisers, who listen to student problems every day, recognize the importance of having good mental health facilities to cope with them. Of course, different universities design their facilities in different ways. Like everything else in higher education, they vary enormously from school to school. Some universities devote extensive resources to student mental health. Others have only the bare bones. Some have a campus mental health center; others house the same services in the general campus health center or university hospital. Many (but not all) work closely with the campus study skills center, helping students with problems like procrastination.

Despite this variation in institutional structure, there are some common themes. One is that mental health services are normally part of your general health coverage (whether that's the campus health center, HMO, or health insurance). Another is that the services are confidential. A third is that most universities provide diagnosis and evaluation, which are essential precursors to effective treatment.

Approaches to treatment, and the resources available for them, vary considerably. Options include medication, short-term individual therapy, support groups, referrals to outside professionals for longer-term treatment, and hospitalization for acute problems. Many universities also offer specialized services, such as those for alcohol and drug abuse, eating disorders, chronic illness, grief, and the trauma of rape or other abuse. Of course, issues of sexuality, including sexual orientation, are especially important to young adults. Some campus centers organize group sessions to deal with male-female relationships, gay and lesbian issues, or bisexuality. Some organize groups on other student issues that have a significant psychological dimension, such as career and lifestyle choices. The mix of these options is different at each university.

Some international students raise a sensitive issue about these services.

> **Tip:** Mental health treatment is part of your health coverage. Services vary considerably from university to university, but most campuses have professionals who have considerable experience working with young adults. They can help if you are having persistent difficulties, feel isolated, or cannot function as well as you usually do.

"Seeking treatment for emotional issues," they say, "is a source of embarrassment or shame in my home country." Some add that their parents' beliefs or religious practices make it difficult for them to seek treatment.

Mental health professionals understand these issues, and they are sensitive to cultural differences which can pose real problems for students. That sensitivity certainly helps, and it does make therapy more effective for students who take advantage of it. But some students are still reluctant to seek treatment even when they are suffering and could benefit from professional counseling and care.

It's easy for outsiders to say, "Seek treatment if you think you might need it. Let medical professionals work with you to decide whether you could benefit and what kind of treatment would be best." That's good advice, but not all students can accept it. Still, deans and advisers who work closely with students know just how important that advice is. They know the value of good mental health resources. That is why they are such strong proponents of having them on campus.

Confidentiality in Medical Care

Information about your prescriptions and medical treatment is kept private. That confidentiality is protected by tight legal restrictions in both the United States and Canada.

There are a few exceptions to this rule of confidentiality, mostly concerning rare issues like a patient who seems likely to take his own life. The main point is that these exceptions are very unusual. The laws are designed to protect patients' privacy.

> **Tip:** Medical records are confidential, with rare exceptions.

Extreme Conditions: The Value of a "Living Will" and a "Health-care Power of Attorney"

One final issue is worth considering: should you make plans now to deal with an extreme medical emergency? What if you are incapacitated and unable to make medical decisions for yourself? For most students, that possibility seems remote. Fortunately, they are right. But remote does not mean impossible. Traumas and serious illnesses do occur. Today, after decades of medical advances, it is often possible to keep seriously ill patients alive for extended periods. Some patients have lingered for years in deep comas, with no hope of recovery. That awful prospect has led more people to ask themselves, "What kind of treatment do I want to receive in such extreme conditions?" And, "If I can't make medical decisions for myself, who do I want to make these decisions for me?"

You can answer these questions with a "living will" and a "health-care power of attorney." A living will says what treatments you want in extreme situations, when you cannot explain these choices yourself. One decision is whether you want a doctor to undertake extraordinary means to preserve your life, even if you have been diagnosed with a fatal or irreversible condition. Another is whether you want life-sustaining care, such as food and water, in these extreme conditions.

A health-care power of attorney designates someone to make medical decisions for you if you cannot.[3] That might be a parent or friend; the choice is yours. In giving them this authority, you can include your explicit instructions about what care you want to receive, as you would in a living will. Without these instructions or someone to act on your behalf, your family and doctors will make these life-and-death decisions themselves. Worse, they may not know what you would want them to do. That puts a terrible burden on their shoulders at a wrenching moment.

The health-care power of attorney and living will are flexible documents, designed to ensure that your wishes are carried out. You can change or revoke them at any time. They take effect only if you cannot make decisions yourself. The documents themselves are relatively simple but, unfortunately, there is not one document that works in all jurisdictions. The laws differ. So, if you want to give medical instructions like this, go online and find the appropriate document for your location.

---

3. Health-care power of attorney involves only medical decisions. It does *not* involve the power to make financial decisions for you.

Organ Donation Card

Along the same lines, consider filling out an organ donor card. If you die, you can help someone else live by giving them your vital organs and tissues. In most states, all you need to do is check a box on the back of your driver's license. Or you can download an organ donor card online. In the United States, the Web address is www.organdonor.gov. In Canada, it's www.giftoflife.on.ca.

> **Tip:** In an extreme medical emergency, you may not be able to make medical decisions for yourself. With a "living will," you can choose the care you want to receive. With a "health-care power of attorney," you can choose a family member or friend to make medical decisions for you, subject to your specified wishes. With an organ donor card, you can give organs and tissues to someone who desperately needs them.

Chapter 23

Campus Life

Universities are not just institutions for teaching and research. They are also social communities where people live, work, and play. They regularly welcome new students and faculty from around the world. What are the best ways to join this cosmopolitan community? How can you participate in ways that enrich your life?

I have already covered some of the most important steps to take, such as improving your language and living close to campus. Now I'd like to turn to a few others. You can find more in chapter 9 ("The Culture of Universities in the United States and Canada"), as well.

Extracurricular Activities

Among the best ways to enter a new university community is to participate in extracurricular activities. Universities here have an extremely wide range of options, from social clubs to drama, from sports to tutoring disadvantaged children. You should survey the options and consider joining at least one, even if you don't have much time for it.

These activities are especially important to undergraduates and a major way they make connections beyond dorms and classes. They give students an opportunity to socialize, contribute, and lead. Just as important, they offer students a chance to put aside their books and lab notes, at least for a moment, and have some fun.

The easiest time to join such activities is when school is starting. That's when you are planning your year, anyway. During orientation week, most organizations set up tables in the student union or main quadrangle to publicize their activities and recruit new members. Each group has a few

> *Tip:* If you are an undergraduate, join at least one extracurricular activity. You'll need to seek them out, and the best time to do that is when they are recruiting during orientation week. They will be happy to show you their materials and explain what they do.

> *Tip:* Joining extracurricular activities is one of the best ways to widen your social circle and make friends beyond students from your home country.

members sitting at their table, speaking with new students about what the group does, what it's like to be a member, and why you should join. The specific activity, such as editing the campus literary magazine, is only one reason to join, and not necessarily the most important one. Often, the most rewarding part is just sitting around, talking with friends after your activities are done.

To get started, visit the information tables during orientation week and sign up for one or two groups that interest you. You can always decide to drop them later, if you don't have time or if you want to switch to another group. You aren't locked in.

Actually, you'll be locked *out* if you do nothing. If you don't sign up early, it's easy to drift along without joining anything. You'll miss out on a lot, including an opportunity to meet students from different countries, different backgrounds, and different religions.

Religion on Campus

All major religions have organizations on campus. They hold regular prayer services, discussion groups, and social events. They frequently organize volunteer activities, such as delivering meals to the elderly or giving blood donations. They also hold ecumenical dialogues, such as those between Catholics and Protestants or Jews and Muslims. All of them welcome students from across the university. Some organize special groups for graduate and professional students. At the University of Chicago, for example, Jewish students have their own organizations in the law school, business school, and medical school, as well as a larger organization devoted mainly to undergraduates.

Whatever your faith, it should be easy to find religious services on campus or nearby. You can ask a classmate, the dean of students, or the international student adviser. The orientation materials should also have a list of campus religious organizations, as well as churches, synagogues, and mosques near campus. All of them are eager to welcome new arrivals.

Graduate Students and Extracurricular Activities

Most extracurricular activities are intended for undergraduates rather than graduate and professional students. Most—but not all. Some graduate students participate in extracurricular sports. Some join religious groups on campus, which include graduate students, faculty, and staff, as well as undergraduates. Still others are active in their department's student organization. Students from all parts of the university join clubs devoted to their home countries. On larger campuses, there are dozens of these national groups.

Doctoral programs are not exactly hotbeds of extracurricular activity, and for good reasons: students are immersed in research and training and gain no advantages on the job market from joining. Still, students in some departments do form small, informal organizations to sponsor social activities and discuss student issues with faculty. Joining a group like the Economics Graduate Students Association is a good way to meet classmates, enjoy a few social events, and learn about shared concerns.

Professional divisions, like the law school or business school, have a more active schedule of extracurricular activities. Students find them useful professionally, as well as socially. They can learn more about their specialty outside of class and network with classmates and working professionals. As officers in their group, they can also demonstrate leadership skills, which might yield some advantages in the job market.

In Wharton's MBA program at the University of Pennsylvania, for example, students organize conferences on "Entrepreneurship" and "New Ventures in Health Care." As charity work, they join Volunteers for Rebuilding Together to renovate homes in poor neighborhoods. There are student groups from specific regions, such as the Greater China Club. Wharton is hardly unusual. Most business schools, law schools, and public policy programs have similar activities with high rates of student participation.

One area where all students can participate—doctoral and professional, graduate and undergraduate—is by attending guest lectures and cultural activities on campus. The variety, quality, and sheer numbers of these events are one of the joys of university life. Every day, there are plays, con-

> **Tip:** Doctoral students usually have a limited schedule of extracurricular activities—perhaps a little sports and a departmental student group. Students in professional schools, such as law and business, are typically more active. For them, extracurricular activities build professional networks, demonstrate leadership, and can help on the job market.

> **Tip:** University campuses are filled with special events, from performances by visiting artists to guest lectures by professors. They are a major resource for students, culturally, socially, and intellectually.

certs, athletic contests, and special lectures by visiting professors, political leaders, and business executives.

Your fellow audience members share your interests, so it's a great place to make new friends. Before and after the event, people mill around, talking, seeing old friends, and meeting fellow students with common interests. Attending events like this is an excellent way to make connections and have a good time doing it.

Dating

Social life on campus is not just about guest lectures and cultural organizations. It's also about dating and forming more serious relationships.

A few quick points. One is that there is not always a sharp line between "having a bite to eat" and "going out for a date." It may not be easy to tell when you are just sharing a cup of coffee and when you are doing something more. The boundaries are often blurred. That can be confusing, but it also encourages new relationships.

Second, there are lots of social events that make it easy to meet men and women on campus. Every weekend (and some week nights), there are parties with music, dancing, food, wine, and conversation. During the week, men and women also get together for study groups.

Third, there is genuine tolerance on campus for all kinds of dating relationships. Students date across racial, ethnic, and religious lines all the time. There are active gay communities. Universities offer a wide-open field for different kinds of social relationships.

Because there are so few constraints, you have to decide for yourself whether you want to date a fellow Korean, a fellow Christian, a fellow

Evangelical Christian, and so on. You can make choices that might not have been open to you when you lived at home.

As you cross these social boundaries, you should recognize that you and your partner may bring different norms and expectations to the relationship. That can be rewarding, exciting, and disconcerting, all at the same time. To forge a relationship that is comfortable and satisfying, it helps to talk about these differences.

Fourth, if your relationship includes sex, then it carries some risks of disease or unwanted pregnancy. It's important for *both* partners to take responsibility for these risks, to discuss them openly rather than assuming implicitly that your partner is handling everything. If you are close enough to have sex, you are close enough to discuss personal issues. It's important to remember that, as effective as birth-control pills are at preventing pregnancy, they do not prevent the spread of HIV or other sexually transmitted diseases. If you want to discuss issues like these with your doctor, you can do it in confidence. Your health plan should cover the medical visit and any testing or prescriptions you need. If you are concerned about emotional or interpersonal issues, including sexual issues, your health plan may also provide access to psychologists, social workers, and other mental health professionals. Like doctors and nurses, they will respect your privacy. (Health issues are covered in more detail in chapter 22.)

Fifth, there is a strong norm that *all* sex should be consensual. That's not just a good idea, it's the law. Forced sex is rape, and it's a serious crime. Sex can be rape even if the students know each other, even if they have been dating, even if they choose to go back to an apartment late at night and have some drinks. When people know each other, coerced sex is called "date rape," but it's still rape. The crucial issue is whether you both wanted to have sex at the time.

It's an entirely different matter if one of you decides *afterward* that it was a bad idea. That is "regretted sex," not rape.

Drinking

Drinking is one of the most vexed issues on university campuses. There are multiple, intertwined issues: underage drinking, binge drinking, drinking and driving, and drinking and dating, and many more—none of them very happy.

The issue of underage drinking is puzzling to many international students. In most countries, after all, you can drink legally at age eighteen. In many European countries, the age is as low as sixteen. In Canada, it's eighteen or nineteen, depending on the province. In the United States, however, the legal age is generally twenty-one. There are some variations from state to state, but the U.S. drinking age is the highest in the world and above the age of most undergraduates.

Because university rules conform to the law, drinking is officially prohibited for most students, on most campuses. The result is a never-ending clash between the laws (and similar university rules) and the students, who want to drink at parties, sporting events, and other activities.[1]

On some campuses, the problem is more serious because undergraduate culture is devoted to drinking and partying. What this means in practice is that the parties begin at some universities on Thursday night and continue straight through the weekend. This is a purely undergraduate phenomenon, but it puts considerable social pressure on students who don't drink heavily and who, from time to time, want to study.

Drinking on campus leads inexorably to problems. Some students stagger away from parties and decide to drive themselves home. They don't always make it. Others get into fights. Still others, their inhibitions loosened, engage in sex that, upon sober reflection, they realize they did not want. A few try to rape women who decline consensual sex, or who were never asked about it in the first place.

Several issues stand out. One is about personal safety and responsibility. Never drive drunk, or ride as a passenger with a drunk driver. Driving under the influence of drugs is just as bad, and, like driving drunk, is a serious crime. If you are driving (sober, I hope) on Friday or Saturday nights, be especially careful about other drivers, who may not be as responsible as you.

Next, learn the laws and university rules. It's important to know what the drinking age is in your city and state, as well as the university's rules for drinking on campus. The rules prohibit recreational drugs, no matter what your age.

Remember, if you are over twenty-one, it is legal to drink but it is illegal (and a very serious matter) to buy liquor for anyone who is underage.

1. The problem is a constant source of aggravation for university officials. Their frustration is the centerpiece of the legendary film comedy about fraternity-house drinking, *Animal House*. As Dean Vernon Wormer explains to one student, "Fat, drunk, and stupid is no way to go through life, son." Excellent advice.

If your university has a "drinking culture" and you don't want to sink into it, you will need to develop friendships and social ties that let you develop an interesting social life in other ways. It is important to think seriously and independently about these issues because, on some campuses, the pressure to drink can push you in uncomfortable directions.

Using the University Library Effectively

Eventually, the parties and dates end, and it's time to crack open the books again. If you need to do research or find some books, you will make the familiar trip to the library.

The main university library is the center of campus intellectual life. All universities have a general research library. Some larger campuses also have smaller, specialized libraries for law, business, science, engineering, or public policy.

How can you use these libraries most effectively? Let me suggest three ways. First, the library is probably the best place on campus to set up a regular study space. It's quiet, centrally located, and full of resources for your studies. If you want to work with fellow students, there are probably special rooms for study groups. If you and some friends want to go out for a snack, there's a junk-food haven nearby.

My advice is to pick a regular study location in the library, probably near your friends. But beware of interruptions. If your friends are too enticing for you to work undisturbed, find a more isolated spot in the library.

Second, when you need guidance about books or journals for your research, speak with a reference librarian. They specialize in topics like medieval Europe or molecular biology, and they order books, journals, microfilms, and databases in their areas. They know what's available at their library and elsewhere, and they know where you should look first. Faculty speak with them often, but students seldom think about doing it. They should. Reference librarians can quickly point you in the right direction for research materials.

> **Tip:** Your study space in the library should be near the resources you need and quiet enough to work without distractions. It's nice to study near friends, but only if you can actually *study* there. If you are constantly interrupted, move a little farther away.

> ***Tip:*** Take a library tour during orientation week and move quickly to set up a regular study space there. Do it in the first week or two of school.

Third, think of the library as both a physical space and an electronic resource. You probably think of it that way already and do much of your reading and research online. That's why you should quickly learn how to access the library when you're off campus. The first step is simple enough. Go to your university's main Web site and click on the library. That opens up some resources, such as the catalog and the reference desk, which are available to everyone, whether they attend the university or not. But the library also maintains costly databases, which are available only to students and faculty. You can access them at the library or from computers off campus if you have a password.

Because the library is so central to your academic life, you should take a guided tour during orientation period. You'll learn where different kinds of books, periodicals, and documents are kept. You'll learn how to use the stacks and check out books, how to order resources from other libraries (through interlibrary loan), and which databases the library currently maintains and which ones it plans to acquire. You'll learn whether your library has reciprocal borrowing privileges with other libraries nearby. You will also learn about their special collections, reference resources, reserve books, and electronic reserve. It's an hour well spent.

Meeting Your Professors

For many international students, the most forbidding and remote area on campus is one they pass every day: their professor's office. There are good reasons to overcome your anxieties. Meeting faculty individually can be one of your most rewarding experiences. It's an opportunity to talk about academic issues, request a recommendation, or get advice about jobs or additional education. The best time to go is during a faculty member's weekly office hours.

> ***Tip:*** Faculty hold regular weekly office hours and expect to meet with students, including some they don't know. International students should take full advantage of the opportunity. Don't wait until you have a problem you need to discuss. Use office hours to discuss your regular academic work.

Gifts

Occasionally, students think they are honoring a professor by giving a very expensive or elaborate present. Actually, faculty members are likely to be embarrassed, confused, and perhaps concerned that the gift is intended as a "sweetener" for a better grade. This is one area where different cultural expectations can lead to misunderstandings.

What gifts are appropriate and inappropriate, then? The answer: small gifts that show your appreciation, along with a personal note. *Don't* give faculty any gifts that are expensive, such as watches, or very personal, such as perfume. *Don't* give any gifts before the semester is finished and your grades are turned in. That might look like an attempt to curry favor or, worse, purchase a better grade. "It's really not right to give these large gifts," one professor told me. Then he laughed and said, "Plus, the students never give me the Mercedes I want."

Small or token gifts are fine, especially if you worked closely with a faculty member. My colleagues and I occasionally receive a box of chocolates or a small item from a student's home country, along with a personal note of thanks. Little treats like this are nice, but they are certainly not required or even expected.

What is always appreciated is a personal message saying how much you liked a course. Professors enjoy hearing that, but you shouldn't do it until the course is over and graded. Later, after you return to your home country, you might want to write to a professor you worked closely with. I know from personal experience that faculty enjoy getting brief e-mails and an attached photo or two, showing what is new in your life. I just got a wonderful one today from a former student. It included a picture of his new baby.

> **Tip:** Don't give expensive or very personal gifts to professors, and don't give them anything during the semester. After a course is over, it is always appropriate to send a note saying how much you enjoyed the class and how much you learned. If you worked closely with a professor, you could give a small gift, but it's certainly not expected.

Chapter 24

Telecommunicating: Phone Calls, Internet, Cable TV, and More

The single most important thing to know about telephone, television, and computer services is that they are changing rapidly—*very* rapidly. You might study all the options and learn how to call Tokyo at the lowest possible rate today, only to find out next month that there is a new, cheaper way.

The second most important thing to know is that your friends, especially other international students, have probably asked the same questions and already figured out some answers. They, too, have been searching for the cheapest way to call overseas or whether there's any TV channel that carries sports from back home. That makes them a great source of information. If you discover the answers first, you can help them.

> ***Tip:*** Whatever arrangements you make for communicating, you should occasionally check to see if there's a new and better way. One of the best ways to find out is to ask other students.

Telephone: Local, Long Distance, and Cellular

You can choose from a wide variety of companies to provide phone service, whether it's local, long-distance, or cellular service. All companies offer a range of plans, some for people who use their phones constantly, others for light users. The only way to know which is best for you is to do the research, match it to your calling needs, and see whether any company offers special discounts this month.

Some plans offer a flat monthly charge for all local calls, or for all calls

> ***Tip:*** Because there are so many phone companies and so many monthly plans, you need to evaluate your communication needs and compare prices carefully. Since prices change rapidly, you may need to reevaluate your arrangements every few months.

> ***Tip:*** When you sign up for a new phone plan, ask if you can keep your existing number.

inside the United States or Canada. Others provide a fixed number of minutes, say 1,000, and then charge a fee for each extra minute. Some (but not all) allow you to "roll over" your unused minutes and use them the following month.

Most cell phone plans offer free calling to family members who use the same cellular company. Some offer free calling to everyone in their network. All offer discounts on fancy cell phones or PDAs (like Blackberry or Treo), but you have to sign up for a one- or two-year contract to get them.

Unfortunately, you not only have to sort through these options, you might need to do it again in a few months since prices keep changing. If you do decide to switch phone providers, remember that you can usually keep your old phone number. You have to request it, though, and fill out a form. It's worth asking, so you don't have to call all your friends and give them your new number.

Signing Up for a Phone Plan

When you sign up for a phone plan, ask how quickly they can activate it. Sometimes they can do it within a few hours; sometimes it takes days. For identification, they will ask for a copy of your driver's license and perhaps your passport and visa. They will also ask for your Social Security Number (or, in Canada, a Social Insurance Number) to check on your credit. That's easily supplied in Canada, since international students are issued those numbers. In the United States, however, international students cannot get Social Security Numbers, and the companies usually don't accept Individual Taxpayer Identification Numbers (ITINs). Without a Social Security Number, most cell phone companies simply do not extend credit plans. Instead, they offer prepaid contract plans, which requires no credit check and no annual contract. You choose your own phone, pay the company an initial activation fee, and then pay a fee at the beginning of each month, ranging from around $20 to $100, depending on the number of minutes and other services you buy. If you run out of minutes, you can buy more.

International Phone Cards

International calling is also a competitive business, and the costs are declining, though they are still much higher than domestic long distance. If you make international calls often, you'll want to check prices at all the major companies, such as AT&T, T-Mobile, and Verizon in the United States, or Rogers or Telus in Canada, before you sign up for phone service. It may be cheaper to use prepaid calling cards (which can also be used for domestic calls) or VoIP (Voice over Internet Protocol).

All the major phone companies sell calling cards, but so do many smaller outfits, and usually for less money. These entrepreneurs buy millions of minutes at wholesale prices and then sell them to individual customers on calling cards. You'll want to compare their prices for calling your home country. Fortunately, there are search engines, such as www .active-phone-calling-cards.com, which automate the comparison.

You'll also want to check out the cards' other features. Are they easy to use? Can you activate them quickly and easily? Is there an expiration date for the calling card minutes? On some cards, the minutes expire after a few months, whether you use them or not.

See if they offer international "call back arrangements." That's important because it might cost only 5¢ a minute to call from Berkeley to New Delhi, but twice as much to call the other direction. Using "call back," your friends and family in India can phone you at the 5¢ rate.

> **Tip:** Calling cards are often the cheapest way to call internationally. You should not only compare prices from various providers, you should consider the convenience and other features.

Phoning over the Internet

One of the cheapest phone options is VoIP, which uses your computer's broadband connections for long-distance calls, either in North America or internationally. It works only if you have DSL, cable, or T1 connections.

Tip: Using VoIP over your broadband connection may well be the cheapest way to call overseas.

When VoIP began a few years ago, it was clunky and inconvenient. Voice quality wasn't so great, either. All that has changed for the better. Now, once you sign up for the service, you can use ordinary landlines or cell phones to call any other phone. The quality is about the same as normal phone service. VoIP simply provides a cheap route between the two phones.

You can purchase the same add-on features you do with regular phone service, such as voicemail, call waiting, caller ID, call forwarding, and conferencing.

As with calling cards, you'll want to compare prices, particularly the cost per minute and the surcharge, if any, for connecting each call. There may also be some minor costs to begin your new service. You can compare costs with the same search engine used to compare calling cards.

Cable TV, Satellite Dishes

Every city has a few local television stations, which are available free to viewers. You can receive them with a small, indoor antenna. Unfortunately, you will get only four or five channels, each of them affiliated with a major network. If you want dozens and dozens of channels, you have to pay a monthly fee to a cable company (such as Comcast) or a satellite service (such as DISH Network or DIRECTV).

Cable companies install a wire to your house, which you then connect to all your TV sets. Depending on the type of sets you own, you may also need to rent an electronic box for each one to receive all the cable channels.

Satellite dishes must be installed and, in North America, must have an unobstructed view of the southern sky. You can install the dish yourself or hire a professional.

Choosing between Cable and Satellite

Cable is more expensive, but it's also more convenient and reliable. For an extra fee, the cable company can also provide you with a broadband connection for your computer. Satellites offer more channels for less money and have more international channels. Both systems work well with video recorders, TiVo, and other devices.

What questions should you ask before choosing? Here are some of the most important:

- How much does it cost to install the service? Do you offer any special "sales" prices? Do I have to sign a contract, perhaps for a year or more?
- How many channels do I get in the basic package, and what's the monthly cost?
- What premium packages do you offer? (They will undoubtedly offer several.) How many channels does each include and at what monthly cost?
- Do you have special packages with international and foreign-language programming? Depending on your interests, you might also ask about sports programming, children's programming, and so forth.
- Does the service also include digital music channels?
- How many TV sets can I hook up to the service and still get good reception on each?
- Do you transmit the signals in analog or digital form?
- How many high-definition channels do you offer (assuming you own an HDTV).
- What happens if there's a problem with the signal or the equipment? What will it cost me if someone needs to come to my house and repair a malfunction? What kind of warranty do you offer on the dish and receiver?

Computer Accounts, Web pages, Blogs, Podcasts, and Online Services

You'll want to set up a university computer account as soon as you arrive. Your school knows that and has procedures to facilitate the task. Just ask someone at the registrar's office or the international student adviser's office.

You undoubtedly have other e-mail accounts, but you still need a university e-mail address. First, it's the way faculty and university administrators communicate with students. With a couple of clicks, they can send e-mails to everyone in a particular class or department. Students receive that mail only if they have university addresses. Second, you'll need a university address—and perhaps a related ID and PIN—to access the university library's databases from your home computer. You probably will need

> **Tip:** Get a university computer account and e-mail address soon after you arrive, but don't cancel any other e-mail and Web services you like.

it to access other electronic resources, such as Moodle or Blackboard for your courses. Finally, you may need it to gain access to wireless networks on campus. Secure networks require a university computer account and PIN.

Getting a university e-mail account doesn't mean you should cancel any other Internet accounts. I recommend keeping them. After all, your friends already know your address on Gmail or Hotmail. These personal accounts are valuable for some things, like business activity, that really don't belong on the university system. A few transactions are okay; dozens and dozens are not. It's fine to use the university network to buy a bicycle on eBay. It's not fine to run your online bicycle business on the university servers. Do that somewhere else. The university's network is intended for research and personal communications.

The same is true for Web pages. Even if your university provides them, you may prefer to set yours up at Google or Yahoo. Simple sites are free, but if your site gets lots of traffic, you might wish to upgrade to a commercial hosting service, such as EarthLink.

One difference between university Web pages and those at Google or EarthLink is that your school has no control over off-campus accounts and much more limited oversight responsibilities. The same is true for any blogs or podcasts you create. If you set them up off campus, you have more control and autonomy.

Privacy Online: Not Very Likely

What you don't have online is privacy. Others can access what you post.[1] You can and will be held responsible for it. Students sometimes forget that and post explicit diaries or candid pictures of their drunken revelry at MySpace or Facebook.

You shouldn't flout the law and university rules anyway. It's especially dim-witted to post the evidence on a public site. And, believe me, these are

---

1. Secure, password-protected sites offer some privacy, but they can be hacked or accessed by law enforcement.

> **Tip:** Remember, online postings are effectively public. If you don't want everybody to see it, don't post it.

public sites. "If you don't want it to be my business," said one Illinois police officer, "then don't post it." That's actually his job, to "keep tabs on anybody posting possibly incriminating information."[2]

Remember, social networking sites are not open only to your friends. They're open to everyone—the dean of students, potential employers, your government at home, and anyone else who's interested.

Mail and Packages

With so much attention lavished on electronic communications, it's easy to overlook snail mail. But it's fun to receive a postcard or letter occasionally, and you may want to send a few to friends back home.

The postal services here are fine. Just be sure you use the correct postage and write "international air mail" on every letter you send to another country. Otherwise, it may go by surface mail—literally, on a slow boat to China—and arrive when your children are ready for university.

If you are sending packages internationally, check to see what kinds of documents should accompany them and whether any duties are required. You need to choose between surface mail and air mail. Once again, surface mail is much cheaper and much slower.

For package delivery, you can choose from a variety of commercial delivery services, as well as the government post office. FedEx, UPS, and DHL are extremely fast and reliable, for both domestic and foreign deliveries. They all have online tracking systems, so you can follow your package from the time you drop it off until it arrives and is signed for. If you send packages frequently, you can set up an online account with one of these carriers and print out mailing labels on your computer.

> **Tip:** Be sure to mark letters "international air mail." For packages, you must choose between air mail, which is fast but expensive, and surface mail, which is slow but cheap.

2. Jimmy Greenfield, "All Up in MySpace," *RedEye* (edition of *Chicago Tribune*), March 28, 2006, p. 6.

Chapter 25

Dealing with Problems

We all face problems, sometimes serious ones. Foresight, prudence, and effort can avert many of them, but nothing can eliminate them entirely.

In this chapter, I want to discuss problems that occasionally confront international students and explain where to turn for help. I want to make four basic points.

- If you face an immediate danger, such as a fire or a robbery in progress, call 911. It's the universal number for emergency assistance in the United States and Canada. It's a free call from cell phones or landlines.
- The international students office can help with many problems, but not with all of them. You may get assistance elsewhere on campus, or the university may not become involved at all.
- You are largely responsible for your own activities off campus, just as local students are.
- International students face many of the same problems local students do, and they should turn to the same sources for help. That might be a professor, doctor, lawyer, or other professional.

Later in the chapter, I will show you exactly who to contact when specific problems arise.

Dial 911 for Emergencies

If you face an emergency, or observe one, such as a serious automobile accident or a toxic chemical spill, dial 911. Try to stay calm so you can explain exactly what the problem is and where it is located. For example, you might tell the 911 operator, "I just saw a car and bicycle collide. The bike rider looks like he's seriously hurt. The accident is at 61st Street and Broadway." Or, "My baby is having real trouble breathing. Something is seriously wrong. I don't know if she's choking or what." The operator might ask you a few questions to determine if there really is an emergency and who should be sent to help.

Operators at 911 are trained to make these decisions and make them quickly. They can dispatch police, fire trucks, ambulances, emergency medical technicians, "hazmat" teams (to deal with hazardous materials), or whoever else is needed.

Use 911 only for serious, urgent problems. If a problem is less pressing—perhaps a car that was broken into last night—you should dial the regular number for police or medical assistance.

Campus Police

Most universities maintain their own police forces to ensure a safe campus. At some universities, they also patrol the surrounding neighborhoods.

To reach the campus police quickly, you need to know their phone number. It's a good idea to program it into your cell phone. After all, their officers and patrol cars are already on campus, so they might be able to reach you faster than city police.

Most campuses also have emergency phone boxes, connected directly to the campus police station. If you need help or see someone else who does, simply open the emergency box and push the button. You'll be speaking with a campus police operator, who can send campus officers or report the problem to 911, which will send city police or other emergency services. It's a good idea to learn where these emergency phone boxes are as you learn your way around campus.

At night, when students may be concerned about their safety walking home or across campus, some universities (but not all) provide police escorts to students who request them. They might drive you to your dorm,

> ***Tip:*** Learn the phone number for the campus police and add it to your cell phone.

> ***Tip:*** Learn where emergency phones are located, especially along the routes you regularly walk.

> **Tip:** Ask whether your university provides safety escorts for students, faculty, and staff.

library, bus stop, or parked car. Other universities don't provide individual rides but ask patrol cars to drive alongside you as you walk. If you are unsure whether your university offers this service, or whether the escort goes beyond the campus (say, to your home nearby), simply call the campus police and ask.

Campus Resources: Going Beyond the International Student Adviser's Office

Fortunately, most problems don't require the police or fire department. Even so, the problems can be troubling: an angry, unhappy roommate, for example, or a financial problem that threatens your tuition, or an illness that prevents your taking an exam on time. Who should you talk with about your problem? Who can give you thoughtful, confidential advice?

In some cases, your first call should go to the international student adviser, but not always. If you cannot take a scheduled exam because you are sick, you should e-mail your professor directly. There's no need for the international students office to become involved. If you are suffering an emotional problem, such as depression, you should speak with your university's student mental health center. They are part of your health plan, have trained counselors, and treat all cases confidentially. The international students office won't even learn about it, unless you tell them.

If you live in a dorm and have problems with a roommate, try to work them out between yourselves. If that fails, you can talk with someone who supervises dorm life, beginning with the resident assistant (RA) and possibly working your way up to the head of your dorm. If you live off campus, the university may not offer assistance.

If you suffer from drug or alcohol problems, you can seek expert counseling from student mental health, your HMO, or your hospital. You might also join a support group like Alcoholics Anonymous. Even if these problems occur "on campus," none of them involves the international students office, though that office might be able to direct you to the right resources.

If you face a serious problem late at night or on the weekend and need

> **Tip:** You already know what an important resource the international student adviser's office is. Still, it is not meant to handle every issue. Sometimes, you should call your professor or academic adviser, your doctor, or perhaps a psychological counselor. For emergencies at nights or on weekends, call the "duty dean."

help from the university, you can call the dean on duty. Someone from the dean of students' office is always "on call," available to handle emergencies whenever they arise. The "duty dean" is a rotating job shared by experienced members of the dean of students' staff. The dean of students' office works closely with the international student adviser, but the two offices are usually separate.[1]

For some difficulties, the international student adviser's office can offer valuable advice or assistance, or can point you to other resources on campus. In many cases, though, you should simply do what local students do and contact the duty dean, RA, or doctor yourself. In fact, most problems facing you as an international student are the same as those facing your local classmates, and you should try to resolve them the same way. You should make the same call, see the same advisers, and pursue the same remedies. Of course, if you aren't sure what to do, the international student adviser's office can offer experienced advice.

Off-Campus Problems

When problems occur off campus, the university might not become involved at all. They are not like intrusive parents, supervising every aspect of your life. It's your responsibility, not theirs, to manage most issues and most problems.

The university knows—and you should, too—that you are more than a student. You are also a renter, driver, parent, patient, borrower, traveler, bank customer, and many other things. The university doesn't take responsibility for these aspects of your life, whether you are an international student or a local one. Unless the problem directly affects your studies or the university itself, their staff probably won't assist you, advise you, or, for that matter, punish you.

1. At most universities, the international student adviser's office is separate from the dean of students' office. But universities vary, and some may consolidate all student advising functions in the dean of students' office. Even if the offices are separate, they work together closely.

Tip: If you have problems that are *not* related to your health, education, or visa status, then you will probably need to get help outside the university.

Tip: Universities do not provide legal advice to their students, faculty, or employees. For that, you need to hire a private attorney who will represent your interests.

If your landlord wants to evict you, for example, you need to call a real estate lawyer, not a university lawyer. The university will not give you legal advice, which would expose them to liability (in case they gave you the wrong advice). It's not their job anyway.

If you need a lawyer, it's your responsibility to engage one. It's possible that someone at the university will suggest a lawyer, but it's more likely they won't. As far as the university is concerned, the legal problems of its students, faculty, and staff are their responsibility.

On the other hand, you might get help from your embassy or local consulate. It's often a good idea to call them when you need assistance off campus.

The embassy's role underscores a crucial point. Although international students may be treated like all other students, they are sometimes in a different position and may face different consequences if things go wrong. Being suspended from school is a clear example. It's bad news for anyone, but it's much worse for international students because it violates the student visa requirement. To stay here, you must be enrolled as a full-time student. Otherwise, you must leave the country. Your spouse and children will have to leave, too, since their visa status is linked to yours.

Five Problems Facing International Students

In my discussions with international students, they report several recurrent problems. First, they sometimes get into trouble because their standards of appropriate behavior are different. Some differences are grounded in their educational experience. Their school training stresses values and practices that may occasionally diverge from ours. Other differences are rooted in broad cultural values, such as the role of women or religion in society. Sometimes, they simply don't know the standards that apply in North America or at North American universities.

In other chapters, I have given examples of these differences and misunderstandings. One concerns plagiarism (chapter 8, "Avoiding Plagiarism and Doing Honest Work"). What some students consider solid work, repeating exactly what the professor thinks, is considered pedestrian and may be outright plagiarism if it copies the professor's words and ideas without proper quotations and citations. Another concerns date rape, a concept that is relatively new in North America and doesn't exist at all in some countries. The view here is that coerced sex is rape, even if the two people know each other. (See chapter 23, "Campus Life.")

Second, international students are often reluctant to use local resources such as counseling services, again because of their cultural values. A number of international students and faculty have told me that it is especially hard for them to ask for psychological help. They may not know who to ask. They may feel ashamed. Or they may feel inadequate because they can't handle the problem themselves.

Of course, it's not just international students who find it difficult to seek psychological help. Local students do, too. But depression, anxiety, or eating disorders are not signs of personal failure or poor self-control. They are recognized medical problems. If you face problems like these, you should get treatment for them, just as you would for other medical problems.

Third, international students may err in handling some problems because they haven't dealt with them before or haven't dealt with them here, where arrangements may be different from those in their home countries. Health care is a good example. Most international students have never purchased health insurance or dealt with an HMO. It's not surprising, then, that they find it confusing and occasionally make mistakes as they navigate these unfamiliar waters.

Fourth, they often face language barriers. That can be particularly troublesome in legal and financial matters, where the stakes are high. If you are caught in a legal dispute and your English isn't excellent, you should hire a translator, or request one when dealing with police and the courts. But you can't hire a translator for everything, and you'll undoubtedly face some situations where slang terms, fast talk, and regional accents will simply perplex you.

Fifth, as I already noted, international students may face more serious consequences than local students for poor grades or misbehavior. That's not because of prejudice or discrimination. It's because international students are here on visas that require them to remain in school. Being suspended or expelled is bad enough for students from Kansas. For students from Korea, it's far worse. They will have to leave the country unless they quickly enroll in another school.

Who to Call When You Need Help: A Quick Reference Table

Here's a quick reference guide for troubleshooting. My goal is not to solve a particular problem, but to explain where you should look for help. Who should you telephone first?

Problem	First calls to make	Explanation
Fire	911	
Medical emergency	911 or go directly to the emergency room or trauma center	911 can send an ambulance and emergency medical technician.
Crime (emergency)	911; university police	Call the one that will respond fastest first.
Crime (nonemergency)	Regular police number	Do not call 911 for nonemergency issues, even if they involve police.
Family emergency at home; you may need to fly back	The international student adviser's office, the dean of students' office, and your academic adviser. After that, if you have time, contact professors with whom you are taking classes and tell them why you need to leave town.	Explain your family situation to your academic adviser or the dean of students' office as clearly as possible. If there's no time to contact your professors, ask your adviser or a trusted friend to do it. Do *not* leave campus without telling someone and explaining your reasons. If you need emergency funds to travel, you should speak with the dean of students' office. They may have special money for such cases or, if they do not, may point you to another office that does. Unfortunately, there is no guarantee that money is available. Sometimes your national embassy can also help. It's certainly a good idea to call them.

Illness (nonemergency)	Your primary care physician or HMO walk-in clinic	Do not use the emergency room for nonemergency illnesses.
Need to postpone a paper or exam because of minor illness	The professor. You can use e-mail or meet during office hours to explain.	Undergraduates, in particular, may be asked to document the illness. Professors may or may not give extensions or penalties for late papers. It's their choice whether to mark down late assignments. Whether they do often depends on whether you show that the problem is real and serious.
Need to postpone a paper or exam because of scheduling conflict	The professor, by e-mail or in person	You probably will *not* be given permission, but you can ask. You should explain your reasons and do so as far in advance as possible.
Doing poorly in a course	The professor, in person; after that, you might wish to contact the university study skills center or writing center.	This is what office hours are for. Explain your problems and ask for guidance. If you have general difficulty writing, see the university's writing center. If you have trouble studying or taking notes, see the university's study skills center.
Problems writing papers	Professor in course; university writing skills center	If your problem is related to a specific course, talk with the professor. If you have more general problems with writing, see the university's writing center. They cannot help you with the substance of the paper, but they can show you how to organize it and write it more effectively. If your problem is related to difficulties using English, you'll need to work with an ESL teacher on writing.
Emotional distress, including anxiety, eating disorders, depression	University student mental health center or resources provided by your health insurer	Confidential treatment, normally covered by health insurance

Sleep disorders	Physician	There may be a sleep disorder clinic at your medical center or nearby. Check with your physician.
Roommate difficulties	Your roommate, calmly, in person. If that fails and if you live in university housing, speak with a resident aide or housing officials.	If you live off campus, the university usually does not provide help.
Financial emergency	International students office, dean of students, or your embassy or consulate	The university may or may not have funds for emergency loans. Likewise, some consulates can help financially, but others cannot.
Parking ticket	Pay it promptly unless you think it was given in error. If you wish to protest the ticket, you'll find the instructions for doing so written on the ticket.	If you delay paying the ticket, you will also have to pay late penalties. If you accumulate several unpaid tickets, your car will be towed or disabled. You can recover it only after paying all accumulated tickets and fines, plus an additional charge for towing.
Legal issues (criminal): DUI, moving violation, criminal charges, arrest, incarceration	An attorney specializing in criminal law, and possibly your embassy or consulate	For most cases, you need to hire an attorney, preferably one who specializes in the type of crime you are charged with. The local bar association has a list of these specialists. You might also get names of attorneys from the international student adviser or dean of students' office. If you cannot afford to hire a lawyer, the court will appoint and pay for one if you are charged with a crime. Some cities also have legal assistance organizations that will advise you at no cost. Your local embassy or consulate has experience dealing with these issues and is a good place to call.

Legal issues (civil): eviction notice, eviction, discrimination (off campus)	An attorney specializing in housing, civil rights law, or other civil litigation	For civil issues, you normally have to pay for your own lawyer. Look for one who specializes in the issues you face. At some universities, you might be able to get free assistance from your law school's legal clinic.
Discrimination (on campus)	University office that deals with issues of race, gender, religion, and sexual orientation. If you are unsure whom to contact, check with the dean of students' office or human resources office and they will direct you. If you are still not satisfied, you may wish to contact an attorney.	Universities are committed, by law and by their own values, to equal opportunity. They have officials to ensure it. On the academic side, they may be associated with the office of the university president or provost. On the staff side, they are associated with the human resources office.
Drug or alcohol problems	Your physician or the university's student mental health center	There are alcohol treatment programs on many campuses, plus support groups like Alcoholics Anonymous
Rape, including date rape	Emergency room (for the medical issues); police and campus police (for criminal issues); later, you may wish to contact student mental health to talk about the assault	If you have been forced to have sex against your will, you should go to the emergency room for medical treatment. They will treat you and take fluid samples to document the sexual activity. (This can prove you had sexual contact with a specific individual, but it cannot prove whether that contact was forced or consensual.) You should also contact the city police and university police to report the assault. You may also wish to talk with the student mental health center to receive counseling. Note that these three agencies have different purposes. The emergency room provides urgent medical treatment. The police (and, later, the courts) deal with the crime. The mental health center helps victims cope with the psychological trauma.

Homesickness	Resident aides (if you live in a dorm) plus counselors at student mental health center if you are depressed or unable to work effectively	Besides speaking with RAs and counselors, it often helps to speak with other students. That includes students from your home country, but it should not be limited to them. There are usually several support and discussion groups available on campus. Whether you are homesick or not, it's a good idea to join a diverse set of student groups and activities.
Suspension from school; expulsion from school	Dean of students; international students office; your embassy	Since student visas require full-time enrollment, suspension or expulsion will result in the loss of your visa.
Charges of visa violation; other immigration issues	International students office; your embassy; an immigration lawyer	The international students office is responsible for dealing with the university side of visa issues, such as providing students with paperwork to show they are enrolled. But they cannot help with legal issues. For that, you'll need to hire your own attorney. Be sure to hire a competent, experienced specialist in immigration law.
Charges of plagiarism, cheating, or academic dishonesty	Professor of class, followed by the dean of students. You may also want to speak with the international students office (though they are not the primary office responsible for this issue).	Being charged with plagiarism or cheating could lead to failing a course or being expelled, depending on the university's approach and the severity of the violation. Expulsion leads to the loss of a student visa.
Unresolved problems at the university	Ombudsman	Most universities have an ombudsman whose job is to listen to student complaints about problems on campus and assist in resolving the difficulties.
School problems for your child	Your child's teacher and then the school principal	If you need guidance on whom to speak with and what requests are reasonable, you should ask the international student adviser's office. There may

		also be a campus association of young parents (or perhaps international student spouses) who can offer advice.
Finding daycare	Friends at the university; possibly the university's human resources or benefits office	The international student adviser's office will also know some of the resources available. So will fellow parents on campus.

Professional Specialties: Who Can Help with Which Problem?

Let's look at these issues again from a different perspective. This time, we'll ask which professionals are best equipped to deal with specific problems.

Professors are the first people to contact if you are having difficulty with a course, and the only people to contact if you want to turn in a paper late or take a makeup exam. If they accuse you of an academic violation, such as plagiarism, you should speak directly with them before talking with the dean of students or judicial review board. Normally, professors deal with the academic problems of students in their own classes.

Deans are senior university officials who deal with academic and student affairs, including student problems. Two deans are particularly important for international students:

- the *dean of students,* who deals with both local and international students; and
- the *dean of international student affairs* (or head of the international students office).

These deans handle a wide range of student issues and problems. The dean of students handles violations of academic integrity and may be involved with financial issues, such as scholarships and teaching assistantships. The international students office plays a central role in orienting new students from around the world, helping them settle into university life, and dealing with the university side of visa issues.

The *duty dean* (sometimes called the "on-duty dean") handles emergency student issues at night or on weekends. The position rotates among members of the dean of students' office.

The *campus ombudsman* holds a special position designed to help resolve problems between students and faculty or between students and the university administration. If you have a persistent problem, such as the university's reluctance to provide halal food for Muslims, and are not getting results through normal channels, you might talk with the ombudsman. (Not every campus has this position.)

There are a variety of specialized staff resources to help with specific problems.

ESL teachers are specialists in language instruction and can help students who are having difficulty writing papers in English.

The student mental health center has counselors, psychologists, and psychiatrists on staff to work with students. They usually deal with students individually, but they sometimes organize therapy groups to discuss common problems, from eating to writer's block. The mental health center is the first place to turn for help with depression, homesickness, and other emotional problems. They may also have specialists who deal with rape and trauma, alcohol and drug abuse, and eating disorders.

Resident assistants and the university housing staff deal with housing problems on campus, from rooms that are too cold to intractable disputes between roommates.

Private attorneys are your principal resource for all legal issues, from allegations of drunk driving to landlord-tenant disputes. University attorneys will not advise to you on these private matters. (They may or may not be willing to recommend a private attorney to you.) If you have been charged with a crime, you are entitled to your own attorney. You can hire one yourself or, if you cannot afford to do so, the government will appoint one for you and pay the costs. For civil matters, such as rental disputes, you are welcome to hire your own lawyer, but you are not "entitled" to one. If you need to hire an attorney, be sure to hire a specialist in the issue you are dealing with.

Your *HMO or health insurance plan* is your chief resource for medical care, other than emergencies.

Your *embassy or local consulate* can help with passport and visa issues. They can probably point you to an attorney, a translator, or other resources. If you need emergency financial help, perhaps a ticket to fly home to a sick parent, they may be able to provide assistance, though there is no guarantee.

APPENDIX 1

A Glossary of Words and Phrases for International Students

Universities, like most modern organizations, communicate in their own special language. The dorms and classrooms echo with shorthand terms, abbreviations, and lingo. You need to know what these words and phrases mean if you want to join the conversation or even figure out what people are saying.

Take this sentence, which you might hear outside a lecture hall: "She doesn't have to worry about the drop/add dates because she's just auditing the course for prelims." What? That means: "She is not taking the course for credit or grades. She is simply attending [auditing] it to help prepare for the graduate exams [prelims] in her discipline. Because she is not formally enrolled in the course, she doesn't need to worry about the university's final dates each semester for enrolling in the course or dropping it from her schedule [drop/add dates]." Now you can see why students use shorthand.

I'll help you decode sentences like that, filled with slang and abbreviations. Below, I've listed the key terms and offered explanations. Besides the phrases you'll hear around the university, I have included some useful terms for financial, legal, and medical issues, for shopping, and a few for immigration. I have marked them in the left margin:

($) (FINANCIAL INFORMATION)

(⚖) (LEGAL INFORMATION)

(℞) (MEDICAL INFORMATION)

(🛒) (SHOPPING INFORMATION)

(Ⓐ) (IMMIGRATION INFORMATION)

You might need them when you open a bank account, consult a lawyer, or schedule a doctor's appointment.

If a term is composed of numbers, such as the 1099 tax form, I've listed it as if it were spelled out ("Ten Ninety Nine"). If a term is known mainly by its initials, such as ESL (for "English as a second language"), I have listed it that way. In the next chapter, I have included an extensive list of terms that are known mainly by their initials, like ESL and GPA (for grade point average).

Many of the terms listed in the glossary are discussed in greater detail in the text. Check the table of contents or the index to find these more detailed discussions.

A final word: I have concentrated on terms that apply widely across the United States and Canada. Your university undoubtedly has a few words and phrases all its own—its nickname for the sports stadium or the library, for example. You'll want to learn those, too, as you learn your way around campus.

Glossary of Useful Terms for International Students

ABD: The nickname for students who have completed all requirements of a doctoral program except the thesis. They are labeled "All But Dissertation" (ABD). There is no real degree by that name, but you'll hear it often enough to think there is.

($) **ABM card:** In Canada, a small plastic card used to withdraw cash, deposit checks, or conduct other banking transactions at an automated banking machine (ABM).

In the United States, where the machines are called "automated teller machines," the cards are called ATM cards.

Academic calendar: The university's formal schedule, listing the dates when classes begin and end, as well as exam periods, vacation days, breaks between semesters, and graduation day. Because these calendars are available one or two years in advance, international students can use them to plan trips home.

Academic year: The normal period when school is in session and classes are offered. For most universities, the academic year begins in August or September and ends in May or June. It excludes the summer, even though most universities are open and offer some optional courses then.

Academic probation: The status of students who are not in good academic standing because of poor grades, incomplete courses, or inadequate progress toward their degrees. They can remedy these problems and return to good standing, but they must do so promptly, usually within one semester. If the problems remain, a student may be suspended from school temporarily or dismissed entirely. That's a disaster for international students, because their visas require them to remain full-time students.

Accreditation, or academic accreditation: Certification that a university (or a program within the university) meets accepted academic standards, as determined by an official committee of outside experts. These standards cover the quality and breadth of academic offerings, faculty education levels, treatment of students and faculty, and so forth. National and regional organizations evaluate universities according to well-established criteria and make their findings public.

All students, including international ones, have a vital stake in university accreditation. Degrees from unaccredited universities are not worth much. To ensure that your degree comes from a reputable institution, ask the university which accrediting bodies have certified their degree programs. This information should be readily available and easily compared to that of other schools.

Take as an example a fully accredited school like the University of Michigan. The whole university is accredited by the appropriate regional body for midwestern states: the North Central Association of Colleges and Schools. Within the university, many individual programs are accredited by specialized bodies. The University of Michigan's BA and MA nursing programs, for example, are accredited by the Commission on Collegiate Nursing Education and are approved by the state's Board of Nursing. Within the nursing school, some special programs have earned their own separate approval or certification. The nurse-midwife program, for instance, is approved by the American College of Nurse-Midwives.

Such accreditation assures students that these programs meet high standards and assures employers that job applicants have been educated in strong, reputable programs.

Adjunct professor: The title given to some teachers who are

- not regular members of the faculty, *or*
- regular faculty members who do some teaching in one department but hold their main academic appointment in another.

Neither type votes on hiring, promotions, and curriculum in the department where they hold an adjunct appointment.

Adjuncts who are *not* regular faculty are sometimes hired to teach specific courses or bring practical expertise to the classroom. For example, a practicing attorney might be hired as an adjunct professor to teach classes in criminal law. Such appointments are sometimes called "clinical professors."

Other adjuncts are professors who hold regular appointments in one department but occasionally teach courses in others. For them, the title "adjunct" is a courtesy appointment. Consider, for example, a professor of political science who specializes in political psychology. If she teaches an occasional course in the psychology department, she might be given an adjunct appointment. Her title would then be "professor of political science and adjunct professor of psychology." If she conducts a lot of research and teaching in psychology, she might be given a full joint appointment in both departments. With a full appointment, she could vote on faculty appointments, curriculum, and other departmental issues in *both* departments.

Adviser: A university staff member or professor who offers guidance and counsel to students, particularly about which courses to select, how to improve academic performance, and how to apply for graduate schools or jobs.

Advisers come in many shapes and sizes and don't always have the formal title of "student adviser." Most universities assign each incoming student an academic adviser, who may be faculty or staff. Other advisers are attached to specific departments, such as student advisers in economics or biochemistry. Still others deal with particular kinds of students, such as prelaw students or international students. Besides helping students choose courses, these advisers are available to discuss academic problems and direct students to resources around the university.

Advanced placement, or AP courses: College-level courses taken in high school. Doing well in AP courses shows that students are both ambitious and well educated, which helps them gain admission to selective universities. Some universities give students undergraduate credit for AP courses. Others do not give college credits but do allow students with AP credits to skip introductory courses or satisfy various course requirements.

Affirmative action: The policy of granting benefits, such as preferential admission to a university, based on an individual's racial or ethnic background (or, sometimes, their gender).

The rationale is that these special benefits compensate for long-standing disadvantages facing the same group. So, for example, African Americans were brought to the United States against their will, held as slaves and, after being freed, were subject to systematic discrimination. This pernicious history has continuing effects, and affirmative action is meant to address them.

Affirmative action is controversial, largely because it forces the classification of individuals as members of groups, confers benefits on the entire group, and, by definition, poses disadvantages to nonmembers. Two students who have the same grades, the same standardized test scores, and the same income would be treated differently if one receives affirmative action preferences and the other does not.

One form of affirmative action has now been ruled illegal: admissions quotas. Quotas are policies that set aside a specific number of admission spots, government contracts, or desirable jobs for members of certain groups. In recent years, before admissions quotas were ruled illegal, they were used as a form of affirmative action to help disadvantaged groups. In the first half of the twentieth century, however, quotas were used in the opposite way, to restrict admission of certain groups, notably Jews, to levels well below what they would have achieved by merit alone.

Alma mater: The generic term for a student's school, usually the one attended as an undergraduate. It may also refer to the school's traditional song. "My alma mater is Yale." Or, "Oh, no, he's going to sing the Princeton alma mater." Latin for "nurturing mother."

"As is": Notice that a product, such as a used car, is being sold with whatever flaws, defects, or breakage it happens to have and without any warranty.

Associate's degree (AA): An associate of arts degree, offered by two-year colleges. A student may take the AA as a final degree or transfer after receiving the degree to a full four-year college and complete a bachelor's degree there.

($) **ATM card:** Small plastic card used to withdraw cash, deposit checks, or conduct other banking transactions at an automated teller machine (ATM).

In Canada, where the machines are called "automated banking machines," the cards are called ABM cards.

Attendance (class attendance): Regular presence at class meetings. Although most classes do not "take attendance" (that is, mark each student present or absent), your presence is essential to your learning.

There are other incentives to attend regularly, as well. Students will fail a test or quiz if it is given when they are absent without a legitimate excuse, such as illness. Students who don't attend seminars regularly cannot join in class discussions, which are considered in the overall grade. Finally, a few classes may actually *require* attendance and reduce the grades of students who do not attend regularly. This is particularly true of smaller introductory courses for undergraduates, such as freshman English composition.

This emphasis on attendance is in marked contrast to European universities, where many classes are large lectures and attendance is purely optional.

(⚖) **Attorney:** A professional qualified to advise clients about their legal rights and obligations, file legal documents, pursue civil remedies in court, and defend clients against criminal accusations. Each U.S. state and Canadian province certifies lawyers, who have the right to speak privately with their clients. The only exception to this rule of "client confidentiality" is when lawyers know a client is breaking a law or intends to do so. In that case, lawyers must report the violation to the court. For a more complete entry, see "lawyer."

Audit: Taking a course for no grade and no academic credit, purely for its educational value. With the professor's permission, auditors may choose whether to take exams and write papers. Usually there is no charge for auditing, but it does require the professor's explicit permission in advance.

If you want to "sit in" on a course like this, you should talk with the professor first. Ask whether you can and, if so, what your role and obligations will be. You might have to do all the reading, for example, or not speak unless called upon (to give priority to students enrolled in the class).

($) **Available funds:** See the entry for "bank balance."

BA, BS: The two principal undergraduate degrees: the Bachelor of Arts (BA) and the Bachelor of Science (BS). Either degree can be called a "baccalaureate" or "bachelor's degree." Sometimes, the name of the student's major (or academic specialization) is added, such as a "BA in English literature" or a "BS in physics."

BA/MA, or joint BA/MA: A program allowing an undergraduate to earn a master's degree (MA) in conjunction with an undergraduate degree (BA) program. Joint BA/

MA programs are not offered in all fields or by all universities. The programs usually take one year less than completing BA and MA degrees consecutively.

Because these joint programs are intensive and demanding, they are restricted to top students. BA/MA students are highly qualified and highly motivated undergraduates, who use the programs to earn master's degrees much faster and at lower cost than they could in separate MA programs.

Baccalaureate or bachelor's degree: General name for an undergraduate degree, either a BA (Bachelor of Arts) or BS (Bachelor of Science).

($) **Bank balance (vs. "available funds"):** The total funds in your account, based on your deposits and withdrawals.

There is an important subcategory of the total balance: the "available balance" or "available funds." That is the amount of money that can be withdrawn from the bank immediately, if you wish. As soon as you deposit cash, for instance, the funds are available for withdrawal. When you deposit a check, however, the funds can be withdrawn only after the check has "cleared," this is, after it has been presented to the bank on which it was written and the funds transferred to the bank where it was deposited. Your total bank balance includes *all* deposits, including checks that have been recently deposited. Those checks are not included in the "available balance" until they have cleared.

To illustrate, let's say that you open a new account at Citibank. You start with $0 in the account and deposit $100 in cash. Your balance becomes $100, and all of it is available for withdrawal. Now you add another deposit, a $50 check from the Bank of America. Your balance is now $150, but you cannot withdraw the extra $50 until that check deposit has cleared (that is, until the check is presented to Bank of America and the $50 has been transferred to your account at Citibank). Your "available balance" is $100 until the check clears.

($) **Bank routing number:** The nine-digit code identifying each U.S. bank and used for sending electronic fund transfers to that institution. To transfer funds to a U.S. bank customer, the sender needs to know two crucial numbers: (1) the routing number for the recipient's bank and (2) the recipient's account number at the bank.

BCL: Bachelor of Civil Law, the degree awarded in Canada to students who specialize in civil code rather than common law. (Common law students are awarded an LLB.) Law programs in Canada are intended for undergraduates. In the United States, students attend law school only after completing a four-year college. The U.S. degree is a JD (standing for Juris Doctor).

Whatever the title of the law degree, students in both the United States and Canada must pass a state or provincial bar examination to qualify to practice law.

Block quotations: A quotation running several sentences or more, set off from the regular text in an indented paragraph (or "block"). While shorter quotes are identified by quotation marks, longer ones are identified by this special indented format and do not include quotation marks. Where a quote is denoted by a block quotation or quotation marks, it must also include a proper citation.

Blue book value: The standard selling price of a particular make and model of used car, adjusted for condition, mileage, and equipment. The term refers to the *Kelley Blue Book*, a reference guide to the used-car market. "Blue book value" is often used as a starting point for bargaining between car buyers and sellers.

Board of trustees: The university's ultimate decision-making body, concerned with major decisions, financial issues, the direction of the institution, and selection of the university president. The board does *not* make decisions about hiring, firing, or promoting individual faculty. Rather, it is charged with legal responsibility for the university as a whole. It is usually composed of senior business executives, politicians, civic leaders, philanthropists, scientists, and leading scholars and administrators from other universities.

The term "board of trustees" is used in most universities, but some use other terms, such as "board of governors," "corporation," or "regents."

Bounced check: A check that is not honored because the check itself is improper or the account on which it is written lacks sufficient funds. A slang term, but a commonly used one. If I write a check for $200 and have only $100 in my account, the check will "bounce." The check will be returned ("bounce back") to the person who deposited it, marked "insufficient funds" or "not sufficient funds." A check can bounce for three reasons: (1) the check is fraudulent; (2) the check is not completely filled out and signed; or (3) the account on which the check is written does not have sufficient funds available.

Bursar's office: The university office that issues bills, collects tuition and fees, and accepts money to be added to student ID cards. An unhappy place to go.

Bursary: A monetary award to students in Canada, based on their financial need.

Call numbers: The unique identifying number for each book or document in the library. This list of numbers is available and searchable in electronic form. Until the 1990s, the catalog was composed of paper notecards. Although the records are now digital, the old version still lingers in memory. You will occasionally hear older people call this database "the card catalog." For many years, that's exactly what it was.

Campus cash cards (or university cash cards): Cards used to purchase items on campus, such as meals or photocopies, using funds deposited with the registrar. Also known as "flexible dollars" or "flex dollars," they work like debit cards on campus. The cards themselves are often the same as student IDs. Additional funds can be added to the card at any time.

Canada Pension Plan (CPP): A mandatory system of insurance to support retired or disabled workers, surviving spouses, and minor children who have lost a parent. Workers and employers are required to pay into the system. For workers, these deductions are made automatically from each paycheck. Equivalent to U.S. Social Security.

Canada Revenue Agency (CRA): The national taxation agency in Canada, equivalent to the Internal Revenue Service (IRS) in the United States. Besides the national income tax, Canadians have to pay taxes to their provincial governments. International students have to pay them, too, if they earn taxable income in Canada.

Career placement office (or "career services" or "placement services"): Organization at each university to help students find permanent jobs, summer jobs, and internships with businesses, government agencies, and nonprofit institutions. The only jobs they do not handle are academic jobs. Placement for those is done through individual departments.

The career placement office not only collects student résumés, it distributes them to potential employers, sets up job interviews, and offers advice to students. It also provides a variety of other practical services, from résumé evaluation to practice job interviews.

Many universities maintain more than one placement office. They have a central office for most students and specialized ones for the business school, law school, education school, and other professions.

($) **CD (or certificate of deposit):** A certificate of deposit, for savings placed at a bank for a predetermined, fixed period (six months, a year, two years, or more). Funds can be withdrawn before the certificate expires, but only by paying a financial penalty. Some CDs offer a fixed rate of interest. Others have "floating rates," which go up or down along with other interest rates in the economy. When customers buy a CD, they must choose the length of deposit (maturity) and whether the interest rate will be fixed or floating.

In Canada, a similar arrangement is called a "guaranteed interest contract," or GIC.

Certificate programs: Nondegree programs that give students a document saying they completed the course of study. These are not formal degrees like a master's. Certificate programs are briefer than graduate degree programs and more specialized. Examples include certificates in real estate marketing, project management, or book editing. Many are designed for midcareer professionals. Depending on the program requirements, students might enter these certificate programs with a BA degree or an MA in a related field.

Chair (chair of a department, also an endowed chair): (1) The head of a university department or committee. The head of the economics department, for example, might be called the "chair" or "chairman." The term "chairman" is used less often now, because women frequently hold these leadership positions. (2) The name for a senior professorial position, often with its own endowment to pay for salary and research. This title may be called a "named chair" or "endowed chair" and is awarded to leading scholars by their universities. Joseph S. Nye, for instance, is the Sultan of Oman Professor of International Relations at Harvard University.

Some universities have more money for these endowed chairs than others and, hence, more chaired professors. Among them, some positions carry larger endowments or more prestige. The most prestigious are typically "university professors" or "distinguished service professors." (Nye holds these titles, too.)

Named chairs are not necessarily the heads of departments or committees. In fact, they usually are not. In other words, a professor might hold a named chair but not be the chair of her department. Conversely, she might be the chair of a department and not hold a named chair. Or she might hold both.

($) **Check (spelled "cheque" in Canada):** A written order to pay a recipient a specific amount from a customer's account at a financial institution, such as a bank. The recipient is known as the "payee." The customer who writes the check is the payer (or payor).

(Ⓐ) **Citizenship and Immigration Canada (CIC):** Canada's national authority for passports, immigration, student visas, and work permits for foreign nationals.

Class hour: (1) The time at which a course meets, such as 10:00 a.m. Each university sets its own regular meeting times for classes. (2) The standard measure of a course load, computed by the number of hours a class meets each week. An academic hour normally lasts fifty minutes, but counts as a full class hour. Thus, a one-hour course meets from 10:00 a.m. until 10:50 (leaving students ten minutes to get to their next class). If a student has four courses that each meet for one hour daily on Monday, Wednesday, and Friday, she would be taking twelve class hours. These are also known as "credit hours."

Class ranking: A list of students in the order of their grades, or an individual student's place on that list. This comparison could refer to a specific course ("I finished in the top 10 percent of my statistics class") or to a much larger group, such as all first-year law students ("I finished in the top quarter of my entering class"). Ranking is based exclusively on students' grade point averages (GPAs).

In high schools, some class rankings are adjusted to compensate for more difficult subjects, such as Advanced Placement courses. Universities don't do that.

International students are often surprised to find that, in the United States and Canada, GPAs and class rankings are considered very important for graduate students as well as undergraduates. In many countries, admission to a selective school is proof enough of a student's ability. In North America, however, employers and others look closely at a student's academic performance, even at the most elite schools.

(🛒) **Classified advertisement:** A small ad, normally placed by an individual (rather than a large company), listing products or services for sale. Often used to sell used furniture, clothing, sports equipment, etc. Classified ads were a mainstay of newspapers for many years. They still appear in newspapers, but the most popular sites are now online.

Closed-book exams: Tests in which students cannot use their books, notes, photocopies, hard drive, PDAs, or Internet access. They must rely entirely on what they already know, unaided by books or technology. In open-book exams, by contrast, students can use all these outside resources, provided that they properly cite their sources and clearly indicate any quotations, as they would in a paper. Unless you are told otherwise, you should assume an exam is closed-book. You are always welcome to ask the professor and, if you are unsure, you should. Whether an exam is open-book or closed, you cannot ask friends for help with any questions. That's cheating.

Clinical professor: Title for some teachers whose primary expertise is based on their jobs and practical experience rather than on their scholarly research. Most professional schools—law, business, medicine, nursing, public policy, architecture, engineering, and education—use some clinical faculty to prepare students for jobs in their fields. Medical schools, for example, employ both research faculty, who hold standard academic appointments, and practicing physicians, who may be given clinical appointments if they concentrate on the practice of medicine rather than on research and publications. Clinical professors generally hold term appointments without tenure, but there are some exceptions.

Coeducational (or coed): (1) A high school, college, or university that includes both men and women. For example, "Princeton was all-male until the 1970s, when it went coed." (2) Occasionally, a term referring to a female student, although it sounds like an antique phrase from a 1940s movie: "Who is that coed I saw you with?"

($) **Collection agency:** A private company hired by lenders (or by loan guarantee agencies) to recover debts from borrowers who have defaulted or fallen behind in their payments. Sometimes, a lender actually sells the loan to the collection agency, which makes money only if it collects. Not surprisingly, dealing with them is no fun at all.

College: In the United States, a school that focuses on undergraduate education, as distinct from a university, which includes both undergraduate and graduate programs. Some colleges, like Williams or Swarthmore, are independent educational institutions with only undergraduate programs. Others, like Yale College, are situated within larger institutions (in this case, Yale University) that include graduate and professional programs.

In Canada, by contrast, the term "college" is not used for undergraduate education. It is used, as it is in England, for schools that prepare students to become undergraduates.

Commencement: The ceremony where degrees are awarded. Even though the event is called a "commencement," it is actually held at the end of the university's year, in May or June. The conceit is that it is the commencement of your life beyond the university.

Committee: A group appointed to supervise an academic program or to deal with a topic, issue, problem, or event. Most university committees are made up of faculty and administrators, although some also have student members. There are two main types of committees, with radically different responsibilities: (1) degree-granting committees, composed of faculty, and (2) administrative or advisory committees, composed of faculty, administrators, and/or students.

Degree-granting committees can award BAs, MAs, or PhD's, just as academic departments do. Take the University of Chicago's Committee on International Relations. With a faculty drawn from various departments, it supervises a master's program, sets course requirements, and grants MA degrees. This particular committee is not authorized to grant BAs or PhD's, although other university committees are.

Students in such committees take two kinds of courses: some specially tailored for its students; others offered by various departments and approved as part of the committee's degree program.

The University of Chicago has similar degree-granting committees in human development, cinema and media studies, evolutionary biology, immunology, and so on. Faculty is normally drawn from existing departmental appointments, although some committees in some universities can hire their own faculty.

Administrative and advisory committees, on the other hand, handle the usual administrative tasks of running a large institution. They do *not* grant degrees. Most universities have regular committees to deal with academic fraud, student discipline, employee benefits, biosafety, computation, honorary degrees, the care and use of animals in research, and so on.

To deal with issues that arise occasionally, universities also appoint temporary, ad hoc administrative committees. An ad hoc faculty committee might recommend the selection of a new dean or the expansion of undergraduate enrollment. An ad hoc committee of faculty, administrators, and students might be asked to recommend options for child care at the university.

Community college: A two-year college, offering an associate's degree. For some students, that degree marks the end of their formal education. Other students transfer to full four-year colleges and complete their BA degrees. For many years, community colleges were known as "junior colleges."

Commuter college: An informal term for universities where most students live at home and travel to school each day, rather than living on campus. Commuting is almost always cheaper for students who already live nearby. It is certainly more convenient for older students, who have spouses, children, and full-time jobs. Not surprisingly, these commuter schools have fewer social and cultural activities on campus.

While commuter schools have a full range of courses, many focus on programs that provide job skills or lead to career advancement—practical programs that are well suited to their student body. For example, a commuter college may have a large program in criminal justice, directed at students who want to join the police or who already have a job there and want to be promoted.

All large cities in the United States and Canada have at least one commuter college and many have several.

Conditional admission: Admission to a university or to a particular program that is subject to a student's completing some coursework or meeting other requirements.

Confidentiality: Legal protection against the disclosure of information. There are strict laws and regulations that prohibit doctors and lawyers from disclosing information given to them privately by their clients. The goal is to ensure that clients can speak candidly to their attorneys or physicians.

The laws governing confidentiality are strong, but there are some exceptions. When a client informs a lawyer that he intends to break the law, the lawyer is obliged to reveal that to the courts. Similarly, doctors, nurses, and other health professionals have legal obligations when patients have certain contagious diseases, when they think a patient might endanger themselves or others, or when they think a child might have been abused. In these rare but important cases, professionals are generally required to violate confidentiality and disclose the information to proper authorities.

Consignment shop: A special type of second-hand store, where the goods still belong to their original owner until they are actually sold. The shop takes goods "on consignment" from their owner and offers them for sale to the public. If the goods are sold, the proceeds are split between the shop and the original owner. If the goods are not sold within a specified period, such as three months, they are returned to the owner.

Cooperative education (coop education): An integrated educational program, offered by some universities, combining a paid job with academic coursework. Although international student visas do not normally allow paying jobs off campus, they usually do permit students to hold jobs that are part of cooperative education programs. Be sure to check with the international student adviser's office to make sure a particular coop job qualifies.

Copay: The portion of each medical or pharmacy bill for which you, rather than the insurance company, are responsible. The copay is a fixed dollar amount for each bill and is specified by your insurance policy or HMO coverage. When you fill a prescription, for example, you may be required to pay $15 each time; your insurance company or HMO pays the remainder. This is essentially the same as an insurance "deductible."

Corequisite: A course that must be taken concurrently with another one, or before it. A rarely used term and a rarely used concept. Prerequisites are much more common. They refer to a course that must be taken *prior* to enrolling in a more advanced one.

Cosign or cosigner: Someone who signs a lease or other financial document along with you and is responsible for it if you fail to meet your obligations. If you, a roommate, and your mother all sign a lease, *each* of you is individually responsible for the entire amount.

Students may need a cosigner for three reasons. One is if they are not legally old enough to sign the documents. The "age of emancipation" is set by state law and varies from eighteen to twenty-one. If renters are still minors, they can't be held legally responsible for their agreements, so an adult needs to sign. Another reason is that they may have a bad credit record or none at all. The absence of a credit record is considered the same as a bad record. The landlord or lender, naturally concerned about receiving the rent each month, might refuse to complete the transaction without an additional guarantor—one who has a solid financial record. Finally, even if you are an adult and have a good financial record, some landlords and lenders simply want to get additional signatures as security. They might be willing to rent the apartment without these signatures, but (as they see it) there's no harm in asking.

If you do need a cosigner, make sure that the lease is not a "continuing agreement." If the agreement simply continues "as is" when you renew it, then so does the cosigner's guarantee. He or she is still responsible. That might not be necessary after you've leased an apartment for a year and built up a good record. So, if you renew a lease, ask to sign a new agreement without a cosigner.

Core curriculum (or core requirements): A course or set of courses required of all students. Different parts of the university may have their own core curricula. For example, all entering freshmen may be required to take a specific course in English literature or biological science. Later, all students who choose to major in, say, statistics may be required to take a basic course in that subject or prove they already know the material. Similarly, many graduate programs have a small set of core courses required of all students in a particular field.

Counselor: Someone who advises students. There are two main types of counselors or advisers, and they have quite different responsibilities: (1) academic counselors, who review students' progress and advise them which courses to take, and (2) therapeutic counselors, who assist students with difficult personal and emotional issues. They are psychiatrists, psychologists, social workers, and psychiatric nurses who provide confidential services, usually through the student mental health center or university hospital.

All universities have both kinds of counselors. When students enter school, they are assigned an academic counselor. Psychological counseling services are available by request and are usually covered (or partly covered) by student health insurance.

Course catalog: A complete listing of university classes. It may also include a description of their content and their meeting times. Once available only in hard copy, it is now offered online, as well. The convenience of the electronic catalog is offset by the computer system's uncanny ability to crash when you really need it.

Course credit: Recognition by an academic institution that a student has passed a course. Different universities total course credits in different ways. Some simply count the number of courses a student passes. "So far, he has two course credits in economics." Others count credits by the number of hours a course meets each week. A course that meets for one hour on Mondays, Wednesdays, and Fridays for one semester would count as three credit hours. If the same course met only on Mondays and Wednesdays, it would count as two credit hours. "To complete her major, she still needs six credit hours in physics."

Course load: The number of courses a student is taking or the total number of credit hours for these courses. For example, "I'm taking a three-course load." Or, "I've got a fifteen-hour load." These measures determine whether a student is considered full-time or part-time, a crucial distinction for international students, since their visas require enrollment as full-time students.

Course number: The digit and letter system used to identify courses at each university. The numbers and letters are often used to identify the level of a course (such as graduate or undergraduate) or the area of the university where it is offered. These systems differ at each university.

At the University of Chicago, for example, a 100-level course is a freshman core course. A 200-level course is a departmental course for upper-level undergraduates. A 300-level course is a standard graduate course. A 400- or 500-level course is an advanced graduate seminar or workshop. Besides these numbers, Chicago uses initials to represent departments, such as PS for political science. So a course labeled PS398 is a graduate-level course in political science.

Course registration (and limits on course registration): Enrollment in a specific course or, alternatively, the time when students can enroll in courses. "I'm registering for this course" means I'm signing up to take it. "Registration lasts a couple more days" means the enrollment period for all courses lasts two more days.

Registration for a particular course might be limited by the size of the room or a professor's desire to teach a small seminar rather than a large lecture. Registration might also be limited to students who have fulfilled certain prerequisites. For example, an advanced course in capital markets might allow students to register only if they have completed prior coursework in microeconomics, calculus, and statistics. Any of these limitations might mean that you cannot register for a course you wish to take.

Cramming: Intense preparation immediately before an exam. Slang. "I stayed up all night cramming for today's test."

Credit bureau: National company that collects and sells information about whether individuals pay their bills promptly and fully. There are three major U.S. credit bureaus that collate information from lenders, vendors, and other sources, and then sell that information to anyone who wants to check someone's credit, such as credit card companies, landlords, or automobile dealers. (See the entry for "credit rating.")

Credit card, debit card, ATM card, ABM card: Small plastic cards used to purchase goods and services, withdraw cash, or, in the case of ATM or ABM cards, conduct other banking transactions.

Credit cards are used to make purchases or withdraw cash, using borrowed money. The user repays all or part of the borrowings each month. For any unpaid balances, there are interest charges (usually high ones), plus fees for any late payments.

Debit cards work differently. When the card is used, payment for each transaction is withdrawn immediately from the user's bank account. The card is a kind of instant electronic check. No loans are involved, so the user can purchase as much as his bank balance permits—and no more. For the same reason, the card does not build a user's credit rating.

ATM cards in the United States and ABM cards in Canada are used at automated teller machines to withdraw cash, make deposits, and conduct other banking transactions. Each bank has its own network of teller machines, which are usually free for the bank's own customers. Customers of other banks can use them, too, but they must pay a service charge of $1–$2 for each transaction.

Credit hours: One measure of a student's course load, figured by the number of hours a class normally meets each week. For example, a course that meets for fifty minutes (considered a "class hour") every Monday, Wednesday, and Friday counts as three credit hours. Many universities use credit hours to measure student course loads, full-time enrollment, and progress toward a degree or major. The number of credit hours also affects a course's tuition cost.

($) **Credit rating:** The standard measure of an individual or corporation's ability to service debt. It is based on prior payments, income, savings, and other financial information. A borrower who repays debts on time builds a good credit rating.

International students who are new to the United States and Canada usually have no local credit experience and, hence, no rating. Unfortunately, lenders consider "no rating" to be the same as a "bad rating." That has two implications. First, it is hard for newly arrived students to get credit cards or borrow money. Second, it is important to build a good local credit history as soon as possible.

In the United States and Canada, three large companies handle all consumer credit ratings: Equifax, Experian, and TransUnion. (Their Web addresses are simply their names, followed by .com.) Their giant databases consolidate and summarize an individual's transactions. They provide this information, particularly a summary credit score, to lenders, such as credit card companies, mortgage agencies, or banks. Lenders use this information to decide whether to provide credit to potential borrowers and whether to charge them high rates to reflect greater risks of slow payment or nonpayment.

In recent years, U.S. laws have made credit ratings more transparent. Borrowers now have a right to see their own credit rating (known as a "credit score"), review the credit agency's information about them, and correct any misinformation in the records.

Curriculum vitae (also called a "CV" or "vita"): A complete listing of a student or faculty member's academic accomplishments, including education, employment, publications, unpublished papers, grants, fellowships, and awards. If a scholar was the principal investigator (PI) on a grant or a senior researcher in a laboratory, that would be included. So would important academic service like organizing a convention program. A younger scholar might also list convention presentations and conference papers, though a senior scholar (who has made countless presentations) would probably omit them. Unlike a résumé, which is an abbreviated listing, the CV is comprehensive.

Cut a class: Skipping attendance at one session of a class. Slang. "I was up late last night, so I cut my nine o'clock French class." Some teachers base grades partly on class attendance or participation, so cutting a class may result in a lower grade. It may also mean an unauthorized absence from a test or quiz, which usually results in a grade of zero for that assignment. Cutting a single class is *not* the same as dropping or withdrawing permanently from a course.

Date rape: Forced, coerced, or other involuntary sex between partners who have some prior social relationship. The idea here is that rape can occur among people who know each other, not just among strangers.

This concept is widely accepted in the United States and Canada, and it has important legal implications. If a student alleges she was raped, it is not a sufficient defense to reply, "Well, she agreed to come back to my room at 3 a.m. so she must have known what we were going to do." Agreeing to visit another student's room, however late the hour, does *not* imply consent to have sexual relations. Neither does drinking together, kissing, or even fondling each other.

Involuntary sex is sometimes the result of secretly administered drugs, which render the victim unconscious or confused. Known as "date rape drugs," these odorless, tasteless chemicals are mixed into alcoholic drinks. Whether the comatose victim is raped or not, administering the drug itself it is a serious crime and a moral outrage.

Dean: A senior university official responsible for academic or administrative matters or for student affairs. The term may be confusing because universities have so many deans, with such varied responsibilities. There are two main types of deans: (1) academic (2) nonacademic (or administrative). The dean of the social sciences, for example, supervises that entire academic division and is one of the top scholarly positions in the university. The heads of various departments, such as political science and economics, report to this dean, who has wide-ranging authority over faculty appointments, financial matters, and strategic planning for the division as a whole. The same is true for the dean of the law school or the dean of arts and sciences. These are senior academic posts.

The dean of students, on the other hand, is a senior administrative position, not a scholarly one, even though a professor may hold it. This dean has extensive responsibility over student matters but none over faculty appointments or research at the university. The same is true for a dean of admissions or dean of international students.

Dean's list: A list of undergraduates who excelled academically that semester.

 Debit card: Small plastic card that works like an electronic check to withdraw funds from a user's bank account. See the entry on "credit cards" for a more complete discussion.

 Deductible, insurance deductible: The fixed dollar amount an insured policyholder is required to pay personally for *each* insured event, such as an auto accident, a trip to the doctor, or a prescription. Although the insurance company pays most of the cost, you must pay some of it yourself, beginning with the first dollar of expenses. After you have incurred expenses equal to the deductible, say $100 or $500, the insurer pays the remainder (or a portion of the remainder, such as 80 percent). The amount you pay is known as the "deductible." In medical care, it may be called a "deductible," "copay," or "copayment."

Let's say you bought a car insurance policy with a very low deductible, $100. If you have a minor accident costing less than $50, you'll pay all the costs yourself. If the accident cost $500, you'd pay $100 (the deductible); the insurance company would pay the remaining $400. If the accident cost $5,000, you'd still pay $100 (if that was your deductible) and the insurance company would pay $4,900.

If you had a higher deductible, say $250, then the insurance company would pay nothing on a $50 accident or even a $240 accident. If the accident cost $1,000, the company would pay $750. Naturally, policies with higher deductibles like this cost much less.

Defense (or dissertation defense): An oral examination of an individual student, covering a complete draft of the master's thesis or doctoral dissertation. The examiners always include the student's thesis committee. Some universities also include other faculty, known as "external examiners."

The focus is not on verbal agility but on the quality of the written work. The student must be able to explain the subject matter, the principal conclusions, and the intellectual choices involved in the research project. The committee may ask the student to defend the findings against alternative interpretations.

Students almost always pass, but that is because the thesis adviser will not schedule the exam until she deems the thesis passable. Still, many examining committees recommend (or require) changes in the draft before passing it.

Defense Language Proficiency Test (DLPF): Computerized exams to evaluate native English speakers' ability to read foreign languages and to understand them when spoken. Designed for the U.S. Department of Defense (DOD), the test is now in its fifth version (DLPF 5) and covers more than thirty languages. Although the tests are meant for the military and other U.S. government personnel, where they lead to better jobs and bonus pay, their standards inevitably affect other language-teaching programs.

Deferral: Accepting a university's offer of admission but asking to postpone actual enrollment, usually by one semester or one year. A university may choose to grant the request or not. Even if they grant it, they still must choose whether or not to guarantee the same offer of financial aid. Any student considering deferral should discuss these issues with the university and relevant department and resolve them *before* making the final decision. It is prudent to get the agreed terms in writing so there is no confusion when you enroll later.

Degree student: A student enrolled in an academic program and working toward a recognized degree, such as a Bachelor of Arts or Master of Science. Degree students are distinguished from students who are taking courses but not seeking a degree. Non-degree students are sometimes called "at-large students," "special students," or other terms.

Department: A section of the university, specializing in one discipline or subject, with its own faculty members and students. Faculty may be associated primarily with the department, or they may do some teaching and research there but hold their primary appointments in other departments. An economics professor might teach one course at the law school, perhaps on industrial organization, and hold an adjunct professorship there.

Within a department, faculty set standards for undergraduate majors and graduate degrees (consistent with university rules), admit graduate students, appoint new faculty, and make tenure decisions. Undergraduates are normally admitted by the university, not by a specific department, but some selective departments choose whether or not a student will be permitted to major in their subjects.

Department of Motor Vehicles (DMV): The most common name for the state agency that issues drivers' licenses, automobile license plates, and photo identification cards for nondrivers. All states and provinces have departments like this, though their names differ.

Designated driver: Someone at a party who avoids alcohol and drugs in order to drive friends home safely.

Diploma mill: The nickname for a company selling specious "academic degrees" that do not entail significant coursework and are not approved by reputable accreditation agencies. It is a fraudulent commercial transaction, for both the buyer and seller. The seller is a fake university, providing no educational services. The buyer is a fake student, using the degree to deceive employers, customers, and clients.

Direct deposit: An electronic funds transfer, often used to pay wages or pensions directly to an employee's bank account. These arrangements are faster and more secure than issuing paper checks, which must be endorsed and deposited, and therefore can be lost or stolen. Many employers, including universities, make direct deposits for their workers, but you need to ask. You'll also need to fill out the required forms, which include your bank account number and the bank's routing number.

Distance learning: An alternative term for online courses.

Distribution requirements: A rule that students must take courses in several different academic areas. At Northwestern University, for instance, all undergraduates must take at least one course in each of six broad areas, such as natural sciences, historical studies, and literature and fine arts. The purpose is to ensure that all students receive the rudiments of a liberal education.

Later, when students choose a major or go to graduate school, they usually face another set of distribution requirements, but this time *within* their chosen discipline. Again, the purpose is to ensure breadth of knowledge. For example, a graduate program in political science might require that all students to take at least one course in international relations, one in comparative politics, and one in political philosophy.

To avoid confusion, the university or department classifies each course as falling within one area or another so students know in advance whether taking a particular course fulfills a distribution requirement.

Double major (also known as "dual major" or "joint major"): Specializing in two subjects and fulfilling the requirements for both as undergraduate majors. For details, see "Dual major."

Drop/add: The period at the beginning of each semester when students can change courses freely, adding new ones they wish to take and dropping old ones. This period might last a week or two, depending on the university. Students are not charged for courses that are dropped, and they do not appear on the university's official transcript. In these respects, dropping a course is significantly different from withdrawing, which is done later in the term and usually does appear on the transcript, either temporarily or permanently.

The drop/add period has important benefits for all students. They can use the drop/add period to explore courses without committing themselves for the entire semester. They can sample a course for several sessions, see what the course covers and how the professor conducts it, and then choose whether to take that course or a different one. It's a savvy way to select courses, and international students should take full advantage of it.

DSL: Technology protocol for delivering broadband Internet using traditional copper telephone wires. Requires a telephone landline in your apartment. As an alternative, you can use cable for broadband.

DUI, DWI: Frequently-used initials for drunk driving. The initials stand for two similar terms: "Driving Under the Influence" and "Driving While Intoxicated." To prevent such dangerous behavior, police promote the use of a "designated driver," a friend who avoids drinking in order to drive everyone home safely.

Dual major (also known as "joint major" or "double major"): Specializing in two subjects as an undergraduate. Dual majors must meet the requirements in both fields, but they are normally allowed to count a few courses and papers twice (that is, as fulfilling the requirements in both fields). For example, when a dual major in chemistry and biology takes a biochemistry course, it might count toward the completion of requirements in both fields. Such rules obviously differ across departments and across universities. Any student considering a dual major should review the rules carefully and speak directly with academic advisers in *both* fields. Do it as early as possible.

A dual major is said to receive a "joint degree" in two subjects, for example, a "BS in mathematics and physics." The terms "dual major," "joint major," and "double major" are equivalent. Different universities simply use different terms.

Elective: Courses that are optional rather than required. A typical degree program sets a total number of courses, requires several specific courses, and lets students choose others. Students "elect" which optional courses to take, though the choices may be limited to a particular set of courses or specific level of difficulty.

Electronic funds transfer (EFT): Payment system in which banks and their customers transmit funds via computer, rather than by checks or cash. In effect, an electronic check, also called "direct deposit." When an employee receives wages by EFT, for example, the employer transfers funds to the recipient's bank account by a computer transaction. It's a safe, sure, instantaneous way to deposit funds, and it eliminates the effort of going to the bank and depositing checks.

The United States and Canadian governments make many of their payments that way, including the distribution of student loans. To receive such a transfer, a student must have a bank account.

You can also use EFT to make payments, either automatically or at your discretion. You might set up automatic payments to your cable company and write discretionary electronic checks to your credit card company each month.

Electronic reserve: Required course readings, which the library makes available to students online. These electronic documents supplement the library's physical reserve readings—books and photocopied articles available for short-term loans.

Reserve readings are usually assigned course materials, which many students need to read at about the same time. Libraries cope with this high demand by buying more copies, shortening the borrowing period, photocopying assigned articles, and scanning articles or chapters so they can be read online.

ELL: English language learner. Non-native speakers taking courses to acquire English.

ELPT: English Language Proficiency Test, for students who are not native English speakers.

EMBA: Executive Master of Business Administration. An MBA for current executives, who generally take classes at night and on weekends so they can continue their current, full-time jobs.

(℞) **Emergency Room:** The portion of a hospital intended to treat sudden illnesses or injuries that need immediate medical care. Some hospitals also have a special emergency room for trauma victims such as automobile accidents or shootings.

Because hospital emergency rooms are open around the clock and do not require appointments, they are sometimes misused for ordinary doctor visits. They shouldn't be. Visits to the emergency room are very expensive and are covered by HMOs and insurance only when the patient has serious, unexpected medical problems. For less serious or less pressing problems, make an appointment with your doctor or use your HMO's "walk-in hours," when doctors on duty see patients without appointments.

Emeritus professor: A retired faculty member. Many continue to conduct research and work at their campus offices. A few even continue to teach and advise students. However, they no longer receive regular salaries and no longer vote on university or departmental matters.

($) **Employment Insurance (EI):** Canadian program that pays workers during brief periods of unemployment and supports their retraining, if needed. Funded by mandatory deductions from wages.

ESL: An acronym for "English as a second language." The term is used in the United States, Canada, and Australia. ESL programs are now offered routinely by universities, nonprofit agencies, and businesses. Courses are available at several levels, from novice to advanced, and may include specialized courses on "business English" or "English in the health professions." Courses are also available to help speakers reduce their native accents, an important goal for teachers and business executives.

ESOL: An acronym for "English for speakers of other languages." The same as ESL (English as a second language), but more commonly used in the UK, Ireland, and New Zealand.

ETS: Educational Testing Service, the nonprofit organization that administers TOEFL (Test of English as a Foreign Language) and TSE (Test of Spoken English), as well as other tests. Information about them is available at www.ets.org

Exam period: One or two weeks at the end of the semester (or quarter) when tests are given and longer papers are due. Course meetings are *not* held during this week.

Exams or examinations: Tests designed to assess student knowledge, progress, and ability; usually involves assigning grades, though not always. Exams come in many shapes and sizes. Some require students to write long essays. These are, in effect, short papers. The student may be told exactly what to write about or allowed to choose among several topics. Other exams ask the student to answer many short questions. The questions are answered either by

- choosing one of three or four possible responses ("multiple choice"),
- agreeing or disagreeing ("true/false"), or
- completing a short sentence ("fill in the blank").

A student might also be asked to identify names, places, events, chemical formulas, mathematical equations, or other topics by writing a few sentences. These identification exercises are called "ID questions." Exams often combine several short questions with one or two longer essay questions.

Exams may be either "closed-book" or "open-book." Closed-book exams do not permit students to use any notes, books, or electronic sources. Most exams given in the classroom are closed-book, but it always pays to check. Open-book exams permit the use of outside sources, which should be properly cited or explicitly quoted, as they would be in a paper.

It is vital for students to know, in advance, whether an exam is open-book or closed. In either case, a student may not receive help from another student or give such help. That's cheating for *both* students.

Expulsion: Prohibition from attending the university, because of either failing grades or serious misbehavior. Unlike suspension, expulsion carries no implied promise of readmission at a later date. It is the most serious penalty a university can impose on a student, and each university has its own rules and procedures for doing so. Expulsion has grave consequences for international students, since their visas require them to be registered as full-time students. (See also the entry for "suspension.")

Externship: (See the entry for "internship.")

Extracurricular activities: Sports teams, music groups, ethnic and religious organizations, social clubs, and charity work (such as tutoring poor children) in which students voluntarily participate outside class. Students do not receive grades, academic credit, or pay for extracurricular activities, but they may list them on their résumés.

U.S. and Canadian campuses host a wide range of such activities. Many students participate, especially undergraduates. Extracurricular activities can be a major asset on the job market, especially if the activity is relevant to professional skills or demonstrates a student's leadership skills. Potential employers routinely ask applicants about their extracurricular activities and any leadership positions they have held.

F (or failure): The lowest grade given for a course. Equal to a grade point of zero (0) and known colloquially as "flunking." Failed courses do not count toward the requirements for graduation, but they are included in the student's GPA.

Factory outlet (factory outlet mall): A store that is owned by a manufacturer, selling its own products at discounted prices, or a shopping center featuring such stores. All products at factory outlets are new. Some are overstocks, others are discontinued models or last year's styles. Some may be clearly marked as "irregular" or "factory seconds." They have minor flaws and cannot be sold at full price because they are not "first quality."

Factory seconds (manufacturer's seconds; irregulars): New products that failed to pass the manufacturer's quality inspection because they have minor flaws or blemishes, which do not interfere with the product's intended use. They are marked as "seconds" or "irregulars" and sold at reduced prices, either at factory outlets or at other discount stores.

Family Education Rights and Privacy Act (FERPA): A U.S. law requiring that student education records be kept private. Grades, honors, disciplinary actions, and other information cannot be disclosed to potential employers, graduate schools, or anyone else outside the university without the student's written permission.

Federal government: The national government in the United States or Canada. Both are federal systems, meaning that power is shared between the central government (in Washington or Ottawa) and the states or provinces (such as Ohio or Ontario). Sometimes, people refer to "Washington" or "Ottawa," meaning the federal government. "Washington is allocating more funds for scientific research this year."

Fees: Charges made each semester for university services, in addition to tuition. Many universities charge a "student activities fee" to cover music, movies, parties, and other entertainment events. Registered students, who have paid the fees, can then attend the events at low cost or sometimes for free. Different fees cover campus buses, parking on campus, health insurance, use of the computer network, and so forth.

Depending on the type of fee, it might apply to all students, only to undergraduates, or only to students who live on campus. Some, like the cost of parking on campus, apply only to students who request the service.

($) **Fee waiver:** Permission, given by the university, to avoid paying some student fees. Some fees can be avoided without a waiver since they apply only to students who request a particular service, such as a campus bus pass or parking permit. Other fees are normally charged to every student and can be avoided only be requesting a specific waiver. Students who take online courses, for example, can usually avoid paying needless fees for transportation or social activities on campus, *if* they make a request. At many schools, students with financial need may request waiver of some fees. Each university has its own rules and procedures to decide which waiver requests are granted.

Field exams: Major examinations in graduate school, usually given after the second year of doctoral programs and covering several areas of the discipline. The terms of these exams differ among graduate programs, but their common aim is to ensure that students have mastered the main elements of their discipline.

Field exams are sometimes called "qualifying exams" because passing them is necessary to stay in the program and qualify to write a doctoral dissertation. Not all doctoral programs require these exams.

($) **FICA:** The Federal Insurance Contributions Act, used to fund U.S. Social Security pensions and Medicare (old-age health insurance) by mandatory deductions from wages. FICA taxes, which are slightly over 15 percent of earned income, are paid jointly by the employer and employee. This means employee paychecks are automatically reduced by about 7.5 percent.

(🛒) **Flea market (swap meet):** A marketplace where small vendors sell inexpensive new and used items, often outdoors in the summer and in plain, indoor locations, such as a warehouse, in the winter. The low overhead contributes to low prices, which buyers and sellers haggle over.

Flea markets are sometimes called "swap meets" because they originated as bartering sessions, where neighbors swapped items with each other. Today, nearly all sellers are small merchants who purchase their products and sell them for cash.

Flexible dollars or "flex dollars": Funds deposited with the registrar and used to purchase items on campus, such as meals or photocopying. The funds are accessed by using the student's ID, which works like a debit card on campus. Additional funds can be added to the card at any time, usually by beleaguered parents.

Foreign Language and Area Studies Fellowship (FLAS): Major source of U.S. government funding for graduate students who study selected areas of the world and their languages. FLAS funding is available only to full-time students who are U.S. citizens or permanent residents, or are becoming citizens. International students are not eligible.

($) **401k, also 403(b)(7):** Retirement savings programs for employees at some U.S. businesses and nonprofit institutions. Employees can direct some pretax earnings into these accounts and invest them in stocks, bonds, and other instruments at their own discretion, within the limits of the employer's plan. Typically, employers match some or all of the employee's monthly contributions. The funds accumulate tax-free and are taxed as income only when they are finally withdrawn after retirement. Early withdrawals are possible, but are usually penalized.

For-profit companies use 401k plans; nonprofits, including universities, use 403(b) (7) plans. The two retirement programs are virtually identical, despite their different numbers. The university's office of employee benefits (or human resources) can advise employees on their eligibility to participate and the terms of their university's plan.

411: The number dialed to request the phone numbers for individuals and businesses, locally or nationally. Termed "directory assistance," there's a fee for using it (added to your monthly phone charges). You can do this without cost on your computer, but online databases are not as up-to-date as directory assistance.

Fraternities, sororities: Undergraduate social organizations, where members typically live, eat, and party. Also known as "Greeks," since they are identified by two or three Greek letters, such as Kappa Alpha. Fraternities are for men, sororities for women.

On some campuses (but not on others), fraternities and sororities are the center of college social life. Their houses are often near each other on "fraternity row" and "sorority row." Freshmen are recruited each autumn during "rush" period, when new students meet current members at special parties. Those chosen as future members are called "pledges."

Freshman, sophomore, junior, senior: Names given to students at each year of undergraduate education.

Freshman	First-year undergraduate
Sophomore	Second-year undergraduate
Junior	Third-year undergraduate
Senior	Fourth (and final)-year undergraduate

The same terms are used in high schools, so a ninth grader is a freshman, a twelfth grader a senior. Students who have completed an academic year are said to be "rising" to the next year. So, after completing sophomore year, a student is called a "rising junior." These terms refer to coursework actually completed, not to years spent in school. So, if I went to school part time and took three years to complete my freshman requirements, I would enter my fourth year of study as a sophomore (not a senior).

Graduate schools do *not* use these terms. Students are referred to as "first-year," "second-year," and so on (*ad infinitum* for some graduate students).

Frosh: Nickname for freshman, a first-year undergraduate. Slang.

Fulbright grants: A major U.S. government program to support two types of research and study: (1) U.S. students and teachers going to other countries for approved research and studies, and (2) international exchange students and teachers coming to the United States for similar studies. The Fulbright program is administered by the Institute of International Education (IIE) and funded by the U.S. government, foreign governments, and private donors.

Full-time student: A student carrying a normal load of courses or credit hours. Each school has its own standards for that load. In most universities, twelve credit hours is a full-time load for undergraduates. That means four courses, each meeting for three hours per week. (A "credit hour" is actually fifty minutes of class time.) The full-time load for a graduate student is slightly less, usually nine credit hours.

Maintaining full-time status is crucial for international students since student visas require it. It is also required of U.S. students receiving federal scholarships.

GED: The General Educational Development (GED) test, given to students who have not completed high school but wish to prove that they have acquired the same knowledge. A GED is considered the equivalent of a high school diploma. GED tests are similar in the United States and Canada.

General education (or "gen ed"): Undergraduate programs requiring students to take several courses spread across the social sciences, humanities, history, and the natural sciences. A course within that curriculum is sometimes called a "gen ed" course.

General education programs, also known as "core curricula," are common in the first two years of undergraduate education. They are designed to give students broad grounding in the arts and sciences. Sometimes the courses are specially designed to introduce students to an important area, such as ethics or evolutionary biology. Sometimes, they are simply introductory courses in various disciplines, with a requirement to take several such courses.

Generic drug: A nonbranded medication that has the same active ingredient and strength as a brand-name drug. Because the generic drug is not subject to patent protection and has no research or advertising expenses, it costs less than its brand-name equivalent. Because generic drugs save money, health plans either require them or pay a larger percentage of their costs.

GIC (guaranteed interest contract): In Canada, a single deposit made at a financial institution for a fixed period (ranging from one month to several years), paying a predetermined rate of interest. Some contracts permit early withdrawal of funds, but charge a penalty for actually withdrawing funds before the contract expires. Other contracts do not permit early withdrawal.

In the United States, a similar arrangement is called a "certificate of deposit," or CD.

GPA (grade point average): The numerical average of a student's grades, usually based on a four-point scale, where an A is worth four points, a B is worth three, and so on. The grade of B+ (B plus) is worth 3/10 of a point more than straight B. B– (B minus) is worth 3/10 of a point less than straight B. The full list is:

A	4.0 points
A−	3.7
B+	3.3
B	3
B−	2.7
C+	2.3
C	2
C−	1.7
D+	1.3
D	1
F	0

Grades are averaged numerically over all the student's courses. If a student took four courses and made an A, B+, B−, and C, that would be 4.0, 3.3, 2.7, and 2, for a total of 12 points. The average for these four courses, then, is 3.0, or a straight B. This example counts all courses equally. If some involved more course hours, they would be weighted more heavily.

The university calculates these averages, and students pay close attention to them, mainly because they are convenient summaries of academic performance. Employers, faculty, and advisers often ask about them. A student might say, for example, "I have a 3.1 overall and 3.7 in my major." Translated: I make slightly better than a B average in all my courses, but I maintain an A− average in my major subject. GPAs are used to calculate student honors (such as the dean's list) and identify student problems (such as academic probation).

Graduate student union: A labor organization composed of graduate students whose goal is to raise their wages and benefits as teaching assistants.

($) **Grant versus loan:** Two forms of student financial assistance. A grant is an outright gift of aid. It does not need to be repaid. A loan does. Aid to individual students often contains a mixture of loans and grants. The most obvious is when a student loan is "excused" (does not have to be repaid) because the student takes a certain kind of job, such as teaching impoverished children. In that case, what was once a loan becomes an outright grant.

Even when loans are not forgiven, they often contain some hidden grant elements. If a student loan rate is 2 percentage points less than the market interest rate, that 2 percent reduction is effectively a grant. Likewise, if a student would not qualify for a commercial loan but is given a student loan because the government guarantees it, then there is a grant element.

Grade inflation: Weakening standards for evaluating student work so that papers and exams receive higher marks today than they would have twenty or thirty years ago. Most studies show that grading standards in North America have slackened over the past three decades. In the 1950s or 1960s, a mediocre paper might receive a C or C+. Today, it is more likely to receive a B. There is considerable debate—and no real consensus—on what caused the grading changes.

Grader: A graduate student who marks undergraduate papers and exams in a particular class. Unlike a teaching assistant, who also marks papers and exams, a grader does not conduct regular student discussion sections.

Grades (letter grades, pass/fail/, R, audit): The evaluation mark a student receives for a paper, problem set, lab assignment, exam, or entire course. The top grade is normally an A, though some schools permit an A+ (A plus). Below that are A– (A minus), B+, B, B–, C+, C, C–, D, and F (fail). All these are known as "letter grades." They can be readily converted to a numerical scale to calculate grade point averages (GPA). An "A" is equal to 4, a B to 3, and so on.

Some schools allow other grades as well, or allow them for specific courses. The most common is "pass/fail." If a student takes a course pass/fail, then any letter grade above "F" is simply marked as "pass." Students sometimes choose to take courses pass/fail to lessen the pressure for high grades or to explore courses in new subjects that might lower their overall average. Normally, a professor has to give permission for a student to take a course pass/fail, and most require that the student make that decision early in the course, rather than wait to see whether the letter grade is high or low.

Students do not receive academic credit for courses they fail (F). Those courses do not count toward the total courses or credit hours they need to graduate. The grade of D is not failing, but, depending on the school, it may not count as passing, either. Whether a "D" is credited as passing a course (and counting toward graduation requirements) depends on the university.

For individual assignments, a professor or teaching assistant might give a student a mark such as A–/B+, which means the assignment is on the borderline between the two grades. Such hyphenated grades are not permitted on the official transcript.

An auditor is someone who attends a course with the professor's permission but does not receive a course grade. Most schools do not show audited courses on the official transcript, but a few do, with a special mark such as "R" (for "registered"). Auditors are not normally charged for attending.

Greeks: The informal (slang) name for fraternities and sororities or for their student members. So called because fraternities and sororities are identified by two or three Greek letters, such as Zeta Beta Tau.

Gray market (or grey market): Legitimate, new products (not counterfeits) sold by distributors who are not authorized by the manufacturer. Gray-market channels almost always sell products for less. But they carry some risk to consumers. Because the sellers are unauthorized, the manufacturer may refuse to honor the warranties or decline responsibility for the products.

Products sometimes enter the gray market because they cost significantly less in one country or region. A distributor can purchase them there, ship them abroad, and sell them for higher prices. Lacking the manufacturer's warranty and product support, prices for gray-market goods must be lower than those from authorized dealers. If they were not, consumers would simply buy from authorized dealers.

⊕ **GST (Good and Services Tax):** Canadian national sales tax of 7 percent, applied to nearly all goods and services. Similar to VAT (Value Added Tax). The national GST is in addition to provincial sales taxes.

Three eastern provinces combined the GST with their own sales taxes to create the HST, the Harmonized Sales Tax. Nova Scotia, New Brunswick, and Newfoundland and Labrador add their 8 percent local taxes to the 7 percent national tax, creating a 15 percent HST. It applies only in those three provinces.

⚖ **Health-care power of attorney:** A document in which one person delegates the right ℞ to make health-care decisions if he or she is incapacitated. The aim is to allow a relative or trusted friend to make life-or-death medical decisions for someone who is gravely ill and cannot make the decisions for himself. A man might give these powers to his wife, parents, brother, friend, or same-sex partner. Granting this power over health-care decisions does *not* grant any power to make financial decisions for the patient. (See also the entry for "living will.")

℞ **Health insurance:** A policy that pays for standard medical treatment, specialist care, emergencies, and prescription medicine, in return for a fixed monthly fee plus a surcharge (copay) for each doctor's visit or prescription. The alternative to such insurance is membership in a health maintenance organization (HMO).

℞ **HIPAA (Health Insurance Portability and Accountability Act):** Major U.S. law dealing with patients' rights and record keeping in health care. Always referred to by its initials and pronounced "hippa." Passed in 1996 and fully implemented by 2003, the law

- offers strong privacy protection for patients' medical information;
- standardizes medical data so it can be exchanged among health-care institutions;
- allows employees to transfer their medical coverage when they switch jobs, assuring continuity of coverage;
- encourages individual savings accounts for medical purposes; and
- prohibits discrimination against employees based on health conditions.

Historically Black Colleges and Universities (HBCU): Institutions of higher education, mainly in the American South, that served African Americans during the decades of segregation. Some are state sponsored; some are private. Today, segregation is outlawed, and all universities are integrated, including these. Still, at Howard, Morehouse, Spelman, and other HBCUs, the student body is largely black.

℞ **HMO (Health maintenance organization):** One of the main forms of medical coverage for students and faculty in the United States. HMOs are managed-care networks with their own doctors, nurses, administrators, and hospitals (either their own or affiliated with them). As an HMO member, you can see physicians and other health professionals for regular checkups, preventive care, scheduled appointments, and "walk-ins" (unscheduled appointments). If you have medical questions, you can speak to a physician or nurse on call. Prescription drugs are covered. Emergency room visits are covered but require authorization before care can be given.

Honor code: A set of rules, adopted at some universities, in which students formally promise not to lie, cheat, steal, plagiarize, mistreat other students, or engage in anti-social behavior. In most cases, the students also promise to monitor each other and report those who break the rules.

If a student is charged with violating the code, the case is brought before an "honor board," which determines guilt or innocence and the appropriate punishment. At some schools, the board is composed entirely of students. At others, the board includes students, faculty, and staff.

The content of honor codes is not much different from the rules of academic honesty and proper student conduct at other universities. What is different is the responsibility students take on themselves to ensure honesty as a campus-wide value.

Holidays in Canada: See table of Canadian holidays in appendix 2.

Holidays in the United States: See table of U.S. holidays in appendix 2.

Honors, academic honors: A term for superior academic achievement, either in a student's total coursework, major subject, or specific project such as a senior thesis. A student might receive honors on her senior thesis, for example, or graduate with honors in economics. The terms for academic honors vary across universities. In one, a student might graduate with "high honors." In another, the student might graduate "cum laude" (or better yet, "magna cum laude," or best of all "summa cum laude"). These honors are recorded on official transcripts and mentioned in CVs and résumés.

Host family: Volunteers who offer home hospitality and guidance to international students. For high school visitors, host families actually house the students and treat them like family members. For university visitors, host families play a less extensive role, inviting the student to join them for occasional meals and social activities as a way of getting to know the country, its people, and its culture beyond the campus.

Not all universities have established these programs. If they have, students can decide whether or not to participate. Many international students and their host families say it is an enriching experience that fosters lasting friendships.

HST (Harmonized Sales Tax): Sales tax of 15 percent in three eastern Canadian provinces, combining their 8 percent provincial tax with the 7 percent national sales tax (GST). The HST applies only in Nova Scotia, New Brunswick, and Newfoundland and Labrador.

I (incomplete): Indicates a student has not yet completed all the requirements in a course and has not yet received a final grade.

ICE, "in case of emergency": Term for a person to be contacted in case of emergency, whose phone number is programmed into a cell phone under the acronym "ICE." If the phone's owner cannot make the call (perhaps because of a serious accident), then a police officer or emergency medical technician can find the "ICE" contact and call them. This is a recent idea and a very sensible one.

(A) **ICE, "Immigration and Customs Enforcement" (United States):** An investigative branch of the U.S. Department of Homeland Security, with responsibility for border security.

(ID) **Identity card (ID card):** A document (usually a plastic or paper card) indicating who
($) its bearer is, as verified by the entity issuing the document. Occasionally, the ID card contains only the name of the issuing company and the name of cardholder. More often, the card includes the bearer's picture and signature, as well as anticounterfeiting mechanisms such as holograms. The company, university, or government agency that issues the ID often includes a number that is unique to the cardholder, such as an account number at that company. Since ID cards can be forged or fraudulently obtained, the most credible ones are those with strong anticounterfeiting measures issued by government agencies.

ID question (identification question): A brief examination problem, testing whether a student can name or define key topics in the course, such as names, places, events, formulas, or equations. A final examination might combine ID and essay questions, requiring a student to answer, say, ten brief IDs plus two longer essays.

(ID) **Identity Theft:** Stealing someone else's personal information, such as birth date, home
($) address, Social Security or Social Insurance Number, bank account numbers, PIN, and credit card information, in order to impersonate the victim. The goal is usually financial fraud: stealing money from a bank account or charging purchases to the victim's credit card.

To minimize the chances of being victimized, guard your financial data. Don't share it with anyone who doesn't need it for legitimate business reasons. Do not send it by e-mail, which is insecure. Beware of "phishing," where thieves send e-mails pretending to be your bank and asking you to confirm secret financial data.

IELTS, International English Language Testing System: Test of English language ability in four areas: reading, writing, listening, and speaking. The test is given in two formats, an academic one for prospective students and a general one for prospective employees and immigrants.

IM: Acronym for two quite different terms: (1) instant messaging on computers, PDAs, or cell phones, or (2) intramural sports between teams within the same university.

Independent study: A study program (usually a single course) arranged between a faculty member and an individual student. The equivalent of a tutorial and normally taken for academic credit. By taking an independent study course, a student can explore a topic that is not covered by regular courses or delve further into a topic raised in a course.

Independent study courses are available for graduate students and upper-level undergraduates in most large universities. They are commonplace in smaller schools that emphasize teaching. Enrollment in independent study courses *always* requires the professor's permission.

Informational interview: Talking with people who work in a particular company, field, or profession to learn more about it and to build contacts. Informational interviews can be useful for job hunters and can even lead to jobs, but they are not the same as regular job interviews, which are granted to selected applicants for specific positions.

℞ **Informed consent:** A patient's permission to undergo a medical procedure or take a medication, after being told its risks and potential benefits. By signing a consent form, the patient acknowledges that he understands these risks and benefits. Informed consent is required for major medical procedures such as surgery and for any experimental medicines and procedures.

℞ **In-patient:** A patient admitted to the hospital for an overnight stay. By contrast, an out-patient is treated at a hospital or clinic but not admitted for overnight care.

In-residence student: An enrolled student who is taking classes at the university. An in-residence student could be a freshman living in a dorm or a second-year graduate student living in an apartment off campus. In either case, the student is currently taking classes at the university. By contrast, a *non*resident student is enrolled at the university but is taking classes elsewhere, such as a "semester abroad" or "junior year abroad" at an affiliated institution. Students can maintain full-time status whether they are in-residence or not.

Sometimes, "in-residence" is used in a different way, to mean a student whose legal residence is within the same state or province as a public university. A nonresident lives elsewhere. Where you live is important because it affects tuition charges at public universities. Local students pay much less than others. I explain this usage in the entry below, "in-state student; "in-province student."

In-state student; in-province student: A student who resides in the U.S. state or Canadian province of his or her public university and is therefore eligible for reduced tuition. U.S. and Canadian laws are similar in this regard. Public universities, such as the University of North Carolina or the University of Manitoba, charge significantly lower tuition to their residents, mainly because local taxpayers support the universities. Each public university sets its own tuition levels for in-state and out-of-state students.

How long does it take to qualify as an "in-state" or "in-province" student? That depends on the laws in each state or province. Living there while you attend the university does not count toward the status of being "in state" or "in province."

In-state students are occasionally called "in-residence." That can be confusing because the term "in-resident student" has other meanings as well. (See "in-residence student.")

Institutional review board (IRB): A university committee, mandated by U.S. law, that evaluates research proposals to make sure the projects do not harm individuals. Any university research that involves human subjects must be submitted to the IRB for advance approval. That's true for research by students as well as by faculty and staff. In Canada, the equivalent university committee is called a research ethics board (REB).

Instructor: A teaching position, below the rank of assistant professor. Instructors are appointed for fixed terms, usually one to three years. They are not tenure-track; that is, the holders are not granted reviews for possible promotion to tenure. Normally, instructors are not considered full members of the faculty, so they are not eligible to vote on departmental and university matters. Although not all instructors hold doctoral degrees, many do and others are close to completing them. They use instructor positions like postdoctoral fellowships, as stepping-stones to tenure-track jobs.

The title of "instructor," like so many academic titles, is not uniform across universities. What is called an instructor at one university may be called a lecturer, preceptor, or tutor at another.

℞ **Intensive care unit (ICU):** Part of the hospital designed to care for seriously ill patients who need continuous monitoring and round-the-clock medical attention.

Interlibrary loan: An arrangement among research libraries, permitting users at one to borrow books from another in the network. These arrangements are particularly valuable for students doing advanced research, since no single university has every specialized book. To borrow a book or other item through interlibrary loan, see a reference librarian or interlibrary loan specialist at your local library.

Intermural sports (also known as "intercollegiate sports"): Sporting contests between teams from different universities. Distinguished from *intra*mural sports, where teams from the same university compete with each other, often on a more informal basis.

Interdisciplinary: Academic programs that draw upon two or more well-defined scholarly fields, seeking insights based on their integration and cross-fertilization. One example is the use of microeconomics to analyze legal questions. Another is the new field of bioinformatics, which draws on computer science, statistics, and molecular biology.

$ **Internal Revenue Service (IRS):** The national tax agency in the United States, similar to the Canada Revenue Agency (CRA). Income taxes are also levied by most states and a few cities, using their own tax forms and tax collection agencies. Tax obligations do *not* depend on your citizenship or your student status. They depend on where you earn income. If you earn it in the United States or Canada, then you owe taxes there. That includes income earned by international students, although some awards or grants may be exempt from taxation.

Internship: Supervised training in a job or other practical area, either paid or unpaid. Undertaken to gain experience, build contacts, and improve chances of landing a permanent job or admission to a graduate program.

Internships are required in professional training programs, such as nursing or social work, which prepare students for specific jobs. In some programs, students receive academic credit for their internships and have two supervisors, one at the job site and another at the university. Different universities have own rules for these practical training programs, and may call them externships, practicums, or something else.

💲 **ITIN (Individual Taxpayer Identification Number):** A ID number for individuals who cannot receive a Social Security Number because they are ineligible to work in the United States. (Social Security Numbers are limited to those who can work legally.) Although an ITIN cannot be used for employment, it can be used as a unique identifying number on documents such as U.S. tax forms or credit applications. As a unique identifier, it works like a Social Security Number. Application for an ITIN is made through the Internal Revenue Service and requires proof of identity. The best proof is a valid passport.

Intramurals: Sporting contests between teams *within* the same university. Contrasted with intermural (or intercollegiate) sports, which pit athletes or teams from different universities against each other. Intramurals are sometimes abbreviated as IM (or IMs), though that acronym is also used for instant messaging on computers and cell phones.

Invigilator: Someone who supervises an exam to prevent cheating. The term is used in Canada, following the English practice. In the United States, the person is called a proctor, exam proctor, or monitor.

Ivy League: A group of eight elite, private universities in the eastern United States, so called because some old campus buildings are covered with ivy vines. The universities are Brown, Columbia, Cornell, Dartmouth, Harvard, Pennsylvania, Princeton, and Yale.

⚖️ **JD:** Degree awarded by most U.S. law schools; an abbreviation for the Latin term Juris Doctor. For many years, U.S. law schools awarded their graduates an LLB (Legum Baccalaureus). Now, they typically give them a JD. This more august title indicates that, in the United States, students attend three years of law school after they have completed their four-year bachelor's degree. In Canada, by contrast, law is studied in an undergraduate program and graduates are awarded an LLB degree. After receiving their law degrees, U.S. and Canadian students must still pass a state or provincial bar examination to qualify to practice law.

Joint degree program: A graduate or undergraduate program that offers degrees in two or more specialized fields. One common example is a joint degree in law and business. Such programs may be tightly organized, with a well-defined program of study integrating the fields. Or they may be loosely organized, with simple requirements that students take a specified number of courses in each discipline.

Joint major (also known as "double major" or "dual major"): Specializing in two subjects and fulfilling the requirements for both as undergraduate majors. For details, see "Dual major."

Junior faculty: Untenured faculty members.

Judicial review board (or honor code board or similar title): An official university panel that reviews allegations of student misconduct, such as plagiarism or cheating. Some universities use review boards to handle these allegations; others rely on deans of students. The review board may be composed entirely of faculty and administrators or it may include some students. The board can decide if a student should fail a class or be suspended from the university. Some boards deal only with academic issues. Others deal with both academic and nonacademic conduct, such as student drinking.

K–12: U.S. schooling from kindergarten (immediately prior to first grade) through high school graduation (twelfth grade). Students begin around the age of five and graduate at seventeen or eighteen. Schooling beyond the twelfth grade is called "higher education" or "postsecondary education."

Kelley Blue Book ("blue book value"): The standard reference guide to the selling prices of used cars, by make, model, equipment, and condition. Used as a starting point for bargaining between buyers and sellers. "The blue book value of a 2006 Honda Accord like this, in fair condition with low mileage, automatic transmission, and air-conditioning, is $500 more than I'm asking."

Lab assistant or lab TA: A graduate student who supervises and grades students doing laboratory science assignments. Science courses usually combine lab work with lectures or seminars. Lab TAs are in charge of working with students in the lab itself, under the professor's overall direction, and may also lead small discussion sections, grade papers and exams, and work with individual students. In return, lab TAs receive fellowship support or wages. Serving as a TA or lab TA is an integral part of a graduate student's professional training.

Language tables (also language dorms): Eating arrangements where everyone speaks a foreign language to help them learn it. Universities often set up these tables as informal learning tools for language students. At one table, everyone speaks Spanish; at another, Chinese; at still another, Arabic. Tables may meet every day or once a week. Native speakers are generally welcomed as informal teachers. Who better to remind everyone the Urdu word for salt?

Some universities go one step further and set up foreign language dormitories where all the residents speak Russian or German or French. These are living arrangements to promote language acquisition, not special residences for native speakers (although native speakers may be hired as dorm assistants).

Lawyer, attorney, notary, paralegal: A lawyer or attorney is a professional qualified to advise clients about their legal rights and obligations, file legal documents, pursue civil remedies in court, and defend clients against criminal accusations. "Attorney" means the same thing as "lawyer." Each U.S. state and Canadian province certifies lawyers, who have the right to speak with their clients in confidence. The only exception is when lawyers know that clients are breaking a law (or intend to), and they cannot prevent it themselves. In that case, lawyers must report the violation to the court.

There are numerous legal specialties, such as immigration law, employment law, commercial law, and criminal defense law. Practitioners who are experts in one may be novices in others. Students who need legal aid with visa issues, for example, should seek a qualified immigration attorney. They are available in cities and most university towns. Likewise, a student facing criminal charges, such as driving under the influence of alcohol, should seek a specialist in criminal law. Individuals accused of crimes have a right to a lawyer. They can choose their own or, if they cannot afford one, the state will appoint one and pay the cost. There is one controversial exception to this right to a lawyer: some terrorism charges.

A notary is something entirely different. In the United States and Canada, a notary (sometimes called a "notary public") plays a minor legal role, primarily certifying signatures on legal documents. Some documents require such signatures. Before signing such a document, you must locate a notary, show your identification, and then sign. The notary witnesses the signature and then stamps and signs the document. Notaries are licensed by each state and province and are available in every community and on every campus. They charge only a few dollars for their services. Note that in the United States and Canada, most notaries are *not* lawyers and cannot provide legal services or offer legal advice. In some Canadian provinces, however, they can handle a real estate closing. In the United States, a lawyer is required.

Paralegals are trained assistants who work under a lawyer's direction. Although paralegals may assist clients, they are not lawyers and are not qualified to give legal advice or provide legal services independently. For routine legal matters, however, paralegals, working under a lawyer's supervision, can prepare documents at lower cost than lawyers themselves.

Leave of absence: An extended period—one semester or more—when a student is not enrolled at the university. The student or the university may request the leave. Students may request it because they are sick or pregnant, wish to work or travel, or lack funds to pay for the next semester. Universities sometimes request (or require) it because of a student's poor grades or behavior problems.

Students who take a leave of absence need to be certain they (1) have filled out the required university forms for a leave, and (2) understand the terms on which they may resume their enrollment.

Liberal arts (or arts and sciences): The study of the humanities, social sciences, and natural sciences, designed to promote general knowledge of fundamental subjects. The humanities include literature, philosophy, languages, and the arts. The social sciences include economics, political science, sociology, geography, anthropology, linguistics, and history. (History may also be considered part of the humanities.) The natural sciences include mathematics, physical sciences (physics, chemistry, geology, astronomy, astrophysics) and the biological sciences (molecular biology, human genetics, evolutionary biology, cell physiology, and so on).

Many universities in the United States and Canada emphasize a broad liberal arts curriculum for undergraduates. Students must take courses in all major areas, called variously a "core curriculum," "general education," or "distribution requirements," before going on to specialize in one subject: their major. A liberal arts curriculum like this can be distinguished from one emphasizing professional or commercial training. It can also be distinguished from current practices in many other countries, where undergraduates are trained intensively in one subject, such as history or chemistry.

Liberal arts training can also be found in a few MA programs, which offer degrees in broad areas such as the social sciences or humanities. Most graduate programs, however, are focused on a single subject (or a subfield within it) or a well-defined professional field. In effect, they extend the specialized study of the "major" rather than the broader foundation of liberal arts.

Living will (also health-care power of attorney): A document in which a person states the kind of health care he wishes to receive if he is incapacitated and unable to communicate these choices himself.. The aim is to allow a relative or trusted friend to make life-or-death medical decisions for someone who is gravely ill and cannot make the decisions for himself.

LLB: Title for a law degree, from the Latin, Legum Baccalaureus. It is the typical law degree in Canada and is awarded to students who complete an undergraduate program in common law. Students who specialize in civil code receive a Bachelor of Civil Law (B.C.L.).

Canadian legal education differs from its U.S. counterpart. In the United States, students must complete a four-year undergraduate degree before entering a three-year law school. At one time, U.S. law schools awarded LL.B. degrees but most have now switched to J.D. (Juris Doctor). They did not change their educational program, only the name of the degree.

After receiving their degrees, U.S. and Canada law students must still pass a state or provincial bar examination to practice law.

MA, MS, MBA, and other master's degrees: There are two principal master's degrees:

Master of Arts   MA
Master of Science   MS

Many professional schools offer graduate degrees that designate the student's area of expertise. Here are the most common master's degrees and their initials:

Architecture   MArch
Business Administration   MBA
Divinity   MDiv
Education   MEd
Engineering   MEng
Fine Arts   MFA
Health Administration   MHA
Informational Science   MIS
Liberal Arts   MLA
Library Science   MLS

Nursing	MN or MSN
Occupational Therapy	MOT
Physical Therapy	MPT
Public Health	MPH
Public Policy	MPP
Social Work	MSW
Teaching	MAT

There is some standardization, but not uniformity. For example, most social work schools award MSW degrees, but Columbia calls theirs MSSW. An "MA in Liberal Arts" at one school might be an MLA at another.

Major: An undergraduate's principal field of studies. Students choose this specialty ("declare their major") at the end of their freshman or sophomore year, depending on the university, and then complete a number of required courses before graduation.

Graduate students have specializations, of course, but they are not called majors or minors.

Married student housing: University-provided apartments near campus for married couples, where one partner is a full-time student. Usually intended for graduate students and research associates, some universities also allow undergraduates and faculty to rent units. Arrangements differ from one university to another.

Matriculation: Enrollment for coursework at a college, university, or other school.

Meal plan: A dining arrangement for students, offering them multiple meals each week in university dining halls for a package price. For some students, the plans are optional, but for others they may be required (for example, for all students living in dormitories or for all freshmen).

Mentor: A person who provides informal guidance and advice to someone younger or less experienced. Mentoring is a volunteer activity and is not paid.

Students are often mentored by professors or even by experienced graduate students. In the corporate world, senior managers often mentor young executives. Sometimes, these mentoring relationships develop by chance. Sometimes they are actively promoted, as they are by organizations of women and minority executives.

Many universities have mentoring programs in which students volunteer to work with high school students, especially those from disadvantaged backgrounds.

Minor: An undergraduate's secondary field of study, requiring fewer courses than the primary field (or "major"). Majors and minors are usually chosen at the end of freshman or sophomore year. Students are required to choose majors but, in most universities, they are not required to minor in any subject.

Why choose this option, then? Because it signals employers and graduate schools that you have some academic background in a particular field, aside from your major.

The terms "major" and "minor" apply only to undergraduate studies, not to graduate specialization.

Moving violation: A traffic ticket issued for breaking a law while driving, such as speeding, driving under the influence (of alcohol), or driving with an expired license. Moving violations carry high fines, usually raise the cost of automobile insurance (because such drivers are considered less safe), and may lead to the loss of a driver's license. The worst offenses may be punished by jail sentences. Moving violations are distinguished from nonmoving violations such as parking tickets.

MSRP (manufacturer's suggested retail price): The full retail price for a product, indicated by the manufacturer. In competitive retail markets, most products sell below this price. At automobile dealers, the MSRP is also known as the "sticker price" or "full sticker price."

Natural science: A term covering both the physical and biological sciences, and sometimes mathematics. Natural science can be contrasted with "social science," such as economics or sociology.

Need-blind admissions: A university policy of admitting new students based on their qualifications, not their ability to pay. Students with financial need are given grants, loans, and jobs to fund the cost of tuition, books, fees, housing, and food.

911: The emergency number for fire, ambulance, and police throughout the United States and Canada. This number works from both cell phones and landlines and is toll-free. The 911 number should be used only for emergencies. Police and other vital services have separate numbers for nonurgent calls. Using 911 for pranks or hoax calls is a criminal offense.

Nontraditional students: Students who are older than their peers and have been out of school for several years before returning. There are no hard-and-fast rules about the age of nontraditional students. For an undergraduate, it would probably be a student who is twenty-five or older. For a graduate student, it would probably be thirty-five or older.

Universities in the United States and Canada generally welcome nontraditional students. That's certainly true of urban commuter schools, where many students hold jobs during the day and attend classes part-time at night. But it is increasingly true of all universities.

The trend has been fostered by changes in the job market. Professionals, such as psychologists or social workers, are required to take formal courses each year to renew their licenses. Aside from that requirement, many professionals take courses to acquire new skills or keep up with rapidly changing fields. Still others, facing unemployment, return to school to train for different jobs. Finally, there has been a steady growth of active retirees, who decide to head back to school solely for intellectual pleasure. For all these reasons, there has been a steady rise in lifelong learning and with it, a rise in nontraditional students on campus.

Notary: A minor legal official authorized to witness signatures on legal documents, administer oaths, take acknowledgments, and perform other limited tasks. In British

Columbia (but not in the United States), a notary can also handle real estate closings, that is, supervise the final payment on a property sale and the transfer of legal title to the new owner. For a comparison between notaries, lawyers, and paralegals, see the entry for "lawyer."

Office hours: Times when a professor or teaching assistant is regularly available to meet with students. All faculty and teaching assistants hold weekly office hours during the academic year.

Ombudsman, Ombudsperson: An official who helps students resolve their difficulties or complaints at the university or helps hospital patients deal with problems about their medical care or billing. The ombudsman's office also provides students with useful information and works with the university or hospital administration to identify and fix recurrent problems.

Open admissions: A policy adopted by a few universities and community colleges that permits any student who has graduated from high school to enroll as a student. Of course, admission does not guarantee that a potential student can afford to attend college or that he will pass his courses. Predictably, colleges with open admissions need to offer a variety of remedial courses to help weak students prepare for college-level work. (These remedial courses typically do *not* count as university credits toward graduation.)

The vast majority of universities have rejected open admissions in favor of more selective standards. Still, most large cities have at least one college or university, often a community college, that admits all students with high school diplomas or their equivalent.

Open-book and closed-book exams: Two types of exams, differing in whether they allow students to use notes, books, photocopies, or the Internet during the test. In a closed-book exam, students cannot use any outside resources. It's cheating if they do. In an open-book exam, on the other hand, students are allowed to use all these resources. If they do, however, they should clearly indicate what sources they relied upon and should use citations and quotations just as they would in a paper. In both closed- and open-book exams, students cannot ask anyone to help them with their answers.

(℞) **Open enrollment:** The period each year when university faculty, students, and staff select their health-care plan. If they are new to campus, they can generally choose a plan without a health exam or exclusion for previously existing medical conditions. If they are already members of an HMO or health insurance plan, they can renew their current provider or choose a different option, among several offered by the university.

To help with the choice, the university's human resources department provides pamphlets and online documents. The competing providers supply their own information and often present their materials to potential clients at a health-care forum, arranged by the university.

You can also arrange to meet privately with a university benefits counselor and discuss your own situation before making your choice.

Orals (oral examination): An examination in which professors ask questions of an individual student, who responds verbally, rather than in writing. "Orals" is the commonly used nickname for this examination, which is given at the completion of some degree programs.

There are two main types of oral exams. One covers a general area of study, such as political philosophy for second-year graduate students in political science. The other covers a student's own written work, such as a thesis. Oral examinations of a student's written work are usually called a "thesis defense." (See "defense.")

Orientation Week (or "O-Week" or "Frosh O-Week"): A series of informational meetings, activities, and optional exams for new students, held immediately before classes begin. The program is designed to help students learn about the university, meet other students, and explore the campus and surrounding community. Exams are also given to students who, on the basis of prior studies, wish to skip introductory courses and take more advanced ones. For example, a student with an extensive math background might take an exam in calculus to "place out" of the first-year class and begin taking second-year calculus. (Some universities would give the student course credit for placing out of first-year calculus; others would not.)

Since new undergraduates—freshmen—are often called "frosh," the week is sometimes called "Frosh O-Week." (These are slang terms.)

For undergraduates, these activities last several days. For new graduate students, they last only a day or two and are focused more narrowly on their program's academic options and requirements. In addition, there are special orientation programs and activities for international students, designed to familiarize them with their new surroundings and new academic environment. Check with the international student adviser's office about these programs as soon as you arrive.

(℞) **Organ donor card:** A document stating that, in case of death, an individual wishes to give organs and tissues to patients who need them. Organs cannot be donated without such a clear statement or authorization from the donor or nearest surviving relative. To donate, individuals can check a box on their driver's license or request a special donor card. You can download the card online. In the United States, the Web address is www.organdonor.gov/signup1.html. In Canada, it's www.giftoflife.on.ca.

Out-of-state student; out-of-province student: A student who does not legally reside in the U.S. state or Canadian province of his or her public university. These students are typically charged higher tuitions than local residents, often much higher. Of course, both in-state and out-of-state students may be eligible for reduced tuition through scholarships, grants, and subsidized loans. (The same is true in Canada.)

Each state and province has its own laws indicating how long a person must live there to qualify for reduced tuition, and each university sets its own tuition levels for these students. Living in the state or province while enrolled at the university does not qualify a student for local tuition status. For that reason, some prospective students move to a state or province and postpone enrollment until they have qualified as a local resident.

(℞) **Out-patient:** A patient who is treated at a hospital or clinic but is not admitted for an overnight stay. By contrast, an in-patient is admitted for at least one night's care. For example, "The doctor stitched up the wound as a simple, out-patient procedure."

($) **Overdraft or bank overdraft (also "overdraft protection"):** A negative balance in your bank account, which occurs when your withdrawals exceed your available funds. In many countries, consumer accounts come with built-in protection against overdrafts. When a customer has a negative balance, the bank automatically provides a loan to cover it. The amount they are willing to cover depends on the customer's credit line, and, of course, they charge interest on the loan. This kind of "overdraft protection" is *not* usually available for ordinary consumer accounts in the United States and Canada. It may be available on some premium accounts.

(℞) **Over-the-counter medication:** A drug that can be purchased without a doctor's pre-
(🛒) scription. Over-the-counter medicines such as aspirin are not covered by health insurance or HMOs.

Paper mill: The nickname for a company that sells written work to students, who hand it in as their own work. The students are committing fraud, pretending they wrote these papers. They are committing a serious ethical violation and breaching basic university rules of academic honesty. Students who are caught risk failure in the course and, quite possibly, suspension or expulsion from the university. The paper mill, for its part, is in business to facilitate this deception and make money from it.

(⚖) **Paralegal:** A person with legal skills who assists attorneys and works under their direction. Can assist clients with routine legal matters, such as a simple will, usually at less cost than a lawyer. Paralegal training is now well established. There are education requirements, proficiency exams, licensing, and continuing legal education for practitioners. For a comparison between paralegals, lawyers, and notaries, see the entry for "lawyer."

Paraphrase: Explaining another writer's ideas without coming too close to the exact phrasing. Good paraphrasing should include proper citation and not mimic the original language. In contrast, "close paraphrasing" might look like an attempt to evade using quotation marks and thus deny another writer full credit. That is considered plagiarism, even if there is a citation, because quotes should include *both* citations and quotation marks.

Part-time student: A student who is taking fewer courses or credit hours than required for full-time status.

Maintaining full-time status is crucial to international students, since it is generally required for student visas. It is also required for U.S. students receiving federal scholarships.

🛒 **Pawn shop:** A store that lends money to individuals, based on their leaving personal property at the store as collateral; if the loan is not repaid, the property then belongs to the lender, who sells it to retail customers looking for used items. The collateral is referred to as a "pawn" or "pledge," and could be anything from gold jewelry or a old trumpet to a car or motorcycle. Loans are based on the resale value of this collateral. If the loan is repaid, the collateral is returned to the person who pawned it.

💲 **Payroll deductions:** Automatic withdrawals from an employee's earnings. Taxes and Social Security (or Social Insurance) are removed from each payroll check a worker receives. Other deductions are normally made for health insurance and retirement. Some, like taxes, are mandated deductions. Others, like retirement savings, may be negotiated by group contract or voluntarily chosen by an individual employee. In some instances, the employer may be required (by law or contract) to remove a minimum amount for, say, retirement, but employees who wish to save more for retirement can ask for higher deductions.

Total earnings before deductions are known as "gross wages." Those after taxes and other deductions are "net wages." There is, alas, a big difference.

Peer-reviewed journal: Scholarly publications in which articles appear only after they have been approved by experts in the field. Prospective authors submit their work to the journal, which sends it out for evaluation by competent reviewers. The reviewers offer their comments and evaluations to the journal editor. The journal editors consider these responses before deciding whether to publish an article, reject it, or ask for revisions. The request for changes is known as "revise and resubmit." Whatever the outcome, editors normally share the reviewers' comments with the authors but keep the reviewers' identities secret.

The gold standard for peer review is called "double blind." In this process, the author submitting the article does not know which scholars will review it (and often does not know afterward). Nor do the reviewers know whose work they are reviewing. So the process is anonymous on both sides—"double blind." Only the journal editors know the author and the reviewers.

Perks (or perquisites): Special benefits, other than salary, that come with a job. "Perks" is the commonly used slang term for perquisites. These benefits may be given routinely to anyone in a particular job, or they may be specially negotiated. Example: "Her promotion comes with some nice perks: a corner office, a research allowance, and free parking."

Permission of the instructor (or permission of the instructor required): Specific authorization, given by a professor, for a student to take a course the professor offers. Faculty members sometimes limit enrollment in their courses this way so they can make sure each student's academic background is appropriate for the course.

PhD: The standard doctoral degree in the arts and sciences. The title derives from the Latin, Philosophiae Doctor. Some fields award different doctoral titles to reflect their specialty, such as

Business	DBA
Dentistry	DDS
Divinity	DD
Education	EdD
Engineering	DEng
Medicine	MD
Psychology	PsyD
Veterinary Medicine	DVM

These practices are not standardized, however. One university might award its doctorates in business administration a DBA; another might give them a PhD. Most scholars consider these differences to be unimportant.

Phi Beta Kappa: The leading U.S. organization recognizing undergraduate academic achievement.

($) **Phishing:** Financial fraud in which criminals send deceptive e-mails asking recipients
(⚖) for their bank account numbers, credit card numbers, or Social Security information.

($) **PIN or PIN numbers:** A personal identification number (PIN) used for security on financial transactions. The equivalent of a password. Do not share your PINs with anyone. If a credit card, debit card, or ATM card is stolen, the thieves will need the PIN to access your account. Don't give it to them by writing it on the card. Instead, keep a list of your account numbers, PINs, and passwords in a secure place at home, *not* in your wallet or purse.

Placement test: An examination given before entrance into a class to determine a student's level of knowledge. Placement tests are commonly used to assign students to courses at the appropriate level of difficulty. On rare occasions, they are used to award actual course credits. "Because I did well on the French placement test, I don't have to take the introductory course."

Plagiarism: The use of others' words, ideas, drawings, computer code, algorithms, musical compositions, or data without proper attribution. Plagiarism is a serious violation of academic rules, whether you are an undergraduate, graduate student, or faculty member, and it has serious consequences.

Pop quiz: A brief, in-class examination given without prior notice. It is a closed-book test that rewards students who attend class regularly and keep up with assignments. It penalizes those who don't. Quizzes like this are given occasionally in high school and lower-level undergraduate courses, but not in more advanced classes.

(⚖) **Power of attorney:** A document in which one person gives another the power to act
(℞) on his behalf. This power might be restricted (by the document) to a specific act or cir-
($) cumstance or it might be quite general. It can be withdrawn by the person who issued it. The term "power of attorney" is a bit misleading. The individual who receives it does

not have to be a lawyer. He or she is simply authorized to act as your agent. (See also "health-care power of attorney.")

Postal code: Canada's system for identifying postal addresses, using a combination of six numbers and letters. For example: Montreal, Quebec H3A 2T6. The U.S. system is called "ZIP codes" and uses only numbers.

Postdoctoral fellowship (postdoc): Financial support for young researchers who recently received their PhD's. Usually awarded on the basis of a research proposal and faculty letters of recommendation. The donor may be the student's home institution, another university or research institution, a charitable foundation, or the government.

Because the fellowships do not require teaching, they give recipients time and resources to conduct publishable research. Most last one or two years and require residence at the institution awarding the fellowship. A PhD from Indiana University who receives a postdoc from Stanford or the National Institutes of Health will move there to conduct research during the fellowship period.

Although postdoctoral fellowships are not lucrative, they can be quite prestigious. They allow the recipient to conduct research full time and aid in their search for a faculty job or senior research position.

Practicum: (See the entry for "internship.")

Preceptor: A name for tutors or an alternative title for instructors (below the rank of assistant professor) at some universities. Like so many academic titles, this one varies across institutions.

Predoctoral fellowship (predoc): Financial support for graduate students, usually advanced students conducting their dissertation research. The fellowships last one or two years and are awarded on the basis of faculty recommendations and research proposals related to the dissertation. They may be awarded by the student's home institution, another university, research institution, foundation, or government agency. They often require the recipient to conduct research at the university or research institution that makes the award. Because the fellowships do not require teaching, recipients can devote full time to dissertation research and writing. They pay less than postdoctoral fellowships because the recipients have less training.

Preprofessional program: A set of courses preparing students for graduate study in a well-defined field of skilled intellectual work, such as law, business, or medicine. Students often refer to themselves as "prelaw" or "premed."

(Ꝑ) **Preferred provider organization (PPO):** Medical insurance plan such as Blue Cross/ Blue Shield that relies on a network of selected health-care providers: hospitals, doctors, nurses, and other health-care professionals. Sometimes called a preferred provider network (PPN) or medical provider network (MPN). The providers agree on reimbursement schedules below their normal charges, and the insurance company passes on some of the savings to policy holders. Policy holders can still use providers "outside the network" and receive some reimbursement, but it is much more expensive for them than using a provider within the network.

Prerequisite: A course (or courses) that must be completed before taking a more advanced one. Before taking a course in international monetary economics, for example, students might be required to finish a course in microeconomics or international trade, or maybe both. Occasionally, a student is allowed to take these background courses at the same time as the more advanced course. This option goes by the awkward name of "corequisite."

Prerequisites for each course are usually listed in the catalog or the syllabus. Even if a prerequisite is not listed, there still might be an informal or unstated requirement, designed to make sure students are well prepared to take an advanced course. If you are uncertain whether you have the right preparation, simply ask the professor. That is especially important for international students whose course background is different from U.S. and Canadian students. The professor may tell you that you have all the background you need, or she may suggest you take another course before enrolling in hers. In any case, if you are taking advanced courses, it's wise to check with the professor and make sure you have the right preparation.

President of the university: The head of the university and its senior administrative officer. Hired and fired by the university's board of directors, the president is responsible for the institution's operations, financing, and educational direction, but rarely intervenes in specific faculty appointments. Over the past several decades, as university financing has become more challenging, presidents have become much more active in raising funds from private donors, foundations, and legislatures.

The title of "president" is the most common one for university leaders, but a few are called "chancellor," "vice-chancellor," "principal," or other titles.

(℞) **Primary care physician (PCP):** A patient's main contact with the health-care system and the first contact for nonemergency problems. Usually an internist, family practitioner, or other general care physician. The PCP for children is usually a pediatrician; for the elderly, a gerontologist.

Principal investigator (PI): The lead researcher, in charge of a scientific project or scholarly undertaking. The PI is responsible for the project's conception, organization, day-to-day conduct, scientific integrity, and reporting, that is, the findings and publications that emanate from the project.

Prior Learning Assessment & Recognition (PLAR): In Canada, the systematic evaluation of a student's learning outside formal educational institutions. Used to grant academic credit or to place students in appropriate higher-level courses.

Private sector, public sector, nonprofit sector: Three main areas of the economy, often used as shorthand to indicate where students are seeking jobs.

Private	Corporations and business enterprises
Public	Government at all levels: city, state or province, national
Nonprofit	Tax-exempt charities

For example, "I have been working in the public sector, mostly on city budgets, but I'm hoping to get a job in the private sector, probably in banking."

Probation (academic probation): A trial period (usually one semester) in which a student must rectify poor grades or poor conduct to remain at the university. If the problems remain, the student will be required to leave the university for at least one semester and possibly longer. The requirement to leave temporarily is "suspension." The requirement to leave permanently is "expulsion." (See also entries for "suspension" and "expulsion")

Proctor, exam proctor, or monitor: Someone who oversees students taking an exam to prevent cheating. In Canada, this person is also called an invigilator.

Professional schools: Graduate schools that prepare students for skilled, intellectually oriented occupations. Among the most prominent programs offering advanced professional training are law, business, education, medicine, nursing, divinity (or theology), public policy, international affairs, clinical psychology, social work, engineering, architecture, journalism (or communication), library science (or information science), and veterinary medicine.

These programs are typically housed within their own academic units and have their own faculties, headed by a dean. Most professional schools are situated within major universities, although a few are free-standing schools.

All these programs aim to train practitioners. The academic program usually lasts two years (three for law school) and culminates in a master's degree or its equivalent. As part of the training, they commonly offer, or even require, student internships. The goal is to integrate working experience with classroom education.

After graduation, professionals need ongoing training to keep up with their changing fields. They need refresher courses to maintain their skills, courses in new topics and techniques to keep up with major innovations, and more advanced courses to match an individual's growing responsibilities. Professional schools meet these needs with continuing education courses and a variety of mid-career and executive training programs.

In tandem with professional training, some schools also run small doctoral programs to educate scholars in their fields. For example, a theology school that trains students as ministers, religious educators, and church administrators might also have a small PhD program to train professors in those fields.

Professorial ranks: The hierarchical order of faculty titles, beginning at the bottom:

- Assistant professor
- Associate professor
- Full professor

Assistant professors are untenured faculty members, holding term appointments for up to seven years. During that period, they may be promoted to associate professor, either with or without tenure.

Assistant and associate professors who have tenure-track positions are, by definition, eligible for a tenure vote. If the vote is positive, the faculty member receives a lifetime appointment and can be fired only for extraordinary reasons, such as ethical violations or the university disbanding the department. Faculty members who are denied tenure normally leave that particular university and seek appointments elsewhere.

At the top of the hierarchy are full professors. Within that group, some hold even more prestigious titles, those of "named chairs" (also called "endowed chairs").

All North American universities have the standard ranks of assistant, associate, and full professor. Beyond that, there are several other titles for teachers and scholars that vary from school to school and from program to program. Some are considered full members of the faculty, but most are not. They still teach, counsel students, conduct research, and perform some administrative duties. But, unless they are faculty members, they do not vote on other appointments or determine departmental curricula.

The positions of "instructor," "tutor," and "preceptor" are below the rank of assistant professor and are usually not members of the faculty. The positions of "adjunct professor" and "clinical professor" are more ambiguous. At some universities, they are considered faculty members; at others, they are not.

When addressing a teacher, these distinctions don't matter. It's fine to call all of them "professor."

Prospective students or "prospies": Students who have been admitted to a university and have either decided to come or remain undecided. "Prospie" is a friendly slang term for a prospective student. Students normally apply in December to attend undergraduate, graduate, and professional programs that begin the following August or September. Decisions on admission and financial aid are sent out in the winter or spring, and a student may well be admitted to several schools. At that point, prospective students ("prospies") must decide which school to accept. Many wish to visit the schools and learn more about the programs before making their final decisions. Some have already decided to come but want to visit the campus and talk with faculty one more time before enrolling. The schools, in turn, welcome these students to campus on special weekends, when students have a chance to sample campus life and ask questions about their specific programs.

Most international students live too far away to take advantage of these "prospie weekends." But faculty, advisers, and admissions officers are glad to speak with prospies by phone and respond to e-mail questions.

Provost: The most common title for the university's second-ranking administrator, just below the president. In most universities, the provost is effectively the "chief academic officer," concentrating on faculty and research appointments, major educational issues, and related budgetary issues. Deans report to the provost, who is involved in academic issues affecting the whole university. The provost may be involved in fundraising, but it is not a primary responsibility, as it is for a university president.

Public university, private university, proprietary university: Three types of higher education, with different types of financing and administrative control.

Public	Nonprofit institution, financed and controlled by a state or province
Private	Nonprofit institution, financed and controlled by an independent charitable board
Proprietary	For-profit business, controlled by its board of directors; may be independent or part of a larger company

A public university is sponsored and supported by a U.S. state or Canadian province, which provides some financing and maintains ultimate control over the institution. Examples are the University of Texas and the University of Toronto.

Private universities are independent, nonprofit organizations, controlled by their own boards of directors. Although they receive charters from the state and usually some public financing (such as research grants and student loans), they are not part of the state educational system. Like public universities, they depend upon several streams of revenue: tuition, outside research grants, gifts from friends and alumni, and earnings on their endowments. Unlike state universities, however, their budgets are not underwritten by direct allocations of state tax revenues. Examples are Harvard, Yale, and Duke. (Canada has very few such universities.)

Proprietary universities are for-profit institutions, owned by corporations. Like other universities, they provide postsecondary education and may be accredited by the usual bodies. Until recently, most proprietary universities concentrated on job training or commercial skills. Now, however, some offer the full range of university courses and programs.

A university's name does not always indicate whether it is public, private, or proprietary. Take three universities named after large American cities. The University of Memphis is a state school; the University of Chicago is private; and the University of Phoenix is a for-profit company.

Quads: The nickname (slang term) for a university's main quadrangle or square, usually near the center of campus. Stanford and the University of Chicago are among many schools with such quadrangles. Not all universities have such focal points and, for those that do, the name varies. The University of Virginia has its famous Lawn; Berkeley has Sproul Plaza; the University of South Carolina has the Horseshoe.

Qualifying exams (field exams): Major examinations in graduate school, covering several areas of the discipline, usually given after the second year of doctoral programs. The terms of these exams differ from program to program, but their common aim is to ensure that students have mastered main elements of the discipline. They may be called "qualifying exams" or "field exams." Both terms make sense. Students must pass them to remain in the doctoral program and qualify to write a dissertation. By the same token, they test knowledge of several key fields within a discipline. Not all doctoral programs require these exams.

Quarter: A segment of the academic year, usually lasting eleven or twelve weeks. An alternative to the semester system. Universities that use the quarter system divide the year into four portions, three during the academic year plus the summer. The semester system divides the academic year into two segments, each lasting about sixteen weeks, plus the summer. (In either case, the summer is not considered part of the regular academic year, which lasts from August until May, or from September until June.)

($) **Québec Pension Plan (QPP):** Within the province of Québec, a mandatory system of insurance for retired or disabled workers, surviving spouses, and minor children who have lost a parent. Workers and employers are both required to pay into the system monthly. Equivalent to Canada Pension Plan (CPP) or U.S. Social Security.

Quiz: A brief, in-class test, covering recently assigned materials. A "pop quiz" is a short test given without any prior notice. It rewards students who attend class regularly and keep up with readings, lectures, and other assignments. Longer tests, called examinations (or exams), cover more materials and are given only with prior notice, so students can prepare for them.

RA: An acronym with two distinct meanings:
- resident assistant in a dormitory, and
- research assistant for a professor.

Both terms are discussed below, under their full titles.

Reading period: Several days at the end of the semester, just before exams, when classes do not meet. Reading period is a time when students can prepare for examinations or complete longer papers.

Readmission, reinstatement: Permission for a former student to reenter the university. Students who have taken a leave of absence or been suspended may seek readmittance so they can complete their studies. Normally, they must make an explicit request, which university officials review. Because the student has been enrolled previously, the request does not entail a full admissions application, like that for new students.

Each university has its own rules about when returning students must apply for readmission. Short absences might not require readmission, but at some universities, students need to apply after only one semester out of school. At others, they need to reapply only after missing three consecutive semesters.

Recommendation or faculty recommendation: Letter from a teacher or administrator commenting on a student's abilities, achievements, personal qualities, and other qualifications for a job or further education. Such letters are usually confidential. That is, a student has explicitly waived the right to see the letter. That waiver makes letters more candid and therefore more valuable.

The most effective letters are written by faculty who know a student well, have read the student's work, and have given it high marks. For graduate school, fellowships, and academic jobs, recommendations from full faculty members carry the most weight. Faculty members write numerous recommendations for students and expect to be asked to do so. It's a standard part of the job. To do it well, however, faculty need to know what the recommendation is for. Is it for a summer job, a graduate fellowship, or law school? They also need a packet of information about the student: courses taken, grades, extracurricular activities, work experience, honors and awards, and perhaps a research paper the student has written. If you have written a personal statement or research proposal related to this recommendation, include that, too. With all this information at hand, a faculty member can write a serious, thoughtful recommendation.

The letter of recommendation should be stored so it can be used again, if needed. That can be done at your university's career placement office or at a national company such as Interfolio (www.interfolio.com). They keep the records confidential and send them only to employers, universities, agencies, and foundations you request.

One final point: When asking for a recommendation, it is wise to ask directly if the faculty member can write a strong, positive endorsement. If, after reviewing your materials, the professor answers "no," it's far better to find out now than to press your request and receive only a mediocre endorsement. My advice: make it easy for a professor to turn down your request for a recommendation. That way, a professor who says "yes" will know you well enough and think highly enough of your abilities to recommend you with honest enthusiasm.

Reference librarian: A librarian who specializes in providing information to library users, answering their questions, and helping them with individual research needs at the library. A typical question to them might be, "Are there any books or databases about women's roles in the French Revolution?" All university libraries have reference librarians available to help students and faculty.

Referral: Permission for a patient to see a medical specialist; given by a primary care physician and approved by the health maintenance organization (HMO). Because specialist care is so expensive, HMO administrators carefully monitor the use of referrals and sometimes deny requests by primary care physicians to send their patients for more extensive treatment. For patients with health insurance, referrals are not necessary.

Registrar: The university official responsible for keeping student records and providing official transcripts, including each student's grades, enrollment status, academic standing, and so forth, to those the student designates. Student education records are private, and their confidentiality is protected by law. In the United States that law is the Family Education Rights and Privacy Act of 1974, known as FERPA. Of course, a student can ask that records be sent to potential employers, graduate schools, and others.

Registration (and restricted registration): The process of enrolling in the university or in a specific course. Now done online.

A student who is registered in the university still has to enroll in specific courses, but some courses may be restricted in various ways. First, a course might be open only to students in specific parts of the university, such as the business school. Second, an advanced course may require some prerequisites. Without taking these prerequisites, a student cannot register for the advanced course. Third, a professor may wish to screen students personally for smaller seminars before permitting them to enter. Such courses allow "registration only with the professor's permission." Finally, registration may be limited (or "capped") at the size of the available classroom, usually on a "first-come, first-served" basis. Students can avoid some of these problems by registering early ("advance registration" or "preregistration") and by checking the course catalog to see if there are any prerequisites for the course.

A student's registration for the entire term may also be restricted or prohibited because of poor grades, poor behavior, or failure to pay tuition and fees.

Religious affiliation (for universities): A formal connection between a university and a religious denomination. This connection may be very strong, with the denomination playing a major role in the university's direction, or it may be much weaker. All universities with religious affiliations are private, since neither the United States nor Canada has a state-supported religion. Some universities seek to promote religious values in their education, but most do not engage in religious instruction.

Except for institutions that exist to train clergy, a university's religious affiliation does *not* limit its enrollment to students of one faith. A good example is Georgetown, a Catholic institution with strong ties to the Jesuit order. It is well known for its diverse student body and faculty and its open discussion of religious issues. The same is true for Southern Methodist University in Dallas, Texas. Methodists receive no special consideration in admissions or financial aid at SMU. The denomination's influence is greatest at SMU's Perkins School of Theology, which is a seminary of the United Methodist Church.

Other universities, though open to students of all faiths, attract mostly students from the sponsoring religion. At Brigham Young University, for example, nearly all students are Mormons. This strong religious connection is reflected in the university's stated mission "to assist individuals in their quest for perfection and eternal life." Most older universities in North America, especially those in New England, began with strong religious affiliations, but dropped those ties by the mid-nineteenth century.

Remedial courses: Courses below the university level, offered to help students acquire essential knowledge and prepare them for regular college courses. Some universities, especially those that admit students with weak academic backgrounds, offer remedial courses as a service. By taking these courses, students have a chance to catch up on basic subjects such as reading, writing, and mathematics. International students may take similar courses in English as a second language (ESL). Remedial courses do not count toward university degrees.

Request for proposals (RFP): A formal document, issued by a granting agency, government, or firm, soliciting applications to perform a specific task or service. To take a typical example, a nonprofit foundation might issue an RFP asking researchers to apply for grants to study some aspect of urban education. Or the RFP might be much more specific, asking for proposals between $50,000 and $150,000 to study educational achievement by African American girls, aged six to nine, in Philadelphia public schools.

Required readings: Books, articles, and other materials that all students in a course must read. The syllabus lists these readings. It may also list some suggested (or supplementary) readings for students who wish to do more.

Resident assistant or resident aide (RA) or resident head (RH): A student, usually in graduate or professional school, hired to live and work in a campus dormitory and help students deal with various issues related to dorm life (example: problems with roommates). Because RAs live in the dorms, they can meet informally with students and offer advice. They may also notice problems before others in the university (such as a student who seems depressed and is not leaving her room) and can intervene to help. RA's are not usually therapists or counselors, so they refer serious problems to professional specialists. RAs receive free rooms. They may also receive a food allowance and modest wages. The common term "RA" can be confusing because it also refers to a totally different job, that of research assistant for a professor. At some schools, the dorm position is called "resident head" (RH).

Research assistant (RA): A student hired to aid faculty members with their scholarly research. RAs might be asked to find books on a particular topic or take notes on an article. Students with the requisite skills might be asked to read materials in languages the professor does not know. RAs are paid hourly fees from the faculty member's research grants or from other university funds. Occasionally, students volunteer to serve as RAs without pay (if no funds are available) to acquire research experience and work closely with a faculty member. The tasks performed by an RA vary considerably from one discipline to another and, indeed, from one professor to another. Given this variation, RAs find it useful to clarify the professor's expectations before they begin work.

Research ethics board (REB): A university committee, mandated by Canadian law, to evaluate research proposals and make sure the projects do not harm individuals. Any university research that involves human subjects, such as a personal interview or psychological experiment, must be submitted to the REB for advance approval. That's true for research by students as well as by faculty and staff. In the United States, the equivalent university committee is called an institutional review board (IRB).

Reserve readings: Books and articles that can be borrowed from the library only for brief periods because so many students need to use them. University libraries have special facilities to handle these short-term loans (a "reserve desk" or "reserve reading room"). The most common items are required readings for courses. Physical copies of books and articles are now supplemented by "electronic reserves." A digital version of an article or book chapter is produced by the library and made available to students, who can read it online or download it.

Residence requirement: Has two quite different meanings. (1) A rule that students must take a given number of courses or credit hours at their university (and not at any other) to qualify for a degree. This restricts the number of courses a student can transfer from other universities toward a degree. (2) A rule stating how long a person must live in a state or province prior to attending university in order to qualify for reduced tuition, which is available only to local residents.

Résumé: A written summary of an individual's career and personal accomplishments, usually presented on a single page. It covers education, work experience, leadership positions, and volunteer work.

ROTC, ROTP: Voluntary programs at some universities where students train part-time to become military officers. The U.S. program is ROTC. The Canadian program is ROTP. In the United States, members of the Reserve Officers' Training Corps (ROTC) receive pay and scholarship money and, in return, are committed to serve in the armed forces for several years after completing their education. The program in Canada, the Regular Officer Training Plan (ROTP), is very similar. It, too, subsidizes the university education of qualified students in training for the military. Both programs are for citizens only.

Rush: The one- or two-week period when fraternities and sororities recruit new members. A student who has been asked to join and agrees is known as a "pledge" until he or she becomes a full-fledged member. "Rush" is also known as "pledge week."

($) **Safe deposit box:** A small private container stored in a special bank vault and rented by individuals (or corporations) to store their valuable documents, cash, jewelry, passports, and other personal items.

(🛒) **Sales tax:** A tax on the purchase of certain goods and services. Sales taxes are *not* included in the marked price of most items in the United States or Canada, though there are some exceptions, such as gasoline. In the United States, cities and states impose these taxes, but the federal government does not. In Canada, both the federal government and the provinces impose sales taxes. Canada's national sales tax is 7 percent and is known as the Goods and Services Tax (GST). Because sales taxes are not included in the marked price, buyers need to add 5–15 percent to calculate the final price. Tax rates vary because they are set by each city, state, and province.

Satellite campus: A branch site of the university, away from its main location. These branches offer courses for full university credit. They are convenient for many commuter students, but lack the full range of programs and courses available at the main campus.

(🅐) **Satisfactory academic progress (SAP):** Standards, set jointly by the U.S. govern-
($) ment and each university, to show if a student remains in good academic standing and is advancing toward a degree at a reasonable pace. Each university determines its own standards and agrees to them with the government. These standards must then be met by students to continue receiving government-sponsored grants, loans, or fellowships, or to maintain their international student visas. A student who fails to meet these standards is given a "grace period," usually one semester, before funding is stopped. If the student is still not making satisfactory progress by the end of the grace period, then the federal funding is stopped. It can be resumed if the student achieves SAP again.

Each university can readily supply its students with the standards it uses to measure satisfactory academic progress. They're usually online. Students who receive federal funding should review them. So should international students, who must make satisfactory progress to renew their student visas.

SAT, ACT, GMAT, GRE, LSAT, MCAT: Standardized tests used in the admissions process for undergraduate, graduate, and professional schools. These are the main tests and their purposes:

SAT (Scholastic Assessment Test)	Undergraduate admissions
ACT (Initials only; no full name)	Undergraduate admissions
GMAT (Graduate Management Admission Test)	Graduate Business Schools
GRE (Graduate Record Examination)	Graduate Schools in Arts and Sciences
LSAT (Law School Admission Test)	Law Schools
MCAT (Medical School Admission Test)	Medical Schools

There are still other specialized tests for biology, dentistry, education, optometry, and pharmacy schools.

($) **Scholarships, fellowships, grants, loans, bursaries:** Various forms of student financial aid. Student aid packages can vary in several ways:

- overall amount,
- proportion that is subsidized,
- criteria for selection (financial need, academic achievement, athletic prowess, or other qualifications), and
- requirements imposed on the recipient (such as maintaining a specific grade point average or serving as a teaching assistant).

Scholarships are generally awarded on the basis of financial need or academic accomplishment. Some are given for other purposes, such as athletic ability.

Fellowships are financial aid packages for graduate study and advanced research. Most are designed to support research and independent inquiry and do not impose requirements to work or teach. Fellowships awarded before the PhD are called predoctoral ("predocs"); those after the degree are postdoctoral ("postdocs").

Grants are outright gifts of financial aid and do not need to be repaid. (In Canada, some grants made to needy students are called bursaries.)

Loans, unlike grants, must be repaid. But student loans often contain some hidden subsidies, such as below-market interest rates. These subsidy elements are underwritten by government agencies. In fact, their financial guarantees are the only reason most students can borrow in the first place. Students who qualify for these government programs must maintain "satisfactory academic progress" to remain eligible. International students are not eligible for government-sponsored student grants and loans in the United States or Canada.

School: Either the generic term for an entire educational institution, such as a university, or the name given to some major divisions within the larger institution, such as the School of Architecture at the University of Illinois, Urbana-Champaign.

Using the generic term, you might say "My school is the University of Arizona," or "I went to school at Northeastern." As a reference to a major division within the university, you might refer to the "Stanford School of Engineering" or the "Medill School of Journalism at Northwestern University."

Secondary school: High school; that is, grades 9–12. Universities and U.S. colleges are known as "postsecondary education."

Second-hand store (thrift store): A retail store selling used items. Sometimes called a "thrift shop" because shopping there is so inexpensive. More commonly, the term "thrift shop" refers only to second-hand stores operated by nonprofit agencies, where the profits go to charity. So all thrift shops are second-hand stores, but not vice versa.

Section (or course section, discussion section): A subdivision of a larger course that is assigned its own scheduled meetings, usually as a supplement to meetings of the larger course. A large lecture course typically has several discussion sections, which meet weekly and are led by a teaching assistant (TA).

Some courses meet only as sections and do not meet as a whole. An English composition course might have a single title and course number, say English 110, but never meet for lectures. Instead, it is divided into a series of smaller sections, English 110, section 1, section 2 . . . , section 6. Each of these sections meets with its own professor (not a TA). The requirements for these sections are very similar.

Security deposit: The amount an apartment renter must pay to the landlord, to be held as a guarantee that the renter will pay the rent each month, including the last month, and will return the apartment in good condition. Similar deposits are often required for automobile leases.

Security deposits usually amount to one month's rent, though that varies from city to city. It is payable when the lease is signed. If the rent is paid every month and the apartment is not damaged, then the entire security deposit (plus a little interest) should be returned promptly at the end of the lease. Ideally, the deposit is held in escrow (that is, by a third party) and is used only if the renter fails to pay the monthly amount or damages the unit beyond "normal wear and tear." Although security deposits are common, they are also a common source of friction between landlords and tenants. Some unscrupulous landlords refuse to return the money, claiming nonexistent damage. To minimize the problem, it helps to do a little research about the landlord before renting a unit. Does the landlord behave honestly, fix problems promptly, maintain the building in good condition, and return security deposits without complaint?

Semester break: The period between two academic terms from mid-December to early January. Universities also have shorter breaks in the middle of regular terms, including Thanksgiving break. All schools take a week-long spring break, usually in March. Nearly all undergraduates leave campus; some graduate students stay and continue to study.

Schools on the semester system (as most universities are) have three longer breaks during the academic year:

- Thanksgiving (between three days and one week; in the midst of fall semester),
- Christmas (two or three weeks, between fall and spring semesters), and
- Spring Break (one week in the midst of spring semester).

Schools on the quarter system have three similar breaks, but they are situated differently in the academic calendar:

- Thanksgiving (between three days and one week; in the midst of fall quarter),
- Christmas (two or three weeks, between fall and winter quarters), and
- Spring Break (one week between the winter and spring quarters).

Dormitories are usually open during these week-long breaks, but not always, and most campus dining halls are closed. If you plan to stay, you should check in advance.

Semester, quarter: The major divisions of the school year. Most schools are on a "semester system," with autumn and spring terms each lasting approximately sixteen weeks. A few schools use the "quarter system," with autumn, winter, and spring terms lasting eleven weeks each. In both systems, the summer is treated separately and is not part of the regular academic year, even though most schools offer optional summer courses.

Senior faculty: Tenured faculty. In some universities, that means only full professors (since only they are tenured). In other universities, some associate professors are tenured. It is ambiguous whether "senior faculty" includes these tenured associate professors or not.

 Sexual harassment: Unwelcome, intrusive sexual attention or sexually provocative language. Can become a legal issue when harassment occurs in a school or workplace, or when threats are made. Although accusers and accused can be either men or women, the vast majority of complaints are made by women against men. Some twelve thousand harassment cases were brought to the U.S. Equal Employment Opportunity Commission in fiscal year 2006, about 85 percent of them by women.

Harassment charges like these are distinguished from more violent crimes of sexual abuse and sexual assault. Students and employees have legal rights to study and work without being harassed, sexually or otherwise. Beyond these legal rights, most universities prohibit sexual harassment in their codes of conduct for students, faculty, staff, and other employees.

One difficulty with any rules against "sexual harassment" lies in the politically contested definition of the term. There are serious disputes over whether the term is too nebulous and expansive, whether it should cover a person's perception of a hostile, offensive, or intimidating environment (since perceptions can differ and since the accused may not have intended to intimidate or offend), and whether rules against sexual harassment unduly limit rights of free speech and expression.

Sign-up sheet (for office hours): A list of available appointment times, posted outside the office of a teacher or adviser. If a teacher is available from 2:00 p.m. until 4:00 p.m. on Wednesday, the sign-up sheet might list available appointments at 2:00 p.m., 2:15 p.m., 2:30 p.m., and so on. Students sign their names at the open times they prefer. Some schools have electronic versions of these sign-up sheets.

Ⓐ **Social Insurance Number (SIN):** The unique number given to each worker in Canada;
Ⓢ equivalent to U.S. Social Security Numbers. SINs are needed to apply for credit cards
and bank accounts, for instance. All foreign nationals receive SINs that begin with
the number 9. These special numbers have an expiration date and must be renewed.
International students, who have SINs identifying them as foreign nationals, cannot be
employed unless they also receive work authorization from Citizenship and Immigration Canada (CIC). Anyone who works without such authorization, or who knowingly
hires such workers, is committing a crime under the Immigration and Refugee Protection Act.

Ⓢ **Social Security:** The U.S. system of mandatory insurance for retired workers, surviving spouses, and minor children who have lost a parent. Workers pay into the system
each month (approximately 7.5 percent of their wages, plus an equal amount paid
by the employer). These payments are known as FICA (Federal Insurance Contributions Act) and are withdrawn automatically from payrolls. Self-employed workers are
responsible for paying the entire amount themselves. Workers who paid into the system are eligible for monthly pension payments, starting at age sixty-two. Alternatively,
they may choose to start at age sixty-five and receive larger payments. The amount they
receive each month depends on the amount they paid in.

Ⓢ **Social Security Number (SSN):** The unique number given to each worker in the
United States. Designed to ensure that payments into the Social Security system are
properly credited to that individual. The same is true in Canada, where workers receive
a Social Insurance Number. SSNs and SINs are relied on by financial institutions, such
as banks, credit card companies, and credit-rating bureaus (which collect information
about whether individuals pay their bills promptly). Applicants for loans, jobs, scholarships, or even telephone service are routinely asked to provide their Social Security
Numbers.

Stacks, library: The part of the library where books are stored. Most university libraries have "open stacks," meaning that students, faculty, and other researchers can browse
freely and select their own books. Some stacks, such as those containing rare and valuable documents, are "closed." Users must fill out forms requesting the items they want,
and librarians bring them to the users.

🛒 **Store credit:** Funds that can be spent only in a particular store or chain of stores. The
credit is usually generated because an item was bought and then returned, or because
the recipient received a gift certificate for use in that store. Depending on the company's rules, a "store credit" may expire if it is not used within a specified time, such as
two years.

Student body: The students at any school. "The Ohio State University student body
comes mainly from that state."

Student card: A photo identification card issued by the university. It is required for
entrance to library, dining hall, dormitories, and other restricted locations, and is
required to borrow library books. Some cards also allow students to make small pay-

ments on campus. A student might pay the bursar $100 and have that amount added to the card electronically. The card can then be used to pay for meals or photocopying. It is, in effect, a debit card for limited purposes on campus.

Student identification number (student ID): The number assigned to each student for registration and other university purposes. Each university has its own ID system. There is no national system of student IDs in the United States or Canada and no national registry of students. The term "student ID" refers to both the number and the card with the number.

Student union: An important campus building that houses various student activities, bookstores, and dining facilities. As such, the student union is a focus of student life. The term "student union" may be confusing, because "union" usually refers to an organization of workers seeking better pay, better working conditions, and more secure employment. Indeed, teaching assistants at a few schools have organized "graduate student unions" along these lines.

Studio apartment: A small apartment with a single main room, plus a bathroom. The main room contains areas for cooking, eating, sleeping, and socializing. Also known as an "efficiency" apartment.

Study abroad programs (also known as "semester abroad" or "junior-year abroad"): Very popular programs in which American and Canadian undergraduates spend one or two semesters in another country, taking courses at a local university or a branch of a North American university. These programs are common options for undergraduates in North America and are sometimes called "semester abroad" or "junior year abroad" (since the common enrollees are third-year undergraduates). The student's home university counts these courses toward its own graduation requirements. In addition, many U.S. universities have established summer programs in prominent locations, such as London, Oxford, and Paris.

While living and studying in other countries, North American students typically learn local languages, literature, politics, sociology, and history. Most live in dorms or apartments, but some live with local families.

Study groups: A collection of students who meet regularly to discuss academic material and work on class assignments. There are two main types of study groups, and it's crucial to distinguish them. (1) In a "pure discussion" and self-teaching group, each student does her own work individually and receives her own grade for it. (2) A cooperative work group produces a joint product, such as a collectively written paper; normally, all members are responsible for the joint work product and each receives the same grade.

Obviously, there are fundamental differences between the two types of groups. In fact, what is perfectly acceptable in a "joint product" group (with different members contributing to the same written assignment) would be cheating in a "pure discussion" group. Pure discussion groups are most often used in the arts and sciences, since the goal is to train students to work individually. Classes in economics or mathematics might form groups to study problem sets or homework assignments. But students are expected to write their own answers to the questions, not copy them from each other. (That would be cheating, in a "pure discussion" study group.) Study groups like these are often arranged by the students themselves. They pick friends or classmates with similar interests and abilities and meet once or twice a week. Occasionally, the teacher forms the groups and assigns each student to one. However the groups are formed, they are simply study aides and self-teaching arrangements.

Professional schools have different goals. They want to train students to work effectively in groups, since that's what they will do in corporations, nonprofit organizations, and government agencies. To prepare them, professional schools often require students to produce joint work in small groups. The groups themselves are usually selected by the faculty, rather than by participants, but that varies from school to school and from class to class. These joint-work groups face several difficulties: a member might shirk (that is, do less than a fair share of the work), do poor work, try to dominate or control the group, or cheat or plagiarize. Since the work product is a joint effort, all members are held responsible and must deal with the problems. It's usually impossible to solve them by expelling a bad student from the group. So the members have to figure out other ways to cope. That is particularly important if they suspect someone is cheating or plagiarizing, since they will all be held responsible and could fail the assignment or even the course.

How do teachers respond to these issues? First, they want students to sort out the problems themselves, just as they would at work. Second, they ask students for confidential evaluations of other members in the group. This allows faculty to differentiate top students from weak students and award them different grades for the course. Of course, if there are very serious problems within the group, members should speak with the professor and perhaps the dean of students.

Summer school (summer term, summer quarter): An optional academic session, offered for several weeks during the summer months. Most universities offer some summer classes, though rarely as many as they offer during the normal academic year. Summer courses are often intensive, meeting every day for several weeks (rather than two or three times a week for several months, as they do during the academic year).

Students use summer school to speed up their graduation, take intensive language classes, or focus exclusively on one difficult subject (such as a course in organic chemistry, required for all students applying to medical school). Some high school students take university-level courses in the summer, and some undergraduates visit another city and take courses at a different university.

Supplementary readings (or suggested readings): Books, articles, and other materials that a student may choose to read as part of a course but is not required to read. All syllabi list required readings; some also provide supplementary (or optional) readings for students who wish to delve into a specific aspect of the course. Even if a syllabus does not list any supplementary readings, a professor will always provide them for students who ask. If you want to learn more about a specific aspect of a course, just talk with your professor (or send an e-mail) and ask for some supplementary readings.

Survey course: An introductory course that offers a broader overview (survey) of the field, rather than an in-depth treatment of one or two topics.

Suspension: The requirement that a student leave the university temporarily (usually for one or two semesters) because of bad grades or bad conduct. A student who is behind on tuition payments may also be suspended but can usually reenter as soon as the arrears are paid. Students with academic or conduct problems are normally readmitted when their suspensions end. Each university has its own rules and procedures to suspend students and readmit them. Suspension has drastic consequences for international students, since their visas require that they be registered as full-time students. (See also the entry for "expulsion.")

($) **SWIFT bank identifier code number:** An international system of bank identifier codes, the equivalent of a U.S. bank routing number. To transfer funds to a bank customer outside the United States, the sender needs to know two crucial numbers: (1) the SWIFT bank identifier code number for the recipient's bank, and (2) the recipient's account number at the bank. The acronym stands for Society for Worldwide Interbank Financial Telecommunication.

Syllabus: The list of readings, requirements, prerequisites, and expectations for a course, handed to all students at the beginning of the course. In the United States and Canada, syllabi are detailed descriptions of the course, not just lists of required readings.

($) **T1:** The basic Canadian tax form, filled out by the taxpayer (or by a tax preparer you hire) and returned to the federal government along with any taxes due. Taxes are due for the previous calendar year on April 30. The tax obligations apply to everyone who earns money, dividends, interest, or other income in the Canada. Everyone who earned taxable income in the last calendar year has to file, even if they don't owe the government money. International students are *not* exempt. The U.S. equivalent is the 1099 tax form.

($) **T4:** A Canadian document provided to each employee showing his income during the previous year, as well as any tax payments made for him automatically by the employer (which have been deducted from each paycheck). If an employee worked for two companies, then he should receive two T4 forms. They are essential to preparing income taxes. In the United States, the equivalent form is a W-2.

($) **Tax preparer:** A firm or individual hired to fill out tax forms, based on information supplied by the taxpayer. Since tax laws are fiendishly complex, many Americans and Canadians hire either an accountant or a tax preparer such as H&R Block, or they use computer software such as TurboTax to fill out federal, state, and provincial forms.

($) **1099:** The basic U.S. tax form, filled out by the taxpayer (or a tax preparer you hire) and returned to the federal government along with any taxes due. Pronounced "ten ninety nine." Taxes are due for the previous calendar year on April 15. Many (but not all) states also have their own annual tax bill, and so do a few cities. All are due on

April 15. The tax obligations apply to everyone who earns money, dividends, interest, or other income in the United States. Everyone who earned taxable income must file, even if they don't owe the government money. International students are *not* exempt. The Canadian equivalent is the T1 tax form.

Teaching assistant (TA): A graduate student who leads small discussion sections, grades papers and exams, and works with individual students in a large course, in exchange for fellowship support or wages. Lab TAs do the same thing in science courses, where they supervise students doing their laboratory assignments. TAs work under the overall supervision of the professor who teaches the course. In larger courses, there may also be a "head TA," who coordinates work among the teaching assistants. Serving as a TA or lab TA is an integral part of a graduate student's professional training.

Tenure: The right of a faculty member not to be dismissed, except for special circumstances (such as criminal conduct or the closing of an entire department). Tenure is a faculty member's most important promotion and comes only after completing several years as a nontenured professor and a thorough review of the scholar's research, teaching, and service to the university. Full professors are tenured. Lecturers, instructors, adjunct faculty, and assistant professors are not. Associate professors are midway up the faculty ladder and may or may not hold tenure, depending on the university's policy. The main rationale for tenure is that it guarantees a faculty member's freedom of expression and inquiry, which are central goals of the university.

Tenure review: The process by which university faculty and academic officers evaluate scholars for permanent appointments. Tenure review usually refers to the promotion process for faculty members already working at the university. The evaluation covers their research and publications, teaching, and service to the university. (The same evaluation is done before recruiting scholars from other universities, but it is not called "tenure review.")

Different schools weigh these factors differently. Research universities emphasizes high-quality, innovative scholarship and publication; teaching-oriented schools emphasize effective classroom performance. Colleagues and students are asked for their opinions, and leading scholars in the field are asked to write confidential letters, discussing the candidate's qualifications.

A small committee of tenured faculty members from the department is typically convened to review the case in depth. They deliver a written report, summarizing the strengths and weaknesses of the case and recommending that tenure be granted or denied. The department then votes and sends its recommendation up to the academic dean or university-wide committee that deals with tenure cases. The dean or committee reviews all the materials, makes its recommendation, and sends the case for a final decision by the university's provost or president. The university board of trustees is not involved.

Since universities have different administrative arrangements, they don't all handle tenure review in the same way. But there are several features common to all of them.

First, it involves an in-depth review of the faculty member's scholarship, teaching, and service. Second, it includes opinion from both local faculty and outside experts. Third, the reports and discussions are all confidential (although some state laws and court decisions may require eventual disclosure, if a lawsuit is filed). Finally, the review process involves several stages, rising from the department to the highest academic officers of the university.

Tenure track: An entry-level professorial job that guarantees that the holder will be formally considered for tenure, usually after six years. This "tenure review" may or may not lead to promotion. By contrast, non-tenure-track jobs are held for fixed terms, perhaps one or two years. They are not considered permanent and do not lead to a tenure review. The distinction between "tenure-track" and "non-tenure-track" jobs is the most important distinction among junior faculty appointments.

Term papers: The nickname for a major research paper in a class. (Semesters are sometimes called "terms"; hence the name.)

TOSOL (Teachers of English to Speakers of Other Languages): A professional association for specialists in teaching English as a second language (ESL).

Terminal degree program (or terminal MA program): A master's program that is intended to be a student's final degree in that subject, not the midpoint in a PhD program. Take the University of Chicago's Harris School of Public Policy, which offers a master's degree in public policy. The MPP is a professional program, designed to train practitioners and policy analysts, and the degree is a terminal one. By contrast, the University of Chicago's Political Science Department trains graduate students as part of a doctoral program. Along the way, students complete the requirements for a master's and are awarded that degree. A few may decide to stop at that point, but the program is oriented toward doctoral training and is not a terminal one.

Test, examination, quiz: A set of questions or exercises designed to assess a student's knowledge, understanding, skills, achievements, or abilities, usually in a specific class or subject area. Longer, more formal tests are called examinations; briefer, more informal ones are called quizzes and cover less material. Any of these tests may be written or oral, although written ones are much more common. They may be given in class or as take-home assignments; they may permit students to use their books, notes, and computers, or they may specifically prohibit them. Students are always given advance notice of major examinations, but brief quizzes (known as "pop quizzes") are sometimes given in class without prior notice.

Thanksgiving: An important autumn holiday, where family and friends celebrate ("give thanks") at a large meal. Essentially a nondenominational harvest festival. In Canada, it is celebrated the second Monday in October. In the United States, it is celebrated the fourth Thursday in November, about a month before Christmas. In both countries, Thanksgiving is a statutory holiday. It is a vacation day (or longer) at all universities. These schedules vary from school to school, and it's important to check yours.

Thesis: The major research paper at the conclusion of an undergraduate, master's, or doctoral program (that is, a BA thesis, MA thesis, or PhD thesis). The PhD thesis is also known as a dissertation or doctoral dissertation.

Thesis adviser (or thesis chair): Faculty member who chairs a thesis committee and is the student's principal mentor on the BA or MA thesis or dissertation project. Each student selects his own thesis adviser, who specializes in the relevant area. In most universities, the adviser must be a faculty member in the department where the thesis is being written.

For PhD's, there are normally two or three other faculty on the thesis committee, all selected by the student (after consulting with the thesis adviser). For BA and MA theses, there is only a principal adviser, not a full committee. In some departments, however, a second faculty reader must approve the thesis before it is accepted.

Thesis committee: A group of three or four faculty members, selected by the doctoral candidate to supervise the research project. The committee chair is the student's principal mentor on the project, but the other members are valued advisers. The committee plays an important role throughout the dissertation process. At the beginning, it holds a "hearing" (formal meeting) to approve the proposal, which covers the subject, methods, data, and other materials to be used. As the research proceeds, committee members consult individually with the student and review the work in progress. At the conclusion, the committee members must jointly approve the final draft and hold an oral examination on it, where the doctoral candidate explains and defends the work.

Universities and departments have their own rules about the composition of thesis committees. Usually, the thesis chair must be a member of the department in which the thesis is written. Depending on the department's rules, the other committee members might be drawn from other departments or even other universities.

Thrift store (second-hand store): A retail store selling inexpensive, used goods and operated by a charitable agency.

Time card: A form, used to calculate paychecks, showing how many hours a student worked as a research assistant, lab assistant, or work-study student on campus. Either the student fills out the form and the supervisor signs it, or else the supervisor fills it out directly.

Title VI (Title 6): The colloquial name for a long-standing U.S. program that funds universities to study various global regions and train students in their languages. Begun during the cold war and originally focused on the Soviet Union, it is now a major funding source for "area study centers" dealing with the Middle East, South Asia, Latin America, Eastern Europe, and East Asia. Title VI grants are made directly to universities and support their teaching programs, graduate student fellowships, research, conferences, outreach to the local community, programs outside the United States, and more.

Foreign Language and Area Studies (FLAS) fellowships are made under Title VI and help fund graduate students who study selected areas of the world and their languages. FLAS funding is available only to full-time students who are (or are becoming) U.S. citizens or permanent residents. International students are not eligible.

Title IX (Title 9): The colloquial name for a U.S. law that mandates gender equality in education, including sports programs. "Title 9 of the Educational Amendments of 1972" was designed to ensure that women receive equal treatment in all aspects of education, including intramural and intercollegiate sports at universities. To meet that goal, the U.S. Department of Education's Office of Civil Rights issued specific (and controversial) regulations, backed by powerful financial sanctions—the threat to terminate federal aid to all parts of the university. In 2002, the law was renamed to honor its original sponsor, the late Representative Patsy Mink. Despite the new formal name, the law and regulations are still known as "Title 9."

TOEFL: Test of English as a Foreign Language, for students who are not native English speakers. Administered by the Educational Testing Service (ETS).

Transcript, official transcript: The official record of a student's courses, grades, and degrees at a given university, provided by the registrar. Employers and graduate schools often request such official transcripts to confirm statements a student made on a résumé or a CV. To guard against fraud, official transcripts are printed on special paper and include other safeguards against counterfeiting.

Transcripts and other student records are private, and their confidentiality is protected by law. (The U.S. law is the Family Education Rights and Privacy Act of 1974, or FERPA.) Of course, a student can ask that records be sent to potential employers, graduate schools, and others. Most universities charge a small fee to provide these official documents.

Unofficial transcripts, without all these safeguards against counterfeiting, are simply the student's online records, which the student can download and print without cost. Professors sometimes ask for these unofficial records when they write a student's recommendations for jobs or graduate school.

Transfer credits: Academic courses taken at one university but used to meet requirements at a different university, where the student is now enrolled. Universities and individual departments have their own rules limiting how many credits can be transferred.

To illustrate: if a student passed several economics courses at Purdue University and then moved to the University of Notre Dame, she would request that her course credits at Purdue be transferred. Officials at Notre Dame would review the student's transcripts and look at the course materials before deciding which credits to approve. The university would decide how many credits could count toward her Notre Dame degree. Faculty in her new department would decide how many of her Purdue economics courses could count toward their requirements. It is possible that three Purdue courses would count toward the overall university requirements, but only two would count toward the department's requirements.

Transfer student: A student who switches from one university to another in the midst of a degree program. For example, an undergraduate may spend freshman and sophomore years at the University of Michigan and transfer to the University of Illinois for junior and senior years. Most students stay at a single university for their degrees, but transfers are quite common. Naturally, they require a formal application to the new university.

A student who graduates from one university and then attends another for a subsequent degree is not a transfer student. Thus, a student who receives a BA from the University of Washington at Seattle and a law degree from the University of Colorado at Boulder is not considered a transfer student. On the other hand, if a student started a law degree at the University of Washington and completed it at the University of Colorado, she would be considered a transfer.

International students should check current immigration rules to see if transferring between universities or changing programs within a university requires any notification to visa authorities.

Trimester: An academic schedule that divides the year into three segments (approximately fourteen weeks each), with students enrolled for two segments each year. Rarely used in the United States or Canada.

TSE: Test of Spoken English, for students who are not native English speakers. Administered by the Educational Testing Service (ETS), it measures a student's ability to speak in an academic or professional setting.

United States Medical Licensing Examination (USMLE): Multistage licensing test for medical school students and graduates.

University: In the United States, a postsecondary school that includes both undergraduate and graduate education, as distinct from a school that focuses on undergraduates alone. (In the United States, schools for undergraduates alone are known as colleges.) In Canada, the nomenclature is different. There, a university can train undergraduates, graduates, or both. Canadians use the term "college" as the English do, to refer to schools that prepare students for universities.

Upper-level courses: Courses designed for juniors and seniors, rather than introductory courses for freshmen and sophomores. Though the term normally refers to undergraduate courses, it is occasionally used for graduate courses, as well. In that case, upper-level courses would be more specialized courses for students who have already completed introductory-level graduate work.

($) **Utilities:** Basic services for homes and apartments, including electricity, natural gas, heating oil, water, garbage, and sewer service; sometimes includes phones and cable television. Monthly charges for utilities (other than phones) may be included in an apartment's monthly rent, or the tenant may have to pay them separately, as an additional charge. Since that charge can be costly, it is vital to know in advance whether an apartment's monthly rental fee includes utilities or not. Water and garbage service are almost always included in the rental price, but other utilities may not be. It pays to check *before* you sign a lease.

Varsity athletics: Sports in which top athletes from one university compete against their peers from other universities. It means the same as "intercollegiate athletics" and can be contrasted with intramural sports, in which students from different dorms and clubs within a single university compete against each other.

Vehicle identification number (VIN): A unique number printed on key parts of every motor vehicle (car, truck, SUV, motorcycle, and so on). The number is listed on documents of sale and transfer, to prevent easy sale of stolen vehicles and parts. Because each vehicle has a unique identifier, you can also trace repairs, maintenance, and accidents of any used car before you purchase it. Specialized companies sell that information to car buyers.

Vocational: Education that provides work-related knowledge, including commercial, industrial, or technical skills. Professional schools are not termed "vocational" even though they provide work-related knowledge and training.

Volunteer programs: Services provided by students, faculty, and staff who work without compensation. North American universities are filled with charity groups where students volunteer their time, money, and expertise to provide a range of valuable services: tutoring for children, food for the hungry, legal assistance for the poor, counseling for crime victims, and much more.

W (for "withdraw"): A course mark indicating that a student who was once enrolled in a course has left it. In some cases, the mark may be modified to indicate that the student was passing or failing at the time of withdrawal (listed as "withdraw-passing" or "withdraw-failing"). These arrangements vary from school to school. One procedure that does not vary: to withdraw from a course, you *must* fill out a proper form. You cannot simply stop attending the course. If you do, you will still be formally enrolled in the course and, inevitably, you will fail it. So, if you wish to withdraw from a course, fill out the proper form. In some schools, you may need to get the professor's permission to withdraw. Whether you do or not, it is courteous to inform the professor if you are leaving a small class.

W-2 form: A U.S. document provided to each employee showing his income during the previous year, as well as any tax payments made for him automatically by the employer (which have been deducted from each paycheck). In January, each employer provides a separate W-2 form to every worker. If you worked for three employers during the year, then you should receive three forms. They are essential to preparing income taxes. The Canadian equivalent is a T4.

W-4 form: A U.S. tax form, filled out by employees, to determine how much their employers should withhold from each paycheck for taxes.

Waiting list: Students who applied to a university or a particular program and are told that they *might* be admitted in the near future, but only if places become available for them. When they are "wait-listed," they have been neither accepted nor rejected. Whether places become available depends on whether students who have already been admitted decide to accept their offers. If enough of them reject their offers (usually because they decide to go to another school), then some students from the waiting list will be admitted. By using a waiting list like this, a school can achieve its targeted number of acceptances.

Walk-in hours: A regular time each day or week when patients can see a doctor or nurse without a scheduled appointment. Most clinics provide walk-in hours for patients who need to see a doctor sooner than any appointment is available. A patient who uses these services is called a "walk-in." A typical walk-in patient has a cough or fever and needs medical assistance today or tomorrow, not in two weeks when the next doctor's appointment is available. The patient's condition is not serious enough to warrant an expensive trip to the hospital emergency room. The solution: use walk-in hours or consult with the physicians on duty by phone.

Warranty: A commitment to repair or replace a defective product or remedy a deficient service. Some warranties cover the entire life of the product, but they are normally made for a specific period, such as car warranties for five years or 100,000 miles, whichever comes first. The warranty may cover an entire product or service, or cover only some specified parts, such as a car's transmission but not its tires. It may include all necessary parts and service, or cover only the parts. The consumer would then have to pay for any labor (that is, "service") needed to make the repairs.

An extended warranty stretches the commitment beyond the initial warranty period. Consider, for example, a new TV that comes with a one-year warranty. The manufacturer or retail store might sell an extended warranty (for an additional fee) to cover any necessary repairs during the second and third years.

White pages: The common name for the phone directory (or part of the phone directory) that contains numbers for individuals. Landlines are normally listed, but you can request that your number be kept private (unlisted), if you wish. Cell phone numbers are not listed. A separate section of the phone directory, the "yellow pages," lists advertisements for products and services.

Wi-Fi: Wireless local area networks for electronic communication. Wi-Fi is a shortened form of "wireless fidelity," a term that is not actually used. Similar to cell-phone technology, it allows users to send and receive computerized data as long as they are within range of a wireless base station. Increasingly, Wi-Fi networks are encrypted to protect the data of authorized users and prevent unauthorized users from gaining access.

Will, or last will and testament: A legal document stating how an individual's property should be distributed and who should become the guardian for any children after a person's death. In the absence of a will, state and provincial governments have standard laws to distribute property and guardianship of minor children. A will deals only with issues that arise after death. It does *not* deal with such vital issues as the medical care an incapacitated person should be given. That is covered in separate documents known as "living wills" and "health-care powers of attorney" (treated in individual entries above).

($) **Work-study:** A U.S. program to help students finance their education through part-time employment on campus. Eligibility is based on a student's financial need. Operated by the Federal Student Aid program, it is limited to U.S. citizens, permanent residents, and a few others such as refugees. International students are not eligible.

Writing-intensive course: A course with extensive writing requirements, usually several assigned papers, to help students become competent academic writers. Some universities now require undergraduates to complete several such courses. The courses themselves may be in a number of disciplines: history, English, philosophy, sociology, biology, and so on.

Writing lab: An optional service offered by all universities to assist students with their course papers and other writing. Writing labs typically offer brief noncredit courses, such as "How to Write a Grant Proposal in the Social Sciences." Most also offer tutorial help to individual students working on papers. These services are usually free.

It is important to understand what writing labs can and cannot do. They can teach students how to organize a paper, edit a draft, and write more clearly and effectively. They can help students overcome difficulties such as writing blocks. What they cannot do is offer substantive help on a paper's content. For that, students need to consult the professor or teaching assistant in their course.

(🛒) **Yellow pages:** The common name for the phone directory (or part of the phone directory) that contains advertisements for products and services. They are organized by categories such as "cars, rental" and "restaurants."

Today, yellow pages are available in printed form and online. You can find them at Web sites such as yellowpages.com, yellow.com, and superpages.com, as well as the "business search" feature at other listing sites. (See also the entry for "White pages.")

ZIP code: Numerical codes used by the United States Postal Service. The basic code is five digits, such as Cambridge, MA 02138. Each address actually has a nine-digit code, which you can use if you wish. For example: Cambridge, MA 02138-5801. Using the entire code speeds up delivery and occasionally helps the post office find the correct location. The Canadian equivalent is called a postal code.

APPENDIX 2

Abbreviations, Acronyms, Nicknames, Holidays, Floor Numbering, and Clothing Sizes

Chapter Contents

Introduction

The glossary includes a number of terms that are often known by abbreviations or informal nicknames. When students say "O-Week," for instance, they are referring to "orientation week." When they say "AP courses," they mean "advanced placement courses," which are introductory college courses offered in high school. In fact, students use abbreviations and nicknames like these all the time and seldom mention the longer names or explain what they mean. It's just assumed that everyone knows.

But everyone doesn't. What's familiar to students in economics is opaque to students in chemistry. In fact, nobody knows all the terms. International students face an even bigger hurdle, since they are still learning a lot of university lingo. They know academic terms in their home countries better than they know the terms here.

This chapter explains what all these shorthand terms mean. It lists the full names for the abbreviations and nicknames you are likely to see. Most are used around the university, but some of them deal with immigration, financial, and medical issues. If you want detailed explanations for any terms, just turn to the glossary.

I have also included tables for holidays, apartment rental terms, and roommate advertisements. Ads for apartments and roommates are filled with abbreviations, which are impenetrable without a guide. "3br/2ba w/w ac immac imm occ" means the unit has three bedrooms, two baths, wall-to-wall carpeting, and air conditioning; it is in immaculate (that is, excellent) condition and is available for immediate occupancy." The ad took only twenty-three letters. The translation took twenty-three words.

I've also included tables for state and provincial names, which are usually written as two-letter abbreviations. You need these abbreviations to mail letters and packages.

As for the holidays, I've listed *when* they are celebrated and *why* they are celebrated. There are separate tables for the United States and Canada, since some holidays are different. For each holiday, I have also indicated whether most universities take a vacation day or a long weekend. That varies by school, so you'll want to check the academic calendar at your university.

You'll find that students here enjoy sharing these celebrations and, just as important, they enjoy learning about your holidays and sharing them. If you celebrate a harvest festival, akin to Thanksgiving, or an independence day, akin to Canada Day, feel free to invite local students to join the festivities. It's fun, and it offers a wonderful opportunity to be a cultural ambassador.

Initials around the University

AA	Associate of Arts degree
ABD	All but dissertation
ACT	(Acronym only; formerly stood for American College Testing program)
AP	Advanced placement program
BA	Bachelor of Arts degree

BA/MA	Joint bachelor's and master's degree
BCL	Bachelor of Civil Law (Canadian degree for legal specialty in civil code)
BS	Bachelor of Science degree
CV	Curriculum vitae
Dr.	Doctor, either a PhD or a medical doctor
DUI	Driving under the influence (of alcohol or illegal drugs)
DWI	Driving while intoxicated (alternate term for DUI)
ELL	English language learner
ELPT	English language proficiency test
EMBA	Executive Master of Business Administration degree (MBA for executives)
ESL	English as a second language
ETS	Educational Testing Service
FERPA	Family Education Rights and Privacy Act of 1974 (U.S.)
FLAS	Foreign Language and Area Studies fellowship (U.S.)
GED	General Educational Development test (equivalent of high school degree)
GMAT	Graduate Management Admission Test
GPA	Grade point average
GRE	Graduate Record Examination
HBCU	Historically Black Colleges and Universities
I	Incomplete (as a course mark)
ID	Identification number or a card with that number
IM	Instant messaging, or
	Intramural sports
IRB	Institutional review board
JD	Juris Doctor, Latin for a law degree (U.S.)
K–12	Kindergarten through twelfth grade
LLB	Legum Baccalaureus, Latin for a law degree
LSAT	Law School Admission Test
MA	Master of Arts degree
MBA	Master of Business Administration degree
MCAT	Medical College Admission Test
MS	Master of Science degree
O-week	Orientation week
PhD	Doctor of Philosophy degree
PI	Principal investigator
PLAR	Prior Learning Assessment & Recognition (Canada)
Prof.	Professor
RA	Resident assistant or resident aide in a dormitory, or

	Research assistant to a professor
REB	Research ethics board (Canada)
RFP	Request for proposals
ROTC	Reserve Officers' Training Corps
ROTP	Regular Officer Training Plan (Canada)
SAP	Satisfactory academic progress
SAT	Scholastic Assessment Test
TA	Teaching assistant
TESOL	Teachers of English to Speakers of Other Languages
TOEFL	Test of English as a Foreign Language
TSE	Test of Spoken English
USMLE	United States Medical Licensing Examination
W	Withdraw (from a course)

Universities themselves are often known by their initials: OSU for the Ohio State University, IU for Indiana University. But not everyone follows the pattern. Although the University of Chicago is U of C, the University of Pennsylvania is Penn and the University of Mississippi is Ole Miss. The University of California, San Diego, is UCSD, and the University of California, Santa Barbara, is UCSB, but the University of California, Berkeley, is "Cal" (to locals) or "Berkeley" (to everybody else).

Initials for Financial Matters or Shopping

ABM	Automated banking machine (Canada)
ATM	Automated teller machine
CD	Certificate of deposit
CPP	Canada Pension Plan
CRA	Canadian Revenue Agency
EAD	Employment Authorization Document (U.S. immigration)
EFT	Electronic funds transfer
EI	Employment Insurance (Canada)
FICA	Federal Insurance Contributions Act
GIC	Guaranteed interest contract (Canada)
GST	Goods and Services Tax (national sales tax in Canada)
HST	Harmonized Sales Tax (in three Eastern Canadian provinces)
ID	Identification number or a card with that number
IRS	Internal Revenue Service
ITIN	Individual Taxpayer Identification Number
MSRP	Manufacturer's suggested retail price
PIN	Personal identification number
PST	Provincial Sales Tax (Canada)
QPP	Québec Pension Plan (Canada)

SIN	Social Insurance Number (Canada)
SSN	Social Security Number
SWIFT	International bank identifier number (stands for "Society for Worldwide Interbank Financial Telecommunication")
T1	Basic Canadian tax form (equivalent of U.S. form 1099)
T4	Annual form stating an employee's wages (Canada)
VIN	Vehicle identification number
W-2	Annual form stating an employee's wages (U.S.)
W-4	U.S. tax form related to withholding taxes from wages

℞ Initials for Medical Care

HIPAA	Health Insurance Portability and Accountability Act
HMO	Health Maintenance Organization
ICE	In case of emergency (contact information programmed into cell phone) ICE also stands for "Immigration and Customs Enforcement," a branch of the U.S. Department of Homeland Security.
ICU	Intensive care unit
MPN	Medical provider network
PCP	Primary care physician
PPO	Preferred provider organization

Nicknames around the University

Coed	Coeducational institution or a female student
Gen ed	General education requirement that courses must be taken in several fields
Flex dollars	Flexible dollars, deposited with the registrar and accessed through the student ID card; effectively a debit card for campus use
Frosh	Freshman
Frosh O-Week	Orientation week for freshmen
Greeks	Fraternities and sororities, so called because they are named with Greek initials
O-Week	Orientation week
Perks	Perquisites
Postdoc	Postdoctoral fellowship
Predoc	Predoctoral fellowship
Prospies	Prospective students who have been admitted and have either decided to come or are still undecided
Quads	Main quadrangle of the university

Title VI   U.S. law funding university programs to study global regions and their languages

Title IX   U.S. law requiring gender equality in university programs, notably sports

Vita   Curriculum vitae

Abbreviations for U.S. States

AL	Alabama	**NE**	Nebraska
AK	Alaska	**NV**	Nevada
AZ	Arizona	**NH**	New Hampshire
AR	Arkansas	**NJ**	New Jersey
CA	California	**NM**	New Mexico
CO	Colorado	**NY**	New York
DE	Delaware	**NC**	North Carolina
FL	Florida	**ND**	North Dakota
GA	Georgia	**OH**	Ohio
HI	Hawaii	**OK**	Oklahoma
ID	Idaho	**OR**	Oregon
IL	Illinois	**PA**	Pennsylvania
IN	Indiana	**RI**	Rhode Island
IA	Iowa	**SC**	South Carolina
KS	Kansas	**SD**	South Dakota
KY	Kentucky	**TN**	Tennessee
LA	Louisiana	**TX**	Texas
ME	Maine	**UT**	Utah
MD	Maryland	**VT**	Vermont
MA	Massachusetts	**VA**	Virginia
MI	Michigan	**WA**	Washington (state; not the nation's capital)
MN	Minnesota		
MS	Mississippi	**WV**	West Virginia
MO	Missouri	**WI**	Wisconsin
MT	Montana	**WY**	Wyoming

The nation's capital city is abbreviated Washington, DC (for the District of Columbia).

Occasionally, you will see longer abbreviations, such as Mass. (for Massachusetts) or Tenn. (for Tennessee). These were commonly used until the U.S. Postal Service introduced two-letter abbreviations and required that they be used on all mail.

Abbreviations for Canadian Provinces and Territories

AB	Alberta		**NU**	Nunavut
BC	British Columbia		**ON**	Ontario
MB	Manitoba		**PE**	Prince Edward Island
NB	New Brunswick		**QC**	Québec
NL	Newfoundland and Labrador		**SK**	Saskatchewan
NT	Northwest Territories		**YT**	Yukon
NS	Nova Scotia			

Holidays in Canada

Canadian holiday	Date	Explanation
New Year's Day	January 1	
Valentine's Day	February 14	A day to send cards, flowers, or sweets to your boyfriend or girlfriend; not a day off from work, but an excellent evening to go out to a nice restaurant
Good Friday Easter Easter Monday	Varies	Canada celebrates Easter on the date used by Catholics and Protestants; it adds Good Friday and the Monday after Easter as statutory holidays to make a long weekend; Easter Monday is not a statutory holiday in British Columbia
Mother's Day	May: 2nd Sunday	Not a statutory holiday but widely celebrated with presents, cards, and phone calls to mothers and grandmothers
Victoria Day	May: Monday preceding May 25	Official birthday celebration for Queen Victoria and Queen Elizabeth II; federal holiday creates a long weekend
Father's Day	June: 3rd Sunday	Presents and cards to dad and granddad; not a statutory holiday but widely celebrated
Québec National Day; also known as St. Jean-Baptiste Day or National Day	June 24	Celebrated only in Québec province
Canada Day	July 1	Anniversary of Canadian union; formerly called Dominion Day; if July 1 falls on a Sunday, then July 2 is a statutory holiday

Civic Holiday	August: 1st Monday	Not a statutory holiday, but widely celebrated; similar to Labor Day in U.S.
Thanksgiving	October: 2nd Monday	Statutory holiday, celebrated by feasting with family and friends
Halloween	October 31 in evening	Not a day off from work or school; children dress in costumes and collect candy treats from adults in early evening
Remembrance Day	November 11	Statutory holiday to commemorate Canadians who died fighting for their country; to remember them, many Canadians wear poppy flowers, since they are blood red and grew in Flanders, where so many soldiers died during World War I
Christmas	December 25	
Boxing Day	December 26	Statutory holiday; traditional day to give presents to family servants and the poor, following the English custom

Holidays in the United States

U.S. Holiday	Date	Explanation
New Year's Day	January 1	
Martin Luther King, Jr., Birthday	January: 3rd Monday	Leader of U.S. civil rights movement in 1950s and 1960s. Federal holiday; a day off work at some universities and not others
President's Day	February: 3rd Monday	Combines birthdays of George Washington and Abraham Lincoln; federal holiday but not celebrated at most universities
Valentine's Day	February 14	A day to send cards, flowers, or sweets to your boyfriend or girlfriend; not a day off from work, but an excellent evening to go out to a nice restaurant
Easter	Varies (always Sunday)	U.S. celebrates on the date used by Catholics and Protestants; Orthodox faiths celebrate later
Mother's Day	May: 2nd Sunday	Not a federal holiday but widely celebrated with presents, cards, and phone calls to mothers and grandmothers

Memorial Day	May: last Monday	Federal holiday, honoring members of the armed services who died fighting for their country; celebrated by all universities; creates a long weekend; traditional start of summer
Father's Day	June: 3rd Sunday	Presents and cards to dad and granddad; not a federal holiday but widely celebrated
Independence Day	July 4	Federal holiday; everybody celebrates with outdoor cooking and parties
Labor Day	September: 1st Monday	Federal holiday; creates long weekend; widely celebrated; traditional end of summer
Columbus Day	October: 2nd Monday	Honors discovery of "New World"; not celebrated by most universities
Halloween	October 31 in evening	Not a day off from work or school; children dress in costumes and go from house to house collecting candy treats in the early evening; adults buy candy to give away
Veterans' Day	November 11	Federal holiday; originally commemorated the end of World War I; now celebrates all who served in the U.S. military
Thanksgiving	November: 4th Thursday	Family and friends feast to celebrate the first such meal between Pilgrims and Native Americans in Plymouth, Massachusetts; some universities also take off the following day, creating a long weekend
Christmas	December 25	Federal holiday; unlike Canada, the United States does not celebrate Boxing Day on December 26

Apartment Rental Abbreviations

Newspapers have inspired a slew of advertising abbreviations, because they charge for each line or letter. Here, I've decoded the abbreviations for apartment rentals. Afterward, I have included a short list of abbreviations used in roommate ads.

In each city, there are also abbreviations for neighborhoods. In Chicago, for example, Hyde Park can be listed as HP or Hyd Pk. Your university housing office will know them and can help you interpret.

Abbreviation	Full term	Definition
a/c, air	Air conditioning	Air conditioning units in rooms (may also mean central air conditioning)
appl, apls	Appliances	Some combination of the following: refrigerator, range, stove, dishwasher, microwave, and garbage disposal
apt	Apartment	Apartment unit (rather than a house)
avail, avl	Available (example: avail Aug 1)	Date when unit can be occupied
Ba	Bath	Full bathroom (toilet, sink, and bath or shower)
½ ba	Half bath	Toilet and sink but no bath or shower
balc	Balcony	
bkr	Broker	The unit is shown by a broker or agent
bldg	Building	
br, bdrm	Bedroom	Bedroom as a separate room
brk	Brick	
bsmt	Basement	
cent a/c, cac, c a/c	Central air conditioning	One air-conditioning system for whole house or apartment
cpt	Carpet	Usually the same as "wall-to-wall carpeting" (w/w cpt)
condo	Condominium	
dep	Deposit	Money left with the landlord at the beginning of the lease to ensure that the apartment is returned in good condition at the end of the lease
dr, din rm	Dining room	Dining room as separate room
drmn, 24-hr drmn	Doorman, 24-hour doorman	Building has an employee at the front door for safety
duplx	Duplex	Either (1) an apartment with a first and second floor or (2) a row house that shares one wall with another house
d/wash, dw	Dishwasher	
dwnpymt	Down-payment	Initial deposit on house, usually as part of a purchase

eff, effic, effcy	Efficiency	One room apartment, with small kitchen in the room; there is a separate full bathroom (same as a "studio")
e, g, c	Electricity, gas, cable TV	
eik	Eat-in kitchen	A small eating area is in the kitchen
elec	Electricity	
elev	Elevator	
eve, eves	Evening, Evenings	
exp bk	Exposed brick	The interior features exposed brick walls
fee	Fee, broker's fee	Fees paid to rental broker who lists the apartment and shows it to potential renters
flr, flrs	Floor, floors	
fp, fpl	Fireplace	
fr	Family room	Also called a living room (lr)
fridge	Refrigerator	
full ba	Full bath	Toilet, sink, and bath, shower
furn	Furnished	Includes basic furniture, usually a bed, dining room table and chairs, and some living room furniture
gar	Garage	
grt	Great	Advertising hyperbole, as in "grt loc" (great location)
gym	Gym	Gym or health club in the building
hi ceil	High ceilings	Usually ceilings 10 feet or higher
hlth	health club	Health club or gym in the building
hook-ups, hkup	Hook-up facilities for a dishwasher or washer/dryer	Plumbing and electricity have been arranged for a dishwasher or a washer/dryer, but the renters will have to provide the machines themselves
hw, hdwd	Hardwood floors	Oak or maple flooring
hse	House	
ht	Heat	
ht/hw	Heat and hot water	
imm occ	Immediate occupancy	
immac	Immaculate	Refers to condition of unit (allegedly)

inc, with	Included	Included in the unit or already included in the price
inc util	Including utilities	Gas and electricity are included in the rental price
indr prkg	Indoor parking	
indr pool	Indoor pool	Swimming pools are outdoors unless stated as indoors
kit	Kitchen	
kitchenette		Small kitchen
loc	Location or located	
lrg	Large	
lr	Living room	
lux	Luxury or luxurious	
lv msg	Leave message	Leave a message stating you are interested
mi	Mile	
mba	Master bathroom	Large, well-equipped bath area
mbr	Master bedroom	Large bedroom, usually with attached bathroom
mrk	Market	
mo	Month	
mod	Modern	
nego	Negotiable	Key elements of the lease such as rent or occupancy date are negotiable
no fee	No fee to be paid to broker	Broker who lists the apartment will be paid by the unit's owner, not the renter
nr	Near	
obo	Or best offer	Used in some sales ads, such as "$30,000 OBO" (meaning that the seller is willing to negotiate)
off st prking, osp	Off-street parking	Unit includes a parking space
owner occ	Owner occupied	Landlord lives in same building
part furn	Partly furnished	Includes some furniture, such as a bed or dining table, but not full furnishings
pd	Paid	
ph	Penthouse	Top floor of a building
pkng	Parking	Unit includes a parking space
pl	Pool	Outdoor pool

plus util, +util	Plus utilities	Monthly utility costs (for gas, electricity, etc.) are not included in the price
prch, pch	Porch	
prvt	Private	
qt	Quiet	
rec rm	Recreation room	Building or unit has a recreation room
refs req, refs reqd	References required	Tenant must supply names of people ready to say he is a jolly good fellow and will pay the rent
renov, renovtd, nwly renov	Renovated	Newly repaired and updated
rd	Road	
rfdk	Roof deck	Usable outdoor area on roof
rm	Room	
dep or sec dep or secur dep	Security deposit	Money left with landlord at the beginning to lease to ensure the apartment is returned in good condition at the end of the lease
sep	Separate	
sf	Square feet	Standard measure of unit size
sm	Small	Always true, except for things that are really tiny
spac	Spacious	Allegedly
stu	Studio	One-room apartment, with small kitchen in the room; there is a separate full bathroom (same as an "efficiency")
stv	Stove	
svc	Service or services	
terr	Terrace	
twnhse	Townhouse	A row house with two or more floors and usually one or two shared walls, rather than a "freestanding" house with no shared walls
trans, transp	Transportation	
u/g prkg	Underground parking	Indoor parking in an underground garage
unfurn	Unfurnished	No furniture is in the unit
util	Utilities	Electric, gas, water; seldom includes phone or cable TV
vu	View	

w/	With	
w/d	Washer and dryer	Note that "w/d" refers to a washer and dryer for clothes; "d/wash" refers to a dishwasher
wic, wlkin clo	Walk-in closet	A very large closet
w/w, w/w cpt	Wall-to-wall carpeting	
xlnt	Excellent	
yd	Yard	An outdoor area is included with the apartment or house

Abbreviated Terms in Advertisements for Roommates

F   Female

Grad   Graduate student

Hsmts   Housemates

M   Male

NS, n/s   Nonsmoker

NP   No pets

Pref   Prefer

Pref'd   Preferred

Prof   Professional (*not* professor)

Refs   References

Req'd   Required

Rmmate   Roommate

S   Single

Ads for roommates sometimes use abbreviations that are common in the "personals" section (that is, ads to find dates or companions). For example, SWF means single, white, female. "G" means gay, "bi" is bisexual, "b" is black, and so on. An ad might say "SWF looking for F rmmate, pref n/s," which means a single, white, female seeks a female roommate, preferably a nonsmoker.

Floor Numbering in Buildings

In the United States and Canada (except for Québec), the ground floor is also called the "first floor." In larger buildings, it may also be called the "lobby." Because this street-level floor has several names, an elevator might designate it as "1," "G," or "L." The floor immediately above it is usually called the second floor, although in some larger buildings it is called the "mezzanine level." If so, it will be labeled "M" in the elevator.

The basement level is usually labeled "B." A second, lower basement is called a "sub-basement" and is labeled "SB." If these subterranean floors are devoted to parking, they might be labeled as P1 (for "parking, level 1"), P2, and so on.

International Clothing Size Charts

Use these charts as general guides, not exact conversions, since manufacturers and designers vary in how they size shoes and clothes. The same size numbers can run "large" or "small," even within the same company. The best advice is to try on shoes or clothes before you buy them, if you can. If you cannot, perhaps because you ordered them online, then be sure *before* you purchase that you can return anything that does not fit properly.

Men's Dress Shirts

U.S., Canada, UK (inches)	U.S., Canada, UK	Europe, Japan (cm)	Korea
14	(S) Small	36	90
14½	(S) Small	37	
15	(M) Medium	38	95
15½	(M) Medium	39	
16	(L) Large	41	100 (compares to 15½–16)
16½	(L) Large	42	105
17	(XL) Extra Large	43	
17½	(XL) Extra Large	44	110

Long-sleeved shirts come in standard arm lengths for each size. Longer and shorter lengths are readily available in stores.
Sources: http://www.onlineconversion.com/clothing_mens.htm; http://www.cairnsconnect.com/ visitor/clothingsizes.php; http://www.thetravelalmanac.com/clothing-size.htm; http://www .korea4expats.com/article-men's_clothing_size_conversion_chart.html (Korea); http://www .frenchfriends.info/practical_travel/men_clothing_size_conversions (Europe).

> **Tip:** Try on shoes and clothes before you buy. Also, ask before purchase if you can return items that do not fit.

Men's Suits

U.S., Canada, UK	Europe	Japan	Metric
32	42		81
34	44		86
36	46	S	91
38	48	M	97
40	50	L	102
42	52	L	107
44	54	LL	112
46	56	LL	117
48	58	LL	122

U.S. and Canadian suit jackets come in standard lengths for each size, unless they are specially marked as long or short versions. A typical size 42 suit would be marked 42 or 42R (for "regular"). A version for taller men would be labeled 42 Long, or 42L. A version for shorter men would be labeled 42 Short, or 42S. Most stores carry these long and short versions in popular sizes, 38–46. Extra-large sizes, including long versions, are available at "big and tall shops" in cities and large malls. Smaller sizes are more difficult to find, but are available in larger cities and online.

Sources: http://www.onlineconversion.com/clothing_mens.htm (United States, UK, Europe, Japan); http://www.asknumbers.com/ClothingMensConversion.aspx (United States, Canada, UK); http://simetric.co.uk/siclothing.htm (metric); http://www.i18nguy.com/clothing.html; http://www.usatourist.com/english/tips/Mens-Sizes.html.

Men's T-Shirts and Undershirts

U.S., Canada, UK (inches)	Europe, Japan (metric, cm)
Small (34–36)	91
Medium (38–40)	101
Large (42–44)	112
Extra-Large (46–48)	122

Source: http://www.asknumbers.com/ClothingMensConversion.aspx.

Men's Pants

U.S., Canada, UK (inches)	Europe	Japan (metric, cm)
28	44	71
30	46	76
32	48	81
34	50	86
36	52	91.5
38	54	96.5
40	56	101.5
42	58	106.5
44	60	112
46	62	117
48	64	122

Ready-to-wear pants have two standard measurements, the first for the waist, the second for the leg length or inseam. A tall person with a 34-inch waist might want pants that are 32 inches long. He would ask for a 34–32. A short person with the same waist might ask for a 34–28. Some pants for suits and for dress occasions are sold with unfinished leg lengths. A tailor measures you and cuts the exact length. Tailors are available either in the store itself or nearby (the store can tell you where). There is a small additional charge for the tailoring. Tailors can also be used to shorten the legs of finished pants, making a 34–32 into a 34–28, if you need it.

Sources: http://www.usatourist.com/english/tips/Mens-Sizes.html; http://www.asknumbers.com/ClothingMensConversion.aspx (for metric); http://www.motostrano.com/ustoeusicota.html (for Europe).

Men's Sweaters

United States (inches)	Europe (metric, cm)
Small (34–36)	44
Medium (38–40)	46–48
Large (42–44)	50
Extra–Large (46–48)	52–54

Source: http://catalog.hartwell.com/osp/Shop/hartwell?dsp=fitguide

Men's Underpants

U.S., Canada (inches)	28	30	32	34	36	38	40	42	44	46	48
Europe, UK		2	3	4	5	6	7	8	9	10	11	12

Source: http://www.frenchfriends.info/practical_travel/men_clothing_size_conversions.

Men's Shoes

U.S.	UK, India, Australia	Europe	France	Japan	China	Korea (Mondopoint, mm)	Mexico	International
5	4½	37	39	23	38	238	—	37.5
5½	5	37½	40	23.5	39	241	4.5	38
6	5½	38	41	24	39.5	245	5	38.5
6½	6	38½	41.5	24.5	40	248	5.5	39
7	6½	39	42	25	41	251	6	40
7½	7	40	42.5	25.5	—	254	6.5	40.5
8	7½	41	43	26	42	257	7	41
8½	8	42	43.5	26.5	43	260	7.5	41.5
9	8½	43	44	27	43.5	264	8	42.5
9½	9	43½	44.5	27.5	44	267	8.5	43
10	9½	44	45	28	44.5	270	9	43.5
10½	10	44½	45.5	28.5	45	273	9.5	44
11	10½	45	46	29	46	276	10	45
11½	11	45½	46.5	29.5	47	279	10.5	46
12	11½	46	47	30	48	283	11	46.5

Sources: http://www.onlineconversion.com/clothing_shoes_mens.htm (U.S., Europe, Mexico, Japan, UK, France, International, Korea); http://www.orientvisual.com/6inchforever/sizechart.htm (for Chinese sizes).

Women's Shoes

U.S.	UK, India	Europe	Japan	China	Korea	Mexico
5	2.5	35	21	35.5	228	—
5½	3	35.5	21.5	36	231	—
6	3.5	36	22	37	235	—
6½	4	37	22.5	37.5	238	—
7	4.5	37.5	23	38	241	—
7½	5	38	23.5	39	245	4.5
8	5.5	38.5	24	39.5	248	5
8½	6	39	24.5	40	251	5.5
9	6.5	40	25	41	254	6
9½	7	41	25.5	—	257	6.5
10	7.5	42	26	42	260	7

Shoe sizes are not standardized internationally, and various sources do not always agree on their conversions. In addition, sizes from individual manufacturers vary considerably. It is especially important, then, to try on shoes before you purchase.
Sources: http://www.onlineconversion.com/clothing_shoes_womens.htm; http://www.usatourist
.com/english/tips/Womens-Sizes.html; http://www.i18nguy.com/l10n/shoes.html#adult; http://
shoes.about.com/od/fitcomfort/a/wintshoesize.htm; http://www.vpshoes.com/sizechart.htm; http://
www.orientvisual.com/6inchforever/sizechart.htm (for Chinese sizes).

Women's Dresses

U.S.	U.S.	UK	Europe	Japan	Korea
2	XS	4	32	5	—
4	S	6	34	7	44
6	S	8	36	9	55
8	M	10	38	11	66
10	M	12	40	13	77
12	L	14	42	15	88
14	L	16	44	17	—
16	XL	18	46	19	—
18	1X	20	48	21	—
20	2X	22	50	23	—

Sources: http://www.usatourist.com/english/tips/Womens-Sizes.html; http://www.yesstyle.com/
Help/Section.aspx?section=cs&sectionId=737& (Korea); http://www.asknumbers.com/ClothingWom-
ensConversion.aspx; http://www.discoverfrance.net/France/Measures/DF_measures.shtml.

Women's Blouses and Sweaters

U.S.	UK	Europe
32	34	40
34	36	42
36	38	44
38	40	46
40	42	48
42	44	50
44	46	53

Source: http://www.usatourist.com/english/tips/Womens-Sizes.html.

Brassieres

U.S.	UK	Europe	Japan
32 A–D	32 B–DD	85 A–DD	A–D70
34 A–F	34 B–F	90 B–F	A–F75
36 A–F	36 B–F	95 B–F	A–F80
38 A–F	38 B–F	100 B–F	A–F85
40 A–F	40 B–F	105 B–F	A–F90
42 A–F	42 B–F	110 B–F	A–F95

Each brassiere (or bra) has two measurements. The first is the chest circumference just *below* the bust. The second is the cup size. So, a 34B and a 34D have the same chest circumference but different cup sizes.

Source: http://www.usatourist.com/english/tips/Womens-Sizes.html.

INDEX

Page numbers for definitions are in boldface.